KU-245-787

CONTENTS

CHINA

PREHISTORY TO THE NINETEENTH CENTURY

An Illustrated History

J.A.G. ROBERTS

SUTTON PUBLISHING

First published under the title *A History of China. Volume 1: Prehistory to c. 1800* in 1996 by
Alan Sutton Publishing Ltd, an imprint of Sutton Publishing Limited
Phoenix Mill · Thrupp · Stroud · Gloucestershire · GL5 2BU

Revised paperback edition first published in 2000

Copyright © J.A.G. Roberts, 1996

All rights reserved. No part of this publication may be reproduced, stored in a retrieval
system, or transmitted, in any form, or by any means, electronic, mechanical,
photocopying, recording or otherwise, without the prior permission of the publishers
and copyright holder.

British Library Cataloguing in Publication Data

A catalogue record for this book is available from the British Library.

ISBN 0 7509 2564 7

*Cover illustration: detail of warrior from Terracotta Army, Qin Dynasty, 210 BC. Tomb of Qin
shi Huang Di, Xianyang, China. (Bridgeman Art Library, London)*

Swindon Borough Council Library Services	
Askews	
951	£14.99

Typeset in 11/13pt Bembo.
Typesetting and origination by
Sutton Publishing Limited
Printed in Great Britain by
Butler & Tanner, Frome, Somerset.

PREFACE

This, the first volume of a two-volume history of China, has a specific aim and a limited purpose. It sets out to present a clear introduction to the history of China, making use of recent writings and drawing attention to areas of conflicting interpretation. This emphasis implies the omission of much of the detail which may be found in longer conventional histories. It also implies a limited treatment of important aspects of China's history, notably economic history, regional history and women's history, to name but three. Other topics, for example intellectual and cultural history, have been dealt with on an extremely selective basis.

Nevertheless it is hoped that, within these confines, this book will convey the interest and the excitement which has been aroused by the re-evaluation of Chinese history which has taken place in recent years. One reason why this has occurred is because spectacular archaeological discoveries have been made, which demand a reconsideration of some aspects of early Chinese history. A more general reason is that, in the past, few historians have been able to penetrate beyond the limitations of traditional Chinese historiography and as a consequence the long sweep of Chinese history appeared to be little more than a prolonged and repetitive catalogue of one dynasty following another. This impression of Chinese history no longer applies: detailed and exhaustive studies have been made on a number of themes, historical controversies have arisen, and new heights of scholarship and lively writing have been reached. It would be invidious to cite individual examples of this new wave, but many instances of important recent writings are referred to in the endnotes to each chapter and in the bibliography.

When writing about China, there is a perennial problem of how best to transliterate Chinese personal and geographical names and technical terms. The most substantial modern work on China, the fifteen-volume *Cambridge History of China*, has continued the use of the Wade-Giles system, and this remains the favoured system of romanisation for most monographs on China written in the West. However, since 1949, the official romanisation has been that known as *pinyin*, which is now used regularly in western newspapers and which is slowly gaining ground in academic writing. As it is intended that this book should be accessible to a broad readership, *pinyin* has been used. For the sake of consistency, direct quotations which contain spellings in the Wade-Giles system have been amended to *pinyin*.

For the most part Pinyin spelling approximates to the phonetic values of English, with the following notable exceptions:

c   is pronounced 'ts' as in Tsar

i   is pronounced 'ee', except when it follows c, ch, r, s, sh, z, and zh, in which case it is pronounced approximately 'er'

ian is pronounced 'ien'

q   is pronounced 'ch' as in cheap

r   is similar to the English 'r' but is pronounced with the tongue behind the front teeth

x   is pronounced 'sh' as in sham

z   is pronounced 'ds' as in hands

zh is pronounced 'j' as in jasmine

When citing Chinese names, the family name is normally given first, followed by the given name. However, in the endnotes, to maintain consistency with the citation of other names, the western practice of putting the surname last is observed. With reference to Chinese emperors, before their accession they are referred to by their personal names, but thereafter they are designated by their reign titles. For example, the first emperor of the Sui dynasty before he claimed the throne is referred to as Yang Jian, and thereafter as 'the Emperor Wendi', 'the Wendi emperor', or simply as 'Wendi'. When citing non-Chinese names or terms, for example when referring to Mongol or Manchu names, the most common form has been preferred, even if this may lead to inconsistency.

ACKNOWLEDGEMENTS

I owe a debt to the many fellow historians and librarians who have assisted me over the years and also to the many students who have attended my classes on the history of China and who have sustained my interest in the subject with their enthusiasm. In particular I would like to thank the staff of the University of Huddersfield Library Services for their patience in obtaining the range of books on which the study is based. My thanks go also to Steve Pratt of the School of Applied Sciences at the university for his meticulous work preparing the maps. I am grateful to my colleagues in the Department of History for enabling me to take a sabbatical to complete the task. Finally I must again thank my wife Jan for her forbearance over the years occupied by work on this book.

Acknowledgements are also due to the following for the use of illustrations: Phillip Ward, 2, 3; British Library, 5, 26, 28, 31, 34; Oriental Museum, University of Durham, 6; The Cultural Relics Bureau, Beijing, and The Metropolitan Museum of Art, New York, 7; Robert Harding Picture Library, 9, 10; The Nelson Gallery Foundation, The Nelson-Atkins Museum of Art, 8; The Metropolitan Museum of Art, The Dillon Fund, 1977, 16; Staatliche Museen zu Berlin, Preussischer Kulturbesitz Museum für Indische Kunst, 17; Marie Antoinette Evans Fund, Museum of Fine Arts, Boston, 20; Museum of Far Eastern Antiquities, Stockholm, Sweden, 23; The Board and Trustees of the Victoria & Albert Museum, 35.

Every effort has been made by the publishers to trace Phillip Ward.

CHRONOLOGICAL TABLE

Dynasties and rulers	*Events and personalities*
Fuxi (?2852 BC)	
Huangdi (?2697)	
Yao	
Shun	
Xia dynasty (?2205–1776)	
Shang dynasty (?1766–1122)	Shang bronzes
Zhou dynasty (?1122–256)	Zhou feudalism
Western Zhou (?1122–771)	
Eastern Zhou (?771–221)	
Spring and Autumn (771–481)	Confucius (551–479)
Warring States (403–221)	Mencius (372–289)
	Zhuangzi (369–286)
	Xunzi (298–238)
Qin dynasty (221–207)	
Qin Shi Huangdi (221–210)	Li Si and Legalism
	Terracotta army
Former Han dynasty (206 BC–AD 9)	
Han Gaozu (206–195)	
	Mawangdui tomb (*c.* 168)
Wudi (141–87)	First official examinations
	Sima Qian (?145–85)
	Chinese army reaches Ferghana
	Debate on salt and iron (81)
Xin dynasty (AD 9–23)	
Wang Mang (9–23)	'Nationalisation' of land
	Red Eyebrows' rebellion
Later Han (25–220)	
Guang Wudi (25–57)	Ma Yuan suppresses rebellion in Vietnam (42–3)

Dynasties and rulers	Events and personalities
	First mention of a Buddhist community in China (65)
	Rise of eunuchs at court
	Threat from Xiongnu and Xianbei
Lingdi (168–89)	Yellow Turban and Five Pecks of Rice rebellions
Three Kingdoms (220–80)	Setting for *The Romance of the Three Kingdoms*
Sixteen Kingdoms (316–84)	
Northern Wei (386–534)	
	Capital transferred to Luoyang (493)
	Buddhist cave temples at Longmen
Southern dynasties (304–589)	
Sui dynasty (589–618)	
Sui Wendi (581–604)	New capital at Chang'an
	Development of examinations
Yangdi (604–18)	Disastrous campaign against Koguryo
Tang dynasty (618–907)	
Tang Gaozu (618–26)	Reintroduction of 'equal field' system
Taizong (626–49)	Xuan Zang's journey to India (629–45)
	Chinese victory at Issyk Kul (657)
Empress Wu (690–705)	
Xuanzong (712–56)	Tang poetry: Li Bo (701–62) and Du Fu (712–70)
	Defeat at Talas river (750)
	Rebellion of An Lushan (755–63)
	Han Yu's Memorial on the Bone of Buddha (803)
	Ennin in China (838–47)
	Official repression of Buddhism (845)
	Huang Chao rebellion (874–84)
Five dynasties & Ten kingdoms (907–60)	
Qidan Liao dynasty (907–1125)	Overwhelmed by Jurchen (1122)
Song (Northern Song) dynasty (960–1127) Song Taizu (960–76)	Capital at Kaifeng
	Examination system fully developed
Taizong (976–97)	
Shenzong (1068–86)	Reforms of Wang Anshi (1068–85)

Dynasties and rulers	*Events and personalities*
Huizong (1101–25)	Fang La rebellion (1120–2) Jurchen invasion of north China (1125)
Jurchen Jin dynasty (1115–1234)	Yellow River shifts to southern course (1194) Jin overrun by Mongols (1211–15) Jin defeated by Mongols (1234)
Southern Song dynasty (1127–1279)	Capital at Hangzhou Fully convertible paper currency Neo-Confucian synthesis of Zhu Xi (1130–1200)
Ningzong (1194–1224)	Dictatorship of Han Tuozhou (1197–1207) Jia Sidao chief councillor (1259–75) Southern Song capitulate to Mongols (1279)
Yuan (Mongol) dynasty (1279–1368) Khubilai (1260–94)	Yuan drama Marco Polo in China (1275–91) Construction of Grand Canal (*c.* 1300) Red Turban rebellions (1340s) Ming-Han war (1360–3)
Ming dynasty (1368–1644) Hongwu (1368–98)	Execution of Hu Weiyong (1380) Yellow Registers and Fish-scale Charts
Yongle (1403–24)	Maritime expeditions (1405–33) Capital moved to Beijing
Zhengtong (1435–49; 1457–64)	Emperor captured at Tumu (1449) Construction of Ming Great Wall (1472–) First Portuguese reach China (1514) First printed version of *The Romance of the Three Kingdoms* (1522) Single-Whip tax reform (1531–) Manchus capture Fushun (1618)
Tianqi (1621–7)	Dominance of the eunuch dictator Wei Zhongxian Rebellions of Li Zicheng and Zhang Xianzhong (1640s)

Dynasties and rulers	*Events and personalities*
Qing dynasty (1644–1912)	
Shunzhi (1644–61)	Zheng Chenggong (Koxinga) active on Fujian coast
Kangxi (1662–1722)	Oboi regency (1661–9)
	Death of last Ming emperor (1662)
	Rebellion of the Three Feudatories (1673–81)
	Taiwan incorporated into the empire (1674)
	Treaty of Nerchinsk (1689)
	Ding figures frozen (1712)
Yongzheng (1723–35)	Reform of tax system
Qianlong (1736–95)	Pope issues *Ex Quo Singulari* (1742)
	Wu Jingzi writes *The Scholars* (1740s)
	Chinese occupation of Tibet (1751)
	Maritime trade restricted to Guangzhou (1760)
	Rise of Heshen (1772–99)
	Literary inquisition (1770s)
	Wang Lun uprising (1774)
	Macartney mission (1793)
	White Lotus rebellion (1796–1804)

INTRODUCTION

THE PATTERN OF CHINESE HISTORY

Early Chinese views of human history were dominated by a belief that there had been a Golden Age in the past, an age when men lived in harmony and peace. Since that time society had degenerated, but there remained a hope that the standards of the Golden Age might be established again. This hope was nurtured by an emphasis on the cyclical pattern of nature, symbolised by the phases of the moon, and a supposition that natural laws would apply equally to human history. When Chinese history was first recorded, historians related this cyclical motion to the rise and fall of the ruling dynasties, thus developing the idea of the dynastic cycle. In this cycle the key element was human behaviour with its tendency to stray from moral standards. Thus Sima Qian, the Grand Historian, who lived between 145–90 BC, summarised the sequence of dynasties before his time as follows:

> The government of the Xia dynasty was marked by good faith, which in time deteriorated until mean men had turned it into rusticity. Therefore the men of Shang who succeeded to the Xia reformed this defect through the virtue of piety. But piety degenerated until mean men had made it a superstitious concern for the spirits. Therefore the men of Zhou who followed corrected this fault through refinement and order. But refinement again deteriorated until it became in the hands of the mean a mere hollow show. Therefore what was needed to reform this hollow show was a return to good faith, for the way of the Three Dynasties of old is like a cycle which, when it ends, must begin over again.[1]

As a consequence of this view, and because it became the practice of Chinese historians to write the history of the preceding dynasty, Chinese history was divided into dynastic sections. This contrasts with the historical tradition of the west which has tended to perceive events as a linear progression rather than as a cyclical repetition. This has led some western historians to criticise the cyclical concept as a block to an understanding of the fundamental dynamics of Chinese history and to try to replace it with linear interpretations.

Before turning to discuss those interpretations, it should be said that some western historians have argued that there is a degree of validity in the Chinese concept of the dynastic cycle, if it is interpreted as a superficial political pattern overlying more fundamental developments. This view was put forward by E.O. Reischauer, who gave some support to the personal and moral basis of the traditional Chinese view. He pointed out that the founder of a dynasty had to be a man of great ability and force, whereas the later rulers of a dynasty, raised in a luxurious and intrigue-ridden court, were more likely to be weaklings. He added that most dynasties did produce at least one later strong ruler who revived the fortunes of the dynasty. Apart from the personal qualities of the ruler, the character of his government was also liable to degenerate as time passed because of the increasingly violent struggle between factions at court.

But, for Reischauer, more fundamental than the human element in the dynastic cycle were the economic and administrative factors. New dynasties eliminated most of their rivals and established peace. Under these conditions the country prospered, the territory was expanded and the treasury was full. But as the dynasty progressed the expenses of government grew and powerful families exerted their influence to evade taxes. The burden of taxation fell more and more heavily on the peasantry. As the financial situation worsened corruption increased and public works, particularly river defences, fell into disrepair. The final phase of the dynastic cycle was marked by the collapse of frontier defences, by famine, and by peasant uprisings which brought about the overthrow of the dynasty. This led to the establishment of a new dynasty and to the inauguration of a new cycle.[2]

One argument against using dynastic periods to divide up Chinese history has been the observation that some of the most important historical transitions have taken place in the middle of a dynastic period, or in periods of division between dynasties. This argument has been put forward in the context of the Tang dynasty (618–907), and the subsequent period of the Five Dynasties. Almost exactly half-way through the Tang period, as a result of the rebellion of An Lushan, the dynasty suffered a setback from which it never fully recovered. However, in the last years of the Tang and during the Five Dynasties – an age traditionally dismissed as a period of moral and political disintegration – a new type of government emerged and a system of rule was inaugurated which was then bequeathed to the next dynasty, the Northern Song.[3]

Contrasting with the idea of a cyclical framework is the concept of a linear progression, the concept which informs many western interpretations of Chinese history. The most obvious example of this is the Marxian view, with its implicit assumption that all human societies follow the same upward path from primitive society through slavery, to feudalism, capitalism, socialism and finally to communism. It has never been easy, even for convinced Marxists, to apply this progression effectively to the Chinese experience. A great deal of effort has been expended on determining when China was a slave society (supposedly in the Shang period), and when the transition from slave to feudal society took place. More time has been spent on explaining why the feudal period, the beginning of which has been traced back to the time of the Zhou (1122–256 BC) and which is deemed to have lasted until the nineteenth century, continued for so long. To accommodate China's experience of imperialism, the last stage of this feudal period, that is from the nineteenth century to the Communist victory in 1949, has been defined as 'semi-feudal, semi-colonial'.

Another form of the linear approach is to apply to China a version of the tripartite division of history into ancient, medieval and modern, which has become so deeply ingrained in the western view of the development of European civilisation. The most complete version of this was produced by Wolfram Eberhard, who not only subdivided Chinese history in this way, but also characterised each subdivision according to the dominant social class. The first age, from approximately 1600 to 250 BC, was that of feudal society, an aristocratic society based on land ownership and military service. The second age, the Chinese Middle Ages, was a gentry society, which lasted from 200 BC until early in this century. Eberhard defined the gentry as a group of leading families whose wealth derived from the land but who also supplied their educated sons to serve in the imperial bureaucracy. The third age commenced with the fall of the empire in 1911, by which time the gentry group was in the process of decomposition, its position challenged by an emerging urban middle class.[4]

THE NAITO HYPOTHESIS

A particularly influential contribution to the interpretation of Chinese history was made by the Japanese historian Naito Torajiro. He challenged the widely held view that the modern period in Chinese history began with the arrival of westerners, either with the arrival of traders and missionaries in the sixteenth century, or with the opening of China after the first Opium War. He argued that the modern period really began at the time of the Song dynasty (960–1279), for in that period aristocratic society finally disappeared. It was replaced by a society in which the despotic power of the emperor was established and at the same time there was an improvement in the position of commoners, who were no longer slaves (or rather serfs) of the aristocracy. Other important changes which marked the beginning of the modern period were the selection of candidates for official appointment by examination, the development of a monetary economy and the spread of a vernacular culture.[5]

THE DIFFERENTNESS OF CHINA

Marx's theory of history assumed that all societies shared a common experience. However, the western view of China has often started from the contrasting premiss that Chinese society is fundamentally different from the societies of the West. In the eighteenth century it was common to find travellers to China delighting in identifying Chinese 'contrarieties'. The list of ways in which Chinese custom was in direct opposition to western practice included the wearing of white to indicate mourning, and the reading of books from the 'back' to the 'front'.

The perception of China as a society which is fundamentally different from the West has led to a dichotomy which has run through much subsequent western writing on China. On the one hand there is the favourable view, which casts China in the role of a model for Europe. In the eighteenth century the most famous exponent of this view was Voltaire, who regarded the Chinese manner of government, with its reliance on receiving advice from learned men and its enjoinment of religious toleration, as a model to be emulated.[6] In the nineteenth century this was replaced by a hostile view, but the favourable view has re-appeared twice in this century, in the admiration expressed for the Chinese Communists in their wartime resistance to Japan and in the descriptions of the communes and social changes under the Cultural Revolution in the 1960s.

The hostile view depicted Chinese society as oppressive and Chinese history as stagnant. An early example of this was contained in Daniel Defoe's *The Farther Adventures of Robinson Crusoe*, published in 1719, in which the Chinese were described as a 'miserable people'. J.G. von Herder castigated China as an 'embalmed mummy'. Hegel, who saw history as a process of spiritual and mental progress, identified China as the place where human progress had begun, but thereafter the consciousness of freedom born in China had moved westwards, while back in China life went on unhistorically, changing restlessly without advancing.

In the nineteenth century, the most famous exponent of the negative view of China was Karl Marx. His interpretation of Asiatic society was that it was both different from and inferior to that of Europe. In Asia individual initiative played virtually no role and political activity was stifled by 'oriental despotism'. The characteristic feature of such a society was its mode of production, which was qualitatively different from any of the phases which had marked the development of European societies. The Asiatic mode of production was characterised by two features: a multitude of tiny, isolated village communities engaging in small-scale agriculture and handicrafts; and at the top of the pyramid, a despotic state which appropriated part of the surplus produced by the village communities and which took charge of public works, especially irrigation.[7]

Marx's ideas were followed up by Karl Wittfogel in his once-influential book *Oriental Despotism*, published in 1957. Wittfogel classified China as a hydraulic society, a type of society not unique to China, for similar societies had also developed in pre-Spanish America, in East Africa and in Hawaii. Such a society might be compared to or contrasted with an 'industrial society' or a 'feudal society'. In a hydraulic society the farming economy depended on large-scale and government-managed works of irrigation and flood control. Because in a hydraulic society there was an absence of constitutional, societal or cultural checks on bureaucratic power, the term 'oriental despotism' accurately described the Chinese form of government. According to

Wittfogel, China developed the characteristics of a hydraulic society as early as the third century BC, and then evolved into what he termed a 'complex hydraulic society', in which private property and enterprise were tolerated. But merchants and landowners had little influence on the ruling institutions, which in the hydraulic state comprised the autocratic power of the sovereign and the hierarchy of ranking officials and bureaucratic underlings. So society did not change, the state remained the institution of greatest power, and China did not experience the commercial or industrial revolutions of the west.[8]

The idea that the bureaucratic state exerted a baleful influence on the development of Chinese society has been expressed by a number of writers. Etienne Balazs rejected the concept of hydraulic society as too narrow to encompass the complexities of Chinese society, but he agreed that the unlimited power of the imperial bureaucracy had stifled the development of a capitalist economy and had prevented the emergence of a western form of science. This, he said, was the price paid for the homogeneity, long duration, and vitality of Chinese civilisation.[9]

This view of the nature of Chinese society merges with another wide-ranging discussion: why China surrendered her commanding lead over the West in terms of technology and why she did not develop as a capitalist society. Criticism of theories of an Asiatic mode of production, or of a hydraulic society, have pointed out that there is plenty of evidence to show that Chinese society was not static, that, for example, there was clear evidence of vigorous economic growth at various points in Chinese history. Investigation of this suggested that the reason why this did not usher in full-scale capitalism was not the overwhelming power of the state, but the contrary: the imperial state was too weak and too limited to provide the infrastructure which would have enabled capitalist ventures to prosper. A recent study of the state and peasant in the inland province of Hunan suggests that the truth must lie between these two extremes. The imperial state was neither despotic nor laissez-faire. It did intervene in the rural economy, often in a manner that was supportive and constructive, but it did not have the ability to overcome the population rise which had led to a tenfold increase in the population of the province from the fourteenth to the nineteenth centuries; nor could it control the consequences of the commercialisation of agriculture, which were beneficial to some but disastrous to others.[10]

REGIONAL STUDIES

It is inevitable, in a book of this scope, that the emphasis of the discussion should be on national themes, and that as a consequence the history of China is treated as if it were monolithic. In fact China is a continental country and over long periods it has been subject to political divisions. These have included times when the country has been divided into two (for example under the Southern Song and the Jin dynasties) and times of more complex divisions, for example in the so-called period of division, between 316 and 589. At all times regions and provinces, the latter themselves in many cases having the size and population of European states, have merited separate treatment. Recently some of the most interesting work on Chinese history, for example Richard von Glahn's study of Sichuan frontier in Song times, or Hugh R. Clark's investigation of the economic development of southern Fujian, has been done in a regional or local context.[11]

Nor can China, in the period studied in this volume or even today, be described as a single economic unit. One of the most influential studies of the Chinese economy was by G. William Skinner, who subdivided the country into eight macroregions, each containing an economic core area. Each of these macroregions can be distinguished and studied in terms of its population distribution, urbanisation, economic activity, etc.[12] This approach has been applied to the eighteenth century, with lively descriptions of the society of the eight macroregions and of Taiwan and Manchuria, descriptions which bring out vividly 'the pluralism and diversity of China.'[13] But this is a pioneering study and to extend its approach across the whole span of Chinese history is well beyond the scope of this book.

CHAPTER ONE

PREHISTORIC CHINA AND THE SHANG DYNASTY

For long it had been supposed in the West that Chinese civilisation had no prehistory. However, this supposition was swept aside in the 1920s, when the field method of archaeology was introduced into China and important archaeological discoveries began to be made. Since then archaeology has produced a tremendous amount of information on the early history of China. However, much of this information is still in the process of being interpreted and there are many substantial gaps in our knowledge.

LOWER PALAEOLITHIC CULTURES

The first discovery of remains of early man in China came in 1927, when the Swedish archaeologist J.G. Andersson, excavating sites at Zhoukoudian, thirty miles south-west of Beijing, found human fossil remains including five nearly complete crania. These have been ascribed to *Sinanthropus pekinensis*, otherwise known as Beijing man, who possessed hominid features: erect posture and considerable cranial capacity and the capability of making tools and implements, but who was distinguished from *Homo sapiens* by the low skull vault, the great thickness of the skull wall and by other features which made him a relation of *Homo erectus* of Java. From the associated deposits it was apparent that Beijing man hunted deer and possibly made fire and cooked his meat. He was probably a cannibal, eating the flesh, brain and marrow of his own kind. He used vein quartz to make a variety of implements and it has been suggested that the range of artefacts he made is more like the assemblages of southern and eastern Asia than those of Europe and Africa. But this suggestion and another which proposes a morphological link between Beijing man and the modern Mongoloid populations has not been generally accepted. It is not possible to apply new scientific techniques to these fossil remains because they disappeared, en route to the United States, shortly after the attack on Pearl Harbor.

In 1963, and in subsequent years, more early human remains were found in the vicinity of Lantian in eastern-central Shaanxi, about 1,000 kilometres south-west of Zhoukoudian. These remains, although closely related to Beijing man, were more primitive, the cranial capacity being considerably smaller. No habitation sites were identified in connection with these remains, although some stone implements were found which may be associated with them. Stone implements of comparable age have been found at a number of sites near Ruicheng in south-western Shanxi. There is also evidence of human occupation of about the same date at several localities in South China.

MIDDLE AND UPPER PALAEOLITHIC CULTURES

Only a limited number of Middle Palaeolithic sites have been found in China, the most notable being those of the Ordos region and the Fen river valley in Shanxi. It is not clear whether the Middle Palaeolithic transitional stage also occurred in South China.

Much more is known of the Upper Palaeolithic period. In North China sites of this period have been uncovered throughout the Ordos region, that is to say the northern grasslands of the middle Yellow river, and these have become known collectively as the Ordosian culture. Not a great deal of evidence of the physical characteristics of Upper Palaeolithic man is available. The Upper Cave at Zhoukoudian contained three skeletal remains, which yielded a radiocarbon date of 16,922 BC. These remains have been described as 'pre-Chinese', 'un-specialised' Mongoloids resembling American Indians. But information on Ordos stone industries is substantial: at one site in Shanxi more than fifteen thousand pieces of stone implements and flakes were found. The blade artefacts of the culture are identical with the Perigordian and Aurignacian types of western Europe, and exhibit a clear tendency to specialise. Composite implements made of bone shafts and microlithic implements are known and regional variations have been recognised. A number of other Upper Palaeolithic sites have been discovered in south-western China.

The evidence relating to Upper Palaeolithic man in China has given rise to controversy over the origin of the Mongoloid branch of living man. In 1943 Franz Weidenreich and then in 1962 Carleton Coon argued that there was a genetic continuity from Beijing man to modern Mongoloids on the basis of common cranial and dental features, for example shovel-shaped incisors. They proposed that Beijing man was ancestral solely to the Mongoloids and that separate contemporaneous early hominids were ancestral to the other races of present-day man. The alternate view is that all modern men have a common ancestor who was later than Beijing man. Modern Chinese may have developed by direct descent from the people of the Upper Cave at Zhoukoudian, but there is as yet a lack of evidence to bridge the gap between Palaeolithic man and Neolithic man in North China, who displays physical characteristics apparently indistinguishable from the modern Chinese.

NEOLITHIC MAN IN CHINA

It was long commonly believed that the Neolithic way of life – characterised by reliance on farming for food, by the use of pottery, and by the making of stone implements by grinding – had not commenced in China until the third millennium BC, and that it had been diffused to North China from western Asia. However, from the 1950s archaeological discoveries provided evidence of an indigenous Neolithic culture in North China. In the 1960s evidence was found to indicate the existence of parallel Neolithic cultures on the south-eastern coast (the Dapenkeng culture) and the lower Yangzi and Huai river areas (the Qinglian'gang culture).

All three cultures have been the subject of a considerable amount of excavation and writing and the importance of all three has now been established. Nevertheless, the best-known Neolithic sites remain those of the Yellow river valley. The first discovery was made in 1920 by farmers of Yangshao village in northern Henan, near the great bend of the Yellow river. Subsequently, hundreds of sites identified with the Yangshao culture were found over a large area of the Yellow river valley. Typically, Yangshao culture was one practised by settled farmers, living in villages sited in the valleys of the Yellow river drainage system. They cultivated foxtail millet and, to supplement their diet, they collected wild grain and went hunting and fishing. They had domesticated dogs and pigs and a few cattle, sheep and goats, and they may have grown hemp and raised silkworms.

The best-known Yangshao site is that of Banpo near Xi'an in southern Shaanxi. It was a large village which experienced several successive periods of occupation, which has been taken to indicate that its inhabitants practised shifting cultivation, moving away from the village site when the land had been temporarily exhausted and returning when it had recovered. It was quite a large village, containing perhaps one hundred houses, and it was surrounded by a ditch. The houses were of a fairly permanent construction, with plastered floors, wattle-and-daub walls and roofs supported on wooden posts. In the latter period of occupation a longhouse was constructed in the centre of the village. At the east end of the village was a pottery centre and to the north the village cemetery. From the evidence of the longhouse and the arrangement of the cemetery, it has been suggested that the inhabitants had lineage and clan types of kinship grouping and that they had already initiated the cult of ancestors to symbolise lineage solidarity.

The best-known production of the Yangshao culture is its ceramics and in particular the painted pottery used at meals and for rituals. This pottery is handmade and moulded and there is some indication of the use of coiling techniques, but not of the wheel. The decoration is concentrated on the upper part of the vessel and usually comprises abstract designs of large joined spirals. In a few cases schematic human figures or fish are represented.

Outstanding examples of Yangshao pottery have been described as the finest artistic achievement of the Neolithic period in China – so remarkable that it has seemed difficult to explain the sudden and indigenous emergence of so sophisticated a culture. When J.G. Andersson first attempted to classify the regional variations of the pottery which had been found over a wide area of North China, he considered that the Gansu pottery of the far north-west was the oldest regional variety. This led him to suggest that Yangshao culture had come from the West and had reached China through the Gansu panhandle. This supposition was supported by apparent similarities between Yangshao pottery and the decoration of pottery of a similar age found in Turkestan. However, extensive excavation of Yangshao sites, and in particular of Majiayao, has shown conclusively that the Gansu pottery is of a later date than that of the Zhong Yuan, or Central Plain, area of the Yellow river valley. Moreover, it is now known that the Yangshao culture, or more correctly its forerunners, is a good deal older than Andersson had supposed, and dates back to the sixth millennium BC. It seems to have originated in the nuclear area of central Shaanxi, south-western Shanxi and western Henan, and this strengthens the implication that it grew out of the terminal Palaeolithic and Mesolithic cultures of the area, although the links have yet to be established. In short, the derivation of Yangshao culture from the Middle East is no longer a tenable theory. What is now a matter of debate is the relationship between the regions in China where Neolithic cultures developed.

In 1928 the site of Chengziyai, in north-west Shandong, was first excavated. This village appeared to differ from the Yangshao culture villages, in that it was surrounded by a defensive wall of stamped earth. The design of the houses too was somewhat different and the inhabitants made greater use of polished stone implements. Most strikingly they produced a distinctively different type of pottery, which was thin, hard and burnished black, with angular shapes rather than the rounded contours of Yangshao pottery and which showed the beginnings of the use of the wheel. This culture has become known as Longshan, after another site in Shandong.

At first archaeologists recognised the Longshan culture as distinct from that of Yangshao and regarded it as localised in the east, whereas Yangshao was the Neolithic culture of the Central Plain – an interpretation which became known as the 'two-culture theory'. However, when the site of Miaodigou II was excavated, Longshan pottery was found at a level above that of the painted pottery. Consequently a second theory, the 'nuclear theory' was propounded which proposed that the Longshan culture was later than the Yangshao and that in fact it derived from it. However, this interpretation was difficult to reconcile with the evidence of the pottery: Longshan pottery is unpainted and many of the vessels are footed, unlike the Yangshao ware. This led to the view that the appearance of Longshan ware was evidence of the intrusive influence of a different and unrelated culture – a view which was confirmed when carbon-14 dating became available. It has been suggested recently that the true relationship between the two cultures is that Longshan culture was long established south of the Yellow river, that it extended into the Central Plain and that in its later development it became the dominant culture of the region.[1]

THE XIA DYNASTY

According to early Chinese historians, and in particular to Sima Qian, who died in about 90 BC, Chinese history began with a sequence of three early rulers, followed by a succession of five emperors. The first of the three rulers was Fuxi, whose reign traditionally began in 2852 BC, and who was credited with the domestication of animals and the institution of family life. The third was Shennong, the divine farmer, who taught the people settled agriculture. These figures, who were described as half-human, half-animal, were clearly mythological. Their successors, the five emperors, were culture heroes. Huangdi, the Yellow Emperor, supposedly reigned from 2697 BC. It was he who introduced ceramics and writing. The fourth and fifth emperors of the sequence, Yao and Shun, were particularly esteemed as model rulers. Yao was said to have devised the agrarian calendar. Regarding his son as unworthy of the throne he appointed as his successor Shun, a poor peasant renowned for his devotion to his father, and he in turn became a model ruler. Shun continued Yao's practice and also chose a paragon, a man named Yu, as his successor. It is at this point that Chinese history begins to supplement the archaeological record, because Yu was believed to have founded a dynasty called the Xia, the traditional dates of which are 2205–1766 BC.

The Xia was the first of the three ancient dynasties, sometimes known as the *sandai*. The other two were the Shang and the Zhou, whose recorded dates were respectively 1766–1122 BC and 1122–256 BC. Chinese historians traditionally regarded these dynasties as sequential, each dynasty being overthrown by its successor. A recent evaluation of their relationship in the light of archaeological evidence suggests that they were only successive in terms of their relative political eminence, that Shang was already a powerful political entity prior to its subjugation of Xia, and Zhou was an important state before its overthrow of Shang. According to this interpretation the geographic dominion of the three dynasties may be accepted as having been Xia in the centre, Shang in the east and Zhou in the west. They are regarded as having shared essentially the same culture.

This re-evaluation has supported the view that the Xia dynasty, which was long regarded as belonging to legend rather than to history, did exist at approximately the times given in the early records. The late Central Plain Longshan culture has been dated to about 2000 BC, and the obvious inference is that the two are identical. In particular, the culture found at Erlitou, east of Luoyang in Henan has been identified with the Xia. Further, the evidence of pottery typology is consistent with the view that the Henan Longshan culture was the predecessor of the Erlitou culture.[2]

THE SHANG DYNASTY

According to tradition the Shang dynasty was established in 1766 BC when Cheng Tang – Tang the Completer – overthrew the tyrannical last ruler of the Xia and restored humane and virtuous government to the empire. Archaeological evidence has not confirmed this, and the dates of the Shang dynasty and the circumstances of the transition from Xia to Shang dominance are uncertain. One particular issue which remains unsolved is whether the important sites discovered in 1950, at Zhengzhou in northern Henan, belong to the early Shang or should be identified with the previous dynasty.

Despite these uncertainties there can be no doubt that the Shang dynasty, which shared a common culture with the Xia and which probably had its centre of activity somewhat to the east of the Xia sphere of activity, replaced the Xia as the most powerful political entity in north China between the dates ascribed to it by tradition. During that time the dynasty occupied a series of capitals, the most famous of which was Anyang in north Henan, the site of which was initially excavated between 1928 and 1937. It was this excavation which determined once and for all the historic existence of the dynasty, which previously had been accredited only by legends. Not only did these excavations produce extensive information relating to the physical features of the Shang capital, they also uncovered very substantial quantities of inscriptions on bone and bronze which have made it possible to build up a detailed picture of the nature of the Shang state as it existed in the middle and late Shang dynastic periods.

This state was a form of theocracy headed by a succession of kings whose main functions were probably ritual rather than political. The throne was passed from elder brother to younger brother as well as from father to son in a succession of thirty rulers. Their names were recorded by Sima Qian and their existence has been substantiated by archaeological finds. Rulers were served by officials whose titles indicate that they performed a variety of specialised functions. Although Shang culture spread over a large area of north China, it is unlikely that the control of the Shang kings extended nearly as far. What is more probable is that over much of the area authority was exercised by aristocratic leaders who accepted to some extent the leadership of the Shang kings, but who ruled in their own areas. These leaders defended the frontiers of Shang territory, supplied the manpower required for both military and construction purposes and collected tribute for the court. Surrounding the area of established and permanent Shang authority there was an outer zone ruled by tribal chieftains, friendly to the Shang, whose authority over their own people had been confirmed by investiture according to Shang political theory.[3]

At Anyang, in the enclave at Xiaotun, was situated the ceremonial and administrative focus of the Shang state. This comprised three sections, the functions of which are believed to be understood. The most northerly and perhaps the oldest section consisted of fifteen rectangular houses on stamped-earth foundations, which have been taken to be the residences of the ruling élite. The middle section contained twenty-one halls, constructed above a complex system of drainage channels and a large number of human burials. These are believed to have been the ancestral temples of the royal lineages. The most southerly section was the site of seventeen stamped-earth foundations, considered to have been the ceremonial heart of the enclave. This included a stepped structure which was almost certainly the foundation of a sacrificial altar. The scale of these structures, the evidence of elaborate planning, the extensive sacrifice of humans, the use of stamped-earth techniques and the innumerable oracle bones found on the site all point to this being the ceremonial centre of the royal house of the Shang dynasty.

About three kilometres north of Xiaotun is the site of Xibeigang, described as the royal cemetery of the Shang monarchs. The excavation of this site has revealed eleven very large cruciform graves and 1,222 small graves. It has been suggested that these are the graves of the eleven Shang kings who are recorded as having ruled from Anyang over a period of 273 years, and it has been estimated that the digging of each pit required at least seven thousand working days. The excavation of these graves has provided the most dramatic evidence of the nature of Shang kingship. The burials were accompanied by a large number of human sacrifices, the bodies, frequently with heads and torsos separated, being found around the central chamber and on the ramp leading down to it. The royal tombs contained a rich selection of Shang art. In the best known tomb, number 1001, was found an outstanding collection of stone sculptures and bronze artefacts.

SHANG BRONZES

This mention of bronze artefacts leads naturally to a discussion of one of the outstanding cultural achievements of the Shang period, that is the production of ceremonial bronze vessels which are remarkably sophisticated in terms of both technology and design. Chinese collectors had long identified the Shang period with the production of these vessels, but it was only with the excavation of Anyang that this ascription could be proved correct. However, the initial response to the discoveries by western archaeologists, who were puzzled by the lack of any examples of more primitive bronze casting, was that the technology for the creation of the bronzes must have derived from outside China, that is from west Asia.

More recent studies[4] have greatly strengthened the argument that the beginning of metallurgy in China, even though it came much later than in the West, was the result of an indigenous discovery. In the case of bronze technology, the particular argument which has been put forward is concerned with the technical repertoire of the Shang craftsmen. Noel Barnard pointed out that early Chinese bronzes show that craftsmen were acquainted only with direct casting in piece-mould assemblies and the casting-on to the vessel of pre-cast members such as handles and lugs; they knew nothing of sheet metal working, annealing and other techniques and did not use many of the tools which had appeared in the West. When it came to casting, Chinese craftsmen outclassed their western counterparts, but in the more general field of metal technology they lagged far behind. This, and the indication that the forms of Shang bronzes appear to derive from pottery styles, amount to strong evidence in support of the view that the Shang bronzes were the result of independent development.

Apart from the discussion relating to the origin of bronze technology, the principal interest of the bronzes relates to their aesthetic qualities and the indications which these offer of the nature of Shang society. Much of the production of bronze items was connected with conspicuous consumption. The main categories of production were ritual vessels, luxury items sometimes to be deposited in tombs, and weapons. Various classifications of these items have been made and chronological and stylistic sequences have been suggested. The high point of sequence is seen as coming in the late Shang and early Chou period. One of the characteristic forms was that of the *jue*, a ritual vessel standing on three legs, apparently intended for the warming of wine. The surfaces of these vessels and other ritual vessels were commonly covered with stylised surface decoration, the most common motif being that of a mythical creature lacking a lower jaw, known as the *taotie* mask.

Many of the vessels carried an inscription which indicated the reason why they had been cast and the purpose to which they were to be put. Vessels were often cast for the performance of sacrifices to ancestral spirits. As time passed inscriptions tended to become longer and by the early Chou period there are many examples of inscriptions which recorded that the vessels had been cast by persons who had received gifts from their feudal superiors and were to be used in ceremonies to reinforce that relationship.

THE DEVELOPMENT OF WRITING

It was in the Shang period that the Chinese system of writing became fully established. Examples of incised potters' marks go back to the Banpo site and to the Yangshao culture of the fifth millennium BC. It is uncertain whether these marks should be taken as among the earliest forms of Chinese characters, as similar markings are found elsewhere on neolithic pottery. However, pottery from Jiangzhai, Lintong *xian*, for which the date 4000 BC has been proposed, is inscribed with graphs which appear to have broken away from the simple single-element structures of the inscriptions at Banpo and to be sufficiently advanced in structural form to be regarded as primitive characters.

Pottery sherds from Dawenkou culture sites, which have been dated between 3000 and 2500 BC, carry inscriptions which go beyond primitive marks or pictorial representations of objects to include composite ideographs which convey concepts such as 'morning' or 'hot'. As such composite ideographs have been found on two different sites, it has been suggested that the meaning of the graphs was widely understood by people of that time. Here, it appears, is the beginning of a form of writing which could transcend differences of dialect. Moreover, here too is important indirect evidence of the independent development of the Chinese writing system. Simple ideographs have been used at various times in various cultures worldwide, and although there is no evidence to support the suggestion, it might be supposed that the art of writing had been diffused to China from the West. However the composite ideograph, which brings together several elements to form a single graph, is the essence of the Chinese writing system. Its early appearance in the context of the development of pottery inscriptions strongly suggests an indigenous origin. Moreover, the emergence of this writing system in the nuclear area implies the subsequent centrifugal diffusion of the system throughout the Chinese sphere.[5]

In the Shang period the written record of inscriptions on pottery and bronze vessels is greatly augmented by the survival of writing on bone, turtle shells and bamboo. The bone inscriptions are often to be found on the shoulder blades of cattle or sheep, which were used for a form of divination called scapulimancy, a practice already established in the Longshan culture. The divination consisted of interpreting the cracks which appeared in the bone after it had been heated. In the Shang period this became a sophisticated practice. The bone was treated in advance and questions were inscribed to be answered by interpreting the cracks which appeared subsequently. These oracle bones are evidence of the ceremonial practices of the time and an indication of the presence of a specialist group of augurs. To date, at least 107,000 oracle bone pieces have been assembled in more than eighty collections. Three thousand separate graphs have been identified, about half of which may be translated with varying degrees of accuracy.[6] The inscriptions which the bones bear provide much of what is known about the organisation of the Shang state.

THE SHANG STATE

Much of our knowledge of the Shang state refers to the Late Shang or Anyang period dating from approximately 1200 BC to 1040 BC. At that time the state had its main centres along the Yellow and the Huai rivers and exercised some authority up the Wei river valley in the territory to be known as the Zhou homeland.

Within this area and between these dates, the Shang rulers presided over a form of patrimonial domain. According to Paul Wheatley, who first elaborated this interpretation of the Shang state,[7] it operated through a combination of traditionalism and arbitrariness. The king regarded himself as the earthly instrument for the accomplishment of Heaven's designs. His lineage occupied a central position in the state's political, economic and ceremonial structures. The ruler treated all political administration as his personal affair and the officials, whom he had appointed on the basis of his confidence in them, performed their duties as a form of personal service to the ruler. The officials fell into three groups: the first comprised the secretariat – the councillors, including the great minister, who were in charge of agriculture (that is to say the arrangement of the agricultural calendar), the management of palace affairs, and the organisation of feasts and other matters; in this group too were the diviners and ceremonial specialists, including the court chroniclers. The second group was that of the civil officers who were appointed to various offices and who were distinguished according to rank. Finally there were military officials, who also had specified duties.

The above was the organisation of the royal domain. However, it is clear that in the Late Shang state authority was delegated by granting benefices in return for services rendered to the throne. The holders of benefices were granted titles, in return for which they performed certain duties, in particular the defence of Shang territory by the supply of manpower for military and construction purposes and by the collection of tribute for the court. It is interesting to note that a number of women were beneficed under these arrangements. In addition to these benefices, there was an outer ring of territories held by chieftains friendly to the Shang, whose authority was confirmed by investiture according to Shang political theory. This practice illustrates the process of sinicisation, the process of becoming Chinese, which was reinforced by the spread of the written language and the performance of cults related to ancestors.

Even allowing for the power of the Shang ceremonial, it is clear that the Shang state exercised only a limited control over much of the territory which lay under its influence. A recent analysis of oracle-bone inscriptions has provided fascinating, if incomplete, detail of the functioning of its authority.[8] The coercive power of the state derived from the king's armies and those of a few close supporters, and there are numerous divinations on the possible outcome of sorties made by these forces. However, the Shang diviners did not divine about expeditions which did not involve the king as well as his allies. This is taken as evidence that the military power exercised by the Shang state was dynastic: the allies of the Shang would only fight if the king fought beside them. State power was exercised in the capital and in the few places which were regularly visited by the king. Elsewhere the state might be seen as a thin network of pathways and encampments laid over a hinterland which rarely knew the king's presence.

A particular example of the nature of Shang authority, and one which is of especial interest because of subsequent developments, concerns the relationship between the Shang state and the people of Zhou who probably lived north of the Wei river. Many of the divination inscriptions refer to the Zhou in terms which imply that they were members of the Shang state: for example, they received orders from the king. On the other hand, it is clear that the Zhou were not at the heart of the Shang state, and the Shang had little direct contact with them. One reason for this was distance, the Zhou centre being 625 kilometres from Xiaotun, but the relationship also underlines

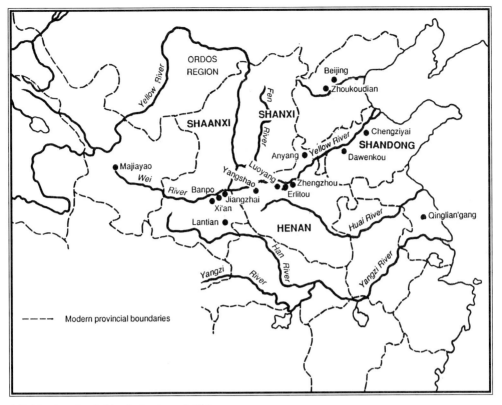

1 Prehistoric and early historic sites in north China

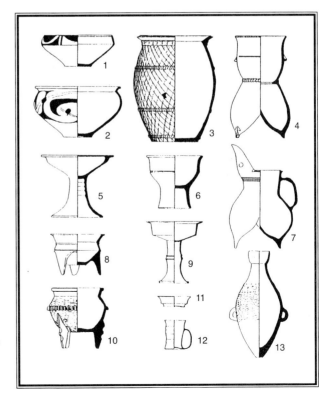

2 Neolithic pottery types of north China,
first half of the second millennium BC;
types 1–4 are Yangshao and types 5–12
are Longshan

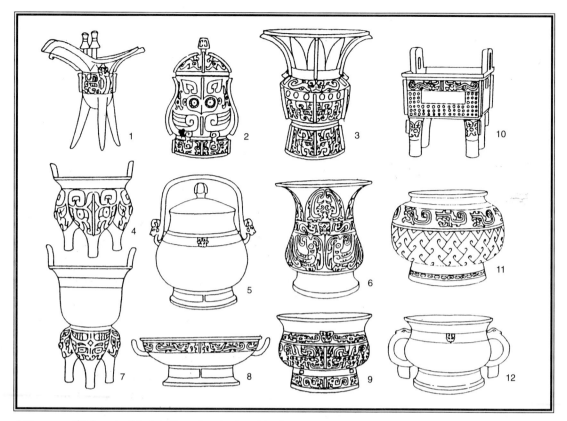

3 Bronze sacrificial vessels of the late Shang dynasty; type 1 is a jue

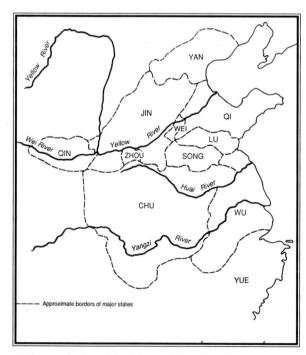

4 China at the time of Confucius (c. 551–479 BC)

5 Zhuangzi drumming on a bowl and singing after his wife's death; nineteenth-century woodblock (O/C 15331.e.12)

the argument that the Shang state, if such a term is acceptable, exercised only a limited influence over the territory with which it is associated. Perhaps it should be described as an incipient state, a dynastic lineage, ruling in a patrimonial style over a central and perhaps shifting nucleus, and exercising intermittent influence over surrounding groups.

Shang society showed considerable class differentiation. At the top was an élite comprising the king and the royal lineages. There is evidence of an aristocratic culture in some of the burials and it is clear that military skills were valued. The Shang army comprised two main corps, one of infantry and one of chariots, and some aristocratic tombs contain chariot burials. The evidence of the use of chariots, either for hunting or for war, provides the strongest proof of direct contacts between China and the West. Although the domesticated horse had been known in Mesopotamia from the first half of the third millennium, it only became popular and was used to draw a war chariot from about 1500 BC. A mere two and a half centuries later the use of the horse chariot in China was recorded on oracle bones. Moreover, the design of the Shang horse chariot closely resembled that developed in the West.[9]

Below the aristocracy was a specialist group composed of craftsmen, and particularly those who worked in bronze. It seems probable that particular handicrafts were the prerogative of individual kinship groups. These artisan groups had a lifestyle which set them apart from the peasantry. In particular they lived in above-ground stamped-earth buildings, containing two rooms and sometimes provided with a window, altogether much superior to the dwellings of the peasants.

At the bottom of the social pyramid were the peasants. It has often been alleged that Shang society was a slave society and for Marxist historians this description has been axiomatic. There certainly was a great gulf between the aristocracy and the peasants. Peasants lived in primitive semi-subterranean dwellings. Their burials were extremely simple and contained only the most meagre display of possessions. The evidence of the great tombs, the construction of which required many thousands of man hours, and of the numerous human sacrifices – usually found in multiples of ten, offers some support for the slave society view. However, most western writers have rejected that interpretation and have argued that peasants were not slaves but serfs. In some cases, at least, those sacrificed were prisoners of war, sometimes found to be suffering from malnutrition.

CHAPTER TWO

THE ZHOU DYNASTY

By tradition, the Zhou dynasty is dated from 1122–256 BC[1] and this immensely long period is subdivided into three parts: the Western Zhou period, 1122–771 BC, the earlier part of the Eastern Zhou period, from 771–481 BC, which is known as the Spring and Autumn period after a work of that name which records the events in the state of Lu in those years; and the Warring States period, which lasted from 403–221 BC. This era has long been regarded as the crucial formative stage in Chinese history. Of it Herrlee G. Creel once remarked, 'It would probably be generally agreed, for most practical purposes that the Chinese tradition may be said to have begun with the Zhou'.[2]

THE WESTERN ZHOU

According to the tradition enshrined in the historical record, the overthrow of the Shang dynasty and its replacement by the Zhou came about because of the transfer of the mandate of heaven. The Zhou rulers were granted the mandate to enable them to rescue the suffering people from the wicked last king of the Shang. In the account given by Sima Qian, in the *Shiji*, the *Historical Records*, compiled a thousand years later, the Zhou ruler the Earl of the West, otherwise known as King Wen, was a paragon of virtue. He excited the jealousy of the last Shang monarch, who, on one occasion imprisoned him. When King Wen died his son King Wu, known for his martial qualities, attacked the Shang and overthrew them. The account of the conquest which has been handed down indicates that events took a dramatic turn. The Zhou troops numbered only 50,000 and they were met by a Shang army of 700,000 men. However, the Shang troops revolted against the cruelties of their ruler and went over to the other side. The last Shang ruler died amidst the flames of his palace.

Other scraps of evidence do not add a great deal to the traditional account. It is likely that the Zhou state was populated by people who had not completely accepted Shang culture. According to Mencius, 'King Wen was a Western barbarian'.[3] A more exact interpretation of Zhou ethnic origins was put forward by Wolfram Eberhard, who suggested that the ruling house of Zhou 'may have been related to the Turkish ethnic group'.[4] However there is no linguistic evidence to support this theory. The archaeological evidence suggests that the Zhou may have displayed some cultural differences, perhaps because they had developed their state in harsher surroundings. Nevertheless, they derived from the same Longshanoid culture which had produced the Shang. Relations had existed between Shang and Zhou over a number of generations. By the reign of King Tai, grandfather of King Wen, it is evident that a degree of sinicisation had already taken place and Zhou rulers may have accepted Shang overlordship. The reason for the Zhou attack on the Shang state may never be known, but the relative ease with which the dynasty was brought to an end suggests that its rulers were no longer able to rely on the loyalty of their leading vassals. It has been suggested recently that the Zhou victory depended less on the issue of loyalty than on military technology. At the decisive battle of Muye the Zhou army was led by three hundred chariots. Chariots were new on the battlefield; their significance was not so much as a fighting vehicle, but more as a mobile platform from which aristocratic warriors could command their troops.[5]

A variety of opinion has been expressed over the significance of the change from Shang to Zhou: should it be regarded as a major discontinuity, or were the main elements of the Shang state continued under the successor state? According to Franz Michael, the fall of the Shang and the establishment of the Zhou was more than a dynastic change, it was the end of an era. The age of magic and the belief in Shangdi, the ruler of the spirits and the ancestor of the Shang, was overturned. In its place the Zhou established a rational explanation of a moral universe. In particular two new concepts were introduced by the Zhou: the concepts of *tian* or heaven, and of *de*, human morality or man's proper conduct in harmony with the moral principles of the universe.[6]

Other writers have argued that there was continuity. Jacques Gernet wrote that

the complex process of evolution which leads from the archaic monarchy – the main characteristics of which persist at the beginning of the Zhou period – to the centralized state and the imperial unification does not present any real break in continuity.[7]

The historical and archaeological record lends support to this view. The conquest of the Shang was followed by the enfeoffment of the son of the last Shang ruler as a vassal of the Zhou king. However, to ensure his good behaviour, two of the king's brothers were appointed to keep watch over him. Shortly after that King Wu died, and although he was succeeded by his son, real power fell into the hands of his brother, the famous Duke of Zhou. Jealousy over the duke's rule led to an uprising in which the Shang heir died. This was followed by the duke leading a military expedition to the east, on which, it was claimed, he extinguished fifty states and enfeoffed seventy-one of his followers. At this point the duke also established a new capital near Luoyang, although the old Zhou capital, near present-day Xi'an, remained the seat of the Zhou administration.

On the whole, the archaeological evidence supports the case for continuity rather than for major change. Chang Kwang-chih noted the constants relating to the construction of cities and the practices relating to burials. Even more convincing is the evidence of the bronze art of the period. The study made by Bernard Karlgren of the stylistic evolution of the ritual vessels concluded that the art of the Western Zhou was still essentially the same as the Shang, but with small innovations.[8]

A more substantial dispute has arisen over the nature of the Zhou state as established by the Duke of Zhou and developed by his successors. Traditional Chinese historiography treated the Xia, Shang and Western Zhou states as unified empires, similar in authority to those of more modern times. However, in *La Chine antique*, published in 1927, Henri Maspero depicted China under the Zhou as a far more primitive society, 'à demi sauvage encore'. He believed that in political terms it was only a loose federation of vassal states and that the establishment of a real state in China at that time was still impossible.[9]

Maspero's view was challenged by Herrlee G. Creel, who presented a detailed argument in support of the view that the Western Zhou kings ruled an empire rather than a tribal society and that they had developed a rather tightly controlled, relatively centralised government. Creel's argument began with a consideration of the organisation of royal government. He noted that the Zhou rulers claimed to be continuing the good practices of their predecessors. Nevertheless, according to Creel, the evidence suggested that there was innovation and in particular the development of a proto-bureaucratic form of administration. He identified three types of officials, administrative, functional and military, and noted the post of chief minister, whose role was not easy to define as much remained within the personal control of the king. Officials were not true bureaucrats, for they still derived much of their living from their fiefs, but they did display bureaucratic tendencies, particularly in their addiction to the use of written records.

To control an empire, it was essential that the government should have developed certain mechanisms, and Creel went to great lengths to identify the evidence which showed that this was so. He pointed out that a unified state required a financial system. After reviewing all the evidence relating to commercial activity and finance, he concluded that it was probable that there was a considerable amount of trade in the empire, that media of exchange of various kinds – in particular cowrie shells and silk – were in use, and that extensive financial operations were carried out by the government. He also noted the probability that a system of justice had been instituted. According to Creel, even though no Zhou code of law has survived, there is no reason to doubt that laws existed, that the king was the chief dispenser of justice, that legal procedures were followed and that crimes such as theft were punished severely.

FEUDALISM IN EARLY CHINA

The debate over the character of the Western Zhou state is related to the more general issue of feudalism in early China. The suggestion that the term feudalism, a term which was coined to denote the social and economic relationships in western Europe during the mediaeval period, should be applied to the China of a thousand years earlier, was first proposed by Guo Moruo. For Guo and for other Marxist historians it formed part of an analysis of the development of Chinese society which began by identifying Shang society as slave society, and which identified the transitional point from slave to feudal society as having occurred during the Zhou period, perhaps coincidental with the shift from the Spring and Autumn stage to that of the Warring States.

The argument that Zhou society was a feudal society is based on two explanations of feudalism: the dynamic version which defines feudalism as a form of society which is liable to arise under certain conditions, and the static version which refers to the institutions and relationships within a society. In the Chinese context the dynamic version is represented by the interpretation of the Shang/Zhou change which emphasises the collapse of a powerful Shang empire, the foreignness of the Zhou and the military character of the conquest. Once the Zhou had overthrown the Shang, they found that they did not have the resources to rule the empire directly and so territory was parcelled out to Zhou leaders and allies who had participated in the conquest, and also to indigenous clan leaders who had submitted to the Zhou and were permitted to retain their lands. This led to the creation of a large number of small states, at least one hundred of which are known to have existed in the eighth century BC. Characteristically each state consisted of a walled capital, surrounded by tilled lands and separated from the next state by a 'no man's land, peopled by "barbarians"'.[10]

The descriptive version of feudalism is a more detailed interpretation, which relies on western studies of feudalism to provide a model with which the Chinese version may be compared. The model commonly adopted is that put forward by Marc Bloch in *Feudal Society*. This contained two essential elements: the institution of the fief, a delineated territory allocated to an individual who might exercise limited or unlimited control over it; and the institution of vassalage, the relationship denoted by the requirement on the holder of the fief to provide military aid to the ruler and the obligation of everlasting loyalty.

The descriptive version of feudalism begins with the concept that all land belonged to the king and he alone had the right to dispose of it. There was evidence of this in a poem in the *Shijing*, that is the *Book of Songs*:

> Everywhere under vast Heaven
> There is no land that is not the king's.
> To the borders of those lands
> There are none who are not the king's servants.[11]

It continues with reference to the existence of a fixed hierarchy of nobility of descending rank bearing specific titles. The Chinese terms *gong, hou, bo, zi* and *nan* are usually translated as duke, marquis, earl, viscount and baron. Each of these nobles was invested with a territory and the confirmation of his possession took the form of a ceremony of investiture which took place in the Zhou ancestral temple. The new vassal was presented with a jade sceptre and a tablet bearing the terms of his enfeoffment, and received other valuable gifts including bronze vessels. Rulership was hereditary and the ceremony was repeated when the son succeeded his father. In return for being granted land, nobles had to attend audiences at court, provide assistance for major construction projects and supply troops to assist the king in the event of barbarian attack. The feudal relationship was not confined to the king and nobles: nobles in turn subdivided their domains among their relatives, their officials and their courtiers, and made similar grants of land in exchange for service.

Zhou society displayed other features which made it comparable to that of feudal Europe. The aristocracy was a class clearly differentiated from the mass of the population. It did not engage in trade and it obeyed an elaborate code of ritual comparable to the code of chivalry of European knighthood. Above all it was committed to war, and the typical aristocrat went on campaigns with his four-horse chariot supported by a company of foot-soldiers. Of the commoners, the great mass of them were peasants, who were bound to the land as serfs; in times of peace they were forced to hand over a portion of their crop to their lord and to provide labour services; in times of war they had to serve their lord as foot-soldiers. The system of land tenure is imperfectly understood, because of shortage of evidence. However, it is often suggested that the 'well-field' system, later described by Mencius, was practised at this time. The Chinese character for a well resembles the pattern for a game of noughts and crosses. Under this system of land distribution, the produce of the central square, which was cultivated by the group of peasants, was reserved for the lord, whereas the produce of the surrounding eight squares was retained by individual peasant families for their own use.

This description of Zhou society has been subjected to many qualifications, which in some cases have amounted to a rejection of the application of the word 'feudal' to the Chinese situation. The most obvious point to make is that of shortage of evidence. Many of the statements contained in the description derive from sources much later than the Western Zhou period and reflect a strong tendency in such sources to describe the period as a golden age and to imply a degree of uniformity and order which most probably did not exist. Another qualification is that whereas in European feudalism the relationship between lord and vassal was a contractual one, under the Western Zhou the relationship was very often one of kinship ties and if no kinship tie existed it was usually created by marriage. This led Charles O. Hucker to say that 'all the feudal lords were expected to accept the king as head of a vast extended family and to feel themselves beholden to the Zhou ancestral spirits as its founders'.[12] As time passed, the blood ties to the Zhou became more remote and the kinship ties were loosened. As the Zhou rulers extended their area of influence, new political units were created and grants were made to vassals who were not relatives.

If the description 'feudal', is appropriate, it should used in the light of special features of China's experience. For example, Wolfram Eberhard employed the term 'superstratification' to denote the form of feudal society which had developed under the Zhou, because in that case a conquering federation had imposed itself on an already stratified society. Eberhard added that the conquering federation was a foreign one. Owen Lattimore pointed out that a special kind of feudalism developed in the frontier zone in which Chinese and nomads met. Derk Bodde argued that a fully-fledged feudal system could only have come into existence some time after the Zhou conquest, when it extended to sub-infeudation, that is it integrated not only the ruler and his vassals but the entire population into the feudal pyramid.

The most recent study of the Western Zhou period, which makes extensive use of archaeological evidence, is that of Hsu Cho-yun and Katheryn M. Linduff. They describe Zhou feudalism as 'a multilayered feudal structure that accommodated both conformity in the ruling mechanism and diversity in practice'.[13] The structure had been developed to enable the Zhou to establish its influence over the Shang and the vassal states, and subsequently over an area which spread south of the Yangzi and into the southern coastal regions. The backbone of the feudal system which was developed was the *zongfa* or kinship network. This term, which literally means 'law of kindred', referred to Zhou practice regarding patrilineal descent and exogamy, which has been seen as breaking with the Shang custom that the royal inheritance should pass to a younger brother rather than to the eldest son. Power was delegated into the hands of vassals, but the feudal relationship was strengthened either by kinship bonds or by matrimonial ties. As a consequence, the ruling class of the Zhou was tied into a 'vast extended household'. Evidence of the strength and general acceptance of these kinship bonds is to be found in cemeteries which have been excavated, which indicate that the dead were buried in an orderly fashion reflecting the ranked structure of kin groups.

POLITICAL DEVELOPMENTS IN THE WESTERN ZHOU

As mentioned above, the feudal structure developed in the Western Zhou was a response to the needs created by the conquest of the Shang and subsequent expansion. It is possible to indicate how this expansion was achieved. In former Shang territory the Zhou appointed a new ruler from the Zhou royal lineage who was expected to seek the collaboration of the Shang élite. For example, in the state of Wei, the younger brother of King Wu and the Duke of Zhou was appointed as ruler, and he was urged to honour Shang traditions and to enlist the services of Shang elders. As the Zhou expanded into the areas peripheral to the Shang state, they encountered a wide variety of non-Chinese peoples. Here the Zhou could not adopt the same model of cultural fusion which they had applied to the Shang people. Nevertheless, they tried to assimilate and accommodate local people rather than to confront and suppress them. Zhou expansion proceeded in all directions from the new capital at Zhengzhou. To the north, the states of Yan and Jin were brought more firmly into the Zhou orbit through a fusion of the Shang and Zhou élites. Further extension of Zhou influence in this direction was barred by the strength of the nomadic groups from the steppes. The most significant expansion was to the east. Here the Zhou had been faced with an uprising and had had to establish their control over populations which were not ethnic Chinese. For example the state of Qi, which occupied much of present-day Shandong, had a diverse population which included non-Chinese peoples such as the Laiyi who were eventually subjugated. To manage such a diverse population, the Zhou rulers supported policies of co-existence and tolerated diverse customs and at the same time they formed coalitions with local groups. Meanwhile to the south descendants of the Zhou royal house were enfeoffed. A gradual fusion of holdings led to the emergence of the state of Chu along the Huai river valley.

While this political expansion and consolidation was taking place, two broader trends may be observed. The first was the diffusion of elements of Zhou culture throughout much of modern China. To the north-west Zhou influence reached into Gansu and to the south-west into Sichuan. It made its way south across the Yangzi, reaching as far as the Zhu river valley. In many cases the cultural diffusion was of a superficial nature. In Sichuan, for example, Zhou influence was later overwhelmed by a revival of non-Chinese culture. But elsewhere the diffusion of Zhou culture was to leave a lasting impact on local populations.

The second trend concerned the matter of identity and the use of the term *huaxia* to denote mainstream Chinese as opposed to peripheral groups. Initially the description *huaxia* applied only to the inhabitants of the Central Plain and referred to the descendants of the Neolithic traditions of Yangshao and Longshan. However the Zhou expansion extended the application of the term, through the process of cultural fusion, to those who accepted the Zhou concept of Chineseness. The Zhou, it will be remembered, had claimed that the mandate of heaven had given them the right to rule. This doctrine justified Zhou expansion and strengthened the identification of the political units created or endorsed by the Zhou with a broader political concept. Herein perhaps lies the beginning of the assumption that what is now modern China should be a single political entity rather than a collection of nation states.

THE FALL OF THE WESTERN ZHOU, 771 BC

The Western Zhou period was one of rapid but unstable expansion. At the beginning of the period Zhou rulers, by a process of conquest, enfeoffment and the transfer of states, had spread their influence over a large part of northern China. In the middle of the period their successors conducted frequent and ambitious campaigns against non-Chinese peoples on the periphery of their territory. For example, King Mu, who reigned in the tenth century BC, made a series of expeditions into Central Asia. His chariot, it was said, was pulled by eight semi-divine stallions and his desire was to leave the track of this chariot everywhere. But after his reign Zhou authority over the regional lords began to decline and by the beginning of the eighth century BC its ability to control the non-Chinese people on the borders was in doubt.

The end came in 771 BC, when the Zhou capital Hao was overrun by non-Chinese from the north in alliance with rebel Chinese states. According to legend King You, the last king of the Western Zhou, had amused his concubine by frequently lighting beacon fires to call for assistance. On this occasion the feudal lords failed to respond to the signal and the king was defeated and killed. But the real reasons for the fall of the Western Zhou were a series of natural catastrophes, including a serious earthquake and a famine, and the decline of the royal administration. The personal failings of the last Western Zhou king may have played a part, and another factor was recurrent pressure from non-Chinese peoples. The dynasty, as originally constructed, was no longer viable. After the death of King You the capital was transferred east to Luoyang and the successors to the Zhou throne played a much more limited role.

POLITICAL, SOCIAL AND ECONOMIC DEVELOPMENTS IN THE SPRING AND AUTUMN PERIOD

The Eastern Zhou period, which is traditionally divided into the Spring and Autumn period, 771–481 BC and the Warring States period 403–221 BC, will be considered first in terms of its political, social and economic developments and in a later section in terms of its philosophical and cultural aspects.

In political terms the early Spring and Autumn period saw northern China divided into perhaps fifteen major feudal states, interspersed with a large number of smaller fiefs. The Zhou dynasty itself occupied a small area around Luoyang and its influence was restricted to the performance of religious and symbolic ceremonies. The major feudal states can be divided into two: those of the Central Plain which were regarded as Chinese, and those of the periphery which were regarded by the former group as barbarian.

Typical of the Chinese feudal states was the state of Qi, which, after it had absorbed some of its smaller neighbours, occupied much of the present-day province of Shandong. After this expansion, Qi under its ruler Duke Huan began to modernise its institutions. A key figure in this was Guan Zhong, who became one of the most renowned statesmen of antiquity. A uniform tax system was introduced, a method of military recruitment enforced and steps taken to develop the commerce of the state.

Another powerful state of this early period was the state of Jin, which occupied part of modern Shanxi. The ruler of Jin had played a part in placing the first ruler of the Eastern Zhou on the throne. The geographical position of Jin allowed for expansion and the mountainous terrain it occupied may have encouraged the development of horse-breeding.

A third example of state building can be found in the southern state of Chu. This state, which was regarded as semi-Chinese, occupied the middle Yangzi region. Despite its barbaric reputation it contained substantial cities, where its leaders buried their dead in style and with the accompaniment of human sacrifices. Although the Chu leaders claimed descent from the royal house of Zhou, from the beginning they had also claimed the title of king. And although the Chu kings granted fiefs to some of their followers, they also introduced a new administrative model, that of the *xian* or administrative district placed under an official appointed by the ruler.

These states were powerful political entities, and they conducted themselves as sovereign bodies. Official contacts between states were frequent and in the early Spring and Autumn period were generally friendly. But the lack of any effective central authority made it difficult to co-ordinate a response to a common threat. Such a threat arose in the seventh century BC with attacks from non-Chinese tribes in the north, and grew more serious when Chu, the major state on the southern periphery, also began to encroach on the states of the Central Plain. In 651 BC, to counter this threat, the central states held a conference. In *Mencius* there is a record of an agreement made on that occasion.[14] The states which participated agreed to a system of collective security and chose one of their leaders to act as hegemon. Duke Huan of Qi became the first of the 'five leaders of the feudal lords' who sought to hold this association together. His successor was Duke Wen of Jin, who was made hegemon in 632 BC. It was alleged that a regulation had been adopted which provided that interstate meetings should be held at regular intervals.[15] At its best the hegemon system was but a weak response to the failure of central authority. The ruler of Chu was not committed to the arrangement and when he became the hegemon the whole purpose of the initiative was lost and the danger of uncontrolled interstate warfare was apparent.

The change in the balance of political power was a reflection of the important social and economic changes which occurred at this time. At the beginning of the Eastern Zhou period, society had been dominated by an élite composed of rulers who for the most part were related to or appointed by the royal house. This élite in turn was served by ministers or officials drawn from the great noble families of the state and holding their position by virtue of their birth. In addition to having a position at court members of the élite were also holders of fiefs where they were feudal lords. The élite group also included those termed *shi*, initially a term denoting a knight or fighting gentleman. Below this group lay the great mass of society: the merchants, artisans and above all the peasants. Peasants were bound to the soil and required to do labour service for the landowner. This was also a society which had slaves. In a society organised on these lines there was very little social mobility.

This situation began to change soon after the beginning of the Spring and Autumn period. After the collapse of Zhou royal authority, a power struggle developed in several states which led to the elimination of some of the noble families. This was followed by the rise of the families of ministers and officials. In the sixth century there began what has been described as the 'crisis of aristocratic society'.[16] By this is meant the collapse of the familial system which had dominated society in the early Zhou period. As the administration of states became more complex, rulers now freed from external obligations sought to centralise their authority. They began to turn away from their reliance on the great families and to enlist the help of the *shi* who became increasingly important as members of a new bureaucratic group. The career of Confucius may be taken as an example of state service and of upward mobility not unusual for the time.[17]

Behind these political changes lay technological and economic advances. The most fundamental development was that of metallurgy. The use of bronze became widespread in the Spring and Autumn period and it was now used for coins, utensils and weapons and also for agricultural implements. At about the same time the use of iron began to spread. The evidence relating to the early development of iron technology in China is incomplete. Under the Shang dynasty, meteoric iron was used to make blades for bronze implements. The earliest known iron implement, a dagger with a bronze handle and an iron blade, has been dated to the early Spring and Autumn period. However, it is only in the latter part of that period that there is evidence of the widespread use of iron, which is much later than the same development in the West.[18] However, in China iron manufacturers quickly started to use the cast–iron process, a faster and cheaper method of producing iron. This technology was not adopted in the West until centuries later. Once iron had begun to be manufactured in China, there was a rapid development of mining and growth of production which in turn had great influence on agriculture and warfare.

Alongside this development occurred a fundamental change in the organisation of agriculture. It will be recalled that under the Shang a form of agricultural commune, the 'well-field' system, was apparently in use. In the Spring and Autumn period, perhaps as a consequence of a rising population and the opening up of new land, any such collective system fell into disuse. In its place came a free market in land and the emergence of landlord-tenant relations. The first explicit reference to this change is to be found in the records of the state of Lu for 594 BC, which refer to the payment of taxes by peasants in place of the labour service which hitherto had been the custom.

Another important development was the growth of commerce, shown most clearly in the spread of the use of money. The earliest coins were produced in the states of Zhou and Jin in the late Spring and Autumn period and were in the form of a spade-shaped tool. There is a record that the King of Zhou in 524 BC had minted large coins, the implication being that smaller coins were already in circulation.[19] Results from the excavation of city sites dating from this period suggest an increase in urbanisation and this in turn supports the impression of a growing merchant class. There is evidence of the gradual improvement of communications both on land and on water. Another indication of the increase in commerce can be found in references to the collection of tariffs on goods crossing state boundaries and of tolls imposed on goods being brought to cities.

TRANSITION FROM SPRING AND AUTUMN TO WARRING STATES

The traditional reason for dividing the Western Zhou period into two at 481 BC was that that year was the last year of the Spring and Autumn annals. Because in the *Zuozhuan* (a commentary on *Historical Records*), the record was extended to 464 BC, the latter date was also used to mark the division. Although the dates merely referred to a break in the historical record, most historians assumed that a more fundamental change occurred at about that time. The most commonly cited aspect of the difference was the increasing frequency of wars – hence the appellation Warring States for the second period. However, after Hsu Cho-yun had analysed the record he concluded that wars were equally frequent in both periods.[20] Other writers countered this conclusion by pointing out that the character of war had changed. Whereas in the earlier period wars had been the pastime of a chariot-riding aristocracy, in the latter period it was a more serious affair, dominated by professional generals commanding a massed infantry force armed with a new weapon, the crossbow.[21] The date usually adopted for the beginning of the Warring States period, 403 BC, is also connected with the increasing severity of the power struggle between the states. In that year the state of Jin fragmented between three contestants. This left seven states, sometimes known as the seven powers: Qin, the eventual victor, in the west, Qi in the east, Yan in the north-east, Chu in the south, and in the north the three successor states to Jin, namely Zhao, Han and Wei.

Marxist historians have explained the progression from Spring and Autumn to Warring States periods In a different way. They have argued that it coincided with the change from slave to feudal society. However, the evidence for widespread slavery in the early Zhou period is very limited – indeed, there are more references to slavery in the time of the Warring States. Certainly there is nothing to indicate that the economy of China up to this time had been based on slavery.[22]

The question remains: how great was the contrast between the two periods? The impression that the Warring States period was one of frequent and destructive wars was a theme dear to Mencius's heart and this may be one reason why that view has for so long been accepted. But it must be said that the figures for casualties given in the traditional accounts are too high to be credible.[23] More importantly, the evidence of population growth and economic expansion which occurred at this time does not seem compatible with the dismal reputation of the period.

POLITICAL, SOCIAL AND ECONOMIC DEVELOPMENTS IN THE WARRING STATES PERIOD

If it is accepted that the division between the Spring and Autumn and Warring States periods is little more than a historical convenience, the fact remains that there are many differences between China at the beginning and at the end of the Eastern Zhou period. The first is that of the balance of power between the states. The seven states which had dominated the political scene at the beginning of the Warring States period had, a century later, effectively been reduced to three: Qin, Chu and Qi. In the third century BC this consolidation continued with the rise of Qin. In 256 BC, Qin deposed the last Zhou ruler and absorbed the remainder of its territory. Finally, in the decade after 231 BC, Qin eliminated its rivals and for the first time established a centralised empire in China.

The common explanation for this change is the decay of Zhou feudalism and the decline of the aristocratic leadership. This was accompanied by a centralisation of power within states. In the feudal states of the early Spring and Autumn period the state resembled a large household. The closest relatives of the ruler filled the highest offices of the state. Before the end of that period the system had begun to break down and it became the practice for ministers, drawn from aristocratic families but appointed by rulers, to hold important positions. This situation in turn began to collapse because of conflicts between ministerial families. Rulers now began to appoint *shi* to significant positions in state politics. This was the beginning of a consolidation of state power which was one of the marked features of the Warring States period. Increasingly rulers began to rely on career experts to carry out policies which were directed at strengthening the state. These new experts needed to be trained and one of the features of states of this period was the emergence of schools in which masters taught their disciples the arts of government, strategy and diplomacy.

Interstate rivalries intensified and it was at this point that the advance in military technology changed wars from limited campaigns fought among aristocratic leaders to more extensive wars involving far larger numbers of foot soldiers. Military conscription systems became common and it was claimed that the largest states raised armies a million strong.[24] In the fifth century BC iron weapons were introduced and the crossbow began to be used. Another important change was the introduction of cavalry which by the third century BC had become the standard auxiliary arm.

Another contrast lies in the matter of social mobility. According to Hsu Cho-yun the transition of an individual from one stratum to another was easier during the Warring States period than during the Spring and Autumn period.[25] It has been demonstrated that a substantial proportion of those who became chancellors or who held other high positions in the states of the Warring States period were self-made men. Others rose from obscure origins through the profession of arms. Many of the generals of the Warring States period came of humble origins, among them Sunzi, otherwise known as Sun the Cripple, because he had had his feet cut off as a punishment. A native of the state of Wei, he became the chief of staff of the state of Qi and author of the famous treatise *The Art of War*.

Despite the intensification of war, all the evidence suggests that the Warring States period was one of substantial economic progress. Recent archaeological discoveries have produced iron objects in great numbers and variety and indicate that iron was now commonly used to make agricultural implements. In *Mencius* the following exchange was recorded:

'Does Xu Zi use an iron pot and earthenware steamer for cooking rice and iron implements for ploughing the fields?'
'Yes.'
'Does he make them himself?'
'No. He trades grain for them.'[26]

The growth of commerce is confirmed by the spread of the use of bronze coinage. In the Warring States period coinage was minted in all the seven major states and three main types have been identified: the spade coinage already referred to, a coinage in the form of a knife found in Qi and surrounding areas, and a round coin pierced by a hole, the forerunner of the copper cash, used in the southern state of Chu. A considerable interstate commerce had developed. At first this was mainly in natural products of the region, but by the Warring States period certain areas had developed specialised industrial products. The state of Han produced swords, halberds and other iron weapons and Qi was well known for a type of purple cloth.[27]

INTELLECTUAL DEVELOPMENTS IN THE EASTERN ZHOU PERIOD

All that has been said about the political, social and economic changes in the Eastern Zhou period may be related to the great flowering of intellectual activity which began in the sixth century BC. It has become a commonplace to see a connection between the waves of rapid change which marked that period – and the disruption which those waves caused – and the proliferation of intellectual activity, much of which concentrated on offering solutions to the problem of ordering society in such changing times.

In proposing their solutions the political theorists of the late Spring and Autumn and Warring State periods were not starting from scratch. Important philosophical concepts, which had been formulated much earlier, shaped the direction of their thinking. The idea of a supreme being, who has the power to distribute rewards and punishments, can be traced back to the Shang period. At first the deity was perceived in anthropomorphic terms, but in the Zhou period the concept changed to an abstract force signified by the use of the term *tian* or heaven. In the Shang period, as previously noted, divination was well established and the famous divination manual, the *Yijing* or the *Book of Changes* may date from the late Shang period. The practice of ancestor worship, in the context of ceremonies associated with the royal clan, can also be traced to Shang times. In the Zhou period well-established families recognised the common descent group and male descendants were expected to perform sacrifices to their ancestors and to ensure the continuity of the lineage by begetting a male heir. Another concept which goes back to the Spring and Autumn period concerns the Chinese view of the cosmos. All things in the cosmos function in accordance with the *dao* or Way and partake of two complementary forces, *yang* and *yin*. In their origin the Chinese characters for these terms may refer to a valley, one side bathed in sun and the other shrouded in darkness. By extension *yang* denotes the sun and male energy, whereas *yin* denotes the moon and the female principle.

Although these concepts remained fundamental to Chinese thought, it was in the late Spring and Autumn period and in the time of the Warring States that the key developments in political and philosophical thought occurred. First and foremost among the teachers and philosophers of that period was Kongfuzi, or Master Kong, known in the West as Confucius. Confucius, whose traditional dates are 551–479 BC, came from the small state of Lu and was of relatively humble parentage; indeed his career may be taken as an example of the rise of the *shi* to positions of influence in the state. What little is known of his personal life may be gleaned chiefly from the *Lunyu* or *Analects*, a collection of sayings and brief anecdotes relating to Confucius compiled by his followers. It appears that Confucius was orphaned at an early age and grew up in poverty. He was a scholar who aspired to public office which he eventually achieved by becoming the police commissioner of the state of Lu.[28] Perhaps because the policy which he proposed to the government was ignored, Confucius abandoned the appointment, and for the next thirteen years he travelled from state to state offering advice to the rulers and seeking employment with them. He returned to Lu in 484 BC and in the last five years of his life he was a teacher.

Confucius's teaching was primarily concerned with how a ruler should govern. He based his advice on the lessons of the past and in particular he looked back to the beginning of the Zhou dynasty as a golden age and to the founders of the dynasty, King Wen and the Duke of Zhou, as models of rectitude. He admired King Wen because he regarded him as displaying the qualities of an ideal ruler, not because of his military achievements, but because of his success as an administrator and his skill in the arts of peace, which enabled him to build up a store of moral power, a prelude to the Zhou succession to the Shang. He cited the Duke of Zhou because he was believed to have instituted the clan inheritance system known as *zongfa*, the kinship network, the form of feudalism which was reinforced either by kinship bonds or by marriage between the royal house and its vassals. It was on this system that Confucius based his ideas about the natural love and obligations which should subsist between members of a family, ideas which were to form so large a part of his teaching on the subject of morality. Nevertheless, despite this admiration and his constant citation of examples from past ages for the instruction of people of his own day, Confucius was not an arch-conservative. He was quoted as saying 'If by keeping the old warm one can provide understanding of the new, one is fit to be a teacher'.[29] For him the past was a source of examples to be applied creatively to the problems of his own day.

One particular example lay in the matter of moral conduct. Confucius referred frequently to men of virtue, using the term *junzi*, usually translated as 'gentleman'. The term literally meant 'prince's son', but for Confucius the qualifications required for someone to be described as a gentleman were not those of birth but those of moral qualities. The *junzi* would practise those qualities which have come down in history as the five constant virtues: benevolence, uprightness of mind, propriety in demeanour, knowledge or enlightenment and good faith. Of these the most important was benevolence or humanity, the supreme excellence in a man of perfect virtue. These virtues were not inherent, they were acquired through self-cultivation and this self-cultivation implied a life of study and a belief in man's perfectibility through learning. The prescription for a *junzi* was in the first instance offered to rulers as a model for conduct and Confucius is always associated with the idea of governing by moral virtue. By extension the qualities were also those to be sought by all who hoped to participate in government and thus Confucius established the idea that rulers should accept advice from scholars on how such government should be instituted.

Another element in Confucius's teaching was associated with the term *li*, usually translated as 'ritual'. He frequently stressed the importance of all those traditional forms which provided an objective standard of conduct. Once he was asked to do away with the sacrificial lamb which was offered at the announcement of each new moon. Confucius refused, saying that whereas his questioner loved the lamb, he loved the rite. By insisting on ritual, and on all those forms of behaviour which upheld traditional forms, matters which might be described as etiquette, Confucius was asserting their continued value in a time of rapid change. Among the forms of ritual, the most important was that of offering sacrifices to ancestors. Confucius certainly endorsed such practices, but he was equally firm in his teaching on the correct relationships which should subsist amongst the living. One of his most famous pronouncements was made in reply to a question from the Duke of Qi about government : 'Let the ruler be a ruler, the subject a subject, the father a father, the son a son'.[30] When Confucius was told that a man had been so upright that when his father stole a sheep, he gave evidence against him, Confucius's reply was 'In our village those who are straight are quite different. Fathers cover up for their sons, and sons cover up for their fathers. Straightness is to be found in such behaviour'.[31]

Soon after Confucius's death the philosopher Mozi challenged some of the most basic of his arguments. He criticised the concept of the gentleman as a pretext for maintaining social inequalities and came close to arguing that all men are equal before God. In place of what he termed the 'partial love' urged by Confucius, that is to say a graded love determined by a system of relationships, he argued the case for universal love, or, as it has otherwise been translated, love without discrimination. One should love every other person as much as one loves oneself and one should love another person's parents as much as one loves one's own. To sanction this belief, Mozi invoked a heaven that was much closer to a personal God than anything endorsed by Confucius. Mozi lived in troubled times. The worst calamities, he said, included the attacking of small states by large states, the plundering of the weak by the strong, and the disdain of the noble for the humble.[32] To combat this Mozi argued a strictly utilitarian role for the state. Its every effort must be directed at satisfying people's material needs, even if this meant abandoning ritual and music. Above all the state should not engage in offensive warfare. Mozi preached pacifism and was said to have intervened personally in attempts to prevent wars and to assist in the defence of states threatened with attack.

Confucius and Mozi, despite their differences, were united in their search for ways of making the world a better place to live in. The philosophy of Daoism, however, turned its back on worldly preoccupations and concerned itself with the individual and his inner life. *Dao* means literally 'the Way' and some of the concepts of Daoism, in particular the idea that man should live in harmony with nature, may date back to the Shang period. Daoism has two key texts, the first of which is the *Daodejing*, or *The Way and Power Classic*, also known as the *Laozi* after its supposed author. Laozi reputedly lived in the state of Chu and was an older contemporary of Confucius. However, there is the greatest uncertainty about his identity – the name merely means 'old man' and there is no corroborative evidence to support the biographical sketch of him which appeared in the *Shiji*. In all probability Laozi was not a historical figure at all.[33] The *Laozi* as a book is very different from the works associated with Confucius or Mozi. Whereas they were concerned with the problems of the world, the *Laozi* is preoccupied with matters of the spirit. Its opening lines proclaim that it is a work of mysticism and poetry:

The way that can be spoken of
Is not the constant way;
The name that can be named
Is not the constant name.

The nameless was the beginning of heaven and earth;
The named was the mother of the myriad creatures.
Hence always rid yourself of desires in order to observe its secrets;
But always allow yourself to have desires in order to observe its manifestations.[34]

Although much of the *Laozi* is concerned with nature and the principle of the *dao*, it also includes references to how the individual should behave and how a ruler should conduct himself. The ideal individual is the sage, and a sage is one who comprehends the Way. The ideal ruler is also the sage, who might be supposed to be able to apply his knowledge of the Way to the task of ruling. However, the question arises: how far should the ruler intervene? In the *Laozi* a key phrase is *wuwei* meaning 'without action', the implication being that the task of the ruler is to avoid doing anything which might upset the natural order. The state is a delicate thing which may be ruined by the least handling. As a consequence, 'Governing a large state is like boiling a small fish'.[35] By avoiding intervention and by setting an example, the ruler might succeed in leading his people to a state of innocence and simplicity.

The second key work of Daoism is the *Zhuangzi*, probably the work of a man of that name whose given dates are 369–286 BC. The *Zhuangzi* is also concerned with the principle of the *dao*, but the emphasis is less on how that knowledge might be put to a mundane use and more on its philosophical aspects. Zhuangzi, who probably lived as a recluse, often seems to want to distance himself from society and in an anarchic or paradoxical way to challenge its conventions. One dialogue in the book describes his behaviour after the death of his wife. He was found sitting with an inverted bowl on his knees, drumming upon it and singing a song. When he was told that his behaviour was inappropriate, he defended himself by saying:

When she died, I was in despair, as any man well might be. But soon, pondering on what had happened, I told myself that in death no strange new fate befalls us. In the beginning we lack not life only, but form. Not form only, but spirit. We are blended in the one great featureless indistinguishable mass. Then a time came when the mass evolved spirit, spirit evolved form, form evolved life. And now life in its turn has evolved death. For not nature only but man's being has its seasons, its sequence of spring and autumn, summer and winter. If someone is tired and has gone to lie down, we do not pursue him with shouting and bawling. She whom I have lost has lain down to sleep for a while in the Great Inner Room. To break in upon her rest with the noise of lamentation would but show that I knew nothing of nature's Sovereign Law. That is why I ceased to mourn.[36]

It has often been said that the doctrines of Confucianism and Daoism complement each other and that a scholar might study the Confucian texts for his career and read the texts of Daoism for relaxation. Certainly the classic texts of Daoism have continued to be read, even though before the end of the Zhou period Daoist philosophical speculation was led astray into the search for the elixir of life. Also many important elements in Daoist teaching were adopted by Confucianism and Buddhism and have lived on in that way.

The late Zhou period has been described as the time of the Hundred Schools, referring to the proliferation of philosophical ideas circulating at the time. There is not space here to refer to them all, but mention must be made of the development of Confucian teaching and of the Legalists whose ideas were adopted by the first unified empire of the Qin.

Confucius had received little recognition in his own day and his teaching had only survived because of the devotion of his followers. Subsequently they added to what he had said and it is the sum of their writings which provided the literary basis of Confucianism. First and foremost among those followers was Mengzi, known in the West as Mencius, whose probable dates were 372 to 289 BC. The main source on his teaching is the *Mencius*, which like the *Analects* is a collection of sayings compiled by his students. Mencius was a declared follower of Confucius and he considered much of what he said to be an explanation of his master's teaching. Nevertheless his reported sayings were also a reflection of his times, which were much more disturbed than those of his predecessor, and they also reflected the intellectual debates of his day. Three aspects of his teaching stand out, the first of which concerns the nature of man. For Confucius this was not an important issue, and the one direct reference he made to the topic was to say 'Men are close to one another by nature. They diverge as a result of repeated practice'.[37] But for Mencius it was fundamental, for his teaching was based on the assumption that man is by nature good, that is to say he possesses certain innate and unselfish tendencies which, if properly cultivated lead towards goodness. In a famous passage Mencius said:

Suppose a man were, all of a sudden, to see a young child on the verge of falling into a well. He would certainly be moved to compassion, not because he wanted to get in the good graces of the parents, nor because he wished to win the praise of his fellow villagers or friends, nor yet because he disliked the cry of the child.[38]

For Mencius to be devoid of the heart of compassion was to lack that which is characteristic of a human being.

Much of what Mencius said was concerned with the application of these tendencies to the good of society. The *Mencius* begins with a famous reference to a conversation between Mencius and King Hui of Liang, on the occasion of a visit which took place in 320 BC.

'Sir,' said the King. 'You have come all this distance, thinking nothing of a thousand *li*. You must surely have some way of profiting my state?'

'Your Majesty,' answered Mencius. 'What is the point of mentioning the word "profit"? All that matters is that there should be benevolence and righteousness.'[39]

Mencius's ideal for the state was benevolent government, that is to say a government that existed for the sake of the people and which sought to provide them with peace and sufficiency. He urged the re-introduction of the 'well-field' system, the system of equal landholding which had perhaps prevailed in the early Zhou period.

The third idea forever associated with Mencius is that of the 'right to rebel'. Mencius explained the right to rule in terms of the mandate of heaven, that is to say the founders of the dynasty had won the approval of heaven by their virtue and had then been granted the right to take the throne. He stressed the obligations of the ruler to lead by example and to rule with benevolence. It was inevitable that Mencius should also address the question of what should happen if a ruler failed in his task, or if he neglected or oppressed the people. Mencius's reply was that he had forfeited the approval of heaven and this gave the people the right to rebel. At first sight this doctrine appears to be democratic – because it imposes a strong obligation on a ruler to take the interests of his people into account – and subversive, because it offers an alternative to suffering oppression. However, because according to the same argument a failed rebellion must be seen as not only treasonable but also impious, it cannot really be said to have inspired many rebellions or to have done much to counter the autocratic tendencies of imperial government in China.

Mention must also be made of the third major contributor to the establishment of the Confucian tradition, although his name is not well known outside China. Xunzi, who lived between 298 and 238 BC, was a high official in the states of Qi and Chu. His collected writings survive in the work known as the *Xunzi*. His most famous philosophical contribution was to contradict Mencius's view on the essential goodness of human nature. For Xunzi the nature of man was evil; his goodness had to be acquired. If a man's evil tendencies were not curbed, strife and injury and cruelty would result. However, goodness may be acquired under the influence of teachers, and under the discipline of laws men may be brought to follow the paths of decorum and righteousness. Xunzi's argument was associated with his rejection of Confucius's and Mencius's ideas of a golden age in the past. Although he lived in difficult times, Xunzi believed that mankind had not changed; what was needed was a commitment to good government and stern control – in other words he was an advocate of authoritarianism.

Xunzi promoted the importance of education and said that it should concentrate on the study of the classics. This was a new idea, indicative of the development and circulation of literature as well as of the establishment of authoritative texts. It is not clear which were the classics to which he referred, but it is to about this time one can trace the identification of a canon of Confucian classics. One listing of the key texts comprised the *Shijing*, the *Book of Songs*, an anthology of poems dating back to the early Zhou period; the *Shujing*, the *Book of Documents*, which reputedly derived from the same date; the *Yijing* or *Book of Changes*, the famous book of divination; the *Spring and Autumn Annals* and the *Liji* or *Book of Rites*, a collection made in the Han period but incorporating earlier materials on rites and rituals. These works were known collectively as the Five Classics. Another listing became known as the Four Books. It comprised the *Analects* and *Mencius* and two extracts from the *Book of Rites*, known as the *Great Learning* and the *Doctrine of the Mean*. Of these books only the *Analects* can in a strict sense be described as the work of Confucius. Some classics entered the canon because they had been used by Confucius as a source of instruction; others, for example the *Great Learning*, were adopted because they expressed ideas which could be traced back to Confucius. Knowledge of these classics was to be deemed essential for the training of a Confucian scholar, beginning with the Four Books and then proceeding to the Five Classics.

One further school of thought must be mentioned here although fuller reference to it belongs in the next chapter. It is the set of ideas which have become known as Legalism. There is a direct link between Xunzi and Legalism, because two of his most famous students, Han Fei and Li Si, were both to become Legalists. However, it must be stressed that Xunzi was no totalitarian and the origin of those tendencies in Legalism must be sought elsewhere.

Han Fei, who died in 233 BC, was a member of the ruling family of the state of Han. It was said that it was because he suffered from a speech impediment that he turned to writing. The *Hanfeizi*, the classic text associated with him, contains a number of essays which he wrote as well as other material. This text is the most complete exposition of the ideas of Legalism. Han Fei brought together a number of disparate ideas into a coherent political philosophy. He knew of the policies of Shang Yang, the fourth-century BC minister of the state of Qin, which will be discussed later. He would also have been aware of Daoist ideas and how, in particular, the Daoist sage-ruler was not placed under any obligation to practise benevolent rule. And he certainly was familiar with the teachings of Xunzi and would have responded to his brand of Confucianism and to his conviction that human nature is evil.

The starting point for Han Fei's thought was his rejection of the Confucian idealisation of the past. He conceded that formerly men could afford to be kind and polite because they were few in number, and under such circumstances rulers might succeed by being benevolent and just. But those days were gone and more difficult times were at hand. He further provoked the Confucianists by arguing that there was no justification for continuing to honour and reward scholars as in the past:

As long as heavy taxes are collected from the farmers while rich rewards are given to the learned gentlemen, it will be impossible to expect the people to work hard and talk little.[40]

For Han Fei the essence of good government was to strengthen the power of the state. If the ruler were to give away any element of his power he ran the risk of creating dangerous rivalries. Legalists identified three things which the ruler must use in order to govern effectively: he must strengthen his power and position; he must perfect administrative techniques, and he must promulgate a precise code of laws. The last point has been taken as the characteristic of Legalist thought. The best-known passage in the *Hanfeizi* is that which asserts that men are naturally spoiled by love, but are submissive to authority:

That being so, rewards should be rich and certain so that people will be attracted by them; punishments should be severe and definite so that the people will fear them; and laws should be uniform and steadfast so that the people will be familiar with them.[41]

In 233 BC Han Fei travelled to the state of Qin, where his erstwhile fellow-student, Li Si, was chief adviser to the king. Perhaps because of jealousy of Han Fei's brilliance, Li Si forced him or induced him to commit suicide. Nevertheless, as will appear, Han Fei's ideas were to outlive him and to have both an immediate and a longer-term influence.

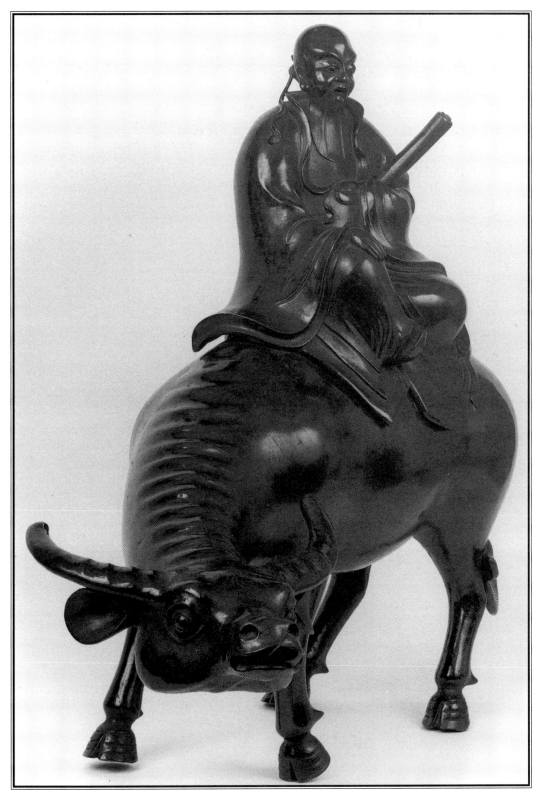

6 Bronze figure of Laozi riding on a buffalo

7 Kneeling archer from the terracotta army

CHAPTER THREE

THE QIN EMPIRE

The span of the Qin dynasty, from 221 to 207 BC, was the shortest in China's dynastic record. Nevertheless the period is generally regarded as of great significance and three particular claims are made for it. The first is that the name 'China', the name to be adopted by the outside world to describe what the Chinese themselves have preferred to call the Middle Kingdom, probably derived from the name Qin.[1] Secondly, the dynasty has recently gained worldwide attention because of the most spectacular archaeological discovery of the late twentieth century: the uncovering of the army of terracotta soldiers guarding the entrance to the tomb of Qin Shi Huangdi, the First Emperor of the Qin. This discovery offers some confirmation of the extraordinary claims relating to the tomb to be found in the *Shiji*, or *Historical Records* compiled by Sima Qian.

Finally, and most generally, is the fact that Qin was the first national dynasty, one which swept away the feudal states of Zhou China and which created a non-feudal, non-hereditary, bureaucratic administration, a change which was described by Charles Hucker as 'a major watershed in Chinese history'.[2] Derk Bodde went even further: for him the year 221 BC, the year the dynasty was established, was 'by far the most important single date in Chinese history before the revolutionary changes of the present century'.[3]

THE RISE OF THE STATE OF QIN

The state of Qin grew up along the Wei river to the west of the Zhou royal domains. This was a frontier region and much of the early history of the state was connected with its struggles with the Rong, a non-Chinese group. In 770 BC Qin helped the Zhou rulers, who also suffered from attacks by the Rong, to remove their capital from Hao to Luoyang, further east. This move marks the division between the Western and Eastern Chou periods. As a reward for this assistance Qin territory was raised to the status of a full principality, and thereafter Qin shared the effective independence enjoyed by the other states of the Eastern Zhou period.

Nevertheless, until the fourth century BC, there was little to suggest that the Qin state would unify China. Qin was regarded as barbarous when compared with the Zhou and perhaps its people had been much influenced by their non-Chinese neighbours. It was said of the Qin state that it had the same customs as the Rong and Di barbarians, 'It has the heart of a tiger or a wolf. . . . It knows nothing about traditional mores, proper relationships, and virtuous conduct'.[4] But then, between 361 and 338 BC, the Qin ruler, Duke Xiao, following advice from an official named Shang Yang, or Lord Shang, transformed the state and set in train those developments which were to lead to the triumph of Qin.

The extraordinary nature of this achievement has long been recognised. In the second century BC the scholar Jia Yi wrote of Duke Xiao:

> He cherished the idea of rolling the empire up like a mat, of lifting up the whole world in his arms and of tying up the four seas in a sack; moreover he had the intention of swallowing up the eight wild countries. At this time the Lord of Shang assisted him; in the interior he fixed models and measures, gave his attention to farming and weaving, and made the necessary preparations for defence and attack; abroad he extended the territory in an uninterrupted way from west to east and fought with the feudal lords.[5]

His minister, Shang Yang, came from the neighbouring state of Wei. It was said that the ruler of Wei once remarked of him '[he] has marvellous talents, – if he be not employed in an official post, it would be better that he were put to death, lest another kingdom obtain his services!' His particular qualification was his commitment to the ideas and policies later to be associated with the school of thought known as Legalism. The Legalists, it will be remembered, rejected the traditional virtues of humanity and righteousness, which had been advocated by the Confucianists. Instead they supported the strengthening of the state, the concentration of power into the hands of a single ruler, and the use of war as an instrument of policy.

Shang Yang's reform programme is not easy to describe accurately. The key text, the *Book of Lord Shang*, which in the past was attributed to him, is now believed to be the work of others, although it may reflect his thinking.[6] One must instead look at the record of achievements when he was the minister. These included the extension of direct state administration, as opposed to devolved administration through hereditary landholders; the abolition of the old fixed landholding system (the well-field system described above) and its replacement by a more flexible system in which the sizes of land units could vary and peasants paid taxes in kind rather than in labour services; and the development of a system of collective responsibility, under which the population was grouped into units of five or ten families, with all members of each unit collectively responsible for the wrongdoing of any individual in the unit (the forerunner of the *baojia* system). His economic reforms were seen by the Marxist historian Guo Moruo as bringing to an end the power of the declining slave-owner aristocrats and as hastening the transition from a slave society to a feudal society.[7]

Another important achievement lay in the codification of the law. Until recently, the earliest Chinese legal code known to have survived dated from the Tang dynasty

(AD 618–907). In 1975 a collection of bamboo slips was found in the grave of a Qin official who had died in 217 BC. Several hundred of these slips were legal documents, referring to a legal code which had been compiled before Qin united China. It is possible that what is recorded on the slips may be the original text as established by Shang Yang.[8]

The collection also referred to a number of aspects of Qin administrative procedure. It has been suggested that any explanation of the triumph of Qin must refer to its geopolitical position on the periphery of the central area, and must emphasise its military achievement. But the explanation must also acknowledge other aspects of the Qin state which the bamboo slips illustrate: the insistence on efficiency and precision; the institution of a fixed routine in administrative procedure; the emphasis on exact quantification and data. This administrative procedure was applied to a state which was politically stable and growing economically. Another important achievement of Qin in the third century lay in the field of agriculture, where there is evidence of the improvement of agricultural production and the conserving of natural resources. Two major projects deserve mention: the canal built by Zheng Guo north of the Wei river, which irrigated nearly half a million acres of land, and the development of the irrigation system on the Chengdu plain.

The achievement of Shang Yang has received very different interpretations over the centuries. In traditional Chinese historiography he has been excoriated. He has been described as a ruthless politician who coerced the people into agriculture and warfare, who introduced a system of governmental surveillance, and who destroyed old institutions, particularly the well-field system. By permitting a free market in land he allowed the rich to become richer and the poor to become poorer. In modern times, Shang Yang's stock has risen. Early in this century he was compared to Solon and to Bismarck. In the 1970s, at the time of the anti-Confucius campaign, he was praised for having dealt blows to divisive forces within the state, for having centralised power, for having enforced ideological uniformity, and for having scorned the literati. In the language of the day Shang Yang was described as having used revolutionary violence in an attempt to suppress the old aristocracy and to introduce radical reforms. Despite his achievements, after the death of Duke Hsiao, Shang Yang became the victim of a counter-revolution, being captured and put to death by 'dismemberment by chariots'.[9] Nevertheless the reformist tendency he had initiated continued after his death.

THE TRIUMPH OF QIN

From the fourth century BC Qin turned its attention away from expansion into non-Chinese areas towards achieving dominance over its rivals to the east. In an era of warring states, Qin achieved notoriety for its willingness to involve itself in war. The *Shiji* recorded its involvement in fifteen major battles or campaigns in the period 364–234 BC. In this contest Qin held an advantage which was to be a recurrent feature of shifts in the power balance in China. This was its situation to the west of the more settled and advanced states, which provided it with natural defences and a secure base from which to attack. The first step in Qin expansion was to undermine the position of the state of Chu to the south – this was achieved in a campaign extending into modern Sichuan.

By the middle of the third century BC the threat offered by Qin to the other states of north China was apparent. When, in 256 BC, Qin destroyed the shadowy survival of the Zhou ruling house, it seemed likely that the state would soon achieve supremacy. However the final triumph of Qin was to be delayed for a further generation of consolidation and of warfare. The key figures of this time were the Qin king, known as Zheng, meaning the Upright, who came to the throne as a youth in 246 BC, and Lü Buwei, who was the chief minister and regent of the state between the years 249 and 237 BC. According to the record Lü was a travelling merchant who became the richest man of his day. He came to power through befriending the heir to the Qin throne; a titillating story relates how Lü had surrendered his beautiful concubine – who was at the time pregnant – to the heir and how thus Lü was the putative father of the child who was to become Qin Shi Huangdi, the First Emperor of Qin. Lü's astonishing rise, at that time an unique instance of a man from a merchant background achieving political power, has been interpreted as a sign of the economic transition taken place in the last years of the Eastern Zhou period. Lü Buwei played an active role in the strengthening of the Qin state by encouraging the construction of canal systems and by patronising the literary arts. The most famous outcome of the latter activity was the work known as the *Lüshi chun jiu*, or *Spring and Autumn of Mr Lü*, an ambitious attempt by scholars working under Lü's direction to produce a compilation of current knowledge on cosmological, political and moral issues, to be used as a basis for the proper conduct of government. Lü also strengthened the military capacity of Qin and weakened the position of the other states by a policy of divide and rule. However Lü was not to live to see the outcome of his preparations. He fell from power in 237 BC after the disclosure that he was continuing his relationship with the First Emperor's mother.

His place was taken by another outstanding politician, Li Si, who was to play the foremost role in the establishment and consolidation of the Qin dynasty. Li Si came from the state of Chu and had been a fellow student of Han Fei. He came to Qin in search of employment and received patronage from Lü Buwei. After Lü's fall from power, a decree was passed expelling alien officials and this might well have led to the end of Li Si's career had he not expostulated to the king in a famous memorial. The decree was rescinded and Li Si was promoted to be Minister of Justice, thus embarking on a remarkable career which was to end only with his death in 208 BC. However, little is known of Li Si's activities in the next decade, although it is probable that he contributed to the triumph of Qin by intriguing against the other feudal states. A more significant contribution to that result – but one which is difficult to pin down – is Li Si's part in promoting the concept of empire to the ruler of Qin. According to the *Shiji*, when Li Si set out for Qin in search of employment, he had declared that 'the king of Qin desires to swallow up the world and to rule with the title of Emperor'. In Derk Bodde's opinion, few men in history have pursued this concept of empire with more rigid determination than did Li Si. Perhaps there was no Qin blueprint for conquest, but a consistency of ambition matches what is known of the character of Li Si. Whenever the opportunity arose he referred to the concept of empire and encouraged the ambitions of the ruler of Qin.[10]

In 230 BC there began the final series of campaigns which, within ten years, were to lead to the elimination of the other states and the establishment of an unified empire. Some of the factors which turned the balance in Qin's favour have already been identified: the geographical position of the state; its ability to attract outstanding figures from other states; the adoption of the ideas of Legalism; the strengthening of its economy and of its administrative institutions; its effective diplomacy preventing the other states from forming a united front to oppose Qin expansion. One other factor has been the subject of debate, namely the military prowess of Qin and in particular the significance of the use of a new weapon, the iron sword. Undoubtedly Qin did have a reputation for using war as an instrument of policy and the *Book of Lord Shang* contained a section on methods of warfare. The last century of the Warring States period was characterised by wars in which Qin played a prominent role both as aggressor and as beneficiary of warfare between other states. It was suggested at one point that the key to its military success lay in the spread of the use of wrought-iron swords which were superior to the bronze swords used by Qin's opponents. However, archaeological evidence has failed to support the thesis that Qin enjoyed enjoyed some kind of metallurgical superiority over its rivals.[11]

THE QIN EMPIRE, 221–210 BC

With the defeat of the feudal states, Li Si seized the opportunity to proclaim a united empire. 'This is the one moment in ten thousand ages', he wrote, 'If Your Highness allows it to slip away and does not press the advantage in haste, the feudal lords will revive their strength and organize themselves into an anti-Qin alliance'.[12] The king assumed the title of *huangdi*, which has been translated as 'sovereign emperor', implying that this was a political, rather than a religious title and that its assumption marked the beginning of a new political order.

What such an order might imply was soon revealed. In a famous memorial, Li Si rejected the idea that the emperor should grant fiefs to his relatives and instead urged the abolition of feudalism. He argued that the original fiefs, which had been granted by the early Zhou kings, had in time degenerated into warring states. To reinstitute a feudal nobility would not lead to peace and would not be advantageous, and the fiefs should therefore be abolished. The memorial was accepted and the rich and noble families of the states were forced to leave their ancestral land holdings and move to the capital at Xianyang, where they could be kept under the watchful eye of the emperor. According to the record, 120,000 families were forced to move. Associated with this measure was the requirement that all the weapons belonging to the feudal lords should be melted down, the metal being used to cast twelve gigantic human figures to be erected in the imperial palace.[13]

In the place of feudal fiefs, the empire was divided into commanderies and prefectures administered by appointed officials. This measure was represented as a novel departure, but there is plenty of evidence to show that this system, which was the forerunner of the modern system of provinces and prefectures, was already partly in existence. The older unit was the *xian* or prefecture (more accurately district), which may have existed in all the seven great states of the Warring States period. Nor was the *jun* or commandery a new administrative unit. When the order dividing the empire into thirty-six commanderies was issued, no less than eighteen of them had already existed as commanderies before the First Emperor's reign. This administrative step was not an innovation, it was the extension of a system of centralised control already introduced before the Qin conquest.

The same centralising thrust and the same move towards uniformity was reflected in other measures. In the *Shiji* it was stated that Li Si 'equalised the written characters, and made these universal throughout the empire'. By this it was meant that Li Si, or more probably a group of scholars working under his orders, carried through a series of reforms of the writing system and ensured that the new style was adopted generally. Variant forms of characters were suppressed and a standard script, known as the Small Seal, was introduced. By this means communication within the empire was facilitated and a strong weapon for cultural integration was forged.

In legal matters the same standardisation prevailed. The Qin law code was applied throughout the empire. Its two basic principles were reasserted. The first was that of mutual responsibility for law-keeping and the obligation to denounce wrongdoers. The second was the reiteration of Shang Yang's principle of making the law so severe that no one would dare to violate it. Fearful punishments, not all of them new, were prescribed, including extracting ribs and boiling in a cauldron.[14]

State intervention also occurred in economic matters. The Qin had a declared preference for agriculture over commerce. The former was seen as the basis of the state's wealth, whereas the latter was seen as non-productive. On occasion steps were taken to round up merchants and to force them to resettle in distant regions. This attitude, it has been suggested, left a prejudice against merchants which has survived in China until modern times. Nevertheless, other steps taken were of benefit to commerce. The currency was standardised, with gold and copper coins put into circulation. Clear regulations were applied to weights and measures. Examples have been found of the two main types of measure: vessels measuring capacity and weights for a balance, and these are inscribed with the imperial edict declaring that measurements should be clear and uniform.[15] Other edicts stipulated that the gauge of the wheels of carts be equal for all parts of China – the purpose being to ensure that the ruts created by the wheels would be equally far apart – and that new roads, fifty paces broad and lined with trees, should be built from the capital to the furthest reaches of the empire in the east and south.

The First Emperor has long been associated with the most ambitious of all building projects, the Great Wall. In the *Shiji* it is stated that the emperor sent a general named Meng Tian to drive the Rong and Di barbarians from the land to the south of the Yellow river. He then built a great wall, or line of fortification using convict labourers transported to the border for garrison duty. It has been generally accepted that this construction was not entirely new, but was more a matter of joining together defensive fortifications already started in the Warring States period. Nevertheless, the major part of the construction has been dated to the time of the Qin empire and the work ascribed to Meng Tian. Its length was said to have extended to ten thousand *li*. Extremely high figures have been placed on the number of persons who would have been required to build the wall and the numbers who perished in its construction. In short the Great Wall has been represented as the supreme example of the ruthless ambition and cruel operation of the First Emperor, which may in turn have contributed to the fall of the Qin empire. However, against this interpretation must be set the view of Arthur Waldron, who has treated the whole issue with great scepticism. He has pointed out that the Great Wall, as we know it today, was not constructed in the Qin period, but in the sixteenth century, under the Ming dynasty. The written records relating to wall-building under the Qin are brief and ambiguous. As a consequence it is not even clear what line the wall followed. Wall construction at this period consisted of earthen ramparts, not stone walls. They were made of local material, required far less labour than stone walls, and did not usually survive for very long.[16]

If the achievement on the northern frontiers of the empire has been exaggerated, the extension of influence to other parts of the country has perhaps been understated. Before the unification Qin had already sent an expedition south to subdue Lingnan, the area of the modern province of Guangdong. In 222 BC an even larger expedition, reputedly numbering half a million men in five armies, was dispatched to conquer the south. Engineers were sent to construct a canal to join the Xiang river in Hunan with the Xi or West river, which flows into the sea near Guangzhou, that is Canton. In 214 BC the expedition suffered a major defeat at the hands of the local population and the expansion was halted temporarily, to be resumed under the Han dynasty.[17]

Mention has already been made of the measures taken to establish a standardised script. This attempt at uniformity may be linked with the most notorious of the deeds of the First Emperor and Li Si, the burning of the books and the burial alive of the scholars. According to the account in the *Shiji*, at a banquet held in 213 BC, a scholar had the temerity to criticise the emperor for not having followed tradition by dividing the empire into feudal fiefs. Li Si responded to this in a memorial in which he inveighed against the scholars of the independent schools who sought to establish a reputation by criticising their sovereign. He accused them of praising the past in order to disparage the present and of criticising enactments of the state. He then made his famous proposal:

> Your servant suggests that all books in the imperial archives, save the memoirs of Qin, be burned. All persons in the empire, except members of the Academy of Learned Scholars, in possession of the *Book of Odes*, the *Book of History*, and discourses of the hundred philosophers should take them to the local governors and have them indiscriminately burned.[18]

Li Si's recommendation was accepted and there occurred a burning of the books which earned the undying contempt of Confucian scholars. It must be said, however, that the scale of the crime and the degree of its effectiveness is in doubt. Li Si was neither the first, nor the last bureaucrat, or ruler, in China to try to destroy literature deemed dangerous by the regime. The attack on literature was not indiscriminate. Texts on medicine, pharmacy, divination, agriculture and arboriculture were entirely spared, as were the historical records of Qin. Even in the case of the proscribed texts, copies could be retained by members of the academy. During the great recovery of books instituted under the Han dynasty, many of the prohibited books were restored, some having been committed to memory by scholars.

The second alleged great crime of the First Emperor supposedly occurred in the following year. Some scholars had complained about the emperor's excesses and as a consequence 460 scholars were executed by being buried alive. The first reference to this event was written a century later. At the very least it is unlikely that the mode of execution was as stated and it is probable that the incident was fabricated to create a legend of Confucian martyrdom.[19]

THE LIFE AND DEATH OF THE FIRST EMPEROR

Zheng the Upright, later to be known as the First Emperor, was born in 259 BC and succeeded to the throne of Qin at the age of thirteen. However it was only after the fall of Lü Buwei in 237 BC that he assumed full control of the state. His relationship with Li Si is far from clear and the relative importance of the parts he and his minister played in conceiving and executing the unification of China can only be a matter for speculation. One view of the relationship between the two was that the emperor was impetuous, emotional and grossly superstitious, whereas Li Si was cold, calculating and eminently rational.[20] What does seem clear is that Li Si was careful to present his actions as the fulfilment of the will of the emperor. Certainly the emperor was an active ruler, one indication of this being the erection of at least seven inscribed stelae which record journeys he made. But, according to the *Shiji*, as his reign progressed, he became increasingly absorbed in metaphysics and magic. He accepted the teaching of the School of the Five Elements – earth, wood, metal, fire and water. According to this teaching each element overcomes its predecessor, flourishes for an allotted time, and then is in turn conquered by the next element in the series. As the element associated with the Zhou dynasty was fire, it followed that that of the Qin was water. The emperor also pursued a great preoccupation of Daoist philosophers or adepts: that of gaining the secret of immortality. His journeys seem to have been as much related to this preoccupation as to affairs of state and it was this hope which took him on a journey to the coast of Shandong in 210 BC. According to the tale recorded in the *Shiji*, the emperor on previous occasions had sent men to obtain the elixir of life which supposedly was guarded by immortals who lived on three supernatural mountains in the middle of the sea. The emperor was told that the reason for their failure to reach the immortal isles was because a great fish had prevented them. So he followed the coast for some time, armed with a large crossbow. When he saw a large fish, he killed it. But soon after that the emperor himself fell ill and died.

Many of the stories recorded about the First Emperor are of doubtful historical value and were probably invented or elaborated to emphasise his superstitious nature and megalomania. However, there is one remarkable piece of evidence which must be taken into account before delivering a final verdict on his personality and ambition. This is, of course, the evidence of the emperor's mausoleum. In the *Shiji* it was stated that work on the tomb had begun as early as 246 BC, and that after the unification of the empire more than 700,000 men had worked on it:

> The laborers dug through three subterranean streams which they sealed off with bronze in order to make the burial chamber. This they filled with models of palaces, towers, and the hundred officials, as well as precious utensils and marvelous rarities. Artisans were ordered to install mechanically triggered crossbows set to shoot any intruder. With quicksilver the various waterways of the empire, the Yangzi and Yellow Rivers, and even the great ocean itself were created and made to flow and circulate mechanically. The heavenly constellations were depicted above and the geography of the earth was laid out below. Lamps were fueled with whale oil so that they might burn forever without being extinguished.[21]

All the emperor's childless wives had been killed and were buried with him. Finally, to preserve the secrets of the tomb, those who had worked on the mausoleum were also sealed up inside it.

The location of the tomb, some thirty miles east of Xianyang, has long been known. The tomb mound rises to about 43 metres and it stands in a rectangular enclosure measuring 2,173 by 974 metres. According to records the tomb had been rifled twice and the assumption was that few of the cultural relics left in the tomb would have survived. A number of pottery figures had been found in the vicinity in recent years, but that gave no warning of the astonishing discovery, made by chance in 1974, of the terracotta army. Subsequent excavation revealed the existence of three enormous pits containing life-sized terracotta figures of soldiers. Pit No. 1 contained about six thousand figures of warriors and horses, outfitted with real weapons, chariots and chariot gear. The arrangement of the figures and their armament indicates that they represent a specific military formation. Pit No. 2 contained a force of about fourteen hundred warriors and horses. The third pit, with only sixty-eight figures, may represent a command unit. There is a fourth pit, but it is empty, and there are no pits where one might have expected to find complementary groups of soldiers to complete the army. This has been taken as indicating that the project was abandoned before it had been completed. Nevertheless the scale and accuracy of the representation is astonishing: each figure was sculptured individually and carefully painted. Even if they were not portraits of individuals, as has been suggested, the craftsmen who created them went to great lengths to differentiate each figure in terms of physical form, expression and dress. Perhaps it will never be possible to confirm Sima Qian's description of the tomb, but the evidence of the terracotta army shows that the extraordinary claims for the ambitions of the First Emperor are based on fact.

THE COLLAPSE OF THE QIN EMPIRE

The empire was not to outlast the death of the First Emperor by long. Difficulties began immediately with a succession dispute, with the heir to the throne being set aside in favour of a younger son. Li Si and the new emperor's tutor, a eunuch named Zhao Gao, played a major role in this intrigue which was followed by the suicide of the original heir and of the general Meng Tian.

The new emperor, usually known as the Second Emperor, was only twenty-one at the time of his accession. He commenced ruling on the lines followed by his father, by making an imperial progression. The aged Li Si restated the principles of Legalism in a famous memorial on 'supervising and holding responsible'. But discontent was rising against heavy taxation, part of which was to pay for the work on the Ebang palace. It was focussed into what has been described as 'the first great popular revolt in Chinese history',[22] headed by a poor Henan farmer, Chen Sheng. He was killed but the rebellion was continued by others.

Meanwhile further intrigues took place at court, resulting in the rise of Zhao Gao and the imprisonment of Li Si, who, in 208 BC was condemned to be cut in two at the waist in the market place at Xianyang. According to the biography of Li Si, Zhao Gao's dominance over the Second Emperor now reached its height. It was said that he had presented a deer to the emperor, while calling it a horse. When the emperor insisted that it was a deer, he was told that he was suffering from delusions. The emperor was advised to go into retirement in a country park and was subsequently forced to commit suicide. He was succeeded by another grandson of the First Emperor, Ziying, who managed to procure the death of Zhao Gao. But by then it was too late to save the dynasty, rebellion had spread and Ziying was captured by the rebels and executed. The Qin dynasty, which was intended to last for ten thousand generations, had come to an end.

EXPLANATIONS OF THE FALL OF THE QIN

Traditional explanations of dynastic change relied heavily on moral factors. The outgoing dynasty was regarded as having failed to observe the dictates of heaven and therefore to have lost the mandate. The last rulers of a dynasty were inevitably portrayed as monsters or weaklings. In the case of the Qin dynasty this moral determinism was expressed even more sharply because of the Legalist outlook of the dynasty and the Confucian persuasion of its critics, which made it more acceptable to express sympathy for the cause of the rebels. The Han poet and statesman Jia Yi wrote a celebrated essay entitled 'The Faults of Qin' which became a classic exposition of this view. He condemned the First Emperor for having discarded the ways of former kings and having burned the writings of the hundred schools. He regarded Chen Sheng and his followers as having been driven to rebellion because of the severity of Qin laws and institutions. They should not have succeeded against the forces of the empire, being armed only with weapons made from hoes and the branches of trees. But Qin had a fatal flaw: it had failed to rule with humanity and righteousness and to realise that the power to attack and the power to retain what one has won are not the same.[23]

In recent times the reputation of Qin Shi Huangdi and the explanation for the collapse of the empire have given rise to controversy. After the 1911 Revolution the emperor was praised because he had rejected Confucianism, regarded at that time as a cause of China's weakness, and because he had unified the country. Later, Marxist historians explained the fall of the Qin in terms of a revolt against oppression by peasants – a revolt which undermined the dynasty, but which was bound to fail because of a compromise with 'landlord class elements'.[24] In the 1970s, in a clear reflection of the political issues of the day, Qin Shi Huangdi was portrayed as a man who had unified China after a long period of civil strife by following the progressive ideology of the time, an ideology which stressed the present and slighted the past.[25]

In the West most historians have emphasised the practical errors of the Qin dynasty rather than its moral failings or class conflicts. Derk Bodde accepted that Qin policies had created a large reservoir of desperate and resentful people who would be ready to join in a rebellion when the opportunity arose after the death of the First Emperor. But he rejected the argument that the rebellion was an indication of a class struggle or of a revolt against the institution of slavery. Instead he suggested that the transformation from Qin state to Qin empire was too much to accomplish in so short a time and so the failure of the empire was inevitable. Signs of tension, including threats to the emperor's life and price inflation, were apparent before the death of the Qin Shi Huangdi. These tensions could not be resolved by his successors in their brief reigns and so the dynasty fell, although many of its achievements, including that of uniting China, were carried over into the Han period.[26]

CHAPTER FOUR

THE HAN DYNASTY

The four centuries of Chinese history under the Han are divided into the earlier dynastic period of the Former or Western Han, dated 206 BC to AD 9, the interregnum of Wang Mang, AD 9–23, and the Later, or Eastern Han dynasty, AD 25–220. In this period some of the most characteristic features of the pattern of Chinese political, social, economic and religious life were established. Before turning to a review of the main events and developments of the Han period, two of these themes will be surveyed briefly.

ECONOMIC DEVELOPMENT IN THE HAN PERIOD

It was during this period that an intensive agricultural economy became confirmed as typical of China. As Hsü Cho-yun put it:

> It appears that once the Chinese stepped upon the path of agriculture, they stayed on that course without deviation. Progress and change occurred from time to time, but agriculture remained paramount in the Chinese way of life.[1]

This concentration on agriculture has been seen as at variance with the potential for economic development, particularly in the realm of commerce, which was a noticeable feature of the Warring States period. The argument that has been put forward is that this potential was forever stifled by the rise of the imperial bureaucratic system. Whether that potential existed or not is an hypothetical question. What is clear is that the key characteristics of intensive agriculture had already been established in the Warring States period. Furthermore, the steady population growth which occurred in the Former Han period, which was not matched by a comparable increase in the area of arable land available, contributed to the development of labour-intensive agriculture.

To be more specific, in the Han period the agrarian economy acquired three characteristic features. The first was that of intensive cultivation, marked by careful field preparation, seed selection, irrigation, the use of manure, crop rotation, multi-cropping and the employment of animal power and of specialised tools. The second was the interdependency of the agrarian economy. By the Han period farm households were connected to a complex economic network which linked the agrarian economy with urban centres. Farmers not only sold their primary produce, but also engaged in a wide variety of secondary activities, which absorbed surplus or under-employed labour. Of these activities the production of textiles was perhaps the most important, and a proportion of these products was also sold. However the system was flexible, the dependence on the marketing system could be reduced and the activities of the farm household could be concentrated on home consumption. This feature linked with a third characteristic of the agrarian economy, the farmer's response to economic crisis. Governments of the Han dynasties were well aware of the importance of maintaining the security and prosperity of the farming population and in general subscribed to the idea that the tax burden should be kept at a low level. However, dynastic weakness led to the rise of landlordism and to heavy rents putting increasing burdens on the peasantry. If drought or flood or other natural catastrophe then occurred, and if self-sufficiency failed to ensure survival, the only alternative was migration. Under the Han government schemes of migration were linked with the establishment of military colonies on the north and north-west frontiers of the empire, thus solving the twin problems of overpopulation and defence. But by far the more important form of migration was free migration to the south, where peasants found a milder climate and more fertile soil. Their movement initiated a long-term trend which was to have reached its apogee in about 1290, when perhaps 90 per cent of the population lived in the area of China defined as the south.

THE NATURE OF THE GODS AND THE WAYS TO PARADISE

In the chapter on the Shang dynasty brief mention was made of religious beliefs and practices. In the subsequent chapter on the Zhou reference was made to Daoism, but much more was said about the development of the schools of philosophy. This might suggest that in China interest in religion and in particular in the afterlife had been relegated to a position of unimportance. Nothing could be further from the truth. Recent archaeological finds, of artefacts interred with the dead and lost texts, have greatly increased our understanding of the religious beliefs of the inhabitants of the Han empire and have demonstrated how essential an awareness of those beliefs is for an appreciation of Han culture.

In the Han period something akin to a revolution occurred in terms of religious beliefs and practices. Michael Loewe expressed the change in the following terms:

By AD 150, the emperors had for some time been offering services to different powers from those worshipped by their ancestors of western Han. There was a new explanation of the workings of the heavens and their wonders; a new view was taken of the miracles wrought on earth and amongst men, as the consequence of an all-embracing order of nature. Men and women saw new ways of attaining a life of eternity beyond the grave and relied on new types of talisman to achieve those ends. The emperor's authority had won new respect which derived not from the results of conquest by force, but from the legitimate power bestowed by a superior. The institutions of state now depended on a common acceptance of a series of holy books, whose texts and interpretation had passed through a lengthy process of controversy.[2]

There is not space here to summarise all the developments of Han religious thought. Instead, to convey the character of those changes, reference may first be made to one of the most important recent finds of the Han period, the excavation started in 1972 of tomb no. 1, that belonging to the countess of Dai, at Mawangdui in Hunan in central China. This tomb, which dates from about 168 BC, contained a rich collection of funerary furnishings which illustrate current ideas on life after death. It also contained the well-preserved body of the countess. At that time man was conceived as having a physical and spiritual form. The physical form might be likened to a candle, while the spiritual form resembled firstly the element which kept the body alight (known as *po*) and secondly the light which the flame cast (known as *hun*), which endowed a human being with intelligence and spiritual qualities. The careful mummification of the corpse may have been intended to provide the *po* with a home to which it could return. The other spiritual element, the *hun* required guidance on its journey to paradise. To help it to complete the journey successfully various talismans were put in the tomb, the most important of which was a painting on silk placed face downwards on top of the innermost of the four coffins. This depicted a journey which would take the *hun* first to the magical island of Penglai, where the soul would receive sustenance to enable it to reach the gates of paradise. The talisman would allow the *hun* to survive the scrutiny of the human warders and animals who guarded the gates and so enter and take up its place in the land of eternity.[3]

The change in religious belief in the Han period may be illustrated by reference to the important series of artefacts known as TLV mirrors. Mirrors had appeared in funerary furnishings from the Zhou period as evidence of wealth and as a form of protection for the deceased. However, the evolution of TLV mirrors may be dated from towards the end of the first century BC to the middle of the Eastern Han period. These mirrors bear complex symbolic features which provide a link between life on earth and life after death. The characteristic pattern is that of a square set within a circle, representing earth surrounded by the heavens. Within the square are placed the terms for the twelve divisions: the divisions of time which, by the Han period, had already been assigned animals to act as their emblems – Rat, Ox, Tiger, Hare, Dragon, Snake, Horse, Sheep, Monkey, Cock, Dog and Boar. Outside the square but inside the circle are set the animal motifs of four of the Five Elements: water, fire, wood and metal. The boss at the centre of the mirror may represent the fifth element, earth. In this part of the mirror are found the markings which resemble the letters T, L, and V, which may refer to marks on diviners' boards and which may indicate that the diviner has been consulted and has advised how the most felicitous disposal of the deceased person might be attained. Finally, the border of the mirror is frequently decorated with a scroll which represents the bank of clouds upon which the soul may mount to join the world of the immortal beings. The purpose of these mirrors was to provide the bearer, whether alive or dead, with a permanent assurance that he or she was situated in a correct relationship with the cosmos.[4]

THE FOUNDING OF THE FORMER HAN DYNASTY

As suggested in the previous chapter, the fall of the Qin dynasty was more the result of the errors of its rulers and chief advisers than a rejection of the principle of an unified empire. However, the transition from one dynasty to another could only come about through an armed struggle and it was inevitable that in that struggle contrasting models of the implications of unification might be discerned.

The first model was that proffered by Xiang Yu, an aristocrat and military leader from the old state of Chu, who led the attempt to overthrow the Qin dynasty and to replace the centralisation of power it represented with a return to the state system. The second model was that associated with Liu Bang, a man of peasant origins from the town of Pei in central China, who astutely offered a continuation of centralised power coupled with moderation and clemency, in contrast to the extremes practised by the Qin dynasty.

Xiang Yu made his bid for power after the defeat of the rebellion headed by Chen Sheng. He and his uncle declared the re-establishment of the state of Chu, an act which precipitated the re-formation of other states of the Warring States period. Such an action forced the dynasty to try to defeat Xiang Yu, but his capture of Julu, a city in northern China, greatly enhanced his military reputation. At this time Liu Bang, who was one of his supporters, was campaigning against the Qin in the west, in the Wei river valley which had been the strategic base from which the Qin had gained control of the country. In 207 BC he entered the Qin capital of Xianyang. Later historians were to stress the restraint of his subsequent actions. He negotiated the surrender of the city and prevented its looting. He announced the repeal of the Qin penal code and replaced it with a famous three-article code which stated simply that: he who killed anyone should suffer death; he who wounded another or stole should be punished according to the gravity of the offence; and that the rest of the Qin laws were abolished.[5] Furthermore, he was astute enough to lay claim to the city archives, which contained the information essential for the establishment of a new administration.

On the other hand, when Xiang Yu arrived, the city was looted and burned and the last king of Qin and his family put to death. Xiang Yu then revealed his preference in terms of a political settlement by announcing that the empire was to be divided into nineteen states, of which he was to be the ruler of one and from which he was to exercise the power of hegemon. This division threatened Liu Bang's position in the Wei river valley and it was at this point that the two men fell out and a civil war commenced. Although Liu Bang commanded inferior forces and by all accounts lacked the military flair of Xiang Yu, he more than made up for this with his political astuteness. When Xiang Yu had the young ruler of the state of Chu put to death, Liu Bang denounced him as a regicide. Although he could claim that right was on his side, Liu Bang's forces suffered several military defeats, and it was only through the energy of his lieutenants that his cause survived. Nevertheless Liu Bang gained allies and in 202 BC he achieved the decisive victory at Gaixia in modern Anhui. He proclaimed himself emperor (posthumous name Gaozu) and named his dynasty the Han, after the Han river and after the title of the king of Han which he had held since 206 BC, which date was taken as the official commencement of the dynasty.

THE REIGNS OF GAOZU AND HIS SONS, 202–141 BC

Liu Bang reigned as the Emperor Gaozu until he died in 195 BC. After his death, the throne was held by minors and real power lay in the hands of the empress dowager, the Empress Lü, until she died in 180 BC, to be succeeded first by another son of Liu Bang, and then by his grandson who ruled as the Emperor Jing or Jingdi until 141 BC.

During those years a remarkable consolidation of political power took place. This was not achieved by the harsh measures adopted by the First Emperor of the Qin, nor by the dispersed system advocated by Xiang Yu, but by pragmatic means. After Liu Bang had gained power, he had granted an amnesty and had demobilised his troops. He was not therefore in a position to coerce those who had been his allies and for this reason he had to accept a major compromise in terms of the administration of the empire. In the west, in that part of the empire encircling the capital Chang'an, direct administrative control in the form of commanderies was continued or developed. In the east, in a vast area stretching from north-east China, along the coast and down to the south, ten kingdoms were established. Initially their rulers were the *de facto* power-holders, often men who had fought on Liu Bang's side in the civil war. Within six years all but one of these men had been replaced by a member of the emperor's family. In addition to these concessions, the emperor conferred the lesser rank of *hou* or marquis on many of his principal supporters. The title was hereditary and carried a stipend derived from taxes raised within the marquisate.

Gaozu died in 195 BC, to be succeeded by his son, then a teenager. This son died in 188 BC and the succession passed to two minors. It was during this time that a classic instance occurred of a recurrent threat to the stability of the Chinese imperial institution: the domination of the empress dowager. During these years the power behind the throne was Liu Bang's widow, the Empress Lü. Confucian teaching emphasised the concept of filial piety. Since an emperor usually succeeded to the throne on the death of his father, filial piety was expressed in terms of duty to his mother. The Empress Lü was not to be the last empress dowager to take advantage of this situation and until her death in 180 BC she strenuously promoted the interests of her family. Her influence did not survive her, for after her death her family was eliminated and her memory excoriated.[6] For ever after her name was cited as evidence of the danger of female rule.

After the Empress Lü's death the empire passed peacefully through the hands of a grandson of Liu Bang, who reigned as Wendi, and of his son, Jingdi. During this period steps were taken to reduce the power of the kingdoms which still formed the eastern part of the empire. In 154 BC a major revolt broke out involving six of the kings in the east and south-east. After its suppression, Han direct control over the empire was extended, a process that was to be taken further as the dynastic period progressed.

The first Han emperor had also initiated two measures which were to place the imperial institution on a more stable footing. The first of these was to develop the bureaucratic form of government established by the Qin. At the highest level the emperor was assisted by three officials, known as the Three Excellencies, and they in turn were supported by nine ministers, each of whom had responsibility for a specified branch of the administration. It was a feature of Han government that senior officials were duplicated. Thus, in the most senior position, that of Chancellor, there were two chancellors, the Chancellor of the Right and the Chancellor of the Left. The bureaucracy was extended to cover the commanderies, the parts of the empire under direct imperial control. Each commandery was placed under a Commandery Administrator who was provided with subordinate staff. All officials in this bureaucracy were ranked according to their nominal salary, which was expressed in bushels of unhusked grain.[7]

The other step was more innovatory. It amounted to the discarding of Legalism as the ideological basis for government and its gradual replacement by Confucianism. Gaozu was far too suspicious of scholars to allow this to happen immediately. On one occasion he did sacrifice at the grave of Confucius, but he did not repeal the Qin decree against the ownership of proscribed Confucian books. Nevertheless the way was open for the development of a fresh justification for imperial power, one based on an ethical view of the rights and obligations of rulers and subjects. The significance of this became apparent a generation later. When Wendi was on the throne Jia Yi, the essayist whose writings on the faults of Qin have already been noticed, urged the emperor to emulate the example of the kings of Zhou, that is to care for his subjects' well-being and to listen to the criticism of his ministers.[8]

The consolidation of Han control was accompanied by the development of policies which earned the dynasty the support of the people. Mention has already been made of the rescinding of the most severe of the Qin laws. In practice the change was less apparent and much of the Qin legal code remained in force.[9] The same was true of the requirement on peasants in terms of taxation and corvée labour, which continued Qin practice. Large numbers of people were conscripted to construct the walls of the capital at Chang'an. Peasants were liable to a poll tax and a land tax, as well as to labour obligations and military service. The rate of the land tax, normally one-fifteenth of the harvest, was halved in 168 BC, and the labour and military service obligations appear to have been less onerous in the early part of the Han period than they had been under the Qin. According to the *Hanshu*, the *History of the Former Han*, these were years of prosperity:

> The government grain depots . . . were all completely filled, while the government treasury and storehouses, moreover, had surpluses of wealth of all kinds. In the capital cash had accumulated in layers of hundreds of millions, [the number of] which could not be checked because the strings [which held the coins together] were rotted.[10]

An indication of the splendour of the dynasty at this time may be found in the ruins of its capital at Chang'an, the city of Eternal Tranquillity. Its construction had been commenced under Gaozu and greatly extended by his successor. The formal layout of the city symbolised the regularity of the imperial order and the view of society as a series of interrelated groups, each placed in its own rightful position in the universe. The city was built to face south, so that when the emperor was seated in his audience chamber he occupied the favoured south-facing position. The walls, which stood 12 metres high, enclosed an area of some 26 square kilometres. Within the city were to be found imperial palaces, parks, markets and ritual structures.[11]

It was during this period of consolidation that the first steps were taken to stabilise and extend the frontiers of the empire. In this the main, indeed overriding, consideration was the relationship with the Xiongnu, inhabitants of an empire to the north of China. It was this people who were once identified with the Huns, although that is no longer accepted. In 209 BC Maodun, a dynamic new leader of the Xiongnu seized power. He rapidly brought together a new confederation of the inhabitants of the steppes and encroached on Chinese territory. This prompted Gaozu in 200 BC to mount a campaign to win the territory back, but he was defeated at the battle of Pingcheng in modern Shanxi and narrowly escaped capture. Thereupon Gaozu changed tactics from war to diplomacy. Two years later the first of a series of treaties was signed between the Han and Xiongnu empires. In each treaty a marriage alliance was arranged between a Chinese princess and a Xiongnu leader and this was accompanied by a handsome gift from the Han empire. These treaties served to reduce the risk of Xiongnu attack and gradually led to the development of a significant border trade.[12]

THE REIGN OF WUDI, 141–87 BC

Michael Loewe, the foremost western historian of the Han dynasty, once remarked that the historical development of the Former Han period could best be understood in terms of two attitudes or convictions which characterised intellectual, religious and political change alike. He named these two attitudes 'modernist' and 'reformist'. The modernist attitude derived from Legalism, but differed from it. Modernists were concerned with the problems of the contemporary world. The reformist attitude derived from Confucian thought but was an extension of Confucianism. Reformists wished to eliminate the political and social abuses of the day by a return to conditions which they believed had existed in the remote past. According to Loewe, modernist policies dominated in the first century of the Former Han and reached their apogee in the reign of Wudi. Thereafter reformist tendencies gained strength and formed the ideological basis on which the usurper Wang Mang claimed the right to the throne.[13]

The reign of Wudi was the longest and most glorious of the Former Han. In the *Hanshu* he was the subject of a panegyric,[14] but not a great deal is known for certain of his personality. He was active in government, supervising work on the defences of the Yellow river and performing the necessary state rituals. But he never accompanied the military expeditions which were a principle source of the glorious reputation of his reign. He embodied a concept of the imperial institution which was committed inflexibly to certain basic principles of rule. An influential expression of this may be found in an essay written by the famous Confucian scholar Dong Zhongshu (*c.* 179–104 BC) and entitled 'The threefold obligation of the ruler'. These obligations were: to serve the basis of Heaven by making the appropriate sacrifices and setting the appropriate moral example; to serve the basis of earth by performing such symbolic acts as ploughing a furrow or feeding silkworms; and to serve the basis of man by establishing schools and enlightening the people by education.[15]

Under Wudi further steps were taken to develop the bureaucracy and important innovations were introduced. Most notable was the beginning of a career open to talent. A dramatic example of social mobility through education was the case of Gongsun Hong, who rose from being a swineherd to occupy the post of chancellor. He had studied the Confucian classics and had tendered advice to Wudi on the conduct of government. The usual way in which officials were recruited was by recommendation by provincial officials or senior ministers. If their recommendations proved unsatisfactory they were liable to punishment. In 124 BC an Imperial Academy was established with a quota of official disciples and students who studied the Confucian classics under the court scholars. After one year the students sat an examination in one of the classics and if they passed they were eligible for appointment to a government post. This has been seen as the start of the civil service examination system.[16]

Wudi's reign coincided with a great surge of intellectual activity in China. It is only

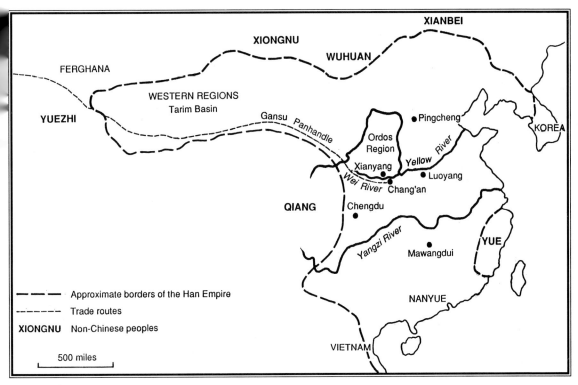

8 The Han Empire

9 Bronze figure of a flying horse, excavated from a tomb at Wuwei, Gansu; Eastern Han dynasty

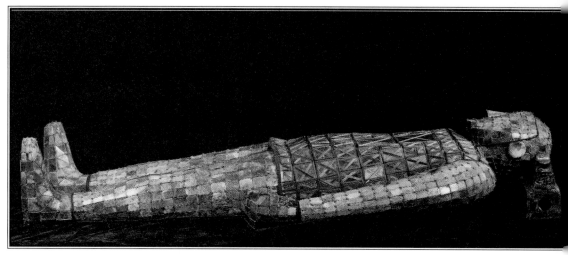

10 *The jade funeral suit of Princess Dou Wan, Western Han dynasty. It was believed that jade would prevent the decay of the corpse*

11 *The Empress Wei in procession with court ladies; restored relief panel from Longman, late Northern Wei dynasty*

possible to mention three examples of this. The first was the compilation known as the *Huainanzi*, assembled under the patronage of the prince of Huainan, who was a grandson of Gaozu. The collection had a distinctly Daoist tendency, containing, for example, a Daoist concept of the creation. But it also displayed perhaps the most characteristic feature of Han thought, its eclecticism. The essays in the book covered a variety of topics and represented a variety of views, and in the conclusion there was an attempt to synthesise what had been said:

> Casting away the foul and impure, drawing forth the pure and silent, it unifies the world, brings order to all things, responds to change and comprehends classes and categories. It does not pursue a single path, nor guard but one corner of thought, bound and led by material things and unable to change with the times. Use it in a corner of life and it will never fail; spread it over the whole world and it will never be found lacking[17]

Mention has already been made of Dong Zhongshu, the leading philosopher of the day, who may be said to have laid the foundations for orthodox Han Confucianism. His concept of the duties of the sovereign has already been noted. His writings, which included the *Chunqiu fanlu*, or *Deep Significance of the Spring and Autumn Annals*, were of great influence in at least three other areas of thought. The first was the theory of portents. Dong Zhongshu pursued the theme that if the emperor, the Son of Heaven, was failing in his duties, portents would appear which indicated Heaven's displeasure. If he failed to heed these, they would be followed by wonders, or 'Heaven's threats', which if ignored would lead to calamity. Secondly, he developed ideas relating to the order of nature, referring in particular to the Five Elements, that is water, fire, wood, metal and earth, to the *yin* and *yang* forces, and to the principle of the *dao* or Way. In Dong Zhongshu's writings these all formed part of one cosmic system, which in turn interlinked with political and ethical theories – heaven, earth and man all being governed by the same forces. Finally, it was Dong Zhongshu who ensured that the traditions and principles associated with Confucius would be accepted as orthodoxy by Wudi and by all succeeding emperors. This in itself was a remarkable change of fortune, after the attempt at the destruction of Confucian literature under the Qin. In Wudi's time not only were the texts restored, but they also became the basis of education and Confucius himself became the model for scholars. It was at this time that the state cult of Confucius was first established, an apotheosis transforming Confucius's thought from ethical treatise to the basis of a state religion.

Two other famous writers lived in Wudi's reign. The Grand Historian, Sima Qian, who died about 85 BC, was the author of the *Shiji*, the first attempt at a comprehensive survey of the history of China. He claimed merely to be completing a task started by his father, who had held the post of Grand Recorder at the court. In fact his ambition went much further, for he aimed to produce a vast and novel account of the past, based on a judicious selection from the records which had survived. In 99 BC Sima Qian spoke out in defence of a general who had been defeated by the Xiongnu, for which offence Wudi ordered that he be castrated – the sentence was carried out because the historian could not afford to redeem the punishment.[18]

The most famous poet of the day, Sima Xiangru, was rather more fortunate. He came from the province of Sichuan and married the daughter of a wealthy iron manufacturer. He became a courtier at Wudi's court and famous for his prose poems or *fu*. One of these contained a rhapsodic description of the Shanglin park, created by the First Emperor near Chang'an, and filled with exotic plants and strange animals. The poem's extravagant vocabulary, which was very different from the simple language of the verse in the Book of Songs, suggested that it was addressed to a minority audience of scholars and courtiers.

This was a period of active government and of state intervention in the operation of the economy. Significant changes were made in the administration of the empire. Many new commanderies were created and a system of regional inspectors established. A massive project to control the Yellow river was initiated. A free market in land was permitted and large estates were acquired, which then provided a major part of state revenue. Land was confiscated from landowners who had attempted to evade tax and then leased to peasants. In cities and towns, markets were controlled and merchants, whose status was low, were placed under various restrictions. State monopolies were established in the manufacture of salt and iron and somewhat later on the production of alcoholic liquors.

At the same time vigorous policies were pursued to prevent any significant challenge to dynastic rule. The administrative changes and the development of the bureaucracy formed part of a process of centralising power which progressively weakened the holders of kingdoms and marquisates. Several of the kingdoms suffered loss of territory and their significance was much diminished from that which they had been accorded at the beginning of the dynasty. Some 178 new marquisates were conferred in Wudi's reign, often as a means of ensuring the loyalty of former opponents, and in 112 BC over one hundred titles were also confiscated. One measure introduced by the emperor, which forced the division of an estate between all the male heirs, was to prove particularly effective against the principle of hereditary power. Coercive measures were also used against merchants who had profited greatly from the laissez-faire policies of the early Han emperors. Their position had improved even further as trade routes to Central Asia were opened up, and there were many instances quoted of merchants rapidly acquiring vast fortunes. Increased economic activity also gave a great boost to manufacturing, especially the production of iron and salt. Entrepreneurs amassed fortunes and then invested their profits in land. When, in 119 BC, the state set up monopolies in iron and salt the intention was not only to take a share of the profits, but also to challenge the accumulation of wealth and power in merchant hands. A similar profit motive may be detected in the introduction of a system of government purchase of surplus products in times of plenty and their sale in times of shortage.

The most dramatic indication of the growing power of the state was the policy of expansion with the effort first directed against the Xiongnu. In 138 BC Wudi despatched Zhang Qian as an envoy to the Yuezhi, a central Asian people known to be enemies of the Xiongnu, with whom he hoped to conclude an alliance. When Zhang Qian returned thirteen years later, having been held captive by the Xiongnu, he brought back invaluable information on Central Asia. He was also said to have introduced alfalfa and the grape to China. In the meantime military expeditions had been launched against the Xiongnu and the leading general of the day, Huo Qubing, achieved major victories over them in 121 and 119 BC. Later in the reign Chinese armies even reached Ferghana and the Pamirs. In the wake of these victories came colonisation of the Gansu panhandle and the development of trade along the Silk Road. At the same time Chinese expansion occurred in other directions. In 108 BC an expedition was sent to Korea which resulted in the establishment of four commanderies in the north of the peninsula. In the south victories were achieved over the people of Nanyue and commanderies were established in present-day Yunnan and Sichuan.

Without doubt the reign of Wudi was, from the Chinese point of view, a period of great progress. A sense of achievement was revealed in 104 BC when the emperor sanctioned the performance of ceremonies at which the dynasty's patron element of water, which had not been changed at the fall of the Qin dynasty, was now altered to that of earth, and the favoured colour became yellow in place of black. At the same time a new expression, Grand Beginning, was adopted for the counting of years.

Nevertheless, serious strains had already become evident and were to increase before the reign was over. Expeditions against the Xiongnu were extremely costly and so too was the effort required to maintain Chinese influence in the far-flung outposts of the empire. In 103 BC an expedition to obtain the 'heavenly horses' of Ferghana had failed and soon after that Xiongnu raiding started again. Trouble was not only apparent on the periphery of the empire, for in 99 BC serious outbreaks of banditry in eastern China forced the government to send special armed commissioners to restore order. In 91 BC the court itself was convulsed by a dynastic crisis which derived from a perennial problem suffered by dynasties, that of the power of the family of the empress. This was exacerbated by another frequent cause of dissension, the issue of the succession. For much of Wudi's reign the family of the Empress Wei had been in the ascendant and members of the family had occupied senior military and bureaucratic positions. The accumulation of problems encouraged the Li family, that is to say the family of Lady Li, one of the emperor's principal consorts, to challenge the dominance of the Wei. Accusations of witchcraft and embezzlement were traded. Open fighting broke out in which, it was said, ten thousand people died, and the Empress Wei and the heir apparent were both forced to commit suicide. At the same time the Li family was virtually eliminated. The one man who did improve his position as a result of the infighting was Huo Guang, a relative of the Empress Wei and half-brother of general Huo Qubing whose successes against the Xiongnu have already been noted. When Wudi fell terminally ill in 87 BC it was Huo Guang who headed the triumvirate which secured the succession of the eight-year-old boy who was to reign as Zhaodi.[19]

LATER RULERS OF THE FORMER HAN DYNASTY

Almost immediately after the death of Wudi, the underlying discontents of his reign came to the surface. In 81 BC a conference was held to discuss the cause of the hardship which the population was suffering. The record of this conference has survived in the *Yan tie lun* or *Discourses on Salt and Iron*. The protagonists in the debate were the modernists and reformists referred to above. The apologists for the government represented the modernist view and their critics that of the reformists. The fundamental issue was defining the aims of a government. The reformists argued that these should be based on principles while the modernists replied that a government must respond to practical and material considerations. The debate then moved on to specific concerns and especially to criticism of foreign policy and state monopolies. Spokesmen for the modernist view replied that the Xiongnu threat had made it necessary to fight a defensive war and that monopolies had been established to protect the people from exploitation. Furthermore, the opening of trade with Central Asia had led to the introduction of many new and exotic products. In return, the critics of government questioned the need to venture so far to the west and described the operation of the monopolies as inefficient and corrupt. The most successful part of the reformists' argument related to contemporary living conditions, which they compared unfavourably with those which had prevailed in the early years of the dynasty. Perhaps this earned them a moral victory in the debate and it is true that, after Wudi's death, state intervention declined and the monopolies fell into disuse.

Among the complexities of the last seventy years of Former Han rule three themes stand out: court politics, foreign policy and the economy. Michael Loewe once remarked that 'the development of Han politics can only be understood in the context of the rivalries and scandals within the palace'.[20] However, the record of court intrigue quickly degenerates into a catalogue of names and does not make for easy reading. Perhaps one incident stands out sufficiently to demand notice and to illustrate the character of these intrigues. This concerned the fate of Huo Guang, the leader of the triumvirate which had arranged the succession to Wudi. As sole survivor of that triumvirate he played a similar role in securing the succession of Xuandi in 74 BC and until his death eight years later Huo Guang dominated the court. However, Xuandi's succession inevitably raised the question of who should be empress. The emperor insisted that his consort, who had already borne him a son, should be elevated to that rank, and her son thus be recognised as heir to the throne. Huo Guang was unable to prevent this, but shortly afterwards his wife secretly procured the death of the empress by poisoning. In 68 BC Huo Guang himself died and as a mark of the great esteem he was held in he was buried in a style hitherto reserved for emperors. His body was dressed in a suit of jade and a settlement of 300 families was established to maintain his tomb. But within two years a power struggle at court led to the elimination of almost every one of Huo Guang's descendants. Moreover, after his death the range of policies for which he stood – the modernist policies of expansion, control of the population and exploitation of resources, were gradually replaced by reformist policies of retrenchment and laissez-faire.[21]

In foreign policy, likewise, the reign of Xuandi has been identified as a turning point. Until then expansion into central Asia had continued, helped by internal quarrels among the Xiongnu and other tribes, notably the Qiang, ancestors of the modern Tibetans. From about 60 BC a new phase of consolidation began, associated with the advice tendered to the emperor by Zhao Chongguo, an experienced general. He drew attention to the danger and expense of relying on military force to sustain the Chinese position, and the difficulty of securing any decisive victory. He suggested instead that the correct policy in the frontier areas was the permanent establishment of sponsored farming settlements. This proposal was adopted and shortly afterwards the office of Protector-General of the Western Regions was created with the task of co-ordinating Chinese initiatives in the region.

Finally there was the matter of the economy, which despite the growth of industry and commerce was still overwhelmingly based on agriculture. A fundamental problem was the growth of large landholdings and the impoverishment of the peasantry. In about 100 BC Dong Zhongshu had submitted a memorial to Wudi advising the limitation of land and slave ownership and recalling the merits of the 'well-field' system. His advice went unheeded and the problem continued to grow with the increase in population reducing the average size of peasant lots.

DYNASTIC DECLINE AND THE USURPATION OF WANG MANG

The last years of the Former Han dynasty illustrated many of the characteristics of what was later recognised as the downward phase of the dynastic cycle. These included extravagance at court followed by an unsuccessful attempt at retrenchment, one measure being a sharp reduction in the budget of the office of music. Another recurrent problem was the deepening conflict between court factions, often representing the family of the empress and the eunuchs. The latter, whose task was to ensure the well-being of the emperor and his women, only occasionally exerted influence in the former Han period, unlike the situation which was to prevail under the Later Han. Other factors which weakened the dynasty were succession disputes and regencies on behalf of child emperors. In the last decades of the Former Han the imperial line of succession from Xuandi failed, and the last three emperors of the dynasty were either invalids or minors.

Other problems added to the sense of crisis. One was the difficulty and expense of maintaining distant frontiers. Before the dynasty fell there was a partial withdrawal from Korea, but the suppression of rebellion in southwest China had imposed a severe strain on the empire's military capacity. There were also strains relating to raising tax revenues with a shift of the tax burden from large landowners to those least able to pay. The concentration of landownership was itself a recurrent difficulty. At the very end of the Han period, in 7 BC, a desperate and unsuccessful attempt was made to rectify this by the forcible redistribution of landholdings. Yet another problem was the neglect of river defences, which led to the disastrous flooding of the Yellow river in 30–29 BC.

The collapse of the dynasty was associated with the dominance of the Empress Wang, the mother of Chengdi, the emperor who reigned from 33 to 7 BC. Although the empress did not wield power herself, her influence was felt through members of her family who held the office of regent. Her nephew Wang Mang was regent while Pingdi was on the throne from AD 1 to 6. Shortly afterwards he claimed the throne, formally declaring himself as the first emperor of the Xin or New dynasty in AD 9.

Few characters in Chinese history have aroused more controversy than Wang Mang. For centuries, in China's traditional historiography, he was denounced as a tyrant, as a hypocrite and as an usurper. Yet earlier in this century the famous scholar Hu Shi hailed him as a pioneer of state socialism, who followed policies similar to those pursued in Russia in the 1920s.[22] More recently he has been classed as a reformist who tried to put into practice a genuine form of Confucianism,[23] or described as a pragmatist who governed China very much as the Han emperors had done before him.[24]

The basis on which these judgments have been formed are the factors which contributed to Wang Mang's rise to power, the measures which he took as emperor and the circumstances which led to his fall. In every case this evidence is limited and is heavily imbued with the horror of usurpers expressed in traditional historiography. As for Wang Mang's rise to power, the allegation was that he achieved this through a combination of ambition and guile, although that might be countered by a justification for his actions. The office of regent had been monopolised by the Wang family for twenty-five years and he had been preceded by three of his uncles. Moreover, Wang Mang had a reputation as a scholar, as a model of filial piety and as a man of modest personal needs. His decision to seize the throne was supported by a claim that twelve auspicious omens had appeared, which showed that heaven had awarded its mandate to him. The court nobility and officials had urged him to accept the offer.[25] Much of this case was astute propaganda and his motives may have been a combination of ambition and an awareness of the probable danger to himself and to his family if he did not seize power.

When in power Wang Mang pursued a range of policies which amounted to a programme of reform, although at times he appeared to be engaged in crisis management. His actions may be summarised under five headings, the first of which was the promulgation of an edict ordering the introduction of an equal landholding system based on the ancient 'well-field' principle. This measure, which has been described as the 'nationalisation' of the land, involved the abolition of private landownership and the prohibition of the sale of land or of slaves. In the edict it was made clear that this was an attack on large landholders and on their exploitation of peasants and that it was intended to return to the practices of the days of the Emperors Yao and Shun. The edict was issued in AD 9 and rescinded three years later, having proved entirely impractical.

A second major step was the reinstatement of the monopolies in salt, iron and alcohol which had been instituted under Wudi and which had been allowed to pass into disuse. At the same time a controlled market was introduced in grain, cloth and silk, with the government purchasing goods when they were cheap and selling them when the prices were high. It is not clear whether this was meant as a relief programme or to raise finance, but what is apparent is the anti-mercantile nature of the measure.

Thirdly, Wang Mang enacted a series of laws relating to taxation and the currency. A tax of ten per cent of income was levied on merchants and craftsmen. Several changes were made to the coinage system, with a large number of new denominations being introduced and an effective devaluation being carried out by allowing a discrepancy between face value and actual weight of the currency. A prohibition on the possession of gold and a requirement that it be exchanged for coinage, a measure probably intended to impoverish the nobility, was also passed.

It was perhaps inevitable that Wang Mang's disputed accession to the throne would be followed by trouble on the frontiers. The most serious danger arose from the alleged demotion of the tribal leader of the Xiongnu, but the threat of trouble was effectively countered by a show of force and a policy of divide and rule. Another area of difficulty was in the Western Regions, where in AD 13 a rebellion resulted in the death of the Chinese protector-general. Once again Wang Mang was able to deal with this, by dispatching a force large enough to re-establish the Chinese position.

Finally, Wang Mang sponsored scholarly research on the Confucian classics. He was patron to the historian Liu Xin and through him encouraged a revival of interest in ancient texts. Wang Mang himself was deeply interested in the record of China's antiquity. He assumed titles from the Zhou period and on occasions claimed to be recreating the ideal Confucian state. In a more practical vein, Wang Mang also encouraged scientific research, permitting a medical dissection to take place; and in AD 19 he encouraged an early attempt at manned flight.

If at least some of these actions might be regarded as achievements, why did Wang Mang's reign come to a premature end? Ban Gu, the historian of the Former Han, was in no doubt: it was because the measures he took were so ill-conceived that he antagonised all classes of society:

> The people could not turn a hand without violating some prohibition. . . . The rich had no means to protect themselves and the poor no way to stay alive. They rose up and became thieves and bandits, infesting the hills and marshes, and the officials, being unable to seize them, contrived on the contrary to hide their presence so that they grew more prevalent day by day. . . . Famine and pestilence raged and people ate each other so that before Wang Mang was finally punished half the population of the empire had perished. . . .[26]

Many writers have echoed Ban Gu and have found fault with the measures taken by Wang Mang. These have been decried as impractical in the case of the land reform, and a cause of confusion, distress and loss of confidence in the case of the currency innovations.[27] The attempt to re-introduce monopolies has been criticised as certain to antagonise the merchants without leading to any financial advantage to the population as a whole. The conduct of foreign relations has been decried as inept. At best Wang Mang has been portrayed as an idealistic intellectual, with many genuine humanitarian impulses, who became corrupted by power.[28] Less charitably, he has been referred to as an over-ambitious ruler whose attempt to bring about change led to abject failure accompanied by ridicule and farce.[29]

In these opinions the common explanation for the collapse of the short-lived Xin dynasty was the innovatory, if not to say revolutionary, domestic policy espoused by Wang Mang. Hans Bielenstein, however, argued that there was nothing new about these measures, for they all derived from past example and in particular from practices dating from the reign of Wudi. Wang Mang was 'a pragmatist who governed China very much as the Han emperors had done before him'.[30] For Bielenstein the essential reason for Wang Mang's fall was a natural disaster, the shifting of the Yellow river to a southern course debouching just north of the Shandong peninsula. This caused a massive loss of life, widespread famine and many people became refugees. It also gave rise to peasant rebellion, the most famous manifestation of which was the rebel group who became known as the Red Eyebrows because they painted their foreheads red to distinguish themselves from the government troops. Wang Mang's forces had several unsuccessful encounters with the rebels, and he then found his position challenged by a gentry-led group, centred on Nanyang in present-day Henan, and led by a descendant of the founder of the Former

Han dynasty. In AD 23 this group inflicted a decisive defeat on Wang Mang, who retreated to Chang'an where he was killed. It took another two years of civil war between rival claimants before Liu Xiu claimed the throne as the first emperor of the Later Han dynasty.

RESTORATION AND RECOVERY IN THE LATER HAN

Liu Xiu, later to be known by his posthumous name, Guang Wudi, occupied the throne until AD 57. During that period, and during the reigns of his successors Mingdi and Zhangdi, the Han dynasty was restored and China achieved a level of prosperity and security comparable to that of the Former Han.

Guang Wudi's first task was to suppress peasant rebellion and to overcome rivals to the throne. The Red Eyebrows had already been weakened by internal division and through clashes with other contenders. In communist historiography the reason for their defeat has been described as the seizure of the fruits of the peasant class struggle by representatives of the landlord class.[31] Liu Xiu, the future emperor, who came from Henan, was a landowner and his most dangerous rival for the throne, Gongsun Shu, was the leader of a powerful family based in present-day Sichuan. Liu Xiu had declared himself emperor in AD 23, but it was not until AD 36 that Gongsun Shu was killed and his capital Chengdu captured.

It was one thing to achieve a military victory, but the more difficult task was to fashion a political settlement that would last. Although Guang Wudi claimed to have restored the Han dynasty, the restoration was only partial. Many of the fiefs of the Former Han were not revived and only a limited return was made to the Former Han practice of nominating the emperor's sons as rulers of kingdoms. Another break with the past was the decision to move the imperial capital from Chang'an to Luoyang, some 200 miles to the east (hence the alternative name of the dynasty, the Eastern Han). Luoyang was to become the most populous city in the world at that time. The most marked discontinuity was in the matter of the national élite. The Former Han had seen the rise of great families to positions of power and influence. Some of these had been displaced under Wang Mang. The restoration, however, 'was not a restoration of the old social order'.[32] Guang Wudi's support had not derived from the great families of the former dynasty but for the most part came from the lesser gentry. Initially this gave him freedom of action in determining how to reward his allies. In the longer term this did not amount to absolute power and all emperors of the Later Han had to look for additional sources of support to remain in power. The political history of Guang Wudi's reign and that of his successors was dominated by attempts to manipulate the rivalry between various factions at court and in the bureaucracy.

In administrative terms, much of Later Han practice derived from the previous dynasty, although there were some changes in terms of the location of power and of cost. The most important development was the rise in influence of the secretariat, which although of lesser formal importance than the three great offices of state, was increasingly relied upon by the emperor. In terms of expense, Guang Wudi, like some other founders of dynasties, was able to make economies by cutting superfluous offices, for example in the palace guard and in the stable and coachhouse establishment. A much larger economy was achieved by reducing the number of counties by 400, a change made possible because of population decline and migration from the north-west.

There is evidence to suggest that the turbulent years of dynastic change accompanied by natural disasters had led to a substantial reduction in population. Two sets of figures have survived, the annual registrations of the population for the purpose of taxation for AD 2 and for AD 140. The first showed the population to number 57.7 million individuals and the latter indicated slightly over 48 million individuals. In the same period there had been a dramatic shift in the regional distribution of the population. At the earlier date 76 per cent of the population lived in North China, but by the later date this proportion had fallen to 54 per cent.

These figures belie a pattern of improvements in agriculture, with the greater use of iron farming implements, the repair and extension of irrigation projects and the increased use of draft animals. The significance of the last-named change was shown in AD 76 when a serious cattle epidemic occurred and this caused large areas of land to be taken out of cultivation. The benefits of agricultural improvement were not shared out evenly, for powerful landowners extended their holdings and grew rich at the expense of their labourers. Much of the migration from the north-west and the Central Plain southwards may have been due to the impoverishment of peasants who could not keep up with technological change or who had fallen into debt. Some confirmation of this situation is to be found in measures taken by the government to assist poor peasants. These included taxing agriculture lightly, helping peasants who had lost their land to resettle elsewhere, and providing direct grants of assistance. It is testimony to the efficiency of Later Han government in the first century AD that it contained the effects of natural disaster while remaining solvent.

In towns and cities too there was evidence of economic improvement. It was in this period that a money economy became fully accepted, with wages commonly being paid in cash and labour services being partially commuted into a monetary tax. Communications were improved and it has been suggested that land transportation in North China was probably as good during the Later Han as it was in any period before modern times.[33] This advance encouraged commercial activity which was subject to less government interference than in the past. Interregional trade flourished and new and improved products such as paper and lacquerware were distributed widely.

In foreign relations, Guang Wudi and his successors achieved short-term glory at the expense of creating disastrous long-term problems. In terms of relations with the

Xiongnu, the policy was one of divide and rule. A southern branch of the Xiongnu was allowed to settle in the Ordos region, but sporadic campaigns were fought against the northern branch, culminating in a major victory in AD 89. This permitted the restoration of Chinese influence in the Western Regions, the key figure in this venture being Ban Chao, brother of the historian Ban Gu. He led an army across the Pamirs, reached the Caspian Sea and sent an envoy to make contact with the Roman Empire. In the meantime, in the north-east, the Han dynasty was involved in dealings with two other important tribal groupings who had been brought into contact with China through the campaigns against the Xiongnu. The Wuhuan lived beyond the Great Wall in modern Hebei and Liaoning. They had formerly been in a tributary relationship with the Xiongnu, but from AD 49 they were drawn into the Han tributary system, their leaders being offered titles and gifts in return for guarding the frontier against their former overlords. As a result they began to settle in the northern commanderies. The Xianbei lived beyond the Wuhuan. They too became clients of the Han with the duty of fighting the Xiongnu, a task which they fulfilled only too successfully. In AD 91 they defeated the northern Xiongnu and occupied their lands, only then to turn against the Chinese. For the next century the Xianbei were to be the main threat on China's northern frontier. Meanwhile throughout the south the Han empire continued to expand. Another famous name in Chinese military history, Ma Yuan, is remembered for his heroic campaign which in AD 43 ended the attempt by two Vietnamese sisters to shake off the Chinese yoke.

THE BEGINNINGS OF DECLINE AND THE CRISIS OF AD 168

A century before it came to an end, the Later Han dynasty was already showing signs of disorder, which were to culminate in the crisis of AD 168. The problems besetting the dynasty may be divided into three, of which the first appeared at court. For a century, starting from 88, a succession of minors had occupied the throne. Effective power was in the hands of a regent, or more often in the hands of the empress dowager. There were frequent examples of contested succession and of violent deaths at court. The most notorious exponent of the latter practices was Liang Ji, brother of the empress of Shundi, who allegedly procured the murder of one infant emperor and made his sister regent for his successor. Over a period of twenty years, until his murder in 159, he accumulated every conceivable post of importance and amassed a fortune estimated at 3,000 million cash. At court at this time the influence of the family of the 'external clans', as the family of the empress was termed, was challenged by the eunuchs, castrated men employed in the imperial palace. Eunuchs, who were often of plebeian origins, owed their influence to their relationship to the emperor whose harem they guarded. In return the emperor looked to them for support against the 'external clans'. Under the Later Han the number of eunuchs at court increased greatly, reaching 2,000, and they began to exercise political influence. Their position improved in 114 when the adopted son of an eunuch was permitted to inherit his fief, and again in 135 when eunuchs were granted the right to hand down noble titles to their adopted heirs. It was a group of five eunuchs who murdered Liang Ji and throughout the reign of Huandi the eunuchs played a prominent role. When Huandi died in 169, a major crisis occurred at the Han court, the outcome of which was a triumph for the eunuchs. For the next fifteen years eunuchs controlled the government and pursued a vendetta against those whom they regarded as having acted against their interests in the past.

The second problem was the growing unevenness in the distribution of wealth. The celebrated scholar Wang Fu lived between AD 90 and 165. A man who never obtained official preferment, he expressed his views on the age in a work called *Qianfu lun* or *Criticisms of a Hidden Man*. In one chapter of the book, entitled 'On excessive luxury', he railed against the social conditions and morals of his day. He noted how agriculture was being abandoned in favour of trade, how people, even the servants and slaves of the aristocracy, ate and dressed extravagantly, and how the administration of justice had become too expensive for the poor to use.[34] Some of this accumulation of wealth derived from large estates and the wealth of some landowners outstripped that of officials. Evidence of this wealth has been found in the thousands of tombs of Han date which have been identified. Many tombs contain pottery models, representing the various possessions of the deceased and sometimes drawing attention to his position as a landowner.[35] But alongside this wealthy minority the great mass of the agricultural population lived in abject poverty, oppressed by taxes and labour services and often in danger of losing the plot of land which represented to them some degree of independence, and without which they would become landless labourers.[36]

Finally there was the problem of the frontier. In the second century AD the dynasty had to face the consequences of previous policies of compromise. One difficulty was that of expense. When the dynasty had restored tributary relations with the Western Regions in AD 73, it had become the established practice for the Chinese to make regular payments amounting to a total of 74,800,000 cash a year to leaders of the tribes in the area and this was a tremendous burden on state finances. An even larger sum was spent on maintaining the southern Xiongnu, now settled within Han territory. Although the Xiongnu presence alongside Chinese settlers was expected to stabilise this section of the frontier, in fact it created a complicated and often dangerous racial situation, the full implications of which became apparent a century later. However it was from the Xianbei in the north that the most pressing threat emerged. In the middle of the century a leader named Tanshihuai created a great steppe confederation of his peoples and between 168 and his death in 180 he inflicted a series of defeats on the Chinese, so destabilising the whole of the northern frontier.

Similarities have been noted between the problems of the Chinese and Roman empires in coping with the threat of uncivilised or nomadic peoples on their borders. It has been pointed out that effective control meant a combination of two factors: adequate military power to dominate such peoples and acceptance of their position by the peoples so dominated. In the Former Han period this combination had been achieved and control maintained. However in the Later Han, with the appearance of Xianbei, who initially lacked a coherent political system with which the Chinese could deal, there was no acceptance of Chinese authority. At the same time the loss of Chinese population in the north, and the weakening of government finances and commitment, undermined the principle of adequate military power. The fact that until the year 177, when an expedition against Tanshihuai ended in disaster, Chinese armies were successful in their campaigns, disguised the extent of the erosion of the Chinese position. By the end of the dynasty, Chinese authority had been driven well to the south and the frontier lands had fallen out of Chinese control. In this region, a century later, were to emerge the barbarian states which dominated North China in the centuries of division.[37]

THE FALL OF THE LATER HAN

Although the Han dynasty did not come to an end until 220, its effective collapse as a dynasty occurred in 189. A discussion of the reasons for its decline and fall must therefore concentrate on the reign of Lingdi, that is on the period from 168 to 189. Some of the reasons for dynastic decline had already become established by the start of his reign: factional fighting at court, great disparities in wealth, and threats on the frontier. Under Lingdi the situation worsened: the sale of high office became established, and Xianbei raiding on the frontier became increasingly frequent. These were later to be recognised as typical features of dynastic decline. So too was a third factor, peasant rebellion, which Marxist writers attributed to the struggle of peasants against the landlord class. However, even Marxist writers would have to admit that the rebellion which challenged the dynasty in 184 was a rebellion of a new type, although it was to have many repetitions, for it was a rebellion which derived its inspiration from religion. Adherents of popular Daoism, perhaps responding to the fact that the year 184 marked the beginning of a new sexagenary cycle in the calendar, rose in a number of movements. There were two main rebellions, the Yellow Turbans, headed by Zhang Jue in the east, and the Five Pecks of Rice (so named after the subscription paid by each follower), headed by Zhang Lu in the west. The inspiration of these millenarian sects was a book dating from the end of the former Han entitled *Taiping jing*, or *The Book of the Great Peace*, which announced the coming of a new golden age of prosperity and equality. This promise attracted a following of many thousands of peasants, who attacked government officials. This provoked savage reprisals, said to have cost the lives of half a million people in the first year alone.[38]

The Yellow Turban and Five Pecks of Rice rebellions, which undoubtedly brought widespread devastation, are often cited as the cause of the downfall of the Han dynasty. However, it must be remembered that the direct threat from these rebellions had been countered by 189 and that there is some doubt whether the rebellions aimed to overthrow the dynasty. To what then should the collapse of the dynasty be attributed? One could say that a dynasty which was already severely weakened suffered a series of hammer blows which ensured its fall. The first blow came on the death of Lingdi when the eunuchs, who throughout the reign had been the emperor's main support, were massacred.[39] The second came in the following year when Luoyang was sacked and the emperor removed to the old capital of Chang'an. By now effective power lay in the hands of the generals, the most famous of whom, Cao Cao was dominant in the north, Liu Bei in Sichuan and Sun Quan in the south. The dynasty survived in name, but only because Cao Cao declined to usurp it. When he died in 220 his son formally ended the Han period by declaring the establishment of a new dynasty, the Wei.

CHAPTER FIVE

THE PERIOD OF DIVISION

Although the Han dynasty did not officially end until 220, its power collapsed in 189. For over three hundred years from that date no single dynasty had effective control over the whole of China. Between 189 and 220 there was a three-way division of power between three Later Han generals. When Cao Cao, the most famous of these, died in 220, the empire was divided into three kingdoms: the Wei dynasty under Cao Pei, the son of Cao Cao at Luoyang; the Wu dynasty under Sun Quan at Jiankang; and the Shu Han dynasty under Liu Bei at Chengdu. The era of the Three Kingdoms ended in 280 when the successors to the Wei dynasty defeated their rivals and as the Western Jin reunited China, at least in name. But in 311 the dynasty's capital at Luoyang was sacked by the Xiongnu and in 316 the state was destroyed.

From 316 to 589 China was divided politically between dynasties of the south which sought to revive the tradition of the Han, and dynasties of the north, generally established by non-Chinese peoples. To describe the political succession in the south, the term the Six Dynasties is used, referring to the dynasties which had their capital at Jiankang, or modern Nanjing. In the north the fragmentation of authority was even more extreme and the period between 316 and 384 is known as that of the Sixteen Kingdoms. But from that time onwards a new power began to emerge, headed by a branch of the Xianbei known as the Toba, who had originally settled in northern Shanxi. In 386 the Toba adopted the dynastic name of the Northern Wei and from then on they became increasingly sinicised. In 493 the Toba emperor established his capital at Luoyang and inaugurated a period of peace and prosperity. In 534, however, the dynasty split and the north again experienced division under dynasties known collectively as the northern dynasties. From one of these emerged a general named Yang Jian, who not only gained control of the north, but also defeated the last of the southern dynasties. In 589 the Sui dynasty reunited China.

THE FALL OF THE ROMAN AND CHINESE EMPIRES COMPARED

The idea that there might be a connection between the fall of the Roman and the early Chinese empires has been current since at least 1788, when Edward Gibbon completed *The History of the Decline and Fall of the Roman Empire*. In that work Gibbon

67

emphasised the role of what he called the barbarian tribes in undermining the two empires and explained this by stressing the contrast between the civilised but effete values of the Romans and Chinese and the rude vigour of the barbarians.

More recently the collapse has been explained as the consequence of systemic weaknesses in the two empires. The key weaknesses which have been identified are first those to do with the economy, with reference to the growth of great and privileged estates run by large landowning families, and the alleged effect of the institution of slavery. Secondly, there are the factors which undermined the culture or ideology which had informed the empire at the time of its rise, which might be defined as a combination of degeneracy and intrusive religion. For Rome, Gibbon had identified the enemies as the increase in luxury and the adoption of Christianity. For Han China, the same allegations have been made about the effects of luxury, the spread of Buddhism, and the attraction of Daoist escapism. Finally there is the matter of the relationship with 'barbarian' tribes on the frontiers. For some writers[1] the fall of the two empires derived from a common event, the rise of a Mongol people called the Avars who, throughout the fifth century, maintained an empire which extended from the boundary of Korea to Lake Balkhash. The repercussions of their expansion were to bring both empires to their knees at virtually the same time. In both empires a fatal weakness had been created by permitting nomadic peoples to settle within the boundaries of the empire and allowing the defences of the frontier to fall into the hands of auxiliary soldiers recruited among the settlers. Financial weakness made it difficult for either empire to sustain an active defence and this ensured that the policy was one of diplomacy and compromise. And so, as the empires also weakened from within, it was only a matter of time until they collapsed.[2]

With the disappearance of central government, China and western Europe entered a prolonged period of division described as a dark age. In each case one half of the former empire experienced political disintegration, while in the other half, either in form of the Byzantine empire or in the succession of empires centred on Jiankang and known as the Six Dynasties, there was an attempt to preserve the traditions of a glorious past and the hope of recovering that which had been lost.

But there the parallels cease because the Chinese empire recovered. The consensus as to why this occurred is that it had qualities superior to those of the Roman empire. These included a stronger ethnic and cultural unity, with special reference to the Chinese writing system, and a greater geographic unity, with China the more compact empire, not divided by major natural barriers like the Alps. It has been suggested that the Han imperial concept was superior to that of Rome: that the ideal of a just and ethical rule by an emperor who held the mandate of heaven, and who ruled through a bureaucracy composed of educated men, had a greater appeal than the personal rule of the Roman emperors implemented through an impartial code of law. Finally, in practical terms, the weight of population and the age and persistence of Chinese culture in the north of the country, where China was at its weakest, proved a decisive factor. The barbarians who invaded China were unable to change this. The majority absorbed the invaders and converted them into Chinese.[3]

THE ERA OF THE THREE KINGDOMS AND OF THE WESTERN JIN

Between 220 and 280 China was divided into three states. Wolfram Eberhard described the two southern ones as 'condottiere states', that is to say states conquered by generals from the north and for a time ruled by those generals and their northern troops.[4] In the south-west, occupying present-day Sichuan, an area which in Chinese history has often become a regional power base, was the kingdom of Shu Han. Its first ruler, Liu Bei, claimed descent from the Han royal family, and his pretensions to be the legitimate successor were later upheld. In its first years Shu Han achieved some success in extending its influence among the non-Chinese peoples of modern Yunnan and after Liu Bei's death in 226, his chief minister Zhuge Liang gained a reputation as a wily strategist. But after Zhuge Liang died in 234 Shu Han, which had the smallest population of the Three Kingdoms, went into decline and was absorbed by Wei in 263.

In the south-east, occupying the Yangzi valley and a vast area to the south, was the Kingdom of Wu. This area had only become sinicised under the Han and the political control of its rulers was tenuous. Some attempt was made to establish foreign relations, and there is a record of Wu making overtures to the state of Yan in southern Manchuria and to Yamato in the south of Japan. In both cases the motive seems to have been to seek allies against Wei in the north. In this the Wu rulers were not successful and the kingdom fell to Wei in 280.

The kingdom of Wei had been established by Cao Pei, son of Cao Cao, that most famous of the generals of the late Han period. From the start the condition of the state was insecure. It retained the style, and the expense, of an imperial court at Luoyang and it tried to protect its trade routes to the north-west. However, it was forced to make heavy payments to the nineteen Xiongnu tribes which had been allowed to settle in the north and its attempts to subjugate the kingdoms of the south entailed further military expenses.

In the meantime, a more subtle change was taking place in the kingdom's political organisation. Under the Later Han a few powerful families had risen to national importance. Large estates had been established and their owners had come to dominate local affairs. With the decline of central authority these magnates had established enclaves of local power. Some of them had also adopted the ideas of a moralistic revival group whose members called themselves *qingliu*, that is the 'pures'. They railed against the dominance of the imperial throne by the eunuchs and by the family of the empress dowager. They argued that this malign influence should be replaced by the appointment of men who were known locally for maintaining traditional moral standards. This view reinforced a tendency to give increased respect to pedigree and to promote to high office those whose ancestors had formerly achieved eminence.

From these changes there evolved a new system of recruiting men to office, known as the arbiter system, which was to be used by new rulers to gain legitimacy and to obtain the cooperation of powerful local families. Under this system an arbiter, a man chosen from the local upper class, was appointed to each commandery, and later also to each prefecture. His task was to classify candidates for office into nine ranks of character and ability: the higher the rank a man received from the arbiter, the higher the office for which he was eligible. This system precipitated a major change in social stratification, leading to the emergence of aristocratic families, whose status depended partly on their local wealth and influence, and partly on their access to office.[5]

Long before this system was properly established, events in the state of Wei demonstrated the fragility of the political situation. Having conquered Shu Han in 263, the ruler of Wei was deposed by Sima Yan, one of his generals and a member of one of the leading families. Sima Yan established a dynasty called the Western Jin and entitled himself Jin Wudi, the 'martial emperor'. During his reign the state of Wu was subjugated and China reunited. Thereafter some attempt was made to rehabilitate a country which had been ravaged by war by disbanding soldiers and attempting to settle them on the land. The need for such a measure was indicated by the sharp decline in the official census of the taxable population, which by 280 had fallen to 16 million from 56 million under the Later Han. But the dynasty was too weak to coerce the great landowners and generals. After the emperor's death in 290 the country lapsed into the civil war known as the Revolt of the Eight Kings. With the disintegration of imperial government, Xiongnu incursions form the north increased, and in 311 they sacked the capital Luoyang.

While historians have often dismissed the period of the Three Kingdoms and the Northern Wei as a period of dreary disorder, in popular culture it has acquired a romantic reputation. This is largely because it is the period depicted in the seventeenth-century novel *The Romance of the Three Kingdoms*, attributed to Luo Guanzhong. In its pages appear fictionalised representations of Cao Cao, Liu Bei and Zhuge Liang. An even more assured place in popular memory was achieved by Guan Yu, a confederate of Liu Bei, who in the sixteenth century was raised to the rank of Guandi, the God of War.

THE SOUTHERN DYNASTIES

After the collapse of the Western Jin dynasty in the north, for two centuries China was effectively divided into two. It is convenient to describe first the developments to the south of the Yangzi. The record began with the establishment in 317, by a survivor of the Western Jin, of a new dynasty known as the Eastern Jin, with its capital at Jiankang. To the capital came many refugees from the north, while at the same time the Chinese population was increasing rapidly, causing tension between old and new settlers and between the Chinese and non-Chinese populations. The dynasty maintained its claim to be the true heir to the Han and sought to reconquer the north, but it was hampered by intrigues at court and rivalry among generals. In 399 the dynasty was faced with a different sort of threat, a popular rising along the southern coast, perhaps triggered off by tension between new and old settlers. Its leaders claimed a connection with the Yellow Turbans of the last years of the Later Han period. The rising was suppressed by an army commander named Liu Yu, who in 420 usurped the throne and established what became known as the Liu-Song dynasty. Under Liu Yu and his successor a period of political stability ensued, but after the fall of the Liu Song in 479 three more undistinguished dynasties were to rise and fall in quick succession. Despite the failure of any of the southern dynasties to recover political authority, this period was one of population growth and the rise of what has been called a manorial system.

THE NORTHERN DYNASTIES

Meanwhile, in the north, there occurred the long period of anarchy known as the time of the Sixteen Kingdoms. During this era, the settled population of north China was invaded and overrun by various tribal groupings coming from the west and the north. Among these, three major ethnic conglomerations have been distinguished. To the west, in the area of modern Gansu, Shaanxi, Sichuan and Qinghai, were the Tibetan Di and Qiang, peoples who were essentially sheep herders rather than horse breeders and whose states were based on a military rather than on a tribal structure. In the north-west were the Xiongnu, traditionally divided into nineteen tribes, and the Jie, both ethnically described as Turkic. Finally, to the north were the Xianbei, whose ethnic origins were variously described as proto-Mongol or Tungus. These ethnic labels must be treated with caution. At most they only refer to the language and culture of the leading tribe within a group or confederation. Tribes with different ethnic characteristics could and did join together in confederations.[6]

The first major incursion into north China in this period came from the Xiongnu and resulted in the capture of Luoyang and Chang'an and the destruction of the Western Jin dynasty. The leading figure in this train of events was Liu Yuan, descendant of Maodun, whose dynamic leadership of the Xiongnu in the early years of the Former Han dynasty, five hundred years previously, has already been noted. Liu Yuan came from a new mould of Xiongnu leadership, one who had acquired a Chinese education and whose concept of empire was not the nomadic empire of the past, but one which laid claim to settled territory and to the imperial throne of China. To support this claim Liu Yuan could point to the intermarriage between the Xiongnu and the Han dynasty, to the fact that his surname was the same as that of the Han, and that at his capital, Pingcheng, Chinese court ceremonial had been adopted and to it he had already attracted educated Chinese. Liu Yuan died in 310, the year before the capture of Luoyang, though his successors established the short-lived dynasty known as the Earlier Zhao (304–20). But Liu Yuan's vision of empire was not shared by other tribal leaders. A new tribal confederation formed under Shi Luo, who rejected the Chinese model in favour of a return to the Xiongnu nomadic state, but who also broke with tradition by usurping the rightful succession and declaring himself ruler of the Later Zhao dynasty.

The second main challenge came from the Tibetan peoples in the west. When the Later Zhao dynasty collapsed, the leader of a Tibetan tribal confederation declared himself emperor of the Earlier Qin dynasty. In 357 he was succeeded on the dynastic throne by a man named Fu Jian, who built up a formidable fighting force, consisting not only of cavalry, but also of infantry, recruited among the Chinese. With this force he was able to conquer much of North China. In 383 he turned his attention to the conquest of the south and to the destruction of the Eastern Jin. This campaign was the most famous of the period. Fu Jian is supposed to have mustered one million men when he descended the Yangzi to capture Jiankang. But his forces were accustomed to open terrain and were unable to adapt to the conditions of the Yangzi valley. They were defeated by the Jin troops at a decisive battle, which led not only to the failure of the expedition, but also to the rapid disintegration of the Earlier Qin empire.

The third instance of the rise of a non-Chinese dynasty, to be called the Northern Wei, was that of the tribal federation known as the Toba. The original Toba state had been destroyed by Fu Jian, but in about 385 it was re-formed in the north of the present province of Shanxi. Its leadership group may have been of Turkic origin, although the federation incorporated Xiongnu and Xianbei tribes and, as the state prospered, an increasing number of Chinese were employed as officials. Towards the end of the fourth century the Toba state extended its control over much of the North China Plain. It then began a process of adaptation and change, including progressive sinicisation, which gave it a strength and permanency which exceeded that of all previous non-Chinese dynasties.

This process had several components. The first was that the Toba developed sufficient military power to ward off rivals, which was achieved initially by the gradual subversion of the tribal system and its replacement by a military administration. This enabled the Toba to extend their influence in two directions. To the north, the settled Toba attacked and defeated yet another confederation of nomadic tribes, known as the Ruanruan, sometimes identified with the Avars who were later to settle on the Danube. There followed a series of successful expeditions which extended Toba influence into Gansu and gave access to the commerce of Central Asia. By 440 the

Toba empire was the most powerful state in East Asia, ruling the whole of north China.[7]

Another factor was the increasing participation of Chinese in the government of the Toba state. From 440, Pingcheng was developed as a capital city. Although still a barbarous place in the eyes of Chinese visitors, it had a huge palace complex, residential wards and religious buildings. Such a city required the service of Chinese officials accustomed to urban life. From 476, when the Empress Dowager Feng, herself from an aristocratic Chinese family, gained paramount power, the advancement of Chinese to high office gathered pace. Between 472 and 499 a series of decrees was issued, known as the Taihe reforms, which were 'a conscious and deliberate attempt to bring the country closer to the . . . ideal of a Han-Chinese, Confucian, bureaucratic monarchy ruling an ordered aristocratic state'.[8] The reforms included the development of a Confucianised bureaucracy and the promotion of Confucian morality, control of Toba religious and social customs, and the introduction of more sophisticated systems of taxation and forced labour. They were accompanied by a change in frontier policy, with a switch away from the aggressive policy of sending powerful forces on raids against the Ruanruan, to one of wall-building, static defence and appeasement. Policies such as these, aimed at sinicisation and undermining tribal customs, inevitably excited the hostility of traditionalist Toba aristocratic families.

An important economic reform had a more complicated purpose. In 477 a plan was accepted for a 'land equalisation scheme', (*juntian*). All land was decreed to belong to the state. Every free man and woman had the right to receive a certain amount of land for their lifetime, but after their death the land would be redistributed. In addition to this allocation, which was defined as 'personal land', people could also hold a small area known as 'mulberry land', to be planted with mulberries and other crops, which land could be inherited. The introduction of this reform has been associated with the impoverishment of the Toba tribespeople who, as they became more settled, could no longer obtain the plunder on which they had previously relied. It may also have been occasioned by the desire to curtail the growing prosperity of the Chinese gentry.[9] Another view of the reform is that it was intended to extend the land under cultivation and to increase grain production, while at the same time curbing the influence of powerful landlords.[10] It has also been described as a return to the policy attempted by Wang Mang in AD 9 to preserve a free peasantry, essential for the maintenance of the tax revenue of the state.[11] The reform was put into practice from 485 and there is some fragmentary evidence relating to its implementation. It was accompanied by the revival of a collective guarantee system, whereby the population was divided into groups whose members were individually responsible for the conduct and payment of tax within the group, a system later to be refined and known as the *baojia*.

Early in 493 the young Emperor Xiao had said of Pingcheng 'This is a place from which to wage war, not one from which civilized rule can come'.[12] Before the end of that year the emperor announced his decision that the Northern Wei capital would be transferred five hundred miles south, to the site of the historic city of Luoyang. The move was probably intended as a further blow to the declining influence of the Toba aristocratic leadership. Luoyang was chosen because of its cultural associations – it was at the very centre of Chinese civilisation – and because it was at the heart of the most populous and wealthy agricultural region of north China. The move itself took time, two years to move the court and the bureaucracy to Luoyang and a further seven years to build the new capital. But then the city grew rapidly, achieving a population in excess of 500,000 and becoming one of the great cities of the ancient world. The inner city measured about 9.5 square kilometres and was surrounded by massive walls, the remains of which measure 25–30 metres thick. The roads were set out on a grid system and the city was furnished with a sophisticated water supply. Beyond the inner city lay an outer city, which contained the residential wards and over five hundred magnificent Buddhist monasteries and nunneries. One such, the Jingming, was an imperial foundation and it served not only a religious function but it also contributed to the revenues of the state. Within its walls the most advanced water-powered grain-processing machinery of the day was in use. This technology may have been developed by captives or émigrés from the south, and its use may have been monopolised by the imperial house.[13] Another part of the outer city was set aside for the large community of foreign traders. Beyond the city lay the imperial domain and an intensively farmed countryside which supplied the city's food requirements. In 534, when the dynasty collapsed, this great city was to be abandoned in three days.

INTELLECTUAL AND RELIGIOUS DEVELOPMENTS: THE TRANSFORMATION OF DAOISM

Before concluding the discussion of the period of division, the important issue of the intellectual and religious trends which had set in at the end of the Han dynasty must be considered. These include the transformation of Daoism and the introduction and rise of Buddhism.

Confucianism derived its strength from its importance as a state cult and because of its role in the training of bureaucrats. With the decline of the Han dynasty, the way was opened for the development of more speculative and individualistic philosophies. In the third century a number of writers developed the ideas of what has sometimes been described as neo-Daoism or philosophical Daoism. One aspect of the movement was known as *xuanxue* or 'dark learning', whose proponents set out to harmonise the Daoist spirit with Confucian social and moral doctrines. Guo Xiang, who died in 312, conceived the sage to be a person who moved between the realm of human affairs and the transcendental world. He wrote a famous commentary on the *Zhuangzi* in which he developed the Daoist theme of non-action, saying:

In the cutting of a tree the workman does not take any action; the only action he takes is in plying the ax. In the actual managing of affairs, the ruler does not take any action; the only action he takes is in employing his ministers. If the minister can manage affairs, the ruler can employ ministers, the ax can cut the tree, and the woodman can use the ax, each corresponding to his capacity, then the laws of nature will operate of themselves, not because someone takes action.[14]

Other groups engaged in *qingtan* or 'pure conversation', which often implied metaphysical discussion. The most famous of these groups was the Seven Immortals of the Bamboo Grove, a group of men of letters who met near Luoyang to hold discussions, to write poetry and play music, and to drink heavily. An important element in Daoist thought was the search for immortality, which led investigators to the study of medicine and inner hygiene and which also encouraged an interest in alchemy. Daoism also became a popular religion, with temples and a priesthood and a pantheon of gods. It was also at this time that the close connection between Daoism and art was established. In his *Introduction to Landscape Painting* Zong Bing (375–443) summed up many of the points of this relationship when he wrote:

And so I live in leisure and nourish my vital power. I drain clean the wine-cup, play the lute, lay down the picture of scenery, face it in silence, and, while seated, travel beyond the four borders of the land, never leaving the realm where nature exerts her influence, and alone responding to the call of wilderness. Here the cliffs and peaks seem to rise to soaring heights, and groves in the midst of clouds are dense and extend to the vanishing point. Sages and virtuous men of far antiquity come back to live in my imagination and all interesting things come together in my spirit and in my thoughts. What else need I do? I gratify my spirit, that is all. What is there that is more important than gratifying the spirit?[15]

THE INTRODUCTION AND RISE OF BUDDHISM

The origins of Buddhism are traced back to Gautama Sakyamuni, an Indian prince who lived during the sixth and fifth centuries BC. Extravagant claims were later made about the earliness of the coming of Buddhism to China. It was alleged that Confucius had known about the existence of Buddha, or that the explorer Zhang Qian had brought back information on Buddhism gleaned on his travels in central Asia in the second century BC. Another story told how Mingdi, the emperor of the Later Han dynasty who reigned between AD 57 and 75, had in a dream seen a golden deity fly in front of his palace. He was told that his dream was of the Buddha and he thereupon sent an envoy to India who returned with the *Sutra in Forty Sections*, thus introducing Buddhism to China.

Less fanciful accounts suggest that some knowledge of Buddhism may have reached China from the kingdom of Scythia in the reign of the Emperor Ai (6 BC–AD 1) and that a Buddhist community may have already been in existence in northern Jiangsu by the time of Mingdi's dream. This community was probably composed of foreign monks and it is likely that most early adherents of Buddhism in China were traders or missionaries, with the conversion of ethnic Chinese coming at a later stage in the establishment of the religion.

Over the next two centuries Buddhism made only slow progress in China, a fact which has been explained on various grounds. Elsewhere in Asia, Buddhism was perceived as the religion of a more advanced culture and its arrival also introduced a written language to an illiterate community. However China already had a highly developed written language and Buddhism was likely to be received with indifference or hostility by the educated classes. Although the political disintegration of China may have been advantageous to the introduction of Buddhism, Chinese culture remained as a powerful obstacle to the adoption of a new religion. Once Buddhism had arrived in China, other obstacles to its spread became apparent. With its doctrine of renunciation of worldly concerns, including those of family ties, Buddhist values were directly opposed to those of Confucianism which emphasised the importance of the family. Another obstacle derived from the translation of Buddhist texts. The Chinese language had a developed vocabulary of religious and metaphysical terms and so, when the concepts of Buddhism were translated into Chinese, endless confusion was created because the words used in translation already had philosophical connotations. No Chinese scholars at this time knew Sanskrit, the original language of the Buddhist texts, and all translations had to be made indirectly. Because Buddhism came to China by two main routes, overland from central Asia and by sea, and because each route conveyed different versions of Buddhism, further confusion was created. Finally, when Buddhist ideas did become available in China, there was a strong tendency on the Chinese part to treat them eclectically, to select, for example, from the range of Buddhist thought only those techniques which could add to the intuitive faculties, which could provide knowledge of elixirs and practices that might contribute to longevity, or which might perhaps coincide with some of the interests of the neo-Daoist movement referred to above.

Nevertheless, probably before the fall of the Later Han dynasty, the *Sutra in Forty Sections* had been translated into Chinese and in the third and fourth centuries other key texts were translated, albeit crudely. The stage was set for that epoch in Chinese history, extending from the mid-fourth to the end of the eighth centuries, which has been called the Buddhist Age.

In the south of China, in the time of the Eastern Jin, Buddhism found its first adherents among those educated Chinese who had been attracted to neo-Daoism. As a representative of what has been described as gentry Buddhism one might refer to Zhi

Dun, who lived between 314 and 366. He was a gentleman scholar who moved among the prominent laymen of his day, engaging in 'pure conversation', in which he introduced ideas derived from Buddhism. Alternatively, as an example of an early Chinese convert to Buddhism one could mention Huiyuan, who lived between 334 and 417. He founded a centre at Lushan, in northern Jiangxi, where monks and laymen practised a devotional creed which was clearly Buddhist, that is to say it was derived from Buddhist thought, and it was not superimposed on existing Chinese practices. In the fifth and early sixth centuries Buddhism continued to progress among literary figures and the aristocracy. Its most famous patron was the Emperor Wu of the Liang dynasty, who ruled from 502 to 549 and who became a convert to Buddhism. During his reign Daoists were persecuted, the emperor calling for the abolition of all Daoist temples and the return of Daoist priests to the laity. He sought to rule in the manner of a Buddhist monarch, taking as his model the Indian emperor Asoka. He built many Buddhist temples, renounced the eating of meat and on occasions served as a menial in a temple. Although the emperor's support of Buddhism remained undiminished throughout his reign, he found himself criticised by Buddhists who thought he was too concerned with earthly matters. He was also taken to task by the opponents of Buddhism who were alarmed by the excessive number of monks and nuns.[16]

In the north the progress of Buddhism was more rapid. Buddhism reached this area more directly, across inner Asia. The rulers of the region were non-Chinese who had none of the cultural reservations which had impeded and influenced the reception of Buddhism in the south. An early example of how under these circumstances Buddhism might easily gain acceptance was demonstrated by the case of Fotudeng, a monk of central Asiatic origin who arrived at the court of the Later Zhao dynasty in about the year 310. He gave a display of occult powers – he produced a lotus out of a bowl of water and, using toothpicks, drew water from dried-up wells – and thus gained the confidence of the emperor. Other rulers were drawn to Buddhism because it provided an alternative to the Confucianism urged upon them by their Chinese advisers. The most dramatic example of this was the adoption of Buddhism by the rulers of the Toba state who were to found the Northern Wei dynasty. Under the second emperor the Buddhist community of monks had already become a significant presence. A government office was charged with their supervision and a monk named Faguo was appointed Chief of Monks. At first this relationship ensured imperial support, but under the Emperor Wu, who reigned from 424–51, Buddhism in China suffered its first major persecution in which several leading Buddhists and many of their followers were killed. The fundamental situation behind this attack was the tension caused by the sinicisation of the Toba state and the hostility felt by Chinese Confucianists towards Buddhism, which was still regarded as a foreign religion.

This proved to be only a temporary setback. An indication that enthusiasm for Buddhism was undiminished was shown in 460 when work commenced on the cliffs at Yungang, about ten miles west of Pingcheng. A half-mile stretch of the rock-face was honeycombed with caves and decorated with carvings of the Buddha, the largest of which measured seventeen metres in height. When, in 493, the Northern Wei dynasty transferred its capital to Luoyang, Buddhism received yet further encouragement. Numerous temples and monasteries were established in the city, many on a lavish scale. Among them was the Yongning monastery which had a nine-storeyed pagoda which reputedly rose 900 feet and was surmounted by a golden pole which added a further one hundred feet to its height. From the pole were suspended golden dishes and bells.[17] The whole building was so extravagantly finished that its cost exhausted the imperial treasury. In the capital, rival translation schools competed in producing Chinese versions of Buddhist texts, including the *Lotus Sutra* and the *Diamond Sutra*. In the surrounding countryside, Buddhist communities supervised agricultural settlements. Seven miles south of the city, at a site on the Yi river, the Longmen cave complex was carved and decorated to create a permanent symbol of Buddhist devotion.

By the middle of the sixth century Buddhism was firmly established in China, and it had gone far along the road towards acquiring distinctive Chinese features. This was evident in Buddhist art. The figures carved in the cliffs at Yungang, and indeed the whole idea of cave temples, indicated Indian influence. But at Longmen the Chinese tradition of linear, as opposed to plastic, pictorial expression re-asserted itself. This tendency to sinicise Buddhism was also apparent in the development of Chinese sects of Buddhism. The Tiantai school, which had a strongly scholastic and philosophical emphasis, emerged in the south in the sixth century. It called upon its followers to practise meditation and to study Buddhist texts, particularly the *Lotus Sutra*. By contrast the adherents of the Jingtu or Pure Land school, which traced its origin back to Huiyuan and to the fourth century, believed that the single act of calling on the Buddha's name was sufficient to obtain salvation. It was this school which was to popularise the worship of Guanyin, the Goddess of Mercy. In some respects these two sects stood in sharp contrast, but they had one feature in common: they both derived from the adaptation of Buddhism to suit the spiritual and political assumptions of China.

THE FALL OF THE NORTHERN WEI AND THE FINAL YEARS OF DIVISION

Despite its achievements, the Northern Wei dynasty was built on shaky foundations and its collapse was to be even more rapid than its rise. Two main fault lines ran under its structure. One was the perennial difficulty of any dynasty of conquest: how to retain its identity after assuming a Chinese form of government. The Toba solution had been for the emperor, his court and the aristocracy to adopt fully the Chinese style and to

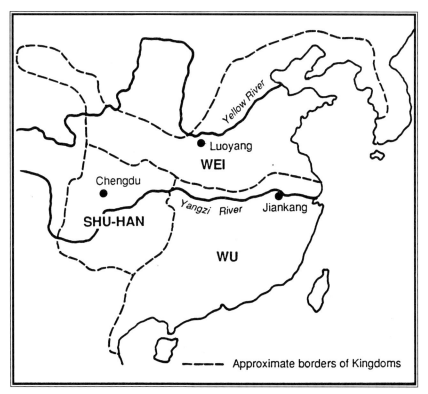

12 *The Three Kingdoms, AD 220–80*

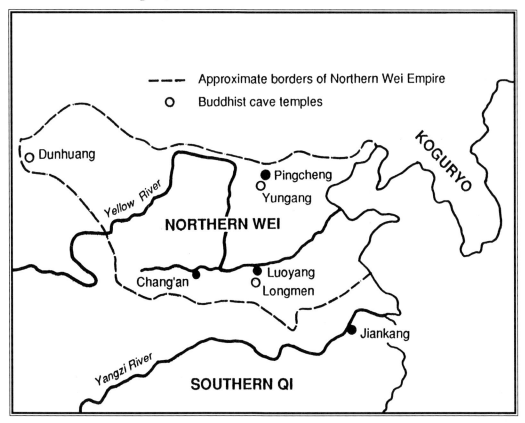

13 *The Toba (Northern Wei) empire, c. AD 500*

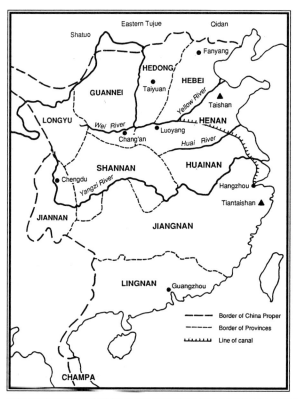

14 *China Proper on the eve of the rebellion of An Lushan, AD 755*

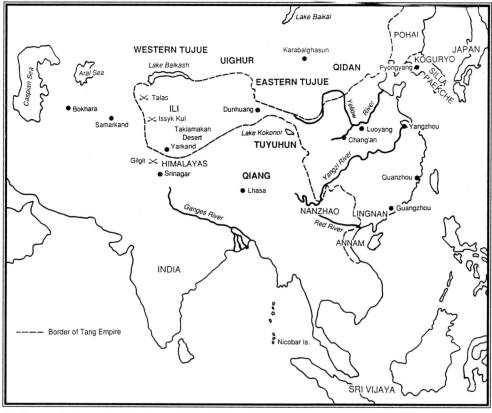

15 *China under the Song, c. 1050*

rule through Chinese officials. On the other hand the Toba people, and their allies in the tribal confederation, retained many aspects of their traditional life style. Because they were separated from their land and herds, the Toba people grew increasingly impoverished and alienated. The other problem was that of the northern frontier which, after the removal of the capital to Luoyang, was distant and difficult to garrison. The armed forces had been weakened by corruption and when, in 524, the Ruanruan crossed the frontier in force, the Toba garrisons mutinied rather than support the dynasty. Even at this point the dynasty might have survived, because the invading tribal groups entirely lacked leadership and a common purpose. But factionalism at court destroyed that chance. In 528 a tribal group known as the Erzhu, who may formerly have come from the state of Sogdiana, perpetrated a massacre of the aristocratic inhabitants of Luoyang. Out of the confusion which followed there rose to prominence a soldier named Gao Huan, who completed the destruction of Luoyang and removed the capital westwards to Ye, taking with him the child-emperor of the Wei. When Gao Huan died in 547 his son usurped the throne and established the Northern Qi dynasty. This brought about a split in the Toba empire, for in the west a separate regime, known as the Northern Zhou dynasty, was established. Once again northern China had lapsed into disunity and the dream of a revival of the Han dynasty seemed more remote than ever.

CHAPTER SIX

THE SUI AND TANG DYNASTIES

The period of division came to an end when a general named Yang Jian, who had usurped the throne of the Northern Zhou, defeated the last of the southern dynasties and in 589 reunified China. The Sui dynasty, which only lasted until 618 when it collapsed, has often been likened to the first empire of the Qin. Both dynasties established a new national unity after a long period of division. In both cases the dynasties were headed by rulers of enormous ambition: the Qin by the First Emperor, the Sui by Sui Wendi and his son Yangdi, all of whom combined a capacity for firm government and constructive design with an inability to foresee the degree of resentment that their actions would elicit. Finally, under both dynasties patterns of rule were established and initiatives taken which were to lead, under the successor dynasty, to a period of prosperity and cultural achievement.

THE ESTABLISHMENT OF THE SUI DYNASTY

In the middle of the sixth century much of China was under the control of one of four dynasties or ruling houses. The springboard for the establishment of the Sui dynasty was the Northern Zhou empire which sprawled over north-western and western China. Its main rival for the control of the north was the Northern Qi. These two states, both of which suffered from sharp racial and economic tensions, were deadly competitors until the Northern Zhou destroyed its eastern counterpart in 577. In central China, along the banks of the Yangzi river, was the much smaller state of Liang ruled by the Emperor Wu, whose conversion to Buddhism has already been noted. In the earlier part of his reign he had some success in centralising power within the state and even showed some aspirations to reunite China. But by the time of his death in 549 the state had collapsed and it was only a cipher when it was overrun by the Northern Zhou in 587. The fourth component was the state of Chen in the south-east, which had been carved out of Liang territory. Chen had ill-advisedly assisted the Northern Zhou in the defeat of the Northern Qi. In 589 the Northern Zhou ruler launched a combined naval and military operation which overwhelmed the Chen troops, while the Chen élite was won over by promises of leniency.

In these operations the prime mover was Yang Jian. He came from an aristocratic family of the Northern Wei, which was probably of Xianbei extraction. His family had been involved in the founding of the Northern Zhou and he was connected by marriage with the leading families of North China, including that of the emperor, for his daughter had married the heir apparent. However in 580, incensed by the misdeeds of his son-in-law, he usurped the throne. There followed a civil war in which Yang Jian owed his success to assistance from a man named Gao Jiong, who was to be his chief minister through much of his reign. In 581 Yang Jian claimed that the mandate of heaven had passed to him and he founded the Sui dynasty with himself being given the posthumous title of Wendi.[1]

Up to this point what had happened was no more than a dynastic coup. But Wendi's ambitions went far beyond this, for he aimed to recreate the imperial tradition of the Han and to have himself recognised as the Son of Heaven. To ensure that his newly-founded dynasty was accepted as legitimate he had forged an edict, purportedly signed by the last Northern Zhou emperor on his deathbed, ordering Yang Jian to take command of the armed forces and to assist the child emperor in carrying on the government. This was followed by other edicts and rituals intended to simulate the mode of succession allegedly followed by the first kings, and to advertise that the new dynasty embodied the continuation of Han tradition. The claim of legitimacy was only the first step in Wendi's campaign to establish his position. The new dynasty also needed to be furnished with an ideology which would sustain its authority and this meant establishing a proper relationship with Confucianism and Buddhism. To assert his support for Confucian morality, Wendi arranged the offering of incentives to those whose conduct exemplified the Confucian virtues and in particular that of filial piety. With regard to Buddhism, which had been under attack under the Northern Zhou, Wendi went out of his way to present himself as an ideal monarch in the Buddhist sense, giving generously to Buddhist foundations, improving the condition of Buddhist clergy and promoting the acceptance of Buddhism as the common faith of the people. Taken together these actions have been described as imperial Buddhism and seen as giving the Sui dynasty an unique character in the annals of the Chinese empire.

Wendi's reign was also memorable for the vigorous practical steps he took to establish a unified state. One of his first decisions, and again a decision heavy in symbolism, was to build a new capital on a new site near the old city of Chang'an. In the edict recommending its construction he wrote 'a capital city is the administrative seat of the myriad officials and the place to which all those within the four seas will turn'.[2] He now had to fulfil that description by reforming central government. Under the Northern Zhou power had been held by a small group of military aristocrats, the majority of whom were non-Chinese origin. Wendi set out to recruit a new élite which would more nearly represent the diverse regions of the new empire, and which would therefore include a higher proportion of Chinese. This he achieved, although the new bureaucracy still retained a preponderance from the north and from the families associated with the imperial line in its senior posts. This élite staffed a central government which bore titles reminiscent of the Han, but that was its only archaic element, for Wendi was indefatigable in maintaining his control of appointments and in demanding a new level of efficiency of his officials.

It was in this context that the essential features of the examination system and the nomination of degrees emerged. In 587 Wendi ordered that all prefectures should send three men annually to the capital as candidates for official appointment. These men were to be examined and ranked in two groups. Eight years later, in 595, the provision of a written examination for the degree of *xiucai*, 'cultivated talent', was mentioned for the first time. This examination tested a candidate's broad general learning; other examinations were devised to test a candidate on a single classical text, and on his general literary ability. It is in the Sui period that the use of examinations to select officials, a system which had been attempted under the Han, became an established practice, although it is uncertain what proportion of officials were chosen by this means.

Whether they were holders of degrees or not, officials after appointment remained subject to regular supervision. One method of checking them was to summon representative officials from each prefecture and call upon them to give, in open court, a report on how their colleagues had discharged their duties. Another means was the appointment of censors who had the task of making tours and investigating the conduct of local officials. The emperor himself made tours and inquired of the local people how well his officials had discharged their duties. Another means of maintaining control of the bureaucracy was the application of the so-called 'law of avoidance', whereby an official was not allowed to serve in his own district of origin.

Alongside these administrative reforms, Wendi also sponsored a major revision of the law, which resulted in the promulgation of the Kaihuang Code, which has been described as 'a remarkable synthesis of the legal traditions of the age of disunity', which proved to be the model for the Tang legal code and thereafter of the successive legal codes of imperial China.[3] At the same time a rationalisation and simplification of the system of local government was carried through. By such means did Wendi assert the power of the ruler, and in so doing established many of the practices which were to be elaborated under the Tang and by later dynasties.

These administrative and legal reforms did not exhaust the list of activities of the first Sui emperor. To finance the costs of government he was forced to improve the system of taxation, which meant an overhaul of the 'land equalisation' or 'equal field' system established under the Northern Wei and a revision of the tax registers. The common people were required to pay taxes of three kinds: a land tax at the rate of three bushels of grain per family per annum, a payment in kind of silk or linen, and a labour service of twenty days labour per annum from each adult male. In order to combat tax evasion the *baojia* system, the system of surveillance, was also revived.

The Sui dynasty derived its power from its conquest of rival dynasties, and it was inevitable that, in the first instance, the maintenance of its military capacity was given great emphasis. But after 590 it became policy to demilitarise the population of the North China Plain. This was achieved in part by an overhaul of the system of recruiting soldiers, and in part by the confiscation of weapons and the prohibition of their future manufacture. Within the empire a system of regional military commands was established which placed the surviving armed forces under central government control. On the frontier military colonies were settled and a programme of wall building was pursued.

Having ensured its internal security, the Sui, like other powerful dynasties, turned to expansion. This involved completing the subjugation of the state of Chen and the destruction of Jiankang, the capital of the Six Dynasties. This was followed by the reassertion of Chinese influence in Vietnam and an abortive attempt to force the state of Champa, in modern times known as Annam, to accept Chinese rule. In the north the main danger was from the people known as the Tujue, ancestral to the Turks. Here Sui success owed more to intrigue and dissension among the frontier tribes than to conquest. The Sui empire had now achieved an extent as great as that of the Han, and was probably more firmly administered, because Wendi supported his conquests with improved communications, the most famous example of this being the construction of a canal linking Chang'an to the Yellow river, thus improving the supply of grain to the capital.

What sort of man was it who engaged in so ambitious a scheme of empire-building? Coming from a northern aristocratic family Wendi retained the preferences of his class for a life on horseback and a disdain for intellectualism. He had been brought up in a Buddhist temple and throughout his life he favoured Buddhism over Confucianism, although he approved the support the latter gave for the harshly authoritarian attitude he adopted towards his sons. Of his conduct of business it was said:

> He labored diligently and concentrated on good government. Every time he held an audience, it could last until late afternoon. He would invite officials of the fifth rank and above to sit and discuss affairs of state, and he would allow the palace guards to eat their evening meal while on duty. Though by nature he was neither benevolent nor enlightened, he was nonetheless a hard-working and perspicacious ruler.[4]

The family culture of the northern aristocrats permitted women a much more active role than that available to Chinese women of a comparable background. Wendi's consort, the Wenxian empress, came from a sinicised Xiongnu clan, that is to say her background was similar to that of the emperor, and this enabled them to form a close working relationship, perhaps unique in the annals of the emperors and empresses of China. In the early years of his reign the empress gave Wendi powerful support and tempered his immoderate rages. However, later in his reign she became increasingly jealous and vengeful, falling out with the emperor's adviser Gao Jiong and contributing to the crisis which ended in the emperor's death.

THE SECOND EMPEROR

One way in which the empress exerted her influence was through the preference she showed for her second son, Yang Guang, who later, as the Emperor Yang, was to earn an infamous reputation. He had been born in 569 and in his early life he had developed a strong interest in the south of the empire, where he had cultivated an acquaintance with both Buddhist and Confucian scholars. In 600 he was party with his mother to an intrigue against the heir apparent which led to his being nominated heir. Two years later the empress died and two years after that the emperor also deceased, in suspicious circumstances. The crime of parricide is held in horror in Chinese history, and because Yangdi was not only the second but also the last emperor of the Sui dynasty, these suspicions, for which there is some documentary evidence, were magnified into a certainty.

The hostile view of Yangdi was based partly on his character, which was depicted as licentious, and partly on his actions, which were represented as the deeds of a spendthrift and a megalomaniac. This view has been challenged by Arthur Wright, who has pointed to his devotion to his wife and to the sensitive landscape poetry which came from his brush. He has shown that, when he became emperor, he followed similar policies to those of his father in terms of appointment to office and performance of rituals and, despite the allegations, he had no great liking for extravagance. However, in other respects he replaced the cautious miserliness of the first emperor with a more ambitious concept of his role as 'supreme autocrat, wise ruler, and cosmic pivot'.[5] Within a year of his accession he had ordered the building, or, along some stretches, the reconstruction, of a canal to link Luoyang to the Huai river. It was said that for this task a million or more workers were mobilised. In 608 work began on another vast project, the construction of a canal from Luoyang to the vicinity of present-day Beijing. Once again vast numbers of men, and for the first time women, were conscripted. These canals were built to perform an important economic function, the shipment of grain and military supplies, and much of the prosperity of the Tang has been attributed to their construction. But at the time the cost, the enforced labour and the extravagant expenditure dominated the accounts.

Although Arthur Wright challenged some aspects of the criticism of Yangdi, he accepted the opinion of the famous Song historian Sima Guang, that an important turning point occurred in the reign in the year 609. It was from that date that Yangdi became increasingly preoccupied with foreign expansion at the expense of dealing with domestic problems. In Wright's opinion his objectives in pursuing this expansion were little different from those of his father, and still conformed with the idea of emulating the achievement of the Han. However, Yangdi and his senior advisers made two basic errors: that of attempting a conquest without first obtaining adequate intelligence and that of refusing to accept defeat.

The campaign which proved a disaster was conducted against the state of Koguryo which occupied what is now north Korea and eastern Manchuria. This area had been under Chinese control during the Han dynasty; it was regarded as a civilised state and also as a potential danger because of the threat of an alliance between Koguryo and the eastern Tujue or Turks, who remained the most potent threat to the dynasty from the north. Early in Wendi's reign an official named Pei Ju had been responsible for foreign and barbarian affairs. He had been relatively successful in controlling the eastern Turks by using a combination of military and diplomatic means. When Yangdi succeeded to the throne, Pei Ju was dispatched to Inner Asia on fact-finding tours, and these were followed by an imperial progress which took the emperor to the far west of his territories. On this tour the emperor discovered that the western Turks had received an embassy from Koguryo. The Koguryo ambassador was instructed to return home and to tell his ruler to send a tributary mission to China immediately, which he failed to do. Pei Ju thereupon advised Yangdi to send an expedition against Koguryo, informing him that Turkish mercenaries were available to support the attack and that Koguryo would quickly submit. Yangdi accepted this advice and in 612, after extensive preparations, a massive force was launched. But the Turkish mercenaries were not available and Pei Ju had seriously underestimated Koguryo determination to resist. Yangdi was forced to withdraw, having suffered heavy losses. In the following year the emperor launched a second attack, which likewise failed. By this time serious rebellions had arisen in China, in one instance headed by a senior official. Nevertheless in 614 a third expedition was launched which also ended in disaster. From that time onwards Yangdi seems to have lost control of events, for he took no effective measures to restore order at home. In 618 he was murdered in his bathhouse by the son of his most trusted general.

It would be an oversimplification to say that it was the failure of the Korean expeditions which brought about Yangdi's downfall, for there were other causes of discontent. The programme of canal-building had been accompanied by other large-scale construction works, including the building of a new capital at Luoyang, and these had been carried out by conscripted labour. Disastrous flooding in the Yellow river valley in 611 was followed by the outbreak of several rebellions in the area. Nevertheless Yangdi's attempt to conquer Koguryo did become a dangerous obsession. Having accepted unsound advice from Pei Ju and having allowed himself to be surrounded with sycophants, he appeared unable to stop the campaigns before they had caused the dynasty irreparable damage. It seemed that in a single reign much of the Sui achievement had been lost, but this was an illusion, for it was on the foundations dug by the two Sui emperors that the Tang dynasty was to reconstitute the empire.

THE FOUNDING OF THE TANG DYNASTY

By 617 the Sui dynasty was in deep trouble. The heavy demands of the Korean expeditions had led to extensive rebellions in the north of China. There was also a real danger that the eastern Turks, who had already made several deep incursions into Shanxi, and who had obtained promises of allegiance from a number of the leaders of rebellion, might invade the country.

It was under these circumstances that a new contender for power emerged. Li Yuan came from an aristocratic family which had become influential under the Northern Zhou, his grandfather having been created the Duke of Tang. When the Tang dynastic history came to be written, his family was supplied with an ancestry which could be traced back to the Han, but it is likely that its origins were less august and that Li Yuan's ethnic background was a mixture of Chinese, Xianbei and Turkish. Early in his career Li Yuan had occupied a series of important military posts, and in 617 he was appointed garrison commander at Taiyuan, a key strategic position in present-day Shanxi, a place which was traditionally regarded as impregnable and from which previously successful assaults had been made on the capital Chang'an.

An answer to the question why Li Yuan became a rebel and ultimately founder of a new dynasty is inextricably mixed with the assessment made of his personality and that of his son Li Shimin, who was to reign as Taizong, the famous second emperor of the Tang dynasty. Most traditional accounts presented Li Yuan as a cautious, plodding figure, who was tricked into heading a rebellion by his ambitious son. In the subsequent events Li Shimin has been credited with the military skills and leadership which gained the throne for his father. However, modern historians, relying on the eye-witness account of Wen Daya in *Diary of the Founding of the Great Tang Dynasty*, have rejected that view and have reinstated Li Yuan as chiefly responsible for his own success.[6] He is said to have conceived the idea of making a bid for the throne before the Taiyuan revolt, being encouraged by a popular ballad which predicted that the next ruler would have the surname Li. It was on his initiative that the next step was taken, which was to neutralise the threat from the eastern Turks by hinting at a willingness to become a Turkish vassal. This obtained Li Yuan Turkish military support and enabled him to start a military campaign which before the end of the year resulted in the capture of the capital. In the following year Li Yuan declared himself the founder of a new dynasty, the Tang. He adopted the reign title of Wude, but is usually known by his posthumous temple name Gaozu.

The transfer of power from Sui to Tang dynasties did not imply any major change in the nature of government. Both royal houses had similar origins in the north-western aristocracy. Both dynasties relied heavily on the aristocracy to supply them with officials. Already under the Sui an attempt had been made to broaden the basis of support by employing more Chinese officials and this was continued in the early Tang period. The state examination system, which had been introduced by the Sui, became the established means of selection. So at first the structure of government was little altered and the emphasis was on continuity rather than on a break with the past.

One reason for the absence of dramatic change was the slow pace of the dynastic succession, which from the outbreak of rebellion in 617 took seven years to complete. Although a number of important military engagements took place, Gaozu's victory depended substantially on the moderation he exercised in dealing with his rivals. Amnesties were granted to those who surrendered to him. Defeated aristocrats were often confirmed in their territories and Sui officials allowed to remain in their posts. The basic structure of central government under the Sui, the three ministries – the Secretariat which drafted edicts, the Chancellery which reviewed and commented on them, and the Department of State Affairs, which put the decisions into effect – was retained and rationalised. There was a general continuity in local administration and in the maintenance of law and order. The Sui system of taxation was largely revived and the equal-field system re-established.[7]

But it would do Gaozu less than justice to imply that the measures he took merely replicated the Sui system. In several aspects of his administration he laid the foundations for the future success of the dynasty. Thus he introduced a new coinage, which was to become the standard currency through the Tang period. He set up a legal commission which, building on the Sui achievement, codified the law and administrative statutes in the form which was not only to remain in force until the fourteenth century, but which was became the basis of the first legal codes in Vietnam, Korea and Japan. He took the first steps on the path which was to lead to the revival of Confucianism and to the attack on the influence of Buddhism. Finally, although he was forced to bribe the eastern Turks to dissuade them from invading the empire, it was while he was on the throne that a start was made to construct an effective defence of the northern border.

Gaozu, however, did not remain long on the throne. A bitter rivalry had developed between two of his sons, Li Jiancheng, the heir apparent, and Li Shimin, his younger brother. The former had his main power base at court and at the capital, where he maintained his own fighting force. The latter, who had a notable record of success as a military commander entrusted with the task of suppressing rivals to the throne, had his power base among the military and civil officials of the Luoyang region. In 626 Li Shimin, suspecting that his brother was plotting against him and believing that his father would take the side of the heir apparent, engineered a coup. In rapid succession Li Jiancheng was murdered, Li Shimin declared heir apparent, and Gaozu himself forced to abdicate to allow Li Shimin to become emperor.

THE REIGN OF TAIZONG

Li Shimin, who is better known as Taizong, his posthumous title, was to remain on the throne until 649. His reign has been described as 'unsurpassed in brilliancy and glory in the entire annals of China'.[8] Despite the fact that he had secured the murder of his brother and the enforced retirement of his father, he was presented as a paragon of virtue and his achievements regarded as a model for all subsequent emperors to emulate.

Modern historians have been unwilling to accept an unblemished portrait. Arthur Wright suggested that a more truthful representation would be to divide the emperor's reign into two halves. In the first decade Taizong adopted the role of 'humble learner of the arts of government'. His attitude to his responsibility was illustrated by a remark which he made in 629:

Recently the number of memorials submitted to us has greatly increased. We have pasted them on the walls of our room so that as We come in or go out We can't fail to notice them. The reason that We are so tirelessly diligent is that We want to understand fully our ministers' sentiments. When we reflect on the principles of government, it is often the third watch of the night (11.00 p.m.–1.00 a.m.) before we fall asleep. We expect our ministers also to use their minds and energies tirelessly to help us realize our hopes.[9]

But after the death of his father and then of the empress, that is to say from 636, Taizong began to behave like the 'supreme autocrat of a rich and powerful empire, increasingly self-confident, self-indulgent and impatient of criticism',[10] a condition which Wright described as 'the pathology of supreme power' and as a pattern of behaviour which had already been demonstrated in the second century BC by Wudi. Whereas in the first decade Taizong had been frugal and cautious, he now became extravagant and capricious, although still occasionally displaying the positive qualities of the earlier half of the reign, those of 'a gifted administrator, a master strategist, a shrewd politician and a loyal friend'.[11]

What did Taizong achieve which has earned him such praise? His reputation undoubtedly rests on his role as consolidator rather than of innovator. It is generally accepted that Taizong built on the foundations laid by the Sui dynasty and restored by his father. Nevertheless this was a formidable part to play and it deserves elaboration.

One aspect of Taizong's brilliant reputation derives from his ability to surround himself with capable ministers, thus establishing a model of the appropriate relationship which should exist between the emperor and those who served him. Taizong carefully cultivated his reputation in this respect, once writing:

The enlightened ruler employs men in the manner of a skilled carpenter. If the wood is straight, he uses it as a shaft for a cart; if it is crooked, he uses it as a wheel. If it is long, he uses it as a roof-beam; if it is short, he uses it as a rafter. No matter whether crooked or straight, long or short, each has something that can be utilized. The enlightened ruler's employment of men is also like this.[12]

The men he employed were indeed different in character and ability. Throughout the reign the emperor's chief confidant was his brother-in-law, Zhangsun Wuji. A second great minister was Fang Xuanling, who had taken the examinations and who became the architect of the system of executive administration and a model of honesty and efficiency. A third important figure was Wei Zheng, who earned the reputation of being an 'unbending moralist and fearless remonstrator', who was to gain the admiration of successive generations of Confucian scholars, not only for his probity, but also for his tireless advocacy of the pre-eminence of civil officials at court.[13]

Under Taizong the principal components of government, which had been created or revived by his father, received further refinement and were to achieve the character of 'ideal institutions' for future generations. At the capital, Chang'an, the central administration was to be found. This comprised the three central ministries: the Department of State Affairs, which in turn comprised the six ministries of public administration, finance, rites, army, justice and public works; the Chancellery and the Secretariat. There were also other government offices, the most notable being the Censorate, whose officials were charged with the investigation of abuses and complaints from the public; and the Supreme Court of Justice, which reviewed the evidence relating to serious crimes and made recommendations to the emperor on the appropriate sentences. Outside the capital the country was divided into administrative regions and these in turn were subdivided into prefectures. Taizong's reforms included a determined effort to reduce the size of the bureaucracy and to strengthen control over the prefectures. The value of service in the provincial bureaucracy, which hitherto had been despised, was affirmed and the emperor made the selection of prefects his personal responsibility. The legal code, which had been compiled first in 624, and which was based on the code of the Northern Zhou, was subject to further revisions to remove anomalies in the prescription of punishment and in some cases to reduce the severity of the penalty.

The same emphasis on consolidation of existing practice can be seen in the financial administration of the empire. In 624 Taizong's father had issued a series of Land Statutes which set out in detail the *juntian* or 'equal field' system which went back to the fifth century and to the time of the Northern Wei. This system, which had been devised in the simpler times of the northern dynasties, with its precise provisions for distribution and redistribution of land, would seem to have been quite inappropriate for the more complex society of the Tang. Nevertheless it remained in force and there are fragmentary records of attempts to apply it and to deal with the problems which were created by the increase in population and the strength of the aristocratic families and monastic foundations. Likewise the provisions for direct taxation remained unchanged, with taxpayers who, it was assumed, had equal landholdings, having equal tax liabilities: a tax in grain, a tax in cloth, and two types of labour service.[14]

What has been said so far of Taizong's reign suggests that it contained little of originality. Its true claim to fame lies not in its innovation, but in its consolidation, which enabled the imperial institution and the Chinese Empire itself to achieve new levels of power and influence. The Tang imperial line had at first merely been a very successful example of a northern aristocratic family. There were other great aristocratic clans, many of which came from the north-east of China. They still regarded status as having been fixed in the fifth century by the Northern Wei under a system known as the *sixing*, or the Four Categories of Clans. In 632 Taizong called for a new compilation of the national genealogy, but when it had been completed and presented to him he was infuriated to discover that the Li clan, that is the imperial line, had been placed in the third class, below several of the north-eastern families. A revised version was prepared, which placed the imperial line in the premier class. This was a clear statement of the superiority of office and ability over lineage. The new compilation did not immediately destroy the prestige of the aristocratic families, but it marked a stage in the decline of their influence.[15]

Another means of enhancing the position of the dynasty was through the development of the examination system. Under Taizong the number and frequency of examinations increased. A system of state schools intended to prepare candidates for the examinations was established, and this led to a marked increase in the number of candidates, some of whom came from the aristocratic families. When Taizong saw a group of successful candidates for the *jinshi* or 'presented scholar' degree leaving the government building in a triumphant column, it is said that he declared, 'The heroes of the empire are all in my pocket!'[16] Undoubtedly he exaggerated, but it is true to say that, in the early Tang period, the expansion of the examination system and the new emphasis on scholarly activity promoted the status of the Tang scholarly élite and enhanced the attraction of an official career.

At the beginning of the Tang period Buddhism enjoyed enormous popularity in China. Numerous monasteries had been established which amassed great wealth and claimed exemption from taxation. Eminent monks declared that the Buddhist clergy owed obedience neither to the state nor to the family. Not surprisingly these pretensions concerned rulers and twice, under the Northern Wei between the years 446 and 452, and under the Northern Zhou between the years 574 and 578, attempts were made to suppress Buddhism. But because of the strength of the popular reaction the repressive legislation was soon repealed. The early Tang emperors were in a stronger position to challenge Buddhism. Gaozu favoured Daoism over Buddhism and even claimed that the royal line was descended from Laozi. His views were encouraged by the sharp criticism of Buddhism expressed by Fu Yi, a Daoist priest who had been appointed chief astrologer. At first it seemed that Taizong was going to reverse that policy, for immediately after his succession he rescinded his father's order for a purge of the Buddhist clergy and a reduction in the number of monasteries. But his true feelings were revealed when he honoured Fu Yi and listened with approval as he delivered a familiar diatribe against Buddhism:

The Buddha was nothing more than a crafty barbarian who succeeded in deluding his own countrymen. Ill-intentioned men in China subsequently perverted the teachings of Zhuangzi and Laozi to serve the ends of Buddhism and dressed up its doctrines in bizarre and mysterious language in order to mislead the uneducated masses. Buddhism offers no benefits to our people; on the contrary it is injurious to the state. It is not that I do not understand Buddhism, but rather that I despise it and refuse to study it.[17]

Taizong was too shrewd to make a direct attack and in 629 he even ordered the erection of seven monasteries to commemorate the battles fought at the founding of the dynasty. But his true sentiments were revealed in 637 when he ordered that henceforth at all ceremonies Daoist monks and nuns would take precedence over their Buddhist counterparts. At about the same time he approved the *Daoseng ge*, the *Regulations Regarding the Daoist and Buddhist Clergies*, which provided harsh punishments for clergy committing various offences. His objective was to reduce the participation of Buddhist clergy in secular life and to confine monks and nuns to their monasteries where they would be occupied with religious observances. By so doing he sought to establish control over the Buddhist church.

Nevertheless towards the end of his life his views altered. This was perhaps because of the admiration which he felt for the monk-translator Xuan Zang, whose epic travels to India in search of Buddhist scriptures had impressed him deeply, if only because of the knowledge Xuan Zang had gained of foreign affairs. Before he died Taizong revised his views on Buddhism and accepted Xuan Zang as his spiritual mentor. He authorised the ordination of 18,500 Buddhist clergy, regretting that he had met Xuan Zang too late to have helped him in the dissemination of Buddhism.

In Taizong's closing years a succession dispute embroiled the emperor and split the court. Initially the heir apparent was the emperor's eldest son, Li Chengqian. His position was undermined by complaints of bizarre behaviour and homosexuality, and because he displayed pro-Turkish proclivities. The emperor was persuaded to shift his favour to a younger son, Li Tai. Li Chengqian attempted a revolt which failed and he was sent into exile. Li Tai in turn was accused of plotting and the emperor was persuaded by his senior ministers to appoint as his heir yet another son, Li Zhi, Prince of Jin. In 649 he succeeded to the throne as the Emperor Gaozong.

GAOZONG AND THE EMPRESS WU

Gaozong was only twenty when he succeeded to the throne. Inevitably the senior officials of his father's court, in particular his uncle Zhangsun Wuji, retained great influence. Another powerful force was the family of the Empress Wang. To add to the emperor's insecurity the early years of his reign were troubled by persistent plotting, which may have been a continuation of the factional conflict of the later years of his father's life.[18]

This situation was to be transformed by the rise of one of the most notorious characters in Chinese history: Wu Zhao, later to become the Empress Wu. She was born in 627 and was brought to the court at Chang'an as a concubine in 640. After Taizong's death she may have become a Buddhist nun. Gaozong, who perhaps knew her before his father's death, flouted convention and started a liaison with her and in 652 she bore him a son. Wu Zhao began an intrigue against the Empress Wang, which culminated in the alleged smothering of the empress's new-born daughter, an atrocious act intended to incriminate the empress. By 655 Wu Zhao had secured the demotion of the empress, her own enthronement, and the recognition of her son as heir apparent.

How can this extraordinary rise be explained? Undoubtedly the Empress Wu was a formidable character, as her subsequent career amply demonstrated. Her ascendancy, however, has also been attributed to rivalry between regional aristocratic groups. Early in the dynastic period the great aristocratic families of north-western China had been dominant, and the Empress Wang had been a representative of their influence. Her downfall, it has been claimed, marked an important shift in the location of influence, for the Empress Wu's support came from families from the north-eastern plain and it was for this reason that she later transferred the capital from Chang'an to Luoyang in the east. Another explanation of her rise attributes it to a class struggle: Wu Zhao, it is said, came from a humble background, and she represented the interests of the newly risen merchant class in a struggle for power with the entrenched aristocratic ruling class. Confirmation for this view is sought in her support for progressive ideas and the preference she showed for the selection of officials by examination, that is to say by merit rather than by birth. It has to be said that both explanations have their weaknesses. The factions at court supporting and opposing the Empress Wang were never as homogeneous as the theory of a power struggle suggests, and other explanations have been put forward for the change of capital.[19] The argument that it was a class struggle is weakened by the fact that the evidence of the Empress Wu's origins do not support the theory, nor is it true that she made greater use of the examination system. Perhaps both theories contain some elements of truth, but a more probable general explanation lies in personal and political alignments at court, which were ably exploited by a strong-minded and ambitious individual.[20]

At first the empress exercised her influence through Gaozong. After 660, when his health deteriorated for long periods of time, she became *de facto* ruler. When Gaozong died in 683 he was succeeded in turn by two of his sons, but power remained in the hands of the empress. In 690 she forsook pretence and usurped the throne, establishing the Zhou dynasty. This lasted until 705, when a restoration of the former emperor took place, the formidable empress dying a few months later at the age of eighty.

A discussion of this period can best be divided by the death of Gaozong. While the emperor lived, much of the empress's efforts were directed at consolidating her position, often, according to hostile accounts, by the most unscrupulous and violent means. Shortly after her enthronement in 655 she heard that the emperor was showing signs of remorse for his treatment of former Empress Wang and a favourite concubine. She thereupon ordered that their hands and feet should be cut off and that they should be thrown into a brewing vat, saying, 'Now these two witches can get drunk to their bones'.[21] Through intrigues she disposed of other court rivals and the group of elder statesmen who had served Taizong.

At the same time she promoted the career of Xu Jingzong, who until 670 was in effect her chief minister. With his help she pursued other policies which also served to advance her interests. Mention has already been made of the transfer of the capital from Chang'an to Luoyang, a move commenced in 657. In 666 she arranged for the performance of the *feng* and *shan* sacrifices on Taishan, the holy mountain in Shandong province. These ceremonies, which had not been performed for over six hundred years, symbolised the complete pacification of the empire and its contented submission to the sovereign. In defiance of all precedent, the empress herself participated in the rites. She also arranged for a revision of the register of prominent clans in the empire, thereby ensuring the inclusion of her clan, the Wu. Another, and more extensive exercise of her influence came through her patronage of Buddhism. From about 660 the emperor had started to take an increasing interest in Daoism and as a consequence several Daoist adepts had achieved powerful positions at court. To counter this the empress advanced the interests of Buddhists. She commissioned the carving of a 56-foot high Vairocana Buddha at the cave temple complex at Longmen, near Luoyang. It was alleged that the features of the statue were those of the empress herself. She also secured the rescinding of an edict which gave Daoists precedence over Buddhists at court ceremonies.

A recital of these developments would suggest that the ascendancy of the empress was a triumph for a vengeful, arbitrary and personal rule which set aside all the principles on which the imperial system was based. However, at a deeper level, the case can be made out that her rise saw not only the continuance, but even the strengthening of those principles. Undoubtedly Gaozong was the beneficiary of the achievements of his predecessors:

[He] inherited a stable state with a smoothly functioning set of institutions, and with a system of administration governed by a centralized system of statute law, in which the authority and responsibility of each office was carefully restricted and defined by law. The military and financial systems had been so devised that direct intervention of the central administration was kept to a minimum. Active government policy was kept within strictly drawn limits: the maintenance of order, military matters, and the administration of the land and tax systems.[22]

The empress made no attempt to interfere with these arrangements, indeed she sought to improve on them – for example, during her ascendancy, an extensive revision of codified law took place.

Perhaps more significantly the examination system for the selection of officials was refined, and a reform credited to the empress was the introduction of a method of concealing from the examiners the names of candidates, so that their identity and social origins could not affect the outcome. It has been alleged that because the empress was not part of the earlier Tang ruling class, she strove to replace that class with a new one, and to achieve this she placed unusual emphasis on the literary examinations as a means of recruiting civil servants. However, such an interpretation oversimplifies a situation in which the composition of the ruling class was more fluid, and the examination system less clearly the source of promotion of a meritocracy, than has been suggested.[23]

Gaozong's reign saw the boundaries of the Chinese state expand to a point previously unsurpassed and never to be exceeded. In 659 the western Turks, having been weakened by internal strife, were placed under Chinese protectorates and the sway of the Tang empire extended westwards to the borders of Persia. At the other extremity, Gaozong capitalised on his father's activities in Korea. In 668 Pyongyang, capital of the north Korean state of Koguryo was captured and the country turned into a Chinese protectorate. However these early successes were not to be sustained, and before the end of Gaozong's reign the central Asian protectorates and the state of Koguryo were slipping away from Chinese control. In the south-west the expansion of Tibet was threatening Gansu and Sichuan, and in the north the revival of the eastern Turks presented a fresh danger.

Frontier defence was a great drain on resources and securing an adequate revenue was an underlying problem of the dynasty. Already in Taizong's reign many households had evaded registration for taxation purposes. Under Gaozong, expensive foreign campaigns and a series of bad harvests aggravated the situation. At the same time prices for basic commodities rose and this was interpreted by officials as signifying that there was too much coin in circulation. The response was to suspend minting coins and to take severe steps against counterfeiting. The years 679 to 683 were a period of serious financial crisis.[24]

THE REIGN OF THE EMPRESS WU

After Gaozong's death, it became apparent that the Empress Wu was determined on power for herself. She ordered the deposition of the first heir to the throne, who had reigned for six weeks as the Zhongzong emperor, and replaced him with his brother. She then took steps indicating her intention to retain control, even to the point of herself claiming the throne. These actions prompted a revolt headed by Li Jingye, which broke out in 684. He and other leading rebels came from prominent families that had fallen into disgrace and had been exiled to the Yangzi region. They had plotted with leading officials at court and when their intrigues were exposed the empress took a terrible revenge and instituted what has been described as a reign of terror. Allegedly deliberately favouring the use men of humble origin as spies and informers, she created a secret police, headed by Zhou Xing and Lai Junchen, who 'earned the same sombre notoriety as Himmler and his aides have gained in modern times'.[25] Many of their victims were members of the upper aristocracy. As a consequence of the terror no official would henceforth dare to challenge openly the actions of the empress. It ensured that when she became scandalously involved with a former pedlar of cosmetics, Xue Huaiyi, and even made him abbot of a Buddhist monastery, none dared accuse her of impropriety.

Nevertheless the empress still hesitated before usurping the throne. Her decision to act may have been prompted partly by another uprising, partly by promptings from her supporters who claimed to have discovered a white stone predicting her future role. She was encouraged by the Buddhist clergy, who hailed her as an incarnation of the Maitreya Buddha. It was also significant that she had assured herself of at least some measure of popular support by making generous gestures towards the common people through a series of Acts of Grace. In 690 three petitions, the last said to contain sixty thousand signatures, were presented to the empress, each urging her to ascend the throne. She consented to the last of these, the emperor abdicated and she became the first ruler of a new dynasty, the Zhou, with the title of 'Holy and Divine Emperor'.

In many ways the Zhou dynasty was a continuation of the Tang, for the empress pursued the policies and practices of her earlier years. Nevertheless her assumption of imperial power did result in important changes of emphasis. For example, she exercised to the full her powers of appointment and dismissal, and as a result the position of chief minister, the title given to the heads of the three central ministries, was substantially undermined. At first she continued to show favour to the Buddhist community and as a demonstration of this she commissioned the construction of a remarkable symbolic building, the Mingtang, or Hall of Light, which was to serve as an audience hall on great occasions. Behind it stood a pagoda of great height containing an enormous wooden Buddha. The construction was supervised by Xue Huaiyi. In the pagoda wild religious rites were performed with the abbot acting as master of ceremonies. But at this point he fell out of favour with the empress and in revenge he burnt down the Mingtang. This event resulted in a distinct shift in the empress's patronage towards Confucianism.

These vast projects undoubtedly put a strain on the exchequer, but the real crisis of the reign began in 695, when a massive uprising occurred among the Qidan to the north-east. They seized the area around modern Beijing and their success encouraged the northern Turks and Tibetans to raid Chinese territory. The empress was forced to buy off the Turks by offering an imperial marriage, thus outflanking the Qidan rebellion. However the problems of the dynasty were not over. In 697 the empress became besotted with two brothers surnamed Zhang who, it was said, dressed in gaily coloured silks and, with powdered and rouged faces, frequented the palace and became so arrogant that they even treated senior officials with disdain.[26] The hostility aroused by their influence forced the empress to declare her wishes on the key issue of the succession, which was that the throne should revert to the deposed Emperor Zhongzong. Even this was not enough to stem criticism and charges of corruption were brought against one of the brothers. When the empress sought to overrule the legal process a plot among senior officials led to the murder of the brothers and the forced abdication of the empress.

What judgments have been passed on the Empress Wu and on this unique period in Chinese history? Because she had defied the principle of male descent and because she had treated harshly those officials who displeased her, the judgment of her in traditional historiography was inevitably condemnatory. Modern historians have taken a different view. C.P. Fitzgerald likened her to Elizabeth I of England, because under her prolonged rule 'China was stronger, more united and richer than ever before in her history'. Through her firm leadership she saved China from another century of civil war and confusion. Her legacy was such that, under her grandson, the Emperor Xuanzong, China was to experience a famous age of poets and artists, a real golden age.[27] A more recent assessment, while not disregarding some of the unsavoury aspects of her reign, emphasises its positive achievements: the development of the examination system as a means of upward mobility and the evidence of improvement in the condition of the mass of the population. Against this however should be set the costs of her ambitious policy of expansion and her failure to provide for a settled succession.[28]

THE REIGN OF XUANZONG, 712–56

For the record of Xuanzong's reign one must rely almost exclusively on the National History compiled by the contemporary historian Liu Fang. He divided the reign into three sections: an early period of consolidation, a central period increasingly marred by court tensions, and a final period in which the emperor withdrew from an active political role, with dire consequences.[29]

The Emperor Xuanzong came to the throne after a period of intrigue. He was young, only twenty-seven years old, a man of attractive personality and considerable firmness of mind. At the beginning of his reign he acted decisively to free himself from the influence of members of the court, to instal ministers of his choice and to pursue his own policies. His first choice of minister was Yao Chong, who, like many of his early appointments, had served under the Empress Wu. Yao Chong's selection, and that of others who were also successful examination candidates, indicates that by now the place of aristocratic families at court was being taken by literati recruited through the examination system.[30]

On Yao Chong's suggestion a ten-point programme of reform of government was instituted – a programme which attempted to revive and stabilise the fortunes of the dynasty. Under these reforms the authority of the chief minister was strengthened and the practice of the open conduct of business was resumed. The operation of the bureaucracy was overhauled to ensure the proper staffing of provincial posts. Legal reforms developed a centrally codified administrative law and the application of uniform administrative rules. Another group of reforms attempted to improve the finances of the dynasty. One problem was the difficulty of supplying the capital Chang'an with grain and this required an improvement in the transport system. Behind this problem lay a chronic situation of recurrent famine and oppressive taxation. To relieve the former, 'price-regulating granaries' were established widely; to combat the latter, some attempt was made to restrict the grant of noble titles which carried with them tax exemptions and at the same time the emperor himself tried to practise austerity.

Finally there was the matter of military reform. Xuanzong had inherited an empire which stretched far beyond the confines of China Proper. Its defence required a very large standing army, estimated at about 600,000 men. Apart from the cost of maintaining so large a military force, the other difficulty lay in delegating command so that a rapid and effective response could be made to any threat to Chinese interests. The solution adopted for this was the establishment of nine major command zones, each headed by a military governor who commanded a large headquarters army, while at the same time administering the military colonies which supported the command zones. This system initially succeeded in stabilising the frontiers, but at the expense of allowing a great accumulation of power in a few hands.

In the middle period of the reign, from 720 to 736, the consolidation continued, but two new issues became important. The first related to the making of senior appointments. Under the Empress Wu many scholar officials had been appointed, perhaps as part of a move to counteract the power of the aristocracy. This practice had been continued under Xuanzong, but from the 720s a struggle began which was to lead to the aristocratic element re-establishing itself in senior positions. Why this shift took place is uncertain, and it should be accepted that the division between the aristocracy and the scholar officials was by no means clear cut. Nevertheless this apparent shift in the balance of power may explain the court rivalries of the time.

The second issue related to the financing of the government. One problem concerned the so-called 'runaway households'. Since the beginning of the dynasty, with greater economic security prevailing, a great agricultural expansion had occurred in the south. This had led to large-scale migration from the north, resulting in peasant families disappearing from the household registers. The first serious attempt to deal with this problem was made by Yuwen Rong. In 724 he proposed a scheme for the general registration of all vagrant unregistered households, which achieved considerable success and which resulted in 800,000 households being registered. However the policy also excited criticism, probably because Yuwen Rong was an aristocrat and his scheme, which was to be carried out by special commissioners directly responsible to the throne, bypassed the regular officials.[31] Another task was to resolve the persistent difficulty of supplying grain to the court when the capital was situated at Chang'an. In 734 Pei Yaoqing was made a minister to implement his own proposal to deal with this problem. His plan involved the establishment of a new commission for transportation and the definition of a new route for the movement of grain to Chang'an which was to be almost entirely by water. It appears that this new route was extremely successful, the amount of grain supplied being more than doubled. This enabled the emperor to confirm Chang'an as the effective capital of the empire and to continue his policies of a greater centralisation of power.[32]

The beginning of the third stage of Xuanzong's reign was marked by the advent to power of Li Linfu who, from 736 until his death in 752, was virtually a dictator.[33] Li was the man to be execrated in history as the source of the misfortunes which were to befall the emperor. He was an aristocrat and a member of the imperial clan and had entered public life through hereditary privilege rather than by examination, though his shortcomings as a scholar were exaggerated. His rise led to the dismissal of Zhang Jiuling, the austere exemplary scholar-official who was said, on the occasion of the emperor's birthday, to have offered his sovereign a compilation of pieces of moral advice instead of an expensive gift.[34]

Li had shown himself to be an efficient administrator and his promotion reflected the emperor's desire to create a strong, centralised and financially sound government.[35] Some of the measures he took have a very modern ring. For example, he discovered that the annual returns relating to taxation, conscription etc., consumed half a million sheets of paper. He devised a more practicable and efficient system, his reform being set out in a compilation known as the Permanently Applicable Directives.[36]

Until the early 740s the measures Li took to improve efficiency were generally acceptable and resulted in a period of prosperity, but from 746 onwards the situation deteriorated. Li became increasingly determined to assert his authority and carried out a purge of his opponents. The emperor, by now sixty years old, had begun to turn his attention from current affairs to personal enlightenment through Daoism and Tantric Buddhism. He had also become infatuated with Yang Guifei, the most bewitching of all favourites in Chinese history, and he had allowed members of the Yang clan to take up powerful positions at court. Meanwhile important changes had been taking place on the borders of the empire. As mentioned earlier, the frontier had been divided into command zones under military governors. In the past its defence had been in the hands of a mixture of troops – some professional soldiers, others convicts and militiamen. In the early eighth century, in response to the demand for more effective defence, these were replaced by much larger contingents of professional soldiers, often of non-Chinese origin whose commanders too were frequently non-Chinese.[37] Among them was a general named An Lushan, himself half-Sogdian and half-Turkish, whose headquarters were at Fanyang, that is present-day Beijing. In addition to commanding a large body of troops and occupying a key position, An Lushan enjoyed the patronage of Yang Guifen.

After a period of relative calm and security, in the middle years of the reign the empire had to respond to threats from the Qidan and the Tibetans. From 750 China suffered a series of military reverses, in the long run the most serious being a defeat at the hands of the Arabs on the Talas river, near Ferghana, the beginning of a collapse of Chinese power in Central Asia.

THE REBELLION OF AN LUSHAN

When Li Linfu died in 752, the implication of these developments became apparent. He was succeeded by Yang Guozhong, second cousin of Yang Guifei, who proceeded to consolidate his position at court and to obtain support from some of the military governors. This brought him into conflict with An Lushan. Yang Guozhong did all that he could to warn the emperor of the danger presented by the general. But An Lushan had the continued support of Yang Guifei, who had supposedly adopted him as her son and may also have been his mistress, and so Xuanzong ignored the warning. Nevertheless it was clear to the general that he was in danger and in late 755, on the pretext that he had been summoned to court to subdue the 'bandit' Yang Guozhong, he led his troops south.

An Lushan's rebellion exposed the weakness at the heart of the Tang empire, for the forces loyal to the throne were no match for An Lushan's mounted cavalry. Within thirty-three days of commencing his march he had captured Luoyang and had declared the establishment of a new dynasty. He would probably have taken Chang'an as well had he not paused, so allowing his opponents to regroup and to win a major victory. The emperor's supporters began to hope that the rebellion might yet be crushed and Yang Guozhong tried to recapture Luoyang, which was a serious miscalculation for it resulted in a disastrous defeat which forced the emperor to abandon Chang'an.

It was at this point that the most poignant of episodes in Chinese history occurred. The emperor's escort held Yang Guozhong responsible for what had happened and they killed him and his family. The commander of the escort then demanded that the emperor himself should order that Yang Guifei be put to death, which sadly he did. The event was celebrated in one of China's most famous poems, *Changhen ge*, the 'Song of Unending Sorrow', by Bo Juyi:

> The Emperor could not save her, he could only cover his face.
> And later when he turned to look, the place of blood and tears
> Was hidden in a yellow dust blown by a cold wind.[38]

The end of the reign came swiftly. The emperor fled to Chengdu in the south-west where he established a court in exile. The heir apparent went north-west and began to rally opposition to the rebels. Realising that his father was no longer capable of ruling effectively, he usurped the throne. To defeat the rebels was a greater task, although it was made easier by the assassination of An Lushan in 757. However it was not until 763 that the rebellion was crushed.

An Lushan's rebellion has commonly been regarded as the turning point in the history of the Tang dynasty, even a turning point in Chinese history. Edwin G. Pulleyblank, in the classic study of the origins of the rebellion, commented:

> Before [An Lushan] China was a vast, unified empire, extending its power far beyond its frontiers. After he raised rebellion it was a shattered and bruised remnant, confined to its own borders, pressed by invaders without, and harassed within by parasitic and lawless armies over which a eunuch-ridden central government exerted a precarious suzerainty. The Tang dynasty never recovered from the blow. . . . Never again did a native Chinese dynasty reach the summit of glory from which An Lushan rudely pushed the Emperor Xuanzong and his brilliant court in 755–6.[39]

It is clear from Pulleyblank's study, and from those studies which have been published since, that the rebellion was the catalyst but not the cause of this decisive change. Pulleyblank rejected the suggestion that the rebellion was an agrarian revolt or that it was triggered by a series of calamities. However he did accept that the changed economic situation was an essential part of the background to the rebellion: an economic revolution which had led to a great increase in trade and the creation of new wealth, had begun 'to crack the seams of the nation's social structure'.[40] Referring to the political background he stressed the conflict of interest within the governing class which has already been identified. Finally, with reference to the military background, he set the rise of An Lushan within the general context of a centrifugal tendency which drew authority away from the centre of the empire to the military commands on its periphery.

More recently C.A. Peterson has sought to distinguish between the background and the origins of the rebellion, which he did not regard as inevitable. He noted the historical tradition which asserted that An Lushan's non-Chinese background and his supposedly barbarous temperament made it likely that he would turn against the throne. He pointed out that the emperor failed to act to counter the potential threat that he posed. He then discussed theories which sought to explain the rebellion by referring to its specific regional features, that is to say why it arose in Hebei. One view was that Hebei, by this time, had received such an influx of non-Chinese that the Tang court had concluded that it could only be held by a 'barbarian', hence the toleration of An Lushan.

Another was that Hebei still nourished a separate consciousness from the government at Chang'an. Peterson, however, suggested that neither explanation was supported by adequate evidence and concluded that Hebei itself was not significant in the origin of the rebellion. What was important was the social and cultural gap between the court and its frontier commanders, a situation which could be exploited by a powerful commander concerned about his own position, for example in the case of An Lushan.[41]

THE LATE TANG PERIOD

Although the rebellion was defeated, it has been seen as having profound consequences. A summary account of these mentions: large scale militarisation with perhaps 750,000 men under arms; the development of autonomous or semi-autonomous governments at provincial level; the rise of men of military background to roles in the official hierarchy; the collapse of the state's financial structure; the final disappearance of the land allocation system; large scale shifts of population; effective loss of control of Hebei and parts of Henan; increased importance to the empire of the Yangzi and Huai valleys and finally the loss of control in Central Asia.[42]

None of this can be gainsaid, but before dismissing the late Tang period as a mere shadow of former glory, reference should be made to important innovations in the matter of financial administration introduced in the decades after the rebellion. Two of these were attributed, at least in part, to an official named Liu Yan, who served under the Daizong emperor (reigned 762–9). It was he who developed the monopoly on salt which by 780 was to provide more than half of the cash revenue at the disposal of the central authorities. He also improved the system of grain transport instituted by Pei Yaoqing, placing it under a Transport Commission and greatly reducing the cost of transport. His reforms, which were seen as encouraging the development of independent agencies, were to be challenged by another innovative official, Yang Yan. To him has been credited an even more important measure: the *liangshuifa* or two-tax system. Put simply this reform consolidated various taxes on property and land and provided that they should be collected twice annually. It enabled the state to derive revenue not only from the peasants, but from all productive classes, a reform even more necessary because of the growth of great estates. The arrangement introduced by this reform was to serve as the basic system of taxation for the next seven centuries.[43]

Two further points may be made to support the view that the late Tang period cannot be dismissed as merely a period of dynastic decline. The first concerns the so-called restoration under the Xianzong emperor, who ruled from 805 to 820. Half a century after the rebellion central government still did not control the provinces effectively. Some of them, particularly in the north and east, were entirely autonomous; others, although administered by court-appointed officials, were only partially controlled from the centre. Xianzong's task was to try to extend his government's effective control and to a certain extent he succeeded. On seven occasions during his reign he used military force against recalcitrant provinces. Such campaigns were expensive and another of Xianzong's achievements was to increase greatly the contribution of the Yangzi valley to government finances. Meanwhile the emperor took steps to restore the morale of the bureaucracy, with some success, although the end of his reign was marred by a dispute with Pei Du, a celebrated official of the period, who questioned the emperor's decision on the appointment of officials. This incident, and claims that towards the end of his reign the emperor grew intolerant and avaricious, have damaged the reputation of a man who was an able ruler, and who, but for his premature death – he may have been poisoned – might have gone further in restoring imperial control.[44]

The other piece of evidence which can be used to adjust the view of the late Tang period is a remarkable document, the diary of a Japanese Buddhist monk known in the west as Ennin. Ennin spent nine years in China, including some five years in Chang'an, and his diary contained detailed descriptions of many aspects of the country, including much information on religion and commerce. He also made many references to the working of government, and this led E.O. Reischauer to remark:

> there emerges a picture of government in operation which is amazing for the ninth century, even in China. The remarkable degree of centralized control still existing, the meticulous attention to written instructions from higher authorities, and the tremendous amount of paper work involved in even the smallest matters of administration are all the more striking just because this was a period of dynastic decline.

This led Reischauer to suggest that this, in a more fundamental sense, was a period of significant political maturation, for the Chinese government had now achieved such a high level of administrative efficiency that the country was never again to undergo the general collapse which ensued after the downfall of the Han.[45]

THE DECLINE AND FALL OF THE TANG DYNASTY

Despite the efforts of Xianzong to curb provincial autonomy, the key problem of the power and independence of the military commands remained. After 820, young emperors were unable to assert their authority, their courts being the scene of factional intrigue and of eunuch influence. In the middle of the century, under an outstanding minister, Li Deyu, effective government was briefly restored and at the same time an attack was made on Buddhism, state support for the religion being a heavy drain on finance. But Li Deyu was dismissed by the next emperor Xuanzong[46] who also restrained the persecution of Buddhism.

Before the end of his reign armed revolts and mutinies had broken out which presaged the fall of the dynasty. These threats were to be eclipsed by the disastrous surge of rebellion headed by Wang Xianzhi and Huang Chao which began in 874. This had its origin in the growth of banditry, particularly in the area between the Yellow and Huai rivers, an area hit by a combination of natural disasters and government exploitation. The two leaders who headed bandit gangs were men of some education, Huang Chao being a failed examination candidate. Their banditry turned into a revolt after government suppression had proved ineffective. The rebellion devastated large areas as far south as the Yangzi. The government, having failed to defeat the rebel bands, tried in vain to buy off its leaders and to encourage resistance by permitting the raising of militia. In 878 more effective commanders of government forces were appointed and they gained a series of victories in which Wang Xianzhi was killed. Huang Chao was forced to move south and in 879 he seized Guangzhou, which he sacked with tremendous loss of life among the foreign community. He then turned north, encountering ill-organised opposition from government forces, and was able to ensconce himself in the lower Yangzi region. At this point he should have been defeated by superior government forces, but inexplicably he was allowed to break through their lines and late in 880 he captured Chang'an, the emperor and the court fleeing westwards to Chengdu. Huang Chao established a new dynasty, but he had little control over his followers, who pillaged Chang'an, and his attempt to win over officials to his side failed. Government forces rallied and besieged the capital. Foreign troops under the command of Li Keyong from the Shatuo, a Turkish tribe, inflicted a series of major defeats on the rebels, Huang Chao being killed in 884.

The emperor returned to the devastated capital, but was quite unable to restore the authority of the dynasty. He died in 888 and neither of his two successors was any more capable of recovering power. In 907 Zhu Wen, a former lieutenant of Huang Chao, declared that that part of north China which he controlled was an independent state under the newly established Liang dynasty. This act confirmed the demise of the Tang.[47]

How has the collapse of the Tang been explained? A recurrent theme is the instability of the Tang court and, particularly in the ninth century, the excessive power of the eunuchs, who were implicated in the deaths of several emperors. A series of minorities and an apparent dearth of capable ministers contributed to a lack of leadership at the centre.

Another explanation relates to the financial position of the government. Despite the introduction of the two-tax system, government revenues remained inadequate to maintain the armed forces it needed to reassert its authority, and had to be supplemented by additional levies which typically fell most severely on the hard-pressed peasantry. The pattern of peasants deserting their lands to take refuge with powerful landowners was repeated. In the key lower Yangzi region, where the tax burden fell most heavily, this pressure led to the growth of social unrest and banditry.

A more fundamental problem, and one which has already been discussed in the context of the rebellion of An Lushan, was the government's loss of power to the military commands on the periphery of the empire. By the early ninth century much of the country was divided into semi-autonomous provinces which had developed their own forms of government and in which the military forces played a major role. Some provinces in the north-east were in effect independent. The independent provinces still recognised Tang sovereignty and the semi-autonomous ones still accepted appointments made by central government. But even this degree of central government influence was to be lost with the disorder which culminated in the great Huang Chao rebellion. Now even the sovereignty of the Tang could no longer command respect and effective control passed to regional states formed from the independent provinces. When one of these, the Liang, usurped the throne, the dynasty came to an end.

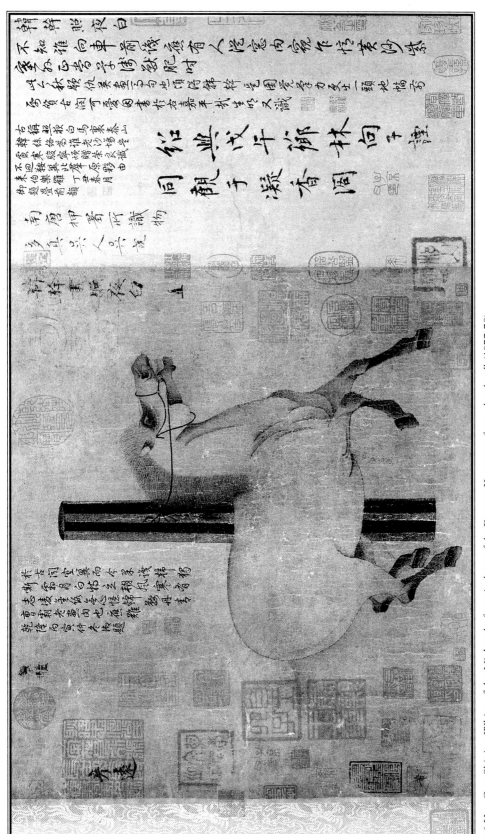

16 Han Gan, Shining White of the Night, the favourite horse of the Emperor Xuanzong, from a handscroll (1977.78)

17 *Uighur prince, from Bauzäklik, Xinjiang, ninth-century fresco*

CHAPTER SEVEN

CHINA AND THE WORLD IN THE EARLY IMPERIAL PERIOD

In the Sui and Tang periods, China's foreign relations underwent a complete transformation. At the beginning of the period only one neighbouring state, Koguryo on the Korean peninsula, could claim to be a stable political entity. Elsewhere China was surrounded by mainly nomadic tribal peoples, who could occasionally form powerful confederations, but who, for the most part, were markedly inferior to China in terms of cultural and political achievement. However, by the end of the period much had changed. In the north-east, in the south, and in the south-west, stable agrarian societies had been formed, the 'Chinese-dominated east Asian cultural sphere had taken shape'. Only to the north did China still share a frontier with nomadic societies, but even these were much more stable and advanced than they had been in the past. This important change was to have a major effect on the development of China's relationship with the outside world.[1]

In this changing political setting, the Chinese empire, ruled for over a century by a powerful dynasty, consolidated Chinese dominance within China proper and extended its influence through much of eastern and central Asia. From the eighth century, particularly after the An Lushan rebellion, Chinese influence declined and by the end of the tenth century part of north China had fallen under foreign rule. A review of these developments may start at the centre and then continue with reference to each of the main zones on the periphery.

CHANG'AN

Chang'an, the Sui and later the Tang capital, was carefully sited near the spot which had been the capital of the Han empire. The modern city of Xi'an occupies the same site. Under the Tang, Chang'an

> was perhaps the world's greatest city – the political hub of a vast empire, the epicentre of Chinese civilization in an age of brilliant creativity, a cosmopolis which attracted merchants and travellers from distant lands, a model for the city-builders of neighbouring states.[2]

The outer walls of this great city enclosed an area of about 30 square miles. The imperial palace stood in front of the northern city gate and in front of this in turn was the administrative centre. The city itself was laid out like a chessboard with the streets running from north to south and from east to west.

Chang'an was indeed the hub of the empire. To the north and east and south it was linked to the rest of China by a canal system, supplemented by a network of imperial roads. Along these roads were post stations for official travellers and inns for merchants. To the west lay the route which in modern times has been called the Silk Road. This took the traveller through the Gansu corridor to the oasis of Dunhuang. There it divided with one route going to the north and the other to the south of the notorious Taklamakan desert. The northern route led, via Samarkand and Bokhara, to the Mediterranean coast; the latter through Yarkand and Srinagar, to India.

By the eighth century Chang'an had a population of about one million, with perhaps another million living in its metropolitan area. Not only was this a vast population, but it was also a cosmopolitan one. In the vicinity of the West Market were to be found Zoroastrian and Manichaean temples, a Christian church and houses of foreign merchants. To the West Market came camel trains from central and western Asia, bringing exotic goods. For example, in 647, after the conquest of the Tarim Basin, a Turkish ruler sent specimens of a new wine-making grape to the emperor. This was the 'mare-teat' grape, an elongated form of grape which was planted in the imperial park in Chang'an.[3] From the south came other exotic fruits, famously the lichee, for which Yang Guifei, Xuanzong's consort, had a craving. They were brought by special courier from Guangzhou.

Chang'an was not alone in having strong links with the outside world. In the eighth century Guangzhou had a population of about 200,000, which included a large merchant class, chiefly Indo-Chinese, Indonesians, Indians, Singhalese, Persians and Arabs.[4] The foreigners lived in a prescribed quarter of the city, were ruled over by specially designated elders, and enjoyed some extraterritorial privileges. Most of China's maritime trade passed through Guangzhou, though not much of it was in Chinese hands. The largest of the ships employed were built in Ceylon and had Persian-speaking crews. Among the goods imported were pearls from India and rhinoceros horn from Indo-China.

TRAVELLERS AND PILGRIMS

While China under the Tang received many foreign visitors, in the same period Chinese awareness of the outside world was greatly enhanced by travellers who crossed central Asia or who ventured over the Southern Ocean. Those who left records of their journeys were in many cases Buddhist pilgrims, who had set out for India to obtain copies of Buddhist scriptures, to visit holy places, or to study at the great

Buddhist monasteries. One of the earliest records was kept by a pilgrim named Fa Xian, who left China in 399, taking an overland route to India and then returning by sea. He spent two years in Ceylon and also visited what was probably Java, before finally landing in Shandong after a voyage of two hundred days.

The most famous Buddhist pilgrim of the Tang period was Xuan Zang, who travelled to India between 629 and 645.[5] It was this journey which was the inspiration of the sixteenth-century novel by Wu Cheng'en entitled *Record of a Journey to the West*, or, in Arthur Waley's translation, *Monkey*. Xuan Zang made a full record of his experiences: how he had left Chang'an by stealth, how he had nearly been murdered by his guide, how he had almost died of thirst in the desert. After he reached India his adventures continued. When travelling down the Ganges he was captured by pirates who planned to use him as a human sacrifice. To this proposal Xuan Zang replied:

As far as my own miserable body is concerned, I have no objection at all to your using it for your sacrifice. But I think I ought to tell you that I came all the way from a far country in order to worship the image of Buddha under the Bodhi-tree and visit the Vulture Park where he preached. I have come for instruction in his scriptures and his Law, and none of these purposes have I yet fulfilled. So that I fear that if you were now to sacrifice me it would be more likely to bring you bad luck than good.[6]

The pirates appeared unmoved by his words, but a great storm arose which terrified his captors who hastened to release him. Xuan Zang continued his pilgrimage to the holy places of Buddhism and assembled his collection of manuscripts. When he returned to Chang'an in 645, he took with him 657 items packed in 520 cases, works which in his remaining years he laboured to translate.

A third famous pilgrim who went to India in search of the law was Yi Jing. He departed from Yangzhou on a Persian ship in 671 and called at the important Buddhist centre of Srivijaya on Sumatra and the Nicobar Islands before landing in Bengal. He visited the holy sites of Buddhism and carried away from India some ten thousand Sanskrit texts. For nine years he remained at Srivijaya, engaged in the task of translation, and then returned to China in 695 to be greeted personally by the Empress Wu when he reached Luoyang.[7]

The efforts of Xuan Zang and Yi Jing, and those of other Chinese Buddhist pilgrims, played an invaluable part in the preservation of early Buddhist culture. Buddhism in India was already under challenge from Hinduism, and many of the texts collected by Xuan Zang were to survive only in Chinese. Before Buddhism in China had come under attack and had suffered a similar decline, Japanese monks in turn had come to Chang'an and had borne home the texts from which Japanese Buddhism was to develop.

SOUTHERN EXPANSION

The southern expansion of the Han people was brought about by two main means, one being the determined thrust under a strong dynasty, using soldiers and establishing bases or military colonies. Alternatively, and possibly associated with periods of confusion in the empire, it came about through the migration of displaced people fleeing from the north and through the establishment of separate regimes in the southern provinces.[8] Underlying these developments was the much less perceptible process of the sinicisation of non-Chinese societies. These movements can be traced in three main theatres: in the extreme south, in the area which is today northern Vietnam, and in the south-west of China, particularly in the province of Yunnan.

In the extreme south, after the early expeditions sent by the First Emperor, the region known as Nan Yue or southern Yue was conquered by the soldiers of the Emperor Wu of the Han dynasty, and a Chinese administration was established in the region. After the fall of the Han the Yue people recovered their independence, but under the Tang Chinese control was reasserted. The present area of Guangdong, Guangxi and part of north Vietnam was designated Lingnan province and large-scale 'development' begun. One means of extending Chinese control was though the system later known as *tusi*, that is to say the appointment of tribal chiefs as officials, which applied a system of indirect rule to ethnic minorities. Another method used was the widespread establishment of *tuntian* or military agricultural colonies. Under the Empress Wu, Lingnan was a favoured place to which to exile opponents and this led to the diffusion of Tang culture in the region. Exceptionally, men from the south achieved distinction under the Tang and this led to a gradual amendment of northern attitudes, from believing Lingnan to be a strange and frightening land to recognising it as part of China. An outstanding example of a southerner who achieved distinction was Zhang Jiuling, who rose to become chief minister under Xuanzong.[9]

Prior to the Tang period Lingnan had been badly affected by malaria, and this and the hostile environment had discouraged settlement. By the end of the Tang period the malarial threat may have declined and southward migration, which had already led to an enormous surge in the proportion of Chinese living south of the Yangzi, now reached the extreme south. Between 606 and 742 the population of the Guangzhou delta rose by over 100 per cent and that of the eastern part of Lingnan by up to 100 per cent. Further massive increases in population occurred in the centuries which followed.[10] This movement is reflected in the linguistic legacy, with Cantonese, the dialect spoken in the region around Guangzhou, most closely resembling the standard spoken language of the Tang period. Following behind the first migratory waves, and forced to take up poorer land, came the dialect group known as the Hakka or *kejia* ('guest people') who to this day call themselves Tang rather than Han Chinese. Although the Yue language, and Yue customs almost entirely disappeared, the Yue population was not displaced and through intermarriage and sinicisation it became virtually indistinguishable from the Chinese immigrants.[11]

As an example of how Chinese settlement of the south evolved one could refer to the case of Fujian province. Chinese migrants first reached Fujian in the late second century AD and formed a settlement on the banks of the Jin river. Over the next four centuries this colony of agriculturalists was enlarged by the arrival of several distinct groups: a group with some claim to membership of the élite society of post-Han China; the possible descendants of an intermediate warrior class of similar origin, and a small artisan class of unknown provenance. On the fringes of the settlement were Han Chinese Buddhist communities and 'boat people' of Chinese origin. The early records contain references to conflict with an indigenous group, but the territory occupied by the colony, between the mountains and the coastal region, was sparsely populated. The main obstacle to growth was the marshy condition of the land near the coast, an ideal breeding ground for malaria-bearing mosquitoes and for parasitic diseases such as schistosomiasis. But by the eighth century a combination of acquired resistance to malaria and gradual progress in the draining of marshes enabled settlement to extend onto the coastal plains, which were ideally suited to wet rice farming, and so it became possible to use the excellent harbour of Quanzhou bay. Further immigration from the north raised the Chinese population to perhaps 200,000, urban settlements were formed and a commercial economy developed. But the most significant change, and the one which was to have a decisive impact in transforming the region into one of the most prosperous in China, came in the ninth century with the start of Quanzhou's trade with the South Seas.[12]

The western part of Lingnan included the Red river basin in present day northern Vietnam. By the time of the Han dynasty, when the region was conquered by the Chinese, this area was already heavily populated and there was no need to bring in Chinese settlers. Instead a few Chinese administrators introduced a Chinese-style administration and the Yue people, in particular the native chiefs, accepted elements of Chinese culture and co-operated with Chinese rule. The peasants, however, were less sinicised and it was they who lent their support to the uprising led by the Trung sisters in AD 39. Chinese rule was restored under the Later Han, was lost again in the period of division and recovered once more under the Sui. Under the Tang the country was named Annan, meaning 'the pacified south', and for two hundred and fifty years it remained under Chinese government. In fact the pacification was never complete and, after a major revolt in 722, China had to maintain a large force in the country to ensure control. In 934, after the fall of the Tang, another rebellion led to the establishment of an independent state. Although the Song attempted to reconquer the former province, the invasion was repelled, and never again was the country to be governed by China.

NANZHAO

For C.P. FitzGerald, the history of Vietnam seemed to illustrate one aspect of the southern expansion of the Chinese people – that it had a natural limit and would be halted when the Chinese reached an area where people of an advanced civilisation had already installed themselves. In Yunnan, as in the case of Lingnan already discussed, he found an example of the opposite process:

> Yunnan thus presents . . . a history of Chinese expansion from its early beginnings with relations between a distant Court and local barbarian rulers, through a period of cultural infusion contemporary with political rejection, and then through the successive stages of conquest, occupation and assimilation.[13]

The first stage of this process had occurred under the Han, when the ruler of the area around Kunming acknowledged the suzerainty of Emperor Wu. Adventurous traders opened an indirect trade route with India and local chiefs became involved in this trade. But then came the period of division and a long hiatus in the process of absorption. In that period what is now Yunnan came under Buddhist influence deriving from Burma, the local tribes adopting Hinayana Buddhism. Under the Tang, west and central Yunnan was for a time divided among six kings. Of these the southern king was to become the dominant ruler, with a capital situated at modern Dali. He, and the ruling class which supported him, were probably of Tai origin, that is to say of the same ethnic background as the people of Thailand, but the Tai were only one of a number of ethnic groups which made up the population of the region. At first the Chinese encouraged these developments and tolerated the rise of the Nanzhao, that is to say the southern king, even though in 731 he had burned his fellow kings alive. In 742 a grandson of the king of Nanzhao married an imperial princess at Chang'an.

This was the high point of Nanzhao's history as a client state. In 751, in the declining years of Xuanzong's reign, Tang forces were sent to punish the kingdom for raiding Chinese settlements in eastern Yunnan. However, the Nanzhao troops won a signal victory which, together with the outbreak of An Lushan's rebellion, ensured that any hope of speedy retribution disappeared. Over the next century Nanzhao grew to become a significant power on China's borders, its territory incorporating northern Burma and western Sichuan.

Only in 879, when a further invasion of Sichuan was repulsed, did this expansion stop and thereafter Nanzhao began to contract. Various reasons have been suggested for why this happened: Burma was a difficult territory to defend and Sichuan, with a dense population, a difficult region to absorb; the Nanzhao state was built on shaky foundations for it had neither ethnic nor cultural homogeneity; Nanzhao political independence was not easy to maintain and when, in the tenth century, the Nanzhao ruling house was deposed and power taken by rulers of Chinese ancestry, the process of sinicisation accelerated. Nevertheless, Nanzhao remained an independent kingdom until the final years of the Song dynasty, and when it was conquered in 1252, it was not by the Chinese but by the Mongols, who incorporated it into their empire. Only in 1382 did the Ming in turn conquer the territory and incorporate Yunnan fully as a province of the Chinese empire.[14]

THE TURKISH EMPIRES OF THE STEPPE

Referring now to Central Asia and to the relationship between China and the nomadic nations of the steppes, a preliminary observation should be made. In the past it was a commonplace to describe the nomads of the central steppe as prowling like wolves, waiting for China to weaken, so that they could rush in and devour it. More recently the metaphor of a mirror has been used to describe the relationship, with the settled society of China and the nomadic society of the steppe reflecting the changes which had occurred in the other society. To develop the metaphor, a comparison has been made between developments in the Tang period and those which occurred earlier, under the Qin and Han dynasties. In the earlier period the unified Chinese state had been matched by the unified steppe state of the Xiongnu. Thereafter the period of division had been matched by disunity on the steppe. Three hundred years later a newly united China under the Sui and Tang was again matched by a succession of unified Turkish empires. This, it has been argued, was no coincidence: 'the state organization of the steppe needed a stable China to exploit'. Periods of division in China were mirrored by periods of division on the steppe, but the unification of China was followed within a generation by a unification of the steppe.[15]

The steppe people who first achieved this unification were the Tujue or Turks. Until the middle of the sixth century they were vassals of the Mongol Ruanruan, their traditional trade being metal-working and their totem, perhaps appropriately, was the wolf. An incident in which the Tujue chief was refused the hand of a Ruanruan princess led to a revolt, with the Tujue allying themselves with the sinicised Western Wei state. While Yang Jian was engaged in establishing the Sui dynasty, the Turks were creating a massive empire which was to extend from Manchuria to the Caspian Sea. The empire owed its existence to its military power and the Turks utilised their strength to extort wealth from China. They traded horses in return for silk, and also demanded lavish gifts for their support. The Northern Zhou made them an annual gift of 100,000 rolls of silk and entertained many Turkish visitors at court. This silk was then traded on to Iran and Byzantium, making the Turks extremely wealthy.

So uneven an arrangement could not endure for long, but some time was to elapse before it was revised in China's favour. Succession disputes made the Turkish empire inherently unstable. In 581 it was divided into two khaghanates, that of the eastern Turks centred on the future Karakorum in Mongolia, and the khaghanate of the western Turks centred on Ili and western Turkestan. At this point the newly established Sui dynasty risked deporting the Turks living at court and refused to continue the silk payments. In retaliation, and in the hope of healing divisions in their ranks, the Turks carried out a major raid on China. Such actions benefited neither side and a compromise was reached. The essence of this was that the Turkish khaghan, in return for receiving aid against rival tribal leaders, formally submitted to China. For the Sui this carried the considerable advantage that their new dynasty was seen as truly holding the mandate of heaven. The relationship was strengthened by the dispatch of a Chinese princess to marry the khaghan and by fomenting rivalry between various Turkish tribes. By the early seventh century the eastern Turks were important allies of the dynasty, used by them as mercenaries against the Qidan to the east. But when Yangdi invaded Korea he discovered that the new khaghan was not prepared to give the expected support. The disastrous campaigns which followed contributed largely to the collapse of the dynasty.

The Turks, however, did not try to capitalise on the dynastic collapse with an invasion. Instead they bided their time until the Tang dynasty was established and then profited from what has been described as the 'outer frontier strategy', under which the Turks raided deep into Chinese territory, yet refused to occupy Chinese land even after great victories. By this means the Tang dynasty, like the Northern Zhou before it, was forced to appease the Turks with lavish gifts and trade privileges.[16]

Then Li Shimin, who was to reign as Taizong, the second emperor of the Tang and effective leader of a strong dynasty, significantly altered the relationship. He came from the north-western aristocratic stock which was only partly Chinese. He was a soldier and an excellent horseman, and in these qualities he was closer to the Turks than to the southern Chinese. On one occasion before he became emperor he had challenged a khaghan to personal combat, such conduct being most untypical of a Chinese ruler. In 626, when the Turks under Xieli invaded the Chang'an region, Li Shimin showed great personal bravery, and through brotherhood ceremonies established personal links with the Turkish leaders. In the following year Xieli found himself facing a rebellion, with the Chinese supporting the rebels. A Chinese army inflicted a disastrous defeat and almost all the Turkish tribes in the east went over to the Tang. New tribal leaders were chosen from among the Turkish élite, the Turkish tribal structure was incorporated into Tang government and Turkish leaders became Tang officials. Li Shimin himself became the 'heavenly khaghan'.[17]

There followed an extraordinary period of Chinese expansion. With the eastern Turks as their faithful allies, the frontiers of Chinese influence were extended even beyond the limits of the Han empire. In a series of campaigns the western Turks were defeated. Before one memorable engagement the Chinese general Su Dingfang said to his troops: 'The fog sheds darkness everywhere. The wind is icy. The barbarians do not believe that we can campaign at this season. Let us hasten to surprise them!'[18] This battle, fought near Issyk Kul in 657, reduced the western Turks to vassals of the Chinese. The Chinese empire now stretched to the borders of Persia.

Yet as the Tang dynasty advanced its frontiers the problems of maintaining its control increased. None of Taizong's successors possessed his skills in manipulating Turkish leaders. Even the eastern Turks grew dissatisfied and revolted. A memorial inscription recorded their grievances:

> Those chieftains who were in China adopted Chinese titles and obeyed the Chinese emperor. They gave their services and their strength to him for fifty years. . . . They surrendered to the Chinese emperor their empire and their own law. Then the Turks and all the common people said as follows: "I used to be of a people who had an empire. Where is my empire now? For whose benefit am I conquering realms?" They said "I used to be of a polity that had an emperor. Where is my emperor now? To which emperor do I give my services and strength?" they said. By saying so they became the foes of the Chinese emperor.[19]

The western Turks resumed the 'outer frontier strategy' and carried out a series of raids into Chinese territory, seizing many captives and extorting vast sums of money. However, by the early eighth century, the age of the great Turkish khaghanates had passed and new situations had developed on China's frontiers.

THE RISE OF TIBET

Before considering the rise of the Uighur, or second Turkish empire, it is appropriate to look at another dramatic development, the rise of Tibet. Little is known of Tibetan history before the seventh century, because of the absence of written records. The early inhabitants of Tibet were known to the Chinese as the Qiang. They were a Mongoloid people who in the north were nomadic but in the south had settled on agricultural land. They followed the Bon religion, a shamanist faith formerly widely prevalent over Central Asia. Early in the seventh century two major developments occurred affecting the Qiang: tribal society gave way to a centralised monarchy, and Buddhism was introduced, which in turn encouraged the development of a writing system. Buddhism at first challenged the Bon religion, but later a synthesis occurred which produced Lamaism.

Between about 620 and 649 the ruler of Tibet was Song-tsen Gampo and it was he who initiated a period of rapid expansion, his possible motive being to placate the aristocracy for their loss of independence by offering them opportunities for plunder. His primary target was the Tuyuhun nomads who used the pastures around Lake Kokonor. In 634, for the first time, the Tibetans sent envoys and tribute to the Tang court. A few years later the Tibetan king, having heard that a Chinese princess had been given in marriage to a ruler of the Tuyuhun, demanded similar treatment. When he was refused he launched an attack into Sichuan which, although repulsed, persuaded the Chinese of the value of a marriage alliance and a Chinese princess was duly sent to Tibet.

There now began a period of intensive sinicisation. Song-tsen Gampo had also asked that men who could read and write Chinese be sent to Tibet, and that members of the Tibetan royal family be permitted to study at the State University. The Chinese princess was a devout Buddhist, and she brought Buddhist monks and Buddhist sacred writings with her to Tibet. Soon afterwards the Tibetans asked for technicians who could teach sericulture, wine-brewing and paper-making, and who could construct grain mills.[20]

In the 660s the Tibetans recommenced their expansion and expelled the Tuyuhun from around the Kokonor. By so doing they 'destroyed the only buffer state between Tibet and Chinese territory'.[21] They twice seized control of the Tarim Basin only to be repulsed by Chinese troops, but still the Tibetan drive continued and by 680 they had gained control of parts of Sichuan. In 696, with the Empress Wu now on the throne, a Tibetan army defeated a large Chinese force less than two hundred miles from Chang'an. The empress, by adroit diplomacy, sowed dissension in the Tibetan ranks, and the immediate danger was averted. Nevertheless the Tibetans posed a very serious danger to the Chinese position in Central Asia. In order to maintain their influence in the Tarim Basin, the Chinese were forced onto the defensive and had to maintain a chain of garrisons and military colonies to safeguard communications.

In 722 Tibetan raiding started once again, but the hostilities culminated in a series of Chinese victories and the Tibetans were forced to sue for peace. In the resultant treaty, negotiated in 730, the Tibetan king acknowledged Chinese suzerainty, embassies were exchanged and a border demarcated. The settlement did not last, and large-scale hostilities occurred again in the 740s and 750s, principally in the Gansu corridor, where the Chinese were defending the approaches to Chang'an from the threat of Tibetan attack. Tibetan expansion was also occurring in the far west, in the Pamirs, but their progress in that region was halted by a spectacular Chinese victory at Gilgit. However, in 755 the Tibetan king died, his successor accepted investiture with Chinese titles and it seemed as if the Tibetan threat had again receded.

Then came An Lushan's rebellion, which forced the withdrawal of Chinese forces – or rather the forces of the military commands which had been set up on the frontiers – and this in turn led to the collapse of the defensive strategy. The Tibetan king decided to take advantage of China's problems by first encroaching on present-day Gansu and Qinghai and then moving on into Shaanxi. In so doing he deprived the Chinese of the horse-breeding and pasture lands essential for the maintenance of cavalry forces. From there, in 763, Tibetan forces attacked and captured Chang'an, which they proceeded to loot. Although they soon withdrew, this was the first of thirteen years of annual

Tibetan attacks which gravely weakened the restored dynasty. In 784, the two sides being exhausted, a peace treaty was signed which contained a definition of the border between the contestants, and which conceded vast tracts of territory to the Tibetans. Within a few years it became clear that this was not a solution to the conflict and China was forced to employ a new strategy, seeking as allies the recently emerged Uighur empire. Shortly afterwards China succeeded in detaching the state of Nanzhao from its habitual support of the Tibetans.

In 821 Tibet and China negotiated a second treaty, which this time was to last. The terms of the agreement were carved in Tibetan and Chinese on a stone pillar which was erected in Lhasa. It was an agreement between 'nephew and uncle', as the rulers of Tibet and China were described, which called for an end to the fighting and established a boundary between the two countries. Even while the treaty was being negotiated dissension had broken out in Tibet. It arose from the attempt of the Tibetan monarchy to use Buddhism as an instrument to establish its authority over the aristocracy, which continued to support the Bon religion. In the 840s a bitter religious strife destroyed the Tibetan monarchy and with it the military power which had for so long threatened China. As a consequence the Tibetan kingdom 'played no significant role in east Asian interstate relations thereafter'.[22]

THE UIGHUR EMPIRE

The long periods of warfare with the Tibetans had destroyed one of the main means used by China to protect her western frontiers, that is to say by the establishment of military colonies. As a consequence a new strategy had to be found to protect China. The means for this was found in the support of the Uighur, a Turkish group closely related to the eastern Turks, who established an empire which lasted from 744 to 840 in the area which is now Mongolia. The relationship which developed between the Uighur and the Chinese was one of mutual benefit: to a weak Chinese dynasty the Uighur provided invaluable military support; while the Uighur received from China an immense revenue and a privileged position in trade. This was a symbiotic relationship, for the Uighur were trusty allies who recognised that it was not in their interest to allow the Tang dynasty to be overthrown.

The Uighur empire was established after a revolt among the vassal tribes had precipitated the collapse of the royal clan of the eastern Turks. The leader of the Uighur, one of those vassal tribes, became khaghan, and to demonstrate that he was in control he sent the severed head of the last Turkish khaghan to the Tang court. At first the Uighur pursued the traditional outer frontier strategy of exploiting China from a distance, but then the rebellion of An Lushan offered them a marvellous opportunity to capitalise on the situation. In exchange for an alliance, and the marriage of the khaghan's daughter to a Tang prince, the Uighur sent a force of 4,000 horsemen to

China. This force played a key role in the recapture of Luoyang, but the price to be paid for assistance was heavy, for the Uighur were allowed to loot the city and in addition were promised an annual payment of 20,000 rolls of silk. When the Uighur had returned home they demanded and obtained a marriage alliance with a Tang princess.

Until the 780s the Uighur periodically campaigned in China, demanding a heavy payment for their services. Thereafter the pattern was more for the Uighur to extort payment from a distance. Some of this revenue came from charging an exorbitant price for horses, which were exchanged for silk. An Arab traveller who visited the Uighur capital reported that the khaghan received annual payments of half a million pieces of silk from China. This immense wealth gave the Uighur leaders extensive patronage, and they were able to establish a much more stable state than any of their predecessors. To the capital at Karabalghasun came Sogdians who provided literate administrators, enabling the running of 'a true city on the steppe'.[23] The sack of Luoyang had led to the khaghan meeting Manichaean missionaries, who converted him. A trilingual inscription on a monument at Karabalghasun recorded that this 'country of barbarous customs, full of the fumes of blood, was changed into a land where the people live on vegetables; from a land of killing to where good deeds are fostered.'[24] Thereafter the Uighur were recognised as the official protectors of Manichaean missions in China. Their claim to be a civilised people was further advanced with the development of a Uighur script and the translation of Manichaean and Buddhist scripts into the Uighur language.

Perhaps this cultural advance and the adoption of a more sedentary existence weakened the Uighur empire. In 840, after the empire had been split by a succession dispute, the Kirghiz tribe from the north seized and looted the capital. The Uighur empire fell and with it went the most dependable support of the Tang dynasty.

THE QIDAN

Meanwhile, in the north-east, another type of tribal confederation had taken shape which was to pose a quite different set of demands on China. The people involved were the Qidan, from whose name the word Cathay was derived. They spoke a language ancestral to Mongolian, though the term Mongol was not yet in use. They were pastoral nomads who came from what in modern times has been named Manchuria and from the area around Rehe. This area was in the marginal zone, that is to say between the open steppe and settled areas. It has long been noted that dynasties of conquest have come from such areas and more recently it has been pointed out that the vast majority of the dynasties of conquest came from the Manchurian marginal zone.[25]

The Qidan first appeared in Chinese annals at the beginning of the fifth century. By the early seventh century they were trying to create an autonomous state on China's frontier, an objective which was not tolerable to a powerful dynasty, and in the early Tang period the Qidan were forced to accept Chinese rule. When in 696 the Qidan revolted, the Chinese, with the assistance of the eastern Turks, suppressed them with such ferocity that their expansion was halted until the beginning of the tenth century.

In the meantime the Qidan began to profit from their proximity to China and Qidan society started to change. They adopted farming, began to produce cloth and commenced living in urban settlements. Traditionally the leadership of the tribal organisation of the eight Qidan tribes was rotated. However, early in the tenth century, Abaoji, the leader of the Yila tribe, broke away from the system. After having completed his term of office he refused to step down and declared himself to be emperor of the Qidan. He thereupon massacred other Qidan leaders and moved to make himself the ruler of a Chinese-style dynasty. Chinese advisers were brought in, and in 916 he adopted a Chinese reign title. He reorganised the military forces, replacing the tribal units with a force personally loyal to him. An imperial bodyguard of mounted archers was formed, its men being drawn from different tribes. At first this was an élite force, but later it became the model for the *ordo* or 'horde', the military formation into which the Qidan people were mobilised.

The Qidan expansion then began. One aspect of this was directed against tribal peoples to the west, first against the Kirghiz in Mongolia, the successors of the Uighur, who were displaced in 924. Two years later the kingdom of Pohai, which extended over northern Korea and part of Manchuria, was overthrown. After Abaoji's death, his son Deguang turned his attention to the south. Following the final collapse of the Tang dynasty in 907, north China had been ruled by the Five Dynasties, a series of ephemeral regimes. In 936 Deguang intervened in the region, supporting Shi Jingtang, a rebellious general, in a bid for power. Shi became the emperor of the Later Jin dynasty and a client of the Qidan, ceding to them territory within the Great Wall in northern Hebei and Shanxi. Such a surrender was a dramatic departure from the practice when dealing with the Uighur, and the humiliating outcome was further stressed by the demand for an annual tribute. When Shi's successor tried to stop the payment of the tribute, he was overthrown, and the Qidan seemed poised to establish themselves as rulers in north China. However, a series of setbacks, including succession disputes and the establishment of the Song dynasty in 960, curbed those ambitions. Nevertheless, despite the efforts of the new dynasty, the Qidan could not be driven out of north China. In 1004, in an agreement known as the treaty of Shanyuan, the Chinese dynasty and the Qidan agreed to a compromise, which left the Qidan, now known as the Liao dynasty, as rulers of part of north China and of territories beyond. A further indication of the limited power of the Song dynasty, was that the Tangut, a Tibetan people, were able to establish the Xi Xia kingdom in modern Gansu.

The Liao empire, which in its first form lasted from 947 until 1125, was a refinement of a type of administration which had been pioneered by the Xianbei in the fourth century and further developed by the Toba in the Northern Wei dynasty. Its essential feature was a form of dualism initiated by Deguang:

> he divided the government into North and South. The Qidan were governed according to their own national system, while the Chinese were governed according to their own system. The national system was plain and simple. In the Chinese system the usage of traditional terminology was preserved.[26]

Under this dual system, features of both Qidan and Chinese society were maintained. On the Qidan side, the survival of the semi-nomadic tradition was evident in the use of no less than five capitals, including modern-day Beijing. The tribal organisation was retained, and the development of it, the *ordo* was improved. The Qidan language was preserved and a codified Qidan law applied. In the areas of China under Qidan rule the Tang system of government remained in force and the Liao emperor performed the functions of a Confucian ruler. The examination system continued in use for the selection of officials. This dual system, which made it possible to rule parts of the steppe and parts of China at the same time, was to provide a model for the later Jurchen Jin empire, and most notably for the Manchu Qing dynasty.

RELATIONS WITH KOREA

To the north-east of China, during the Sui and Tang periods, a unified Korea had emerged. Chinese influence, which had spread into the Korean peninsula in the Han period, had subsequently declined. With the reunification of China the desire to secure this quarter revived and Yangdi, the second emperor of the Sui, three times attempted to conquer Koguryo, the northern of the three kingdoms which then composed Korea. He failed, with disastrous consequences. However, in 663, during Gaozong's reign, Paekche in the southwest was defeated. Five years later, with the assistance of Silla, the third Korean kingdom, Koguryo was also subdued and a Chinese protectorate established at Pyongyang. The country was divided into administrative districts and Chinese officials put in charge of them. When Silla started a movement of resistance against the Chinese presence, this arrangement proved untenable and in 676 the Chinese were forced to withdraw. Silla then created a unified Korean state covering most of the Korean peninsula.

Although independent, the state of Silla, which lasted until 935, was heavily indebted to influence from Tang China. A bureaucratic form of government was introduced, the country was divided into provinces, and a landholding system derived from China was inaugurated. There were also strong cultural links, with the spread of Buddhism, the encouragement of Confucian scholarship and the introduction of competitive examinations. Another indication of the closeness of the relationship which subsisted between Silla and China was that between 703 and 738 no less than forty-five embassies were sent to China. Officials of Korean origin were to be found at the Tang court and many Korean monks settled in China. Large numbers of Koreans lived along the coast from the mouth of the Huai river to the coast of Shandong, many of them being traders and sailors, but others were settlers who formed autonomous colonies.

However, other features of Korean society were antipathetic to a total acceptance of the Chinese model. Korea had an aristocratic order, and the idea of a competitive examination system, which in China had undermined the position of the great aristocratic families, was bound to induce resistance. Confucianism never gained dominance as a state ideology and the concept of the Confucian ruler never took root in Korea.

POHAI

When Koguryo was defeated, a large number of Koguryo captives, including many from the aristocracy, were transported to the north. In time they settled near Jilin in northern Manchuria, in territory inhabited by Tungusic people, and there they founded a state which from 713 became known to the Chinese as Pohai. This state, which at one time extended from the Sungari and Amur rivers into north Korea was, like Silla, organised on the Chinese model. Its administration was based on the Tang bureaucracy, Buddhist influence was strong, and commercial and tributary links were maintained with China. The state survived until it was conquered by the Qidan in 927.

JAPAN

The Tang period was also the high-water mark of Chinese influence on the development of Japan. The use of Chinese writing and the knowledge of Chinese Confucian texts had reached Japan early in the fifth century, and at about the same time technology derived from China, for example improved irrigation techniques, was also introduced. In 538 Buddhism reached Japan via Korea. But it was not until the sixth and seventh centuries, after the reunification of China under the Sui, that the most sustained period of Chinese influence occurred. Two themes predominated in this influence: 'the institutions of government, particularly as perfected under the Tang dynasty, and the doctrines of Buddhism, as institutionalized under the power of the Chinese emperors and the Sinified sectarian orders'.[27] The person most associated with this development was Prince Shōtoku, regent from 593 until his death in 622. In 604 he promulgated a document, known as the Seventeen-Article Constitution, which expressed Confucian ethical and political doctrines and endorsed Buddhism as contributing to the ideal of social harmony.[28] In 702 a compendium of penal laws and administrative practice, known as the Taiho Code, was produced, and once again the model was Tang China. Two other striking examples of borrowing were the introduction of provisions for equal landholding and the practice of choosing officials by means of examinations.[29] Yet in Japan, as in Korea, borrowing from China could only go so far before it met with resistance from indigenous sources. As the power of the Tang empire waned, cultural borrowing declined and these peripheral states increasingly established an independent cultural identity.

CHINA'S RELATIONSHIP WITH THE OUTSIDE WORLD

During the Sui and Tang dynasties embassies from various countries were sent to the Chinese imperial court and students and monks went to China to study religion and culture. The Japanese monk Ennin was a member of the last official Japanese embassy to the Tang court. He arrived in China in 838 and remained there for nine years, studying esoteric Buddhism. His diary provides the first example, and an outstanding one, of a description of China by a foreign visitor. In it he gives details of the preparations made for the dispatch of a tribute mission and the hazards of a voyage to China. Ennin was not at the imperial audience when the tribute was presented, but he recorded that embassies from no less than five countries were received on that day. His diary is packed with details of what he had seen of life in China and it is a major source on Buddhism and its persecution.[30]

The tributary mission to which Ennin belonged represented one form of relationship between China and the outside world. This unequal partnership had its foundation in a myth of Chinese superiority which can be traced back to the formative period of the Chinese empire. At that time the empire was expanding, either through military victories or through the assimilation of surrounding peoples, in a manner which seemed to confirm that Chinese civilisation was indeed superior. In the Han period the language used to describe the relationship between China and those surrounding states, which had accepted Chinese culture and which recognised Chinese superiority, was formalised. Foreign missions to the Chinese court were described as tribute missions. Although tributary missions took gifts to the Chinese court and were rewarded with trade privileges, their essential purpose was perceived as political, as a visible recognition of Chinese superiority. In the Tang period, when Chinese influence was at a high point, the claim for superiority was reinforced by the actuality of power. However, in terms of rhetoric, the justification for superiority was not based on the power balance but on the superiority of China's Confucian culture.[31]

The relationship which developed in the Tang period between China and the nomadic peoples of the steppe had rather different characteristics. For a start, it was a dynamic relationship which altered according to the relative strength of steppe confederations and the Chinese state. Secondly, the relationship was based on economic factors, and in particular on the need of nomadic societies, particularly ones which had achieved a degree of sophistication, to secure grain and quality goods from China. Finally it was a relationship based on the equality, or even on the superiority, in military terms, of the nomadic peoples over the Chinese. The relationship took the form of frontier markets, tributary exchange and intermarriage arrangements, mechanisms first used under the Han and then developed by the Tang. When these mechanisms worked effectively, the northern frontiers were relatively peaceful, but when they broke down the nomadic peoples resumed their alternative relationship, the outer frontier strategy of periodically raiding China and seizing or extorting what they required.[32]

THOUGHT, RELIGION AND CULTURE UNDER THE SUI AND TANG DYNASTIES

THE RISE AND DECLINE OF BUDDHISM

In the sixth century, the whole of northern Chinese society was suffused with Buddhism:

> it penetrated economic life and affected customs at all levels of society. Its monasteries and shrines dotted the landscape; its clergy assumed many social roles; that of preacher and teacher, medical doctor and chanter of magic spells, performers of masses for the dead and guardians of temples that also served as family shrines. Elite families were for the most part Buddhist in belief. They made gifts to monasteries and shrines, used clergy for family and seasonal observances, had the lay vows administered to their sons. . . .[1]

The reasons for this extraordinary growth are by no means certain. In a number of respects Buddhism appeared to be opposed to important aspects of Chinese culture. Whereas the Chinese view of life was that it was to be enjoyed, Buddhist teaching stressed that life was full of suffering and that one should seek release from its repetitive cycle. The Chinese traditionally emphasised the family and in particular its perpetuation through the birth of a son, whereas Buddhists practised celibacy. The Chinese valued productive labour and harmonious social relationships whereas for the Buddhist the objective was enlightenment, which came through a disregard for worldly goods and the abandonment of the household. Furthermore, for the Confucianist it was a requirement to uphold the laws of the state, whereas members of a Buddhist monastic community deemed themselves to be outside the law.[2]

However, from the fourth century onwards Buddhism was to make rapid progress in China. It achieved this at a time of disunity within the state and of uncertainty in men's minds:

> There was no central dynasty motivated by Confucian concepts of government to

oppose the Indian religion. Thoughtful Chinese . . . were looking about for a substitute; they were groping for a new way of life, a new standard of conduct, to take the place of the Confucian ideology which had been found wanting. In this quest they turned to Buddhism to see whether or not this religion could offer some satisfactory solutions to the problems they faced.[3]

An important additional reason for the success of Buddhism in China was that it was not a monolithic faith but a religion which was capable of wide variation and was adaptable to Chinese circumstances. Through the establishment of schools, Chinese forms of Buddhism were developed and characteristic Chinese features incorporated. A common Chinese saying describing the four most influential schools declared, 'The Tiantai and Huayan schools for doctrine, and the Meditation and Pure Land schools for practice'.[4] Of these four schools, the Tiantai did not even exist in India, while the other three, which did have their antecedents in India, developed Chinese characteristics. A brief review of their main features will convey the essentials of Chinese Buddhist thought in this period.

The Tiantai school, which was named after the sacred mountain in Zhejiang, was established by Zhiyi late in the sixth century. His teachings were based on a minute examination of the *Lotus Sutra*, which he regarded as the most complete doctrine among all Buddhist teachings – all other doctrines, although each containing something of value, he considered to be preparatory to it. The sutra taught that the historical Gautama Sakyamuni, who lived in the sixth and fifth centuries BC, was but an earthly manifestation of the eternal Buddha. The Tiantai school offered a doctrine of universal salvation, to be achieved both through intellectual enquiry and meditative practice. The second school, the Huayan or Flower Garden school, had many similarities to the Tiantai school. It was in effect founded by Fazang, the Great Master of Xianshou, and he too was concerned with the universal principle and the nature of matter. It also classified the various Buddhist sects into vehicles, with the perfect doctrine of the Huayan combining what was valuable in all the other vehicles. In this way both the Tiantai and Huayan schools displayed a typical Chinese preference for syncretism. Their philosophical teachings tended to attract an intellectual following rather than popular support.

The Meditation school, known as Chan in China and Zen in Japan and in the West, was by tradition brought to the Northern Wei kingdom by the Indian master Bodhidharma in about the year 520. There, it was said, he practised wall contemplation – sitting in front of a wall – for nine years, before engaging in teaching. In fact Chan Buddhism appears to be a Chinese development, perhaps fusing elements of the Buddhist concept of enlightenment with philosophical ideas derived from Daoism. Chan taught that the Buddha-nature is inherent in all human beings and that nature may be perceived through meditation. In the eighth century Chan Buddhism split into northern and southern schools, the former believing in gradual enlightenment, the latter in sudden enlightenment. The southern school, which rejected all scriptures and which stressed intuition rather than intellect, became extremely popular and has survived to this day.

Also popular was the Jingtu or Pure Land school which emphasised salvation through faith rather than through good works, and thus attracted many simple worshippers. It took its name from the Pure Land or Western Paradise, presided over by Amitabha, the Amita Buddha. According to the shorter version of the *Pure Land Sutra*, the believer can gain access to that land through the repetition of the name of the Amitabha, that is Amituofo in Chinese. In the Pure Land the Amita Buddha has as his chief minister the always compassionate bodhisattva Avalokitesvara, known in Chinese as Guanyin. Through the Tang and into the Song period this figure was depicted as male, but thereafter Guanyin came to be the Goddess of Mercy, clad in white.

The spread of Buddhism represented a major challenge to the authority of the Chinese state. Monasteries were endowed with large parcels of land which were tax exempt. Buddhist clergy, particularly in the south, claimed that they did not owe obedience to the civil authority. The popular support on which the Buddhist church could rely made it difficult, if not dangerous, for emperors to take effective action against it. It was for this reason that Yang Jian, the first Sui emperor, deliberately used Buddhism 'as an ideological force capable of bringing together the country which had been divided for two and a half centuries'.[5]

The early Tang rulers did not display the same enthusiasm for Buddhism. However, because they recognised its influence, they took care to use patronage to conciliate Buddhists by constructing monasteries in key places and by holding services for the dead. At the same time they increasingly applied curbs to the spread of Buddhism. From the beginning of the dynasty Tang emperors had given favours to the Daoist church, and in 637 Taizong challenged the pre-eminent position which Buddhism had come to occupy by issuing an edict that in future Daoist monks and nuns would take precedence over their Buddhist counterparts. Through other measures he confined monks and nuns to their monasteries and restricted them to their religious duties. However, before the end of his reign, and perhaps because of his admiration for Xuan Zang, the Buddhist monk who had brought the scriptures back from India, Taizong withdrew his opposition to Buddhism and authorised the ordination of some 18,500 new monks.[6]

Under the Empress Wu the Buddhist church regained favour. She herself came from a devoutly Buddhist family. The threat of her usurpation of the throne had outraged the Confucianists and alienated the Daoist church, and so it was only natural that she should look to Buddhism for support. Buddhist priests claimed that oracles had identified her as the Maitreya Buddha and had asserted that the mandate of heaven had passed to her. When enthroned she repaid her obligation by reversing Taizong's edict and giving Buddhist priests precedence over the Daoist clergy. During her reign she gave particular favour to the Chan and Huayan schools.

After the empress's death Buddhism again fell from favour. Xuanzong took a harder line than his predecessors, enacting a series of measures to restrict the wealth of the Buddhist church. At the same time he commissioned translations of Buddhist scriptures and offered favours to Chinese and Indian monks, but these were practitioners of esoteric Buddhism, which, like Daoism, used ritual practices to avert disasters.

The An Lushan rebellion, which convulsed north China between 755 and 763, had a major effect on the relationship between Buddhism and the state. On the one hand the dynasty, desperately weakened by the rebellion, was forced to relax its policies towards Buddhism. For example, for a fee it allowed the unrestricted ordination of Buddhist clergy, thus raising short-term revenue while decreasing the number of people liable to taxation. This practice, euphemistically known as 'money for the purchase of scented rice', rebounded on Buddhism – a Buddhist historian later observed: 'The corrupt practice of selling ordination certificates has destroyed our religion'.[7] On the other hand the ravages of war had a destructive effect on the monastic communities near Luoyang and Chang'an. The damage was greater to the philosophical schools than to the popular sects. In the years after the rebellion Pure Land Buddhism not only grew in popularity, but was also introduced at court, where hitherto it had been treated with disdain.

Imperial patronage of Buddhism increased in the years after the rebellion. Daizong (reigned 762–79) authorised vast expenditure on the construction of monasteries and he himself paid reverence to Buddhist relics and encouraged the mass ordination of monks and nuns. His son was less enthusiastic, but was unable to take decisive steps to reduce the heavy cost that the support of Buddhism was placing on the state. Nevertheless he encouraged large translation projects of Buddhist texts. Xianzong (reigned 805–20), took an interest in Chan Buddhism, and gave demonstrations of his own personal piety, most notably in 819 when he had a famous relic, the supposed fingerbone of Buddha, brought to Chang'an so that he could worship it.

It was this event which provoked the celebrated protest by Han Yu, which has sometimes been seen as having initiated the later suppression of Buddhism. In fact, his criticism was neither the first, nor the decisive contribution to that decision. From the beginning of the Tang period voices had been raised against Buddhism. In 621 the grand astrologer and Daoist priest Fu Yi had summarised the commonly-expressed view that the Buddhist monastic communities were a burden on the state. He had urged the emperor to disband the Buddhist clergy and put the monasteries to a better use. Taizong's extravagant expenditure on monasteries had been sharply criticised by a scholar named Gao Ying, who argued that in the past wise rulers had sought merit through good deeds and not by depleting the treasury.[8] An official who served Dezong had estimated that the cost of supplying food and clothing to a single monk was greater than the tax paid by five adult males.[9]

Nevertheless Han Yu's response was significant. He was a famous Confucian scholar, and his 'Memorial on the Bone of Buddha' was an outstandingly vehement criticism of the display of the relic in the imperial palace. He wrote scathingly that 'Buddha was a man of the barbarians who did not speak the language of China and wore clothes of a different fashion'. He understood 'neither the duties that bind a sovereign and subject, nor the affections of father and son'. If the Buddha were still alive he might merely have been granted an audience in an outer hall. Why then, asked Han Yu, after he had long been dead, 'could his rotten bones, the foul and unlucky remains of his body, be rightly admitted to the palace?'[10] For this outburst Han Yu was sentenced to death, his sentence later being commuted to one of exile to the south.

However in 842 the opponents of Buddhism found, in the emperor Wuzong, a ruler willing to take decisive action. In that year decrees were published which called for the expulsion of unregistered monks from monasteries, the laicisation of undesirable monks and the seizure of property belonging to individual members of the Buddhist clergy. Further decrees followed, culminating in 845 with two edicts. One of these prohibited Buddhist monasteries from holding estates and ordered that all monastic wealth be handed over to pay government salaries; the other called for the laicisation of all Buddhist monks and nuns under the age of forty. The Japanese monk Ennin, who witnessed these events, noted that 'the monks and nuns are being exterminated. The scheme is generally the same throughout the land'.[11]

Why did Wuzong act thus? In the Edict on the Suppression of Buddhism he referred to the foreignness of the religion and how recently it had grown in numbers and wealth. He repeated other commonly voiced criticisms:

It wears out the strength of the people with constructions of earth and wood, pilfers their wealth for ornaments of gold and precious objects, causes men to abandon their lords and parents for the company of teachers, and severs man and wife with its monastic decrees.[12]

According to Ennin's account there was a link between the suppression and the Wuzong emperor's preoccupation with Daoism. A major Daoist project, the construction of 'a terrace for viewing the immortals', was being completed when the edict of suppression was promulgated. Nevertheless it is difficult to accept that the suppression was mainly a response to the demands of the Daoist clergy. There is perhaps a stronger case for arguing that it was Confucian officials who led the attack. Buddhist historians have often claimed that Li Deyu, the chief minister, incited the emperor to act. If this was true, and there is some evidence of his involvement, it seems likely that his motivation was political rather than ideological. Even if some stirrings of a Confucian revival had become apparent, this did not amount to a serious challenge to the philosophical aspects of Buddhism.

There remains the question of the importance of the economic motive. All the critics of Buddhism emphasised the cost of state support of Buddhism, and the economic implications of a substantial proportion of the population withdrawing from economic activity and escaping from the burden of taxation. The temptation to confiscate the wealth of Buddhist establishments was clearly there, in particular because the Buddhist church was alleged to have converted much of the nation's precious metal into statues and bells. Nevertheless, it has been pointed out that the actual accumulation of wealth and diversion of human resources by the Buddhist church was much less than might be expected: only one per cent of the population dwelt in Buddhist establishments and these establishments worked no more than four per cent of the cultivated land.[13]

The great suppression was said to have resulted in the destruction of 4,600 monasteries and 40,000 temples and shrines, the laicisation of 260,500 monks and nuns and the confiscation of millions of acres of tax-exempt farmland.[14] Nevertheless it did not destroy Buddhism in China, for under Wuzong's successor something like a restoration of Buddhism took place. However Huang Chao's rebellion was to add greatly to the process of destruction. Buddhist monasteries in almost every part of China were affected, major centres of learning were sacked and the clergy scattered. The schools of Buddhist scholarship fell into disuse, key texts were lost and the transmission of knowledge discontinued.

OTHER RELIGIONS INTRODUCED INTO CHINA

During the Tang period several new religions reached China, including Zoroastrianism, Manichaeism, Christianity, Judaism and Islam. Zoroastrianism reached China from Persia during the reign of the Taizong emperor. The Persian Sassanian dynasty had been overthrown by an Arab invasion and the Persian king sent his son on an embassy to China to ask for assistance against the Arabs. A Persian court in exile was established at Chang'an and permission was given for the building of a Zoroastrian temple. Manichaeism was brought to Chang'an by Uighur merchants in the eighth century and they established a number of temples there and in other cities to serve their fellow countrymen. Manichaeans made no attempt to convert the Chinese population, but this did not protect them from persecution at the time of the suppression of Buddhism. Before the full weight of Wuzong's prejudice had fallen upon the Buddhists, the Manichaeans had their property confiscated and Manichaean priests may have been executed. Similar harsh treatment was meted out to the Zoroastrians.

The Nestorians were a Syrian Christian sect. This form of Christianity (which believed that Jesus had a human as well as a divine identity) had reached China in 635. Its first representative, a monk possibly named Reuben, had presented the Nestorian scriptures to the Taizong emperor, who, it was recorded, 'thoroughly understood their propriety and truth and specially ordered their preaching and transmission'.[15] The first church was built in 638 and the Nestorians received marks of favour from subsequent emperors. An account of Nestorian teachings was inscribed on a monument in 781 and the stone was buried soon after the suppression edict of 845 was promulgated. It was rediscovered in 1625 and may now be seen in the Shaanxi Provincial Museum in Xi'an.

Islam came to China during the Tang period by both the land and the sea routes. A mission from Caliph Othman is recorded as having reached China in 651, and an Arab community, made up of soldiers who had assisted in the suppression of the rebellion of An Lushan, existed in Gansu and Shaanxi from the eighth century. It was from the descendants of these Arabs that the present Muslim population of China derived. In the south Arab traders resided in several ports, where they enjoyed extraterritoriality and the freedom to practise their own religion. However, many of them were to die in the disastrous rebellion led by Huang Chao.[16]

CONFUCIANISM

Of Confucian scholarship during the Tang period it has been said that its main function was to serve the bureaucracy and that learned men devoted themselves to textual exegesis to provide authoritative versions of Confucian texts for use in the examinations. This work was important, 'yet we find in it evidence only of painstaking study and not of creative thought'.[17] More recently a somewhat different view has been expressed. Although much of Tang Confucian scholarship was concerned with the classical and ritual texts and with the compilation of dynastic history, and Confucian scholars displayed an overriding preoccupation with success in the examination system and the pursuit of an official career, there was another side to their activity. This was concerned with the policies to be adopted to deal with contemporary issues, issues which ranged from matters of ritual to defence against the barbarians and economic and financial management. In the first part of the dynasty, before An Lushan's rebellion, much of this activity was state-sponsored, and Confucian scholars participated actively in debates over policy issues. In the later part of the dynasty private scholarship and informal writing became more important and this in turn contributed to the later development of Confucianism.[18]

The best-remembered Confucian scholar of the age was Han Yu (768–824), whose famous attack on Buddhism has already been noted. It has been said of the Tang that 'at no other time in Chinese history did the Confucian tradition come closer to extinction.' It has been claimed that it survived because Han Yu self-consciously took upon himself the task of redefining Confucian values, thus earning the title of the first of the great Neo-Confucians.[19] In his 'Discourse on Teachers' he wrote:

Alas, the teaching of the Way has long been neglected! Hard it is, then, to expect men to be without doubts. The sages of antiquity far excelled ordinary men, and yet they sought teachers and questioned them. But the common people of today, though they are equally far from the level of the sages, count it a shame to study with a teacher. Thus do sages become even wiser, and the stupid more stupid.[20]

According to this view Han Yu was 'a man involved in a life-long attempt to restore political, cultural and religious unity to the Tang world'. He was an innovator, one who represented the dynamic spirit of a new age. However this opinion has been challenged and the essentially conservative quality of Han Yu's thought has been stressed. For example, he had participated in the contemporary debate on whether the heir to the throne should be selected from the imperial sons or on the basis of merit. Han Yu had supported the conservative line which endorsed hereditary succession. With reference to the official educational system, Han Yu had at first appeared to be a reformer, but later, after he had had experience of office, the career values which prevailed in the bureaucracy gained precedence in his mind over the teaching ideals he had developed earlier. Even his stridently anti-Buddhist views did not represent a radical new attitude, nor did they derive from his development as an introspective thinker – the criticism was based on the social and political effects of the spread of Buddhism and echoed the commonly expressed view of officials of his day.[21]

TANG LITERATURE: POETRY

'The splendour and the subsequent decline of the Tang period are reflected in its poetry. Tang China, like Elizabethan England, was virtually a nation of singing birds'. Of this outpouring some 50,000 poems, from the brushes of 2,300 poets, have survived.[22] Later generations have regarded the poetry written during the reign of Xuanzong (712–56) as the apogee of all Chinese poetry, a model which later poets could imitate but could never hope to surpass. The most popular anthology of Chinese verse, the eighteenth-century compilation *Three Hundred Tang Poems*, has ensured that these poems remain familiar to educated Chinese to this day.

This poetic flowering did not come out of the blue. During the period of division poetry had become associated with the life of the recluse. The outstanding example of such a person was Tao Qian (376–427), who had abandoned an official post to take up the life of a farmer. His poems celebrated the joys of the simple country life, and his enjoyment of drinking wine:

> No dust and confusion
>> within my doors and courtyard;
> In the empty rooms,
>> more than sufficient leisure.
> Too long I was held
>> within the barred cage.
> Now I am able
>> to return again to Nature.[23]

After the reunification of China under the Sui, the need for poets to distance themselves from the life of politics and the city grew less and many of the most famous poets of the Tang period served as officials and were familiar with life in the capital Chang'an. It has been said of Tang poets that their motivation to write was quite different from that of their western counterparts. For them, the writing of poetry was not an exclusive vocation, but something which they did under particular circumstances or on a special occasion. In the early Tang period much of the poetry written was court poetry, a response to events at court, composed by that small minority who attended there. By the late eighth century, poetry had been transformed from a minor diversion into an art form. It had become a vehicle for the expression of the feelings of the individual, feelings often related to the poet's moral values, doubts, suffering – feelings often aroused by the experience of absence or exile.[24]

Of the poets of the age, one of the most remarkable was Wang Wei (699–759), for he was equally well-known as a painter. Although he had passed the imperial examinations and had been appointed to office, he was then demoted and required to serve in a lowly position in Shandong. There he wrote in the style of an exile and expressed in simple language his close relationship with nature, a relationship often defined by reference to Buddhist sentiments. He was later reinstated and held a variety of offices until he was captured by An Lushan's rebel army. It was typical of Wang Wei that he did not mention that traumatic experience in his verse. He became famous for his mastery of the brief poem known as *jueju*, the 'cut-short' quatrain, poems which have been described as 'visually complete but intellectually incomplete', which invite the reader to deipher some hidden truth. A poem from the *Wang Stream Collection* illustrates this style:

> The moaning of wind in autumn rain,
> Swift water trickling over stones.
> Leaping waves strike one another –
> A white egret startles up, comes down again.[25]
>> 'Rapids by the Luan Trees'

Li Bo (701–62), often described as China's best-loved poet, was a close contemporary of Wang Wei. He was a precocious poet, always at pains to cultivate his poetic identity – he was 'an immortal, different from ordinary men and privileged to act differently'.[26] His social background is unclear – he came from Sichuan and his family may have been Turkish. It is a testimony to the force of his personality that he was able to impress the emperor and obtain a post in the Hanlin Academy and so become a court poet. There he cultivated his reputation for eccentricity and for wild drinking. Many of his poems refer to this habit. He wrote:

> Once I am drunk
>   losing Heaven and Earth,
> Unsteadily
>   I go to my lonely pillow.
> Not to know
>   that my self exists –
> Of all my joys
>   This is the highest.[27]

But after a few years he fell out of favour at court and spent much of the rest of his life in the Yangzi valley. It was fitting that his most famous poem, and perhaps the best-known poem in the Chinese language, should be written on the subject of absence from home:

> Before my bed
>   there is bright moonlight
> So that it seems
>   like frost on the ground:
>
> Lifting my head
>   I watch the bright moon,
> Lowering my head
>   I dream that I'm home.[28]

'Quiet night thoughts'

The name of Li Bo is forever coupled with that of Du Fu (712–70). The two men are seen as representing the opposed but complementary forces of nature, the *yin* and the *yang*:

Li Bo is the Daoist in this pair of poets, and his constantly recurring symbol is the reflected light of the Moon at night; whilst Du Fu is the Confucian who from early childhood made the Phoenix his symbol, the Fire Bird symbolizing the Yang.[29]

This contrast may be traced to their backgrounds and life experience. Du Fu was born near Xi'an of a family in modest circumstances. He studied hard and took the examinations – and failed, for reasons which have never been fully explained. He met Li Bo and was much influenced by him. He too obtained a post at court, and might have succeeded in gaining official preferment, but for An Lushan's rebellion. The hardship this brought to him and his family darkened the rest of his life. He spent his last eleven years in the north-west, and it was there that his most powerful poetry was written.

It is difficult to do justice to the range and depth of Du Fu's poetry in a few lines. Some sense of it might be conveyed by an extract from a poem called 'Song of Pengya', which in graphic terms described the journey he and his family had made at the time of the rebellion:

> The whole family had been traveling long on foot –
> Most whom we met seemed to have no shame.
> Here and there birds of the valley sang,
> We saw no travelers going the other way.
> My baby girl gnawed at me in her hunger,
> And I feared wild beasts would hear her cries:
> I held her to my chest, covered her mouth,
> But she twisted and turned crying louder in rage.
> My little son did his best to take care of things,
> With purpose went off and got sour plums to eat.
> It had thundered and rained half the past week,
> We clung together, pulling through mud and mire,
> And having made no provision against the rain,
> The paths were slippery, our clothes were cold.[30]

There has been a tendency to regard the Tang period as dominated by these two poets and to see the antithesis between their characters and poetry as defining the two extremes of the poetical achievement of the age. In fact neither poet can be stereotyped so easily, nor can they be regarded as representative of their time. This point can be illustrated by reference to two other poets, both born more than two generations later.

The first of these, Bo Juyi (772–846), has already been encountered, for it was he who wrote the celebrated poem 'Song of Unending Sorrow' which commemorated the death of Yang Guifei, the mistress of the Xuanzong emperor. Bo Juyi had a long and relatively successful career as an official. In 825 he was appointed governor of Suzhon, a post which he found to be no sinecure:

At break of day I confront a pile of papers,
Dusk has come before I get away.
The beauty of the morning, the beauty of the afternoon
Pass while I sit clamped to an office desk.[31]

Nevertheless Bo Juyi found time to be a prolific poet and his poems, written in a simple style and treating of popular sentiments, earned him great contemporary fame. He once wrote to his great friend Yuan Zhen 'from Chang'an to Jiangxi I found my poems publicly written everywhere: in village schools, Buddhist temples, inns, and ships; they were often chanted by scholars, monks, widows, and young girls.'[32] His appeal is illustrated by a short poem which refers to the trade in tropical birds and to the fate of outspoken intellectuals:

Sent as a present from Annam –
A red cockatoo.
Coloured like the peach-tree blossom,
Speaking with the speech of men.
And they did to it what is always done
To the learned and the eloquent.
They took a cage with stout bars
And shut it up inside.[33]

'The Red Cockatoo'

The range of Tang poetry, and the danger of generalising about it, is illustrated by reference to one more poet, Li He (790–816). An old aphorism declared that Du Fu's genius was that of a Confucian sage, Li Bo's that of a Daoist immortal, that Bo Juyi's was human and Li He's ghostly or demonic. Although famous in the ninth century, his taste for morbidity and violence led to him being long neglected. He is now recognised as one of the great poets of the period, an innovator who has been compared with Baudelaire. Some idea of his tone is conveyed by a few lines from 'Don't Go out of the Door':

Heaven is inscrutable,
Earth keeps its secrets.
The nine-headed monster eats our souls,
Frosts and snows snap our bones.
Dogs are set on us, snarl and sniff around us,
And lick their paws, partial to the orchid-girdled,
Till the end of all afflictions, when God sends us his chariot,
And the sword starred with jewels and the yoke of yellow gold.[34]

PROSE AND DRAMA

In the Tang period the distinction between the poet and the writer of prose was not an absolute one, a point illustrated by reference to Han Yu, whose poems appear in the poetry anthologies, but who achieved his enduring influence through his prose. This rejected the existing style known as 'parallel prose' in favour of a simpler, but more archaic form called the 'ancient prose', which took as its model the style of the classics.

As well as his famous memorial on the bone of Buddha, Han Yu wrote dynamic and eloquent essays. When he was exiled to Chaozhou in 819, he found that his district was plagued by crocodiles. This led him to compose his imaginary 'Proclamation to the Crocodile'. In it he described how he had caused an officer to throw a sheep and a pig into the waters where the crocodile lived. He declared that crocodiles had been expelled by the Han, but had returned in the age of division. Their presence was no longer tolerable under the Tang. He, the governor, had been instructed to look after the people of his area, 'but you, crocodile, goggle-eyed, are not content with the deep waters of the creek, but seize your advantage to devour the people and their stock'. He therefore gave the animal an ultimatum – he must either remove to the great sea or be killed with poisoned arrows. Thus, in a short essay, Han Yu demonstrated the effectiveness of his style which combined simplicity with dry humour.

Liu Zongyuan (773–819), a friend and close contemporary of Han Yu is remembered for his satirical fables and biographical sketches. A sketch entitled 'Camel Guo the Gardener' told of a hunchback nicknamed 'Camel', who had an extraordinary ability to make plants grow. When questioned about this he had replied in terms which revealed his Daoist sympathies:

> I cannot make a tree live for ever or flourish. What I *can* do is comply with the nature of the tree so that it takes the way of its kind . . . all *I* do is to avoid harming its growth – I have no power to make it grow.

His questioner then asked whether his philosophy also applied to government. Camel Guo replied cautiously that there might be some resemblance between the art of government and the art of growing trees. 'Wonderful', replied his questioner, 'The art I sought was of cultivating trees; the art I found was of cultivating men. Let this be passed on to all in office!'.[35]

Liu Zongyuan had reason to be critical of how those in office cultivated men. In 805 he was exiled for ten years to southern Hunan, and then from 815 until his early death he was posted as governor to Liuzhou in Guangxi. In his prose he described vividly the scenery of those remote areas, such as the limestone karst features of Liuzhou. Of the curiously-named Mountain of the Transcendents *Go*-game he wrote:

This mountain can be ascended from the west. There is a cavern at its top, and this cavern has screens, chambers, and eaves. Under these eaves there are figures formed from flowing stone, like lungs and livers, and like eggplants – sometimes heaped up below – and like men, like birds, like utensils and other objects, in great abundance.[36]

It was in the Tang period that a colloquial literature developed which was the beginnings of fiction and drama. This literary activity was centred on Chang'an and it took as its subject matter the activities of city-dwellers, dealing with them in realistic human terms. One pioneer in this genre was Bo Xingjian, the brother of Bo Juyi. Having passed the imperial examinations, he served in the capital as an officer in charge of foreign tributes. He wrote 'The Story of Miss Li', the tale of a rich young man who fell hopelessly in love with a young courtesan. Her mother, with her daughter's collusion, ruthlessly exploited the situation and relieved the young man of his fortune. Left penniless, he was forced to earn a living by singing dirges for an undertaker and then his father horsewhipped him for disgracing the family name. At that point Miss Li had a change of heart and encouraged the young man to return to his studies. He eventually achieved the highest success and was reconciled to his father, bringing the tale to a happy conclusion.

The origins of Chinese drama can be traced back to the Han dynasty, but it was only in the Tang period that dances, songs, sketches and acrobatics were combined into drama. An early dramatic form, widely performed from the ninth century, is known as the 'adjutant play'. It had as its recurrent theme the humiliation of an official for accepting bribes. The performance involved both actors and actresses, and included dialogue, singing, costume and make-up.[37]

ARCHITECTURE, SCULPTURE AND PAINTING

Although Chang'an was the greatest city of its age, it did not leave an architectural legacy comparable with that of Rome. Chang'an's buildings were of ephemeral construction, usually built of wood and hence vulnerable to fire. Other reasons explain why more durable buildings were not erected:

Chinese anthropocentrism did not encourage building for the ages or for eternity, and Buddhism – with its illusionist strain – perhaps reinforced this disposition. One should also note that no buildings in Chang'an were built from what we call 'civic pride'.[38]

Nevertheless a few remains of Tang architecture have survived; for example, the foundations of Taizong's palace in Chang'an have been excavated. Little is left of Tang

Buddhist temples, but some idea of their scale and character may be obtained from the Great Buddha Hall of the Todaiji at Nara in Japan, built in the Tang style and in the Tang period, which today is the largest wooden building in the world. Some masonry pagodas have survived, for example the much-altered Great Wild Goose Pagoda at Chang'an, which was climbed by the Japanese monk Ennin in 841. The pagoda derived from the Indian stupa, a Buddhist reliquary tower. In China most pagodas were constructed in wood, to a design resembling the Han timber towers known as *lou*. During the Tang period, the practice of building roofs with uplifted corners, derived from south-east Asia, gradually spread to north China. Applied to pagodas it produced elegant buildings, such as the pagoda at the Yakushiji at Nara which dates from the eighth century, and which was based on a Chinese model.

Both architecture and sculpture were heavily influenced by Buddhism and in both art forms ideas derived from India were to become sinicised. Mention has already been made of the sixth-century cave temples at Longmen, near Luoyang, and of the way in which the carvings there provide examples of how the Chinese tradition of linear pictorial expressions re-asserted itself. Under the Tang a more sophisticated cultural fusion was achieved. An example of this can be found in the sculptured figures of cave-shrines at Tianlongshan in southern Shanxi, carved in the reign of the Empress Wu. Of them it was said:

> In these figures the Indian feeling for solid, swelling form and the Chinese genius for expression in terms of linear rhythm are at last successfully fused and reconciled, to produce a style which was to become the basis of all later Buddhist sculpture in China.[39]

Painters of the Tang period are usually divided into figure painters and landscape painters. Of the former the first important figure is Yan Liben (*c.* 600–73), who was not only a painter but also a prominent official. The best surviving example of his work is a famous scroll depicting thirteen emperors, now in the Boston Museum of Fine Arts. Yan Liben's name is also associated with a series of murals on the walls of the tomb of Princess Yongtai, which was discovered in 1960 near Chang'an. The princess, the daughter of the Zhongzong emperor, was put to death by her grandmother, the Empress Wu. The tomb was built by her grieving father after the empress's death. The paintings, which depict serving girls, are now in poor condition, but of them it has been said that they 'bring us probably as close as we shall ever get to Tang courtly wall-painting as it approached its climax in the eighth century'.[40]

Wu Daozi (*c.* 700–60), who has been described as the Michelangelo of Tang China, is credited with having had the 'power to transform the essentially sculptured ideals of India into the linear, painterly, terms of the Chinese tradition'.[41] He painted with such whirlwind energy that crowds gathered to watch him as he worked. It was said of him:

Wu Daozi's figures remind one of sculpture. One can see them sideways and all round. His line-work consists of minute curves like rolled copper wire; however thickly his red or white paint is laid on, the structure of the forms and modelling of the flesh are never obscured.[42]

No original work by Wu Daozi has survived. However a stone engraving, *The Spirit of Hengyue*, the sacred mountain of the north, to be seen at a Daoist temple at Quyang in Hebei, may be taken as a faithful representation of a design by him. It shows a figure with long billowing hair and scarves and brandishing a spear, which is all energy and movement.[43]

Some court painters specialised in painting horses. The most famous of these in the Tang period was Han Gan (*c.* 715–81), who was summoned by the Xuanzong emperor to paint the imperial horse. Much of this painting, *Shining White of the Night*, which is in the Metropolitan Museum of Art, New York, is the work of a later restorer, who omitted to restore the tail. However, enough remains of the painting to enable the viewer to appreciate the energetic movement and to allow a comparison with Tang pottery figurines.

The Ming artist and art critic Dong Qichang (1555–1636), referring to landscape painting, made a celebrated division between landscape painters of the 'Northern' and 'Southern' Schools. Artists ascribed to the former school were largely professionals and court painters, and those to the latter school were amateurs and scholars. He traced this division back to the Tang period and identified as the founder of the second school the poet Wang Wei, who was said to have been the first painter to have painted landscapes in monochrome ink. No original painting of his has survived, but copies of a handscroll entitled *Clearing after a Snowfall along the River* may provide some idea of his technique. Of the 'Northern' school, Li Sixun (651–716) and his son Li Zhaodao (died about 735) are two of the best-known names. Their paintings were characterised by the use of malachite green and azurite blue. A famous example of this palette, *Minghuang's journey to Shu* attributed to Li Zhaodao, is said to depict the flight of the emperor from An Lushan's rebels in 756.

A notable development in the art of this period can be found in the work of painters such as Zhang Zao and Wang Mo, whose work anticipated that of twentieth-century action painters. The former was said to have painted with worn, blunt brushes, or to have used his fingers, and has therefore been described as the inventor of 'finger-painting'. Wang Mo spattered and splashed his ink onto silk. Such a technique accorded with Chan Buddhist ideas that enlightenment was an irrational experience arrived at through spontaneity and not by careful preparation. Another remarkable style was developed by the monk-painter Guanxiu (832–912), who painted a series of grotesque portraits of Buddhist saints.

DECORATIVE ARTS AND CERAMICS

Whereas Tang painting remained largely committed to Chinese subject matter and style, the decorative arts and ceramics showed clearly the strength of the links between China and the outside world. Chinese silk filled the bazaars of the Middle East, while at the same time Iranian craftsmen brought new weaving techniques to Chang'an. Remarkable examples of these fabrics have been preserved in the caves at Dunhuang on the Silk Road. A wide variety of gold and silver work was produced which likewise showed Middle-eastern influences. A major hoard discovered at Hejiacun near Xi'an included many foreign shapes. One gold bowl had its sides pressed out as lotus leaves; the traced ornament on it showed deer and birds in the Chinese tradition, but the beaded rim on the foot replicated a design used on Iranian silverware.[44]

During the Tang period a wide variety of ceramics was produced and polychrome glazes were developed. From the seventh century, in Hebei province, a high-quality white ware was made out of kaolinitic clay. At about the same time a development in the use of lead glazes led to the production of *sancai*, three-coloured pottery and figurines. Other advances included the production of ceramics decorated with underglaze painting and the perfection of the greenwares known in the West as celadon. The finest examples of this type of ceramics, called Yue ware, was manufactured in Zhejiang. The most coveted examples of it were those vessels which displayed the 'secret colour', that is a particular shade achieved in the glaze.[45]

An important category of Tang pottery was that of figurines and models made to be placed in tombs. These represented the wealth and status of the deceased and were intended to provide for his or her needs in the next world. In the first half of the eighth century enormous quantities of these were produced for tombs around Chang'an and Luoyang. The figurines were made in moulds and glazed with coloured glazes. A general who died at Luoyang in 728 was buried with figurines representing two earth spirits, two Buddhist guardian figures and two civil officials. At the entrance to his tomb were two horses, two camels and three grooms.[46] Other figurines represented foreigners, caricaturing their clothes, large noses and beards.

Porcelain may be defined as a type of ceramic where the clay has become completely fused, which transmits light, and which emits a ringing tone when struck. Several different types of ceramic produced during the Tang period may be described as porcelain. One of the earliest examples was Xing ware, developed in kilns in Hebei from the late sixth century. Another high-quality early porcelain came from Dingzhou likewise in Hebei, the forerunner of the famous Ding ware of the Song dynasty.

CHAPTER NINE

THE SONG DYNASTY

The political developments of the three hundred years after the fall of the Tang are complex, but the main events may be summarised as follows. The period from the fall of the Tang in 907 to the establishment of the Song in 960 is known as the period of the Five Dynasties and Ten Kingdoms. During that time part of northern China was ruled by the Qidan Liao dynasty. The rest of the country was divided into two, the northern part being ruled by a succession of five dynasties and the southern part being fragmented into ten regional states. In 960 a general from the fifth of the northern dynasties seized power and established the Song empire (also known as the Northern Song), which lasted until 1127. Initially Song rule extended over much of China Proper, with the exception of the territory of the Liao empire in the north and the Nanzhao kingdom in the southwest. From about 1038 the area of modern Gansu came under the control of the Tangut Xi Xia kingdom. By the early twelfth century the Liao empire was in decline and in 1122 it was overwhelmed by the Jurchen who established the Jin dynasty. The Jin expansion continued into the rest of northern China, finally stabilising north of the Huai river. The south of China remained under the control of the Song dynasty, now usually known as the Southern Song, with dates 1127 to 1279. Meanwhile, Qidan survivors of the Jurchen invasion had fled west to central Asia, and as the 'Black Qidan' had established the Western Liao dynasty, which lasted until 1211.

THE SIGNIFICANCE OF THE SONG PERIOD

The Tang period, at least until the rebellion of An Lushan, has commonly been regarded as a high point in the history of China. The Song period, however, has been the subject of conflicting verdicts. The traditional view of the period was that the arts of civilisation progressed, but the dynasty suffered from severe political and military weaknesses, for which China was to pay dearly, first with the loss of north China to the Jin and then, in the thirteenth century, with the loss of the entire country to the Mongols.

Some recent analyses have modified or rejected that view. The achievements of the period have been stressed and the age has been compared with the European Renaissance, emphasising the breadth of the changes taking place and their enduring quality. It has been claimed that it was under the Song that the features of Chinese society which were to last until modern times were established. An extensive debate has arisen over the reforms initiated by Wang Anshi in the middle of the eleventh century. This in turn has encouraged research into other aspects of Song society: the evolution of the civil service and the operation of the examination system; social changes and in particular the rise of the gentry; and the economic advances made in this period. At the same time the appreciation of the Song intellectual and cultural achievement has continued.

THE FIVE DYNASTIES AND TEN KINGDOMS

Many historians have noted that whereas after the fall of the Later Han dynasty China experienced nearly four centuries of division, after the fall of the Tang the division only lasted for half a century. This difference has been attributed to the strengthening of the traditions and techniques of centralised rule under the Tang. China would never again be divided into competing political units for even so long as half a century.[1]

In political terms the disintegration of China did not imply a sharp break with the past. The northern dynasties all aspired to reunite China and by 959 the Later Zhou had already brought much of north China back under a single ruler. Moreover the changes of dynasty amounted only to changes in the ruling family. The ruling élite remained unaltered and the civil service continued the routine tasks of government without serious disruption. In the south, in several of the Ten Kingdoms, the same continuity was evident, with the examination system still operating.[2]

Nevertheless the traditional assumption that the Song dynasty merely re-established the Tang system with a few modifications has been firmly rejected. According to an important study by Wang Gungwu key changes took place during the Five Dynasties period which amounted to the creation of a new structure of power. A new central government was formed which incorporated the basic features of the system of military governors, which had emerged in the latter part of the Tang period. The emperors of the Five Dynasties were themselves former military governors. They modelled their courts on their provincial governments, using their retainers as palace commissioners. The governor's private army was transformed into the Emperor's Army and a palace corps created to counter any threat from that army. It was on this platform that the early Northern Song emperors were able to assert control over the central institutions of the state preparatory to conquering the independent states of the south.[3]

The period of division was also one of economic growth and technical innovation, particularly in the south. Perhaps even as a consequence of the relaxation of central control, the small states of the south made rapid progress in terms of commerce. There was an expansion of the trade in tea and the production of ceramics. The shortage of copper, the standard metallic currency, led to the use of other metals including lead and iron and the introduction of 'flying money', the forerunner of a paper currency.

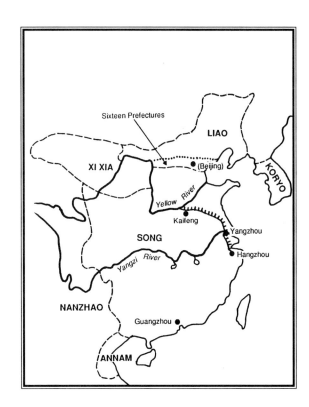

18 *China under the Song, c. 1050*

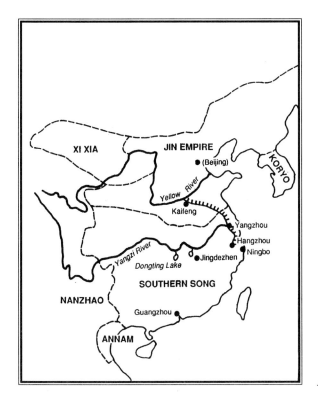

19 *China under the Southern Song and the Jin, c. 1140*

20 The Emperor Huizong (reigned 1101–25), The Five-Colored Parakeet on Blossoming Apricot Tree; *handscroll, Northern Song dynasty*

21 Confucian temple at Suzhou

THE ESTABLISHMENT OF THE SONG DYNASTY

Zhao Kuangyin, a military leader under the Later Zhou dynasty, seized power through a coup in 960. He is known as Taizu, the founder of the Song dynasty. In a restrained and methodical manner, he proceeded to consolidate and extend his control. After half a century of warlordism, his first task was prevent any further military coups. He achieved this by persuading his commanders to retire or to accept minor posts, by creating a professional army loyal to the dynasty and by asserting central government authority over the regional commanders. For the rest of his reign he concentrated on winning over the independent states of the south, with such success that when he died in 976 China Proper, apart from Zhejiang, Shanxi, Nanzhao and the area ruled by the Qidan, had come under Song control. Ever cautious, Taizu did not attempt to challenge the Qidan and even less was he interested in recovering the Tang empire in central Asia. He was succeeded by his brother, the Taizong emperor, who obtained the submission of the regimes in Zhejiang and Shanxi, and received tribute from the Xi Xia kingdom. He then attempted to expel the Qidan, but after two unsuccessful campaigns was forced to make peace and to promise to hand over large quantities of silk and silver in annual payments. So ended the expansive stage of the Song empire, which henceforth relied on a defensive strategy in its dealings with the outside world. Unlike the Tang, the Song empire could never claim to be an universal empire, for even in its dealings with the Qidan, relations were conducted on a basis of equality.

In the meantime the first two Song rulers had taken important steps to strengthen the administration. As rulers of a new dynasty they had the opportunity to innovate and their actions have been seen as having led to an unprecedented accumulation of power in the emperor's own hands. For their capital they chose Kaifeng on the Grand Canal and there they established the organs of government. In many respects these continued the practices of the Tang, but there were some significant changes. As mentioned previously Taizu had managed to assert control over the military, and this was institutionalised by putting military affairs into the hands of the privy council. The chief administrative body was the secretariat-chancellery, which combined two bodies which had been separate under the Tang. Both privy council and secretariat-chancellery were under the personal control of the emperor and his autocratic position was further strengthened by the development of the Censorate, the officers of which kept him informed of complaints. There was considerable overlap between the powers and responsibilities of the various administrative bodies. This arose in part from the emperor's reluctance to carry out too sweeping a rationalisation, but it also served as another means of increasing his personal power.

Supporting these developments were important changes in the recruitment to the bureaucracy and the operation of the examination system. These are connected with what have been seen as key transformations occurring in the late Tang and early Song periods: the subordination of the military to the civil authority and the replacement of aristocratic power with something akin to a meritocracy. Both these aspects of the Song state have been subject to considerable study and more should be said about them.

The development of the bureaucracy was of course based on earlier achievements. Under the Han dynasty a civil service had existed, which had been selected through the use of examinations and which had developed fixed procedures. Under the Tang these processes had been much developed and the system of selection through examinations greatly expanded. Officials were ranked in grades which determined their salaries, and their efficiency in office was subject to regular assessment. Nevertheless it was only under the Song dynasty that these developments reached maturity. Methods of recruitment, appointment and control of civil servants were refined and scholar-officials (*dushu ren*, literally 'persons who read books'), who owed their position entirely to the operation of this system rather than to any hereditary claim to status, administered the country. Through this development 'Confucian China evolved much that has entered the common heritage of personnel administration in the modern state'.[4]

The most important method of recruitment to the civil service lay through the examination system. Under the Song, examinations were held at two levels, the prefectural examination and the metropolitan examination, the latter being followed by a palace examination under the personal supervision of the emperor. At the beginning of the Song period a variety of degrees was awarded to successful candidates, but later the only degree awarded at the scheduled examinations was that of *jinshi*, the doctorate of letters. A number of other significant innovations were made in the early Song period. Under Taizong there was a sharp increase in the number of degrees awarded and this in turn led to an increase in the number of candidates. To cope with this expansion the examination arrangements were overhauled: rules relating to the eligibility of candidates were introduced, certain occupations – for example having been previously a Buddhist or Daoist priest, or having been an artisan, merchant or clerk – were defined as a bar to candidature; residency requirements were enforced to ensure that candidates only took the examinations in their home prefectures; candidates were required to provide evidence of satisfactory character; quotas were established for the number of successful candidates at the prefectural level; and in the examinations measures were taken to ensure the anonymity of candidates' scripts.[5]

Accompanying the expansion of the examination system there was a major growth in the educational provision. Although officially-supported government schools had existed under the Tang, the decline of the dynasty had led to education at local level being much neglected. Early in the eleventh century local officials began to establish new schools. Taking advantage of the spread of printing, these schools were provided with a set of the classics and endowed with a Confucian temple and a piece of land. The Imperial University at Kaifeng continued and expanded the opportunities for higher education which had been available under the Tang. The requirement that it should only provide education for the sons of officials was relaxed. Students of the university received free board and lodging and were exempted from having to take the preliminary prefectural examinations.[6]

The examination system, and the education system which underpinned it, served to provide candidates for the civil service. However, it was not the only source of supply of candidates, for in the Song period it was balanced by the *yin* privilege, or protection system. This allowed certain high officials to nominate members of their family for entry into the civil service. Candidates who availed themselves of this opportunity had to take a placement examination, but this was nevertheless a relatively easy way of entering the service. The protection system supplied over half the successful candidates.

These channels of recruitment produced far more men qualified for office than there were posts available. To deal with this situation, and to ensure control over the bureaucracy, various strategies were adopted. The most important of these was the commission system under which officials were assigned to particular posts for a set period, usually three or four years. As reassignment to the same post was not permitted, this system ensured that an official could not build up a local following. A further check was the 'law of avoidance', which prohibited an official from service in his home prefecture. Yet another control was exercised through sponsorship, a term used to denote the privilege granted to senior officials of sponsoring persons known to them to particular appointments. As these officials were held responsible for the performance of their nominee in office, this has been regarded as an effective way of raising the standards of public service.[7]

The most disputed issue in relation to the examination system and the operation of the bureaucracy is how far it offered a career open to talent. The case for the existence of a meritocracy is perhaps best supported by reference to the early Song period. According to John W. Chaffee, 'By expanding degree numbers, adding a formal prefectural examination, introducing such procedures as covered names and copied examinations, and, under Renzong, promoting education, the early emperors were really trying to create a meritocratic state.'[8]

To what extent did they succeed? Before answering that question one must first note the conflict between the Confucian stress on human virtue and the state's practical need to recruit men of ability. Under the Song there was an attempt to recruit a civil service which had both these qualities. Genuine attempts were made to ensure the impartiality of the examinations, which certainly tested ability, albeit within a restricted range of skills. The importance of virtue was recognised in the sponsorship system and it was not entirely vitiated by the protection system. The latter arrangement, which allowed officials to enable their sons to follow them into the bureaucracy, thus preserving a hereditary practice, also provided officials with a powerful incentive to commit themselves unreservedly to the emperor's service.

There is some evidence to show that candidates from poor backgrounds did have a chance of succeeding in the examination system and of obtaining official appointment.

One study of the family background of prominent officials shows that between 998 and 1126 47.3 per cent of these officials came from families categorised as poor. The very existence of the system promoted the idea of equal opportunity, but it has been pointed out that 'To have about 7,905 (47.3 per cent of a bureaucracy of about 15,000 civil bureaucrats) prominent officials coming from a commoner background in a nation of about one hundred million people is not a specially remarkable achievement'.[9]

REFORM IN SONG CHINA

Far from being complacent about the state of the empire, a number of Song scholars and officials were acutely aware that the previous dynasty had collapsed and that their own dynasty had failed to incorporate the whole of China under its rule. Moreover, in their eyes, the country seemed plagued by certain chronic weaknesses: the concentration of landholding in the hands of people who avoided taxation; the suspect quality of the bureaucracy; the ineffectiveness and expense of the military forces. These concerns led them to make proposals on how the empire might be preserved. For example, in 1039 the writer and teacher Li Gou produced a work entitled 'Thirty plans for enriching the country, strengthening military power, and satisfying the needs of the people'.[10] In 1043–4 Fan Zhongyan, a celebrated scholar and statesman, proposed a ten-point programme of reform which aimed at eliminating entrenched bureaucrats, official favouritism and nepotism, and which proposed examination reform, the establishment of a national school system, land reclamation and the creation of a local militia. Fan was ousted before most of this programme could be attempted, but his proposal for a national school system was followed up and his suggestion for preserving the anonymity of candidates' scripts in examinations was acted upon.

For a reform programme to succeed, it needed an organised body to promote it. However the tradition of Confucian government did not allow officials to form factions or parties. This dilemma led Ouyang Xiu (1007–72), a leading official and one of China's best-known literary figures, to present a famous memorial *On Factions* in which he wrote:

Your servant is aware that from ancient times there have been discussions of the worth of parties. It is only to be hoped that a ruler will distinguish between those of gentlemen and those of inferior men. In general, gentlemen join with other gentlemen in parties because of common principles, while inferior men join with other inferior men for reasons of common profit.

However Ouyang Xiu's defence of factions, which may have owed more to a desire to encourage reform than to a belief in the right to dissent, did not gain acceptance, either in his day or subsequently. Under a system of government in which the emperor had absolute power, political opposition remained indistinguishable from disloyalty.[11]

The reform proposals which have attracted by far the most attention, and which have excited by far the most controversy, were those put forward by Wang Anshi during the reign of the Shenzong emperor, who reigned from 1068 to 1085. Wang Anshi (1021–86), who came from the same part of Jiangxi as did Li Gou, and who was a former protégé of Fan Zhongyan, had occupied several official positions and had experience of practical affairs. In 1058, in a document known as the *Ten Thousand Word Memorial*, he first praised the diligence, humanity and judgment of the emperor. He continued:

> We should expect, therefore, that the needs of every household and man would be filled and that the empire would enjoy a state of perfect order. And yet this result has not been attained. Within the empire the security of the state is a cause for some anxiety, and on our borders there is the constant threat of the barbarians. Day by day the resources of the nation become more depleted and exhausted, while the moral tone and habits of life among the people daily deteriorate.[12]

For Wang Anshi, the way to remedy this situation was a truism of Confucian thought: it was to secure capable men, to assess what should be done and to change the laws to bring them back in line with the ideas of the ancient kings. In a manner typical of radical reformers, he cited Mencius as his authority, yet he broke with precedent by suggesting that the emperor should adopt a proactive role and that officials should have special qualifications rather than be generalists.

In 1068 Wang Anshi was summoned to take over the post of chief minister, which he occupied until 1076 when he was ousted by the conservatives, and which he re-occupied from 1078 until 1085. It was in the early years of his first period of office that he promoted his famous reform programme known as the New Laws or New Policies. These reforms can be summarised under three headings: taxation and the economy, security and military affairs, and the administration.

On taxation Wang's views sounded remarkably modern:

> The deficit of the government nowadays is not due to excessive expenditures alone, but also to the lack of ways to increase incomes. Those who wish to enrich their families merely take from the state; those who wish to enrich the state merely take from the country; and those who wish to enrich the country merely take from natural resources.[13]

Wang's solution was to rationalise taxation, and to try to help the people become more productive. He sought to reduce the concentration of land in the hands of landlords by offering state farming loans to enable farmers to avoid falling into debt. He introduced other innovative measures to improve the state finances, including a tribute and distribution scheme, under which a procurement office was established at Yangzhou. This office replaced the system of collecting tribute in kind, instead buying such goods as the court required in the cheapest market. Another measure, the hired services system, replaced labour services, which had often been evaded by wealthy families, with a graduated tax.

With reference to security and military affairs, Wang's aim was to provide for the state's defence while at the same time reducing the cost to the state of an army of over a million men. His name is associated with the introduction, or rather the revival and improvement, of the system of collective security known as the *baojia*. Able-bodied men from groups of ten households (the *bao*) were to enforce law and order in the neighbourhood and also were eligible to be trained as a militia. At the same time a horse-breeding scheme was set up to enable militia families in the frontier regions to be provided with a horse and fodder.

In his memorial Wang Anshi had stressed the importance of securing capable men for the service of the state. A key objective was to raise the moral status of candidates, and several of his reforms were intended to achieve this. He reorganised the Imperial University, introducing the Three-Hall system, which required students to go through classes before gaining exemptions in the examinations. The apparent purpose of this was to encourage the promotion of candidates of good character rather than those who merely showed cleverness in the examinations. He introduced reforms in the examinations themselves, replacing traditional tests of memory and of formal composition with an essay on the 'general meaning' of the Confucian classics, and with exercises connected to the practical tasks of government. In support of this, he himself wrote commentaries on the classics. In addition he passed regulations placing government clerks on fixed salaries and under strict supervision.

Wang's New Policies were immediately criticised and his reputation ever since has been the subject of controversy. Before his reform programme had even been implemented a member of the censorate attempted to impeach Wang on counts of being overbearing and exceeding his authority. The famous poet and painter Su Dongpo, who at first had been a supporter of reform, later criticised the fiscal reforms and in particular the introduction of state crop loans. He was particularly alarmed by the commission set up by Wang:

Six or seven young men are made to discuss fiscal policies day and night within the bureau, while more than forty aides are sent out to explore the situation. The vast scale of their initial operations has made people frightened and suspicious; the strangeness of the new laws adopted has made officials fearful and puzzled.[14]

Even more damaging was the opposition from the distinguished scholar and statesman Sima Guang. In 1070 he left office because of his disagreement with the New Policies and later wrote memorials calling for their abolition. He was particularly incensed by the hired services system, the *baojia* arrangement, and the establishment of general commanderies which excluded civilian control over army administration. But the emphasis of his criticism, which has echoed down the centuries, was on Wang's character:

> He was self-satisfied and self-opinionated, considering himself without equal among the men of the past and present. He did not know how to select what was best in the laws and institutions of the imperial ancestors and to bring together the happiest proposals put forth throughout the empire. . . . All he wanted was to satisfy his own ambitions, without regard to the best interests of the nation.[15]

Sima Guang was instrumental in bringing about the repeal of many of the New Policies, and the apparent rejection of the proactive style of government which they implied. In fact a number of the proposals – for example the *baojia*, the militia system and the changes in the examinations – were later to be revived and implemented. Wang's reputation was partly restored in the following century by the famous philosopher Zhu Xi. He argued that the need for reform had been widely accepted and that it was only when the reforms provoked criticism that Wang Anshi had become obdurate, rejecting advice and forcing his policies through. Nevertheless it was Sima Guang's condemnation of Wang's character and motives which set the tone for Confucian scholars for generations to come.

In modern times the debate over Wang Anshi has centred on the motivation for and practicality of his reforms. The re-evaluation began in the nineteenth century and was developed early this century by John C. Ferguson who described Wang as a utilitarian, but one who had the interests of the people at heart.[16] Wang's relevance to modern times was picked up by the famous scholar Liang Qichao, who emphasised Wang's far-sightedness and the resemblance of his New Policies to modern ideals.[17] The practicality of his reforms was investigated in the 1930s by H.R. Williamson. He argued that the need for reform was pressing and that the measures conceived by Wang Anshi were intended to relieve the poorer classes and to share the tax burden more equitably. The criticism which greeted the reforms was not because they were inappropriate, but because they attacked the interests of the better off. This line was pursued in Marxist interpretations of Wang, who was described as a man of the bureaucrat-landlord class, whereas his opponents, such as Sima Guang, came from the powerful gentry and big landlord class. His reforms were supported by the dynasty because they offered a solution to two problems: the foreign threat and the danger of a peasant uprising. The remedy he proposed was to implement policies which would contain peasant discontent by winning the support of the middle and small landlord class. His reforms were seen by the powerful gentry and big landlords as an attack on their interests and were consequently frustrated by them.[18]

More recent interpretations have discussed other issues. For the Japanese scholar Ichisada Miyazaki, Wang Anshi's reforms fell into two categories. Some, for example the crop loans, were first-aid measures dealing with social and economic changes; others, especially the *baojia* and the hired-services system, sought to make fundamental social changes. For Miyazaki these reforms related to the major social transition occurring at this time, that is the evolution from an aristocratic to an autocratic society. The reforms were progressive, and may have served to prolong the existence of the Northern Song until 1126 rather than to have advanced its fall.[19] For James T.C. Liu, Wang Anshi was 'a bureaucratic idealist who upheld the ideal of a professionally well-trained and administratively well-controlled bureaucracy as the principal instrument for the realization of a Confucian moral society'. His reforms were not intended to further the interests of a social class, but to improve the performance of the bureaucratic state; they failed because he did not have the support of the bureaucrats themselves and because the system of bureaucratic government was being undermined by the growth of absolutism.[20] Recently Ray Huang has returned to the question of the practicability of the reforms and has concluded that they were premature, in that the attempt to institutionalise monetary management of state affairs was bound to run into insuperable difficulties, because the nation's economic organisation had not yet reached that level of integration which would make such management possible.[21]

THE DECLINE OF THE NORTHERN SONG AND THE RISE OF THE JIN DYNASTY

The reform period extended until the death of the Shenzong emperor in 1086, whereupon a reaction ensued, initially led by Sima Guang. In 1093 the Zhezong emperor came to the throne, and appointed to office Cai Jing, brother of Wang Anshi's son-in-law. He revived the New Policies and extended them to fresh areas and at the same time carried out a witch-hunt against the conservatives. This alternation between reform and conservatism weakened the dynasty. Blame for that decline has also been heaped personally on Cai Jing, who remained in power until 1125. He was said to have pursued his political opponents vindictively, to have tolerated the growth of corruption, and to have encouraged the Huizong emperor to neglect his duties in favour of artistic pursuits.

A further indication of dynastic decline was the rise of peasant rebellion, which may be attributed to various factors, including the increasing concentration of landownership, the mounting burden of tax and the effect of oppressive government measures. The best-known of the rebellions was that headed by Fang La which broke out in Fujian and Zhejiang in 1120. In these revolts the leaders were often men of some wealth who appeared to be supporting the cause of social justice. Fang La was the owner of a plantation of lacquer trees, who turned against the government because of the heaviness of the levies he was required to pay. It is for this reason that the revolts became the basis of the most famous of Chinese novels, *Shuihu zhuan*, known in the West under the titles *Water Margin* and *All Men Are Brothers*. The Fang La rebellion also had a connection with Manichaeism which had survived in this area. It caused great loss of life, said in one source to have amounted to one million dead.[22]

The most important threat to the dynasty was the rise of the Jurchen in the north. When the dynasty had been founded, the Qidan Liao empire extended to include sixteen prefectures in north China. Despite the efforts of the second Song emperor to dislodge them, the Qidan had retained their position, receiving annual tribute from China and developing a dualistic form of government.[23] As time passed the Qidan ceased to present a danger to the Song dynasty. Their population was very small and in the Chinese part of their empire they were in a minority. Moreover as time went on they became increasingly sinicised.

In turn the Liao dynasty fell under threat. The danger came from the Jurchen,[24] a semi-nomadic Tungusic people ancestral to the Manchus, who appeared in eastern Manchuria in the tenth century. Like the Qidan they came from the marginal zone, between the open steppe and the settled areas. Although their favourite pursuit was hunting and they were all skilled horsemen, they also practised agriculture, raised pigs and had small walled towns. Their social organisation was tribal, the basic organisational unit being the lineage, occupying a lineage village. Every adult male was a potential soldier and a body of Jurchen cavalry was a formidable force.[25]

In the tenth century the Jurchen had been subdued by the Qidan and subsequently they had paid tribute to both the Liao and Northern Song dynasties. Part of that tribute had been paid in horses and the development of the horse trade was to have a major role in the rise of the Jurchen. By the twelfth century the Jurchen had adopted metal weapons and had developed the use of horses in warfare. A political struggle among the Jurchen clans resulted in the supremacy of the Wanyan clan. After a period of fighting against Koryo, the dynasty ruling Korea, the Jurchen turned their attention to the Qidan. In 1112 the Liao emperor visited northern Manchuria and gave a feast for the Jurchen at which Aguda, leader of the Wanyan clan refused to perform a tribal dance. This refusal led to the breakdown of relations between Jurchen and Qidan. In 1114 Aguda proclaimed himself emperor of the Jin state and began a campaign against the Liao empire, which had already been weakened by internal dissension. Ill-advisedly the Northern Song added its support to the Qidan, yet within six years the Liao empire collapsed.

In a treaty agreed in 1120, Liao territories were divided between the Jurchen Jin dynasty and the Northern Song. However, the Song court persisted in trying to recover the lost Sixteen Prefectures and various acts of bad faith led to the Jurchen invading China in 1125. By now they had developed formidable military skills. Their mounted horsemen wore heavy armour and sometimes several horses were chained together to form a horse team. They had developed war machines for attacking walled cities and later they pioneered the use of firearms. They also made astute use of collaborators who joined them in the hope of securing a share of the booty. Against this power the Northern Song was outmatched. In 1126, after a protracted siege, the Jurchen captured the capital Kaifeng, and the Huizong emperor and his son were carried off to Manchuria, so ending the Northen Song dynasty. In the years that followed the Jurchen continued to press southwards and it seemed as if only the Yangzi river would block their further advance, for at first the Jurchen had no capability for fighting on water and they were repulsed by the Southern Song fleet. Later the Yangzi was crossed and the Jurchen penetrated as far south as Hangzhou and Ningbo, but a combination of factors – the death of the Jin emperor and the unsuitability of the terrain for the Jurchen cavalry – led to a withdrawal. In 1141 peace was agreed between the Jin and Southern Song, leaving the Jurchen as rulers of most of China north of the Yangzi and the Song as rulers of the south. In addition the Southern Song agreed to pay an annual tribute of 200,000 taels of silver and 200,000 bolts of silk.

THE JIN DYNASTY, 1115–1234

The Jurchen Jin dynasty ruled over much of northern China until it was destroyed by the Mongols in 1234. Its record is a striking example of the problems of non-Chinese rule. It may be compared with that of the Qidan before them and that of the Mongols and Manchus who were to follow in their footsteps. The history of the dynasty may be divided into three stages: a period of dualism from 1115 to 1142, a period of increasing sinicisation until 1215, and a final period of decline.

In the first period the dynasty sought ways of ruling a Chinese population numbering perhaps forty million. Its first stratagem was a form of dualism reminiscent of that used by the Qidan. In Jurchen territory north of the Great Wall tribal administration was retained. In the south Jurchen tribal units were stationed at strategic points, where they cultivated the land and kept a watch over the conquered peoples. There was little benevolence towards either the surviving Qidan or the indigenous population at this early stage. Many Chinese were killed when uprisings were suppressed and perhaps 100,000 Chinese were forcibly resettled in Manchuria. Nevertheless Qidan and Chinese were employed in administrative and military capacities. At the Jin southern capital, Chinese scholars were employed to write proclamations and in 1126 the Chinese bureaucratic system was adopted. Yet further south, in the regions bordering the territory of the Southern Song, the Jurchen tried to set up puppet regimes. In one such state, situated between the Yangzi and Huai rivers, Jurchen generals briefly attempted a Jurchenising movement, forbidding the Chinese to wear native dress and ordering them to cut their hair in the Jurchen style.[26]

From 1142 there was a twenty-year period of peaceful co-existence between the north and the south. During that time many Jurchen moved into China, and were given grants of land and a privileged tax position. Jurchen continued to monopolise military authority and to retain a majority of senior political positions. Nevertheless it was in this period that the Jurchen increasingly adopted Chinese institutions and customs. Hailing, the emperor who ruled from 1150 to 1161, established his central capital at what is now Beijing. He was proud of his knowledge of the Chinese classics and had ambitions to establish a legitimate Confucian dynasty extending over the whole of China. At the same time he ordered the brutal murder of Jurchen nobles who might challenge his claim to the throne which he had usurped, and he planned to conquer the south. He launched the attack in 1161, suffered a reverse, and was assassinated.

His successor Shizong, who reigned 1161–90, ostensibly rejected the sinicisation policies of his predecessor and in some respects attempted to restore the old Jurchen way of life. He made hunting an annual royal activity and encouraged all forms of military exercises. He took several steps to promote Jurchen learning and in 1188 prohibited the Jurchen from wearing Chinese dress. However this nativistic movement did not succeed, in part because it was poorly planned and inconsistent. Shizong's concern for hunting ran contrary to his encouragement to Jurchen to take up farming. The Jurchen language was already dying out when he ordered that the Chinese classics be translated into Jurchen. The policy of centralisation which he continued accelerated rather than fended off sinicisation, and the adoption of the Chinese practice relating to succession was a rejection of Jurchen tribal custom.

So it was not surprising that under his successor Zhangzong further sinicising changes took place. A legal code based on that of the Tang was adopted. In 1191 the ban on intermarriage between Jurchen and Chinese, which had been flouted by both rulers and officials, was rescinded. A final indication of the sinicisation of the dynasty was the prolonged discussion of the appropriate dynastic element, the choice placing the Jin in the line of the legitimate dynasties of China.

A number of events combined to weaken the dynasty. In 1194 the Yellow river shifted to its southern course, causing immense damage. In 1206 the Southern Song minister Han Tuozhou, in an attempt to divert attention from his difficulties at court, declared war on the Jin. The campaign was unsuccessful and Han Tuozhou paid for his rashness with his life. Nevertheless the campaign hampered the Jin efforts against the Mongol threat in Manchuria. At the very moment that the Mongols made their first attacks on China, a succession dispute further weakened the dynasty. By 1215 the Jin had lost Manchuria and much of China north of the Yellow river. There was a pause in the Mongol attacks and a further respite followed the death of Genghis khan in 1227. But in 1230 the new khan Ögödei launched a full-scale attack against the remnants of the Jin empire. Kaifeng, the capital since 1214, was captured by the Mongols after a year-long siege in which both sides used firearms, and in 1234 the dynasty was finally extinguished.[27]

Whatever one might conclude about the reasons for the fall of the Jin dynasty, that of rejection by the majority Chinese population should not be included. Both Chinese and Jurchen defended Kaifeng and it was Chinese who provided the expertise to devise a rocket or flamethrower to use against the invaders. The Jin state was destroyed by the Mongols, with the misguided assistance of the Southern Song. Nevertheless internal weaknesses played their part in this defeat. The sinicisation process had gravely weakened the military capacity of the Jurchen. Paradoxically it could be said that this sinicisation had not gone far enough, for the Jurchen remained an alien minority which had failed to employ to the full the abilities of Chinese scholar-officials to create a durable state.[28]

THE SOUTHERN SONG, 1127–1279

Political developments

Resistance in south China rallied around a younger son of the Huizong emperor, known by his posthumous title Gaozong. He chose to make his capital at Hangzhou, a defensible site which was also at the commercial centre of the new empire. He carried out an internal pacification which eventually brought the whole of southern China, including Sichuan, under Song control. The tactic that he adopted was that of *zhaoan*, meaning 'summoning to pacification'. Leaders of rebel bands were offered the opportunity to come over to the Song side and their soldiers were allowed to join the imperial army. If they did not take up the offer they were liable to be attacked by the pro-government forces. This tactic was employed very effectively by Yue Fei, a young soldier from a humble background, who outwitted the largest of the armed bands which operated around the Dongting lake in Hunan.

However, to achieve a permanent peace it was necessary to come to agreement with the Jurchen. The peace settlement of 1141 was a humiliating affair, for not only did it require the payment of tribute, but also the admission that the Song was a vassal state. It is also remembered for a celebrated confrontation between the advocates of patriotic resistance and those who endorsed a settlement with the invaders. The patriotic cause was represented by Yue Fei who had led several successful campaigns against the Jurchen and who in 1140 had fought his way north to near Kaifeng. He now proposed another attack on Jurchen-held territory. The proposal was rejected by the emperor's chief councillor, Qin Gui, who was already in negotiation with the Jurchen. Yue Fei was arrested on a trumped-up charge and put to death in prison. For this act Qin Gui became one of the most celebrated villains in Chinese history, while Yue Fei came to personify the patriot who puts loyalty to his country before his duty of obedience to his ruler. A poem entitled *Redness All Across the River* was engraved on his tomb. Its words were used in a song which was popular during the Second World War:

> My fierce ambition is to feed upon the flesh of the Huns,
> And, laughing, I thirst for the blood of the Barbarians.
> Oh, let everything begin afresh.
> Let all the rivers and mountains be recovered,
> Before we pay our respect once more to the Emperor.[29]

Gaozong's use of Qin Gui in the peace negotiations was indicative of a pattern of relations between ruler and bureaucracy that was to become typical under the Southern Song. The emperor did not supervise the bureaucracy personally - that was the task of his ministers, and in particular of those who served as his chief councillors. Early in his reign there were often two councillors, who served for short terms in office. From 1139, with the appointment of Qin Gui, the more common arrangement was for there to be a single chief councillor who wielded autocratic power for and on behalf of the emperor. It was Qin Gui who conducted the peace negotiations and who then began to tighten his grip on the government. He dealt with any criticism by arranging for his opponents to be denounced by the *yanguan* or 'opinion officials.[30] At the same time he built up his own power base through nepotism. Such a record suggests a selfish pursuit of power, but it must be added that in the twenty years that followed making peace with the Jurchen, the Southern Song enjoyed political stability and economic growth. Some of this at least should be credited to Qin Gui, although after his death in 1155 Gaozong was quick to blame his minister for any shortcomings that had occurred.

In 1162 Gaozong abdicated in favour of his son Xiaozong although he remained the power behind the throne until his death. In the previous year war had been renewed with the Jurchen. The campaign ended in a stalemate without any recovery of lost territory, but under the peace treaty of 1165 the obnoxious reference to the Southern Song as a vassal state was removed. Until his father's death in 1187 Xiaozong performed his duties conscientiously, but he then he fell into a deep depression and decided to abdicate. That moment marked the beginning of a decisive decline in imperial leadership, for all subsequent emperors showed signs of mental illness or of an inability to perform their duties effectively. As a consequence, in the later years of the dynasty, chief councillors played a key role in government .

The epithet of the Ningzong emperor, who reigned 1194–1224, was 'the tranquil' and of him it has been said that he 'may well represent the most unopinionated and passive emperor of the entire dynasty'.[31] Throughout his long reign two ministers controlled the emperor and the court. The first of these was Han Tuozhou, the nephew of Gaozong's empress, a man without an examination degree, who had first served as supervisor of the Palace Postern, a post which gave him control over access to the throne. Han Tuozhou had close ties with the eunuchs and poor relations with the civil service, who regarded him as unworthy of high office. From 1197 'he reigned as undisputed decision maker at court, the sole formulator of government policy, arbiter of bureaucratic disputes, and shepherd of official advancement'.[32] Such an accumulation of power was bound to lead to his over-reaching himself. He carried out a highly controversial purge of scholar-officials associated with Neo-Confucianist teaching. It may have been the hostility which this evoked which in 1206 prompted him to make his next rash move, an attack on the Jurchen. His plans went badly wrong, for one of his military commanders changed sides and a series of military defeats followed. In November 1207, after recriminations at court, Han Tuozhou was bludgeoned to death by palace guardsmen just outside the walls of the imperial palace. Nobody in authority admitted responsibility for this deed which was probably done on orders from the empress and with the tacit assent of the emperor. Han Tuozhou's end was unprecedented. Confucian propriety recognised the right to express an opinion. A discredited minister might be dismissed, or sent into exile, but not murdered, and it was for this reason that there was no admission of the court's involvement.

The second long-serving councillor was Shi Miyuan, who dominated the court for twenty-five years from 1208. The Shi family came from Ningbo, rising from comparative obscurity under the Northern Song to remarkable prominence under the Southern Song, when it provided three successive generations of chief councillors, only to return to obscurity after the dynasty's collapse. Shi Miyuan was the second of these councillors. He began his tenure of office by reversing the war policy of Han Tuozhou, making a humiliating peace with the Jurchen, the conditions of which included the sending of Han Tuozhou's head to the enemy as a war trophy. He also rescinded the ban on Neo-Confucian teaching. He then took steps to eliminate rivals and consolidate his position, steps which might be criticised as overbearing, but which fell within the expected pattern of behaviour of a chief councillor. However, in 1224, the Ningzong emperor died and Shi Miyuan set aside Zhao Hong, the elder adopted prince, in favour of the younger one who took the throne as the Lizong emperor. Subsequently Zhao Hong was implicated in a rebellion and forced to commit suicide. For this Shi Miyuan was accused of having procured an usurpation followed by a political murder. The subsequent controversy polarised the court and inhibited the development of a policy towards the alarming encroachment of the Mongols on the Jin empire. Nevertheless Shi Miyuan remained in office until his death in 1233, exercising his skill in political manipulation and his caution in handling foreign affairs.

The fourth, and by far the most notorious, of the long-serving chief councillors of the Southern Song period was Jia Sidao. He has been execrated as the archetypal 'bad last minister', the person chiefly responsible for the fall of the Song dynasty. This view, which is that of traditional historiography, has been challenged in modern times.

Jia Sidao (1213–75), who came from a family of medium-grade military officials, first gained office after his sister had entered the Lizong emperor's harem. He earned a reputation for being licentious and also for having a fascination for fighting crickets, a subject on which he wrote a treatise. However he was by no means a mere dilettante. Before appointment to high office in 1259 he had spent twenty years in various provincial and metropolitan posts, where he had gained financial and administrative experience. As chief councillor he carried out several reforms suggestive of a desire to improve standards of government: he took steps to curb the influence of the eunuchs and instituted a system of public letter-boxes where people could place complaints.[33]

However, it was not for his domestic actions that he was to be excoriated, but for his conduct of foreign affairs. In 1234 the Jin dynasty had been crushed by the Mongols, with the assistance of the Southern Song. Soon afterwards the Song found itself defending the rest of China with increasing desperation. In 1251 the Mongol hordes swept through Yunnan as far as the borders of Vietnam. In short, the threat to the dynasty was already very serious when Jia Sidao was appointed chief councillor. The accusation levelled against him was that in 1259, after he had falsely claimed to have gained victories against the Mongols, he negotiated a secret agreement with them in which, in return for a Mongol withdrawal, he promised to make the Yangzi the frontier and for the Song to pay them an annual tribute. This particular accusation has been convincingly refuted – Jia Sidao may have attempted to negotiate, but no agreement was reached. The subsequent decision of the Mongols to retire had nothing to do with the negotiation but was a consequence of the death of the Great Khan Möngke and the need to convoke an assembly to choose his successor.[34] To blame Jia Sidao for the Mongol overthrow of the empire would seem unreasonable, indeed it might be argued that his efforts contributed to the prolonged resistance to the Mongol threat, a resistance more protracted in South China than elsewhere in Asia.

Jia Sidao was also attacked for his promotion of radical agrarian and economic policies. His intention was to increase revenue by taxing large landowners effectively, a policy certain to alienate vested interests. While still a financial commissioner he had taken steps to collect overdue taxes and in 1261 he had proposed measures to prevent the rich hoarding grain. In 1263 he went further by putting forward his infamous 'public field laws'. Under these laws the maximum size of a landed property was restricted according to the rank held by the owner. Holdings of land exceeding these limits were to be bought by the state and converted into public fields, the revenue from which would be used to support the armed forces. The laws were in effect from 1263 to 1275, by which time the revenues from state lands were sufficient to supply the army. However, the cost in loss of support for the dynasty was high, large landowners and government officials were alienated and as a consequence responsive to the overtures of the Mongols. Within four days of Jia Sidao's fall the suggestion was made that the public fields be returned to their owners. By then it was too late, the Mongol armies were approaching and the Song gentry went over to the invaders in large numbers. Jia Sidao was blamed for having promoted a measure which caused this loss of confidence, although in the longer term it might have enabled the dynasty to resist the invasion.

Economic changes

In the Tang-Song era, and in particular in the Southern Song period, China experienced remarkable economic growth. Such was the pace and magnitude of change that writers such as Mark Elvin have referred to it as a 'mediaeval economic revolution'.[35] He described it as having five dimensions. The first was a revolution in farming, particularly in the development of wet-rice cultivation. This was brought about by the systematic application of organic manure; by the introduction of drought-resistant and fast-ripening strains of rice from Vietnam which enabled double-cropping; by improvements in water management and by the development of commercial agriculture. Secondly there was a revolution in water transport: for sea voyages junks, built with watertight bulkheads, used the magnetic compass; even greater progress was made in river and canal transportation, with the development of a national network of waterways. This in turn stimulated a growing interdependence of China's regional economies. At the same time there occurred a revolution in systems of money and credit. 'Flying money', government certificates of credit entitling the bearer to draw an equivalent sum at provincial treasuries, had appeared in the Tang period. This was supplemented by credit instruments and promissory notes. By the twelfth century the Southern Song government was issuing a fully-convertible paper currency and credit systems were well established. Accompanying this were revolutionary changes in marketing structure and urbanisation. Elvin noted that the Chinese rural economy was becoming linked with the market mechanism, that economic advances were bringing about an urban revolution, and that a rising proportion of the population was residing in cities. Finally he argued that in this period China 'advanced to the threshold of a systematic experimental investigation of nature, and created the world's earliest mechanized industry'.[36] To justify this last claim he stressed the spread of printing, the investigation of disease, the advances in mathematics and the appearance of a silk-reeling machine which almost anticipated the technology of the early industrial revolution in the West.

Elvin's argument, which was based on research carried out by Japanese historians, is related to a general interpretation of Chinese history concerning the emergence of capitalism. According to the Japanese historian Naito Torajiro the important economic and social changes which occurred in the Tang-Song era indicated that it was at this point that the 'modern' period in Chinese history began. The implication of this claim is that capitalism, or at least its beginnings, emerged in the Song period. If that was the case, then a reason must be given for why it failed to develop further. One of the most persuasive explanations for this was put forward by Etienne Balazs who argued that the rise of a Chinese bourgeoisie in the Tang-Song period occurred at a time when national sovereignty was divided, and as a consequence the power of the state and that of the ruling scholar-officials was weakened. He admitted that the superabundance of cheap labour in China inhibited the development of time-saving devices, but he argued that this was not the key to why a further development of capitalism did not occur. The real reason was that

what was chiefly lacking in China for the further development of capitalism was not mechanical skill or scientific aptitude, nor a sufficient accumulation of wealth, but scope for individual enterprise. There was no individual freedom and no security for private enterprise, no legal foundation for rights other than those of the state, no alternative investment other than landed property, no guarantee against being penalized by arbitrary exactions from officials or against intervention by the state. But perhaps the supreme inhibiting factor was the overwhelming prestige of the state bureaucracy, which maimed from the start any attempt of the bourgeoisie to be different, to become aware of themselves as a class and fight for an autonomous position in society.[37]

Nevertheless the changes which did take place left an ineradicable mark on the Chinese economy. In the Tang-Song period the population may have doubled, with spectacular growth in the south and east contrasting with limited growth or even decrease in the north.[38] There had been a marked trend towards urbanisation, a massive growth of commerce and the widespread adoption of a monetary economy. Moreover important technological advances had occurred, for example in the production of iron. Iron output increased twelve-fold between 850 and 1050. This occasioned a demand for charcoal which so reduced timber supplies that a precocious development of the coal industry occurred. Coal became a major source of energy for both industrial and domestic use, a development which only occurred in Britain in the period 1540–1640.[39]

Social changes

Mention has already been made of some social changes which occurred in the Northern Song. These changes appear to have completed a process already well under way in the later Tang period, namely the elimination of aristocratic families from positions of power. In their place a new élite had emerged, a professional body of scholar officials, defined by achievement in examinations and by appointment to government office.

The traditional interpretation of this development measured social standing through bureaucratic success and concluded that there was a good deal of social mobility in Song society. More recently it has been argued that beyond the nationally prominent political élite (which might indeed be mobile) there was a locally influential social élite which could dominate a locality for centuries. This revisionary view has been challenged by Richard L. Davies, in a study of the Shi clan of Ningpo, the clan which produced the chief councillor Shi Miyuan. Davies noted that in the early imperial period politically mobile kin groups had usually required at least ten generations to reach the height of their influence, and another ten generations passed before decline set in. However in the Song period, in a society which was more complex and competitive, the entire cycle, of rise, prominence and obscurity, might be completed within ten generations. In the case of the Shi the rise was indeed the product of examination success, reinforced by a family tendency to longevity. There was nothing in this to support the idea of a hereditary élite founded on regional prominence[40] – rather the rise and unimpeded decline of the Shi suggested that 'turbulence within a highly competitive bureaucracy' made it difficult for any kinship group to maintain a position of power for long.[41]

Another important change had occurred in rural society. During the Tang-Song period the tradition that government should control the distribution of land, through the equitable or 'equal field' system, was finally abandoned. It has been estimated that by the end of the eleventh century official and first to third rank households, which constituted a mere 14 per cent of the population of the empire, held 77½ per cent of the land under cultivation. The remainder of the population held only 22½ per cent of the land. However, it is debatable whether the manor was the dominant institution in the Chinese countryside, or whether the small-scale farm worked under a system of private ownership was more typical. It may be that manorial development became more marked as the southern Song period progressed and that it was only a notable feature of certain areas, for example in the prefectures around Lake Tai.[42]

Accompanying rural change was the great increase in urbanisation. Constraints on the growth of towns had broken down in the Tang period and under the Northern and Southern Song towns overflowed their traditional layout into suburbs. Of Southern Song cities, by far the best known was Hangzhou, the 'temporary residence' of the dynasty, known to Marco Polo as Quinsai. In the thirteenth century Hangzhou grew to be the largest and richest city in the world, with a population perhaps numbering two million. The city proper was surrounded by a wall eleven miles in length, it was intersected by canals which in turn were criss-crossed by bridges – Marco Polo claimed that there were 'twelve thousand bridges of stone', in fact they numbered 367. The city was home to the Imperial Palace, to the organs of central government and to the officials who ran them. Hangzhou was also a great commercial city and its population included large numbers of merchants, artisans, workmen and members of the 'low-class professions', for example entertainers and prostitutes. The extensive commercial activities of the city population indicate that another significant social change had occurred in the Southern Song period.[43]

The growth of cities and the spread of printing has ensured that the historical materials describing Song society are plentiful. Consequently more is known of the position of women in Song society than in any previous period in Chinese history. This is an issue which has given rise to disagreement. Until recently the dominant view was that a contrast existed between the position of women under the Tang and that which they occupied under the Song. Under the former dynasty, it was claimed, women from élite backgrounds participated in society with considerable freedom. Some Tang women – the example of the Empress Wu is perhaps not the most fortunate – could be taken as role models. However under the Song the position of women deteriorated: there was the spread of foot-binding and the strong condemnation of the remarriage of widows. It was true that women during the period seemed to enjoy particularly strong property rights, but this was more than matched by the ideological pressure for women to conform to the submissive role endorsed by Neo-Confucian writers.[44]

However Patricia Buckley Ebrey, in her study of marriage and the lives of women in the Song period, emphasised continuity as well as change, for women's lives remained centred on the home throughout the period. Nevertheless important changes did take place which reflected the broader social and economic developments of the time. The commercialisation of cloth production, which involved a good deal of female labour, set a monetary value on women's work; the spread of printing encouraged an increase in literacy among women from scholarly families – literacy seems to have enhanced marriageability; the increased importance for the educated class of making advantageous marriages led to a spectacular increase in the size of dowries, and it was in this context that Song law provided some protection for orphaned girls, allocating to them half a son's share of the estate; more generally, greater affluence encouraged the employment of women as concubines, maids and prostitutes; and in a male society which admired languid women there was the gradual extension of footbinding from the palace and entertainment quarters to the homes of officials. These changes in the role of women may have encouraged Confucian scholars, anxious to fix people in well-defined roles, to emphasise notions of female modesty and widow fidelity, and to condemn women's literary creativity, their claims to property, and their involvement in affairs outside the home.[45]

Intellectual developments: Neo-Confucianism

Under the Southern Song there occurred a Confucian revival which was to have a long-lasting effect on Chinese culture. The antecedents of this movement lay in the Tang period and the writings of Han Yu, in which he had rejected Buddhism as a foreign doctrine and had called for a reassertion of Confucian ethics as a basis for government. During the Northern Song Han Yu's ideas and literary style were revived by Ouyang Xiu who called for a renovation of Chinese society. His call came at the time when the activist Confucianism of Wang Anshi had divided Confucians. His opponents, who have been labelled moralistic conservatives[46] had likened his reforms to Legalism, and their rejection of Wang, made in an atmosphere of dynastic decline, had led to bitter controversy.

At the same time philosophical speculation extended the range of Confucianism. Zhou Tunyi (1017–73) looked back to the *Book of Changes* and also borrowed ideas from Buddhism and Daoism. From these ingredients he constructed a cosmology, a science of the universe, which combined reference to the workings of *yin* and *yang* and the five agents, to explain what he termed the Great Ultimate, the first principle from which all is derived. The heavenly principle, the male element, and the earthly principle, the female element, the two material forces, interacted to engender and transform all. Man received these material forces in their highest excellence, which made him the most intelligent being, capable of developing consciousness. Zhang Zai (1020–77) suggested that a single primal substance, defined as *qi*, and translated as 'material-force' or 'vital energy' composed the entire universe. The world was not illusory, as Buddhists maintained, but composed of this primal material.[47]

These ideas were developed in contrasting ways by the brothers Cheng. Cheng Hao (1032–85), in an essay entitled "Understanding the Nature of Humanity", was concerned with the unity of the human mind and the mind of the universe. His ideas later became the foundation of the Neo-Confucian school of the Mind. The writings of his younger brother Cheng Yi (1033–1107) had the more immediate impact. He adopted Zhang Zai's idea of material-force, but then added a second concept, that of *li* or 'principle', the immutable, immaterial principle in all things that gives them their form. Human nature comprised both principle and material-force. According to Mencius, man was by his nature good. This was the principle, but man's material endowment – his material-force – varied and hence men's character differed. However, Cheng Yi was not a fatalist: he believed that man could cultivate a moral attitude and overcome his shortcomings. This self-cultivation involved the investigation of the principle of things, which sequence of ideas led to the Neo-Confucian School of Principle.

These ideas were later synthesised by Zhu Xi (1130–1200), who brought the concepts of the Great Ultimate, material-force and principle into a single doctrine which was to have an enormous influence. Zhu Xi also established the sequence of the Confucian classics – the Four Books – and wrote commentaries on them. These in time became the central texts for primary education and the examination system. He defined the process of the 'investigation of things' to enable one to acquire moral understanding and to cultivate the inner self. 'Book reading, quiet sitting, ritual practice, physical exercise, calligraphy, arithmetic, and empirical observation all have a place in his pedagogical program'.[48] He taught his ideas at his academy, the White Deer Grotto in Jiangxi, where he acquired an extensive following. In his day his ideas were by no means universally accepted. At a philosophical level he was challenged by

Lu Xiangshan (1139–93), who emphasised meditation and intuition, elaborating on the ideas of Cheng Hao. In 1175 a famous confrontation took place between the two at the Goose Lake Temple. Zhu Xi also fell foul of the chief councillor, Han Tuozhou, who found his teaching, which implied an ideological superiority over the current practices of government, to be subversive, and had his followers banned from the court.

James T.C. Liu, in a striking phrase, described the intellectual and political changes which reached a crisis point in the early twelfth century as 'China turning inward'. After the fall of Wang Anshi the path of reform, which perhaps offered a solution to the crisis of empire, had been blocked. Under the Southern Song the rise of chief councillors, and increasingly autocratic rule, had progressively alienated scholar-officials. Foreign invasion compounded by profound social and economic change provoked a deep uncertainty. This was translated by Zhu Xi and his predecessors into a need to transform Confucianism by incorporating metaphysical concepts: the true Confucian examined himself inwardly, while statecraft became a secondary concern. This redirection of concern affected not only the individual, but also society, for Neo-Confucianism did not extend its empirical approach to scientific investigation. When the Mongol threat became imminent and when they in turn laid claim to Confucian orthodoxy, the Southern Song responded by adopting Zhu Xi's teaching, arrogating true Confucianism to themselves. Of course this did not save the dynasty, but it left the way open for Neo-Confucianism to become the state ideology.

The arts in the Song period: landscape painting and ceramics
The period of the Five Dynasties and the Song dynasty was one of high achievement in a range of arts, but above all one of excellence in landscape painting and ceramics.

It was in this period that landscape painting achieved the maturity which led to its recognition as the dominant form of artistic expression. Under the Tang, the landscape painter Jing Hao (*c.* 855–915) had written a treatise in which he set out the six essentials of painting which were: spirit, harmony, thought, scenery, the brush and ink. In this sequence he proceeded from thought to execution, the underlying implication being that the painter sought not only to represent the true forms of nature but also to reveal their deeper significance.

These principles were followed by Fan Kuan (*c.* 960–1030), whose painting *Travelling amid mountains and gorges*, is a very rare example of a Song painting which has survived. It has been said that:

> It perfectly fulfils the ideal of the Northern Song that a landscape-painting should be of such compelling realism that the viewer will feel that he has been actually transported to the place depicted.[49]

Among the many important artists of the period one should mention the statesman

Su Dongpo (1036–1101), who combined painting with calligraphy, poetry and art criticism, and Mi Fu (1051–1107), also known as a calligrapher. They belonged to a group of artists who were literati, who found their means of self-expression in painting. They subscribed to the amateur ideal, Mi Fu once writing 'In matters of calligraphy and painting, one is not to discuss price. The gentleman is hard to capture by money'.[50]

Some idea of the importance attached to painting in the Song period may be gauged by reference to Huizong, the Northern Song emperor who reigned from 1101 to 1125. He was an accomplished painter of birds and flowers and also supported an academy of painting which rigorously controlled the artists who attended the court. However, the emperor was not able to prevent the development of new styles and unconventional approaches to painting. Among the later members of the academy was Ma Yuan (fl. 1190–1225), who rejected the monumental style of the Northern landscape painters and instead painted evocative scenes of individuals dwarfed by the landscape. Xia Gui (fl. 1180–1224), his younger contemporary at the Southern Song court at Hangzhou, went even further in using expressive brushwork to convey emotion. In this intent, his paintings were not dissimilar to those of Chan Buddhist painters, of whom Mu Qi (c. 1200–1270) is best known in the West for his painting *Six Persimmons*.

With reference to ceramics, in the past it was supposed that the outstanding wares of the time were the product of a few centres which specialised in the small-scale production of particular types of ceramic. Recent excavations at Northern Song ceramic centres have revealed this to be untrue: factories produced a variety of wares, often imitating those made by other centres, and production was on a large scale and governed by economic considerations. The state-sponsored kiln centre at Jingdezhen in Jiangxi province, which began production at the beginning of the eleventh century, became an outstanding example of a centre which combined mass production with high quality.

For connoisseurs, however, the ceramics of the period remain known by their specific names or by their supposed places of manufacture. These included Ding ware, more refined than the Tang product – the bodies of the vessels were so thin that the rims were often bound with metal; *qingbai*, meaning 'blue-white', a type of fine white porcelain, often with incised decoration; Cizhou ware, named after a site in Hebei, but produced right across north China, which featured a slip-painted decoration beneath a transparent glaze; Jun ware, a rather heavy ware characteristically glazed in lavender blue with purple splashes; the black or dark brown Jian ware, produced in Fujian and exported in large quantities to Japan, where it was known as *temmoku*; Guan or 'official' ware, from Hangzhou and Longquan, with a distinctive crackle glaze; and the highly-prized Ru ware, a finer crackleware produced for the Song court for a few years early in the twelfth century. The porcelain of this period has been described as 'both technically and artistically the finest the world has produced'.[51]

CHAPTER TEN

THE YUAN DYNASTY

The Mongol conquest of China came in a series of stages. The Xi Xia kingdom in the north-west was attacked between 1205 and 1209 and the Jin empire of North China was first overrun between 1211 and 1215. The Mongols then turned westwards and seized the Western Liao empire, the state founded by the remnants of the Qidan. After a pause the Mongol attack was resumed, the Jin empire was destroyed in 1234, the remains of the Nanzhao kingdom in the south-west fell in 1253 and Korea was conquered by 1258. The Yuan dynasty was established in 1271 and the Southern Song capitulated in 1279. However, Mongol rule of the whole of China was to last less than a century. By 1351 major rebellions had broken out and in 1368 the Yuan court gave up the unequal struggle and retreated to the steppes.

THE SIGNIFICANCE OF THE YUAN DYNASTY

In traditional Chinese historiography the Mongol conquest was treated as a disaster, and this pejorative view of the Yuan dynasty has been accepted by many western writers. Jacques Gernet, for example, emphasised that this was a Mongol occupation of China. He described how the Mongols had devised a system of economic exploitation and practised racial discrimination, and concluded that their harsh regime and unjust policies had provoked the hatred of the Chinese and had led to their inevitable expulsion.[1] Another charge which has been laid at the Mongols' door is that they caused a major setback to the development of Chinese society, terminating the progress of the Song period, including the economic and technological changes which have been seen as verging on the birth of capitalism, and thus ensuring that the successor Ming dynasty would be an introverted and non-competitive state.[2] It has also been claimed that Mongol rule led to a brutalisation of Chinese politics and that this bore tragic fruit in Ming times, the evidence quoted including the practice instituted by the first Ming emperor of ordering the public flogging of ministers with whom he was displeased.[3]

These views, which are to an extent justifiable, conceal important features of the Yuan dynasty. Many Chinese supported the dynasty because it brought about a reunification of the country. The claim that the Han Chinese despised being ruled by Mongols, and that throughout the Yuan period they wanted to drive them out, ignores the fact that many Mongols remained in China after the Yuan court had left. It is more likely that the Chinese came to accept the Mongol emperors as the legitimate holders of the mandate of heaven. There is evidence to show that Han Chinese culture, far from having been despoiled by the Mongols, as the founder of the Ming dynasty alleged, actually flourished in the Yuan period. A positive view of Mongol rule has claimed that it was more humane than that of the Song, that less use was made of capital punishment and of irregular taxation, that there were no 'literary inquisitions', and that classical scholarship flourished. This revisionary view points out that the verdict on the Yuan of the early Ming period was initially highly favourable, but was reversed after an incident which occurred in 1449 when the Ming emperor was captured by the Oirat Mongols.[4]

The impression which remains is that there is still much to be discovered about the Yuan period. One unresolved mystery concerns population. According to fiscal records the combined population of Song and Jin China amounted to well over 100,000,000, whereas the records of the 1290s indicate a population of roughly 70,000,000. How far that reduction was the product of inadequate recording, how far the result of a demographic disaster, remains unclear.[5] It must also be said that Mongol rule was essentially superficial and that for the great majority of the Chinese population it probably had only a slight impact.

GENGHIS KHAN AND THE CONQUEST OF NORTH CHINA

In the twelfth century the people known to history as the Mongols lived in separate tribes on the steppes of central Asia. Each tribe claimed a common ancestry and the nobles of the tribe regarded themselves as the direct descendants of the tribe's founder. Rulership of a tribe was awarded to an individual by a convocation of the nobles of that tribe. The Mongol economy was based on cattle herding, supplemented by hunting, the Mongols being accomplished horsemen. The Mongols were frequently in conflict with the Tatars, their neighbours to the west, an animosity which was encouraged by the Jurchen Jin dynasty as a means of promoting dissension on the steppe.

The early history of Temujin, the man who was to become Genghis khan, was recorded in the *Secret History of the Mongols*. He was born in about 1167. His father, known as Yesugei the Brave, was a tribal leader who had participated in the struggle against the Tatars. According to the *Secret History* he was poisoned by the Tatars while Temujin was still a child. This grievance, and the ties of friendship and alliance which he developed with other tribal groupings, formed the background of Temujin's claim, made in about 1187, to be the khan of the Mongols. However, it was not until a decade later that with the assistance of the Jin he was able to take revenge on the Tatars. Yet another decade of tribal fighting was to pass until Temujin's position was so strong that at a convocation of tribes held in 1206 he was acclaimed Genghis khan, universal sovereign, ruler of the steppe peoples.

Genghis khan then carried out an extensive reform of the religious, legal, political and above all military organisation of the Mongols. He claimed to be heaven's chosen instrument and assumed that all who stood in his way did so in defiance of heaven's will. It was on this assertion that the Mongol objective of universal rule was based. His wishes took the form of decrees, now for the first time set down in a written form of Mongolian and intended to serve as precedents. He distributed titles and responsibilities and regulated the tribal structure. With reference to military organisation, he elaborated on the decimal system which dated back to the Xiongnu. According to the *Secret History* he created ninety-five tribal units each of a thousand men and each divided into units of tens and hundreds. Together with his own élite corps, the Mongol forces numbered rather more than one hundred thousand men. They fought under their tribal chieftains, operated under strict discipline and were capable of remarkable feats of endurance. This Mongol fighting machine was to create the largest land empire the world has ever seen.

Genghis khan then set in train a series of campaigns which were to take the Mongol forces from Korea to the Black Sea. Between 1211 and 1215, in a series of annual raids, increasingly penetrative attacks were made on Jin territory in north China and the Jurchen homeland in Manchuria was overrun. However, at the very moment that it seemed that the Jin empire was about to collapse, Genghis khan turned his attention westwards and destroyed the Western Liao empire and captured Samarkand and Bokhara. In the meantime Mongol encroachment on China continued and increasingly the Mongols began to take into their service Qidan and Chinese officials, among them Yelüchucai, a Qidan of royal descent, who became a court official and chief astrologer. In 1226 Genghis khan attacked and destroyed the Xi Xia kingdom, himself dying the following year in the course of the campaign.[6]

Genghis khan was succeeded by his third son Ögödei, who took the title of khaghan or emperor, indicating his elevation above his brothers, between whom the rest of the Mongol empire was divided. Under Ögödei a further burst of expansion took place, with Mongol forces invading Korea and reaching Vienna in the west. In 1230 he recommenced the campaign against the Jin, captured Kaifeng in 1233 and destroyed the Jin dynasty in the following year.

Having conquered North China, the Mongols now had to devise a means of ruling it. Up to this point the Mongol practice in China had been that of a nomadic society, exploiting the economy by the imposition of heavy exactions and the enslavement of sections of the population. Large tracts of land were commandeered for grazing and one Mongol nobleman even went as far as to suggest the complete annihilation of the native population and the use of the entire occupied territory as pasture. It was at this point that Yelüchucai made his famous proposal on how the country might be exploited in a more rational way. He suggested, as a first step towards establishing a relationship with the population, the granting of an amnesty to the Chinese who had unwittingly broken Mongolian law. He advised the establishment of a strong central government, the delineation of new administrative districts, and the creation of tax collection bureaux which would supervise the receipt of regular tax payments.

The success of these initial measures encouraged Ögödei to promote Yelüchucai and to allow him to go further in adopting Chinese administrative methods. The next step was the conduct of a national census between 1234 and 1236. For Yelüchucai this was a preliminary to improving the administration, however Ögödei used the information provided to divide North China into appanages for the Mongol princes. This working at cross purposes continued in other respects. Yelüchucai brought Chinese officials into the Mongol service, encouraged the study of the Chinese classics and attempted to re-introduce the examination system. However Ögödei awarded the privilege of farming the taxes of North China to a Muslim businessman and promoted other Muslims to influential positions. By the time of Ögödei's death in 1241, and that of Yelüchucai two years later, the stratagem for ruling China the latter had tried to introduce had been seriously undermined.[7]

THE CONQUEST OF THE SOUTHERN SONG

In 1251 Möngke became khaghan and the encroachment on China resumed. His brother Khubilai conducted an ambitious campaign to subdue the kingdom of Nanzhao. In 1254 raiding of Southern Song territory commenced and Möngke invaded Sichuan in 1258, only to die in the following year. The succession dispute which followed delayed the Mongol assault on the Southern Song for a further twenty years.

Nevertheless it was inevitable that Khubilai, prompted both by the Mongolian concept of universal rule and by the expectation that an emperor who ruled North China should rule the totality of China, would aim to incorporate the Southern Song territory into his domains. However, to achieve this meant overcoming the problems which had restricted the Jurchen to the north: the unsuitable terrain for cavalry, the need to capture walled cities and the threat of Song naval power.

The principal invasion route to the Yangzi valley was along the Han river on which lay the important fortress-town of Xiangyang. The siege of Xiangyang, which lasted from 1268 to 1273, was a decisive contest. With the help of two Muslim engineers, and the use of a vast mangonel to hurl rocks at the fortifications, the walls of the town were finally breached. The conquest of the south was carried out by Bayan, an outstanding general. In 1275 he defeated Jia Sidao, the last chief councillor of the Southern Song and in the following year occupied Hangzhou and received the formal surrender of the Song. However Song loyalists continued their resistance until 1279. They retreated to Guangzhou and were finally forced to put to sea, where Liu Xiufu, the last devoted servant of the dynasty, leapt into the sea with the boy-emperor in his arms and drowned them both.

THE REIGN OF KHUBILAI KHAN

In the meantime Khubilai khan, as ruler of North China, took steps to transform his position from that of Mongol invader to that of Chinese emperor. The process began at his acclamation as khaghan in 1260 at which he promulgated an edict in Chinese, written by his Confucian advisor, which contained a Chinese reign-name. It continued with the construction of capitals, the first at Kaiping in Inner Mongolia, later to be known as Shangdu, the Supreme Capital, and to Coleridge as Xanadu, which was a new town modelled on the Tang capital at Chang'an. Later, on the site of modern Beijing, he had laid out Dadu, the Great Capital, otherwise known as Khanbalik, the city of the khan. Each capital had 'strong historical associations fitting well into the architectural symbolism of a new dynasty.'[8] Despite these claims to Chinese legitimacy, the Mongol court continued to follow nomad practices and moved between the two capitals, spending the summer at Shangdu and the winter at Dadu.

This tension between the assertion of distinctiveness and the danger – in Mongol eyes – of assimilation, remained throughout the Yuan period. Under Khubilai khan the Mongol dream of universal empire began to disintegrate and it became clear that he was the ruler of an east Asian state. The extent of this was determined by the failure of his attempts, made in 1274 and 1281, to subdue the Japanese. The second of these attacks, in which Mongol troops landed on Japanese soil, was frustrated by a storm, the *kamikaze* or 'divine wind' which destroyed the Mongol fleet. Further disastrous failures occurred late in Khubilai's reign when he attempted to coerce the rulers of Champa (in modern Vietnam) and Java.

From 1260 Khubilai had begun to utilise the bureaucratic tradition of the Chinese state. His adviser on this was a former Buddhist monk, Liu Bingzhong, who gave him the famous advice that 'although the empire had been conquered on horseback, it could not be administered on horseback'.[9] He re-established the secretariat and the traditional six ministries. The division between civil, military and censorial branches of government was retained. A system of territorial administration divided China and Korea into twelve provinces. The arrangements resembled those previously in use, although it appears that the delegation of authority was far more extensive. Further steps were taken to confirm the legitimacy of Khubilai as a Chinese emperor. Chinese court ceremonial and Confucian rites were revived and in the early 1260s a national history office was established to collect the historical records of the preceding dynasties.[10] In 1271 Khubilai decided to adopt a Chinese dynastic title, that of *Da Yuan* or 'Great Origin'.

Nevertheless these changes fell well short of sinicisation. In several respects Khubilai himself showed an unwillingness to accept fundamental characteristics of the Chinese state as it had developed. The first was the examination system, which Khubilai rejected as a means of selecting men for appointment to the bureaucracy. For forty years, until the system of examinations was partly revived in 1315, recruits to the bureaucracy came from those who were qualified by status, that it to say because of their family background, or because a member of the family, already a member of the bureaucracy, could exercise the *yin* privilege. Some of these were Chinese, but many came from non-Chinese backgrounds and included many Uighur and Turks. A second essential difference concerned the status and recruitment of the military establishment. Mongol society was highly militarised whereas Chinese society, both in practice and in sentiment, held military values and military men in low esteem. Under Khubilai and his successors the hereditary principle of recruitment was maintained and Chinese forces were recruited in a similar fashion. However, the two elements were never fused and the Mongols never surrendered their military claims to superiority even when the Mongol military machine had ceased to exist.[11] Finally there was the matter of the codification of the law. For centuries China had had a unified legal code and the Jin dynasty, despite being a dynasty of conquest, had adopted a version of the Tang code. The Mongols had brought with them the *jasagh*, the collection of rules and instructions promulgated by Genghis khan, but Chinese society was too complex to be administered through Mongol customary law. Undoubtedly there were great legal difficulties in the way of drafting a code which could be applied to the multicultural society of Yuan China, and this may explain why it was not until 1323 that a compilation of legal documents was promulgated which attempted to strike a balance between Chinese tradition, Mongolian practice, and new social conditions.[12] The fact remained that the Mongols did not accept previous Chinese legal codes, nor could the Chinese accept Mongol customary law.

THE SUCCESSORS OF KHUBILAI KHAN

The last years of Khubilai's reign were clouded by the failure of his foreign adventures, by his ill-health and above all by the problem of succession. In contrast to the Chinese practice of the ruler nominating his successor, the Mongols retained the custom of public acclamation of a ruler from among those eligible to succeed. This gave rise to a recurrent difficulty throughout the Yuan period which weakened the dynasty. Khubilai's original choice of successor was his son Zhenjin but he died in 1285. After Khubilai's death Zhenjin's son Temür was acclaimed khaghan and reigned as the emperor Chengzong from 1294 to 1307. His reign in many respects saw the continuation of policies initiated by Khubilai, and he achieved nominal suzerainty over the whole of the Mongol world. However it was also marked by the onset of administrative inefficiency and corruption. He was followed on the throne by Khaishan (the Wuzong emperor), who rejected much of Khubilai's programme, plunged recklessly into debt and adopted a variety of unsound financial practices to try to recover the situation.

A more settled period of government ensued under Khaishan's brother Ayurbarwada, the emperor Renzong (reigned 1311–20). More than any of his predecessors, Ayurbarwada had absorbed Chinese culture. He employed Confucian scholar-officials in his bureaucracy and in 1315 he partly revived the civil service examinations using a curriculum based on Neo-Confucian texts. However, Mongolian and other non-Chinese groups were given easier tests and a racial quota system was employed. Although the examinations conducted under Ayurbarwada and until the end of the dynasty only recruited four percent of the official appointments, the reform alarmed the Mongol élite.

In the years following his death a prolonged struggle broke out between factions at court, who were divided partly by the stand they took towards sinicisation and partly by the rival claims of the descendants of the two lines from Khubilai. In 1323 a coup took place which put Yesün Temür on the throne, a man whose steppe background made him unsympathetic to Chinese scholar-officials and led him to appoint Muslims to senior positions. When he died in 1328 an even more bloody succession struggle followed which ended with Tugh Temür being enthroned twice. He has been represented as the 'Yuan candidate', that is to say as a Mongol whose commitment was to China rather than to the steppe. He certainly went out of his way to honour Confucius and to promote Chinese culture. Finally, in 1333 Toghön Temür was placed on the throne at the age of thirteen, his reign lasting until 1368 when the Mongol court fled from China.[13]

DISCRIMINATORY POLICIES

One of the most notorious aspects of Mongol rule over China was the application of a 'four-class' system. The population was divided into four ethnic groups in order of descending privilege: Mongols; *semu ren*, that is 'miscellaneous aliens', referring mainly to Western and Central Asians; *Han ren*, the inhabitants of northern China, conquered in 1234, comprising not only Chinese but also including Qidan, Jurchen etc.; and finally and lowest in the order, the *nan ren*, the population of the Southern Song territories acquired in 1279. It is true that the division between the classes was not as rigid as has sometimes been suggested. Nevertheless, discrimination on the grounds of ethnic and political background was an important element in the Yuan social order and it had connotations in terms of bureaucratic appointment, legal treatment and taxation.

With regard to appointments the Mongols certainly practised discrimination in the sense that they never relied on Chinese scholar officials as a class to support their rule. Obstacles were placed in the way of Chinese, even Chinese who had succeeded in the Mongolian version of the examination system, to bar them from high office. Some Chinese literati refused to participate in public life. Nevertheless there were many individual exceptions to this discrimination. Chinese collaborated with the Mongols against the Jurchen and so facilitated the establishment of the Yuan dynasty.

Khubilai employed a number of Chinese advisers, including Xu Heng who was appointed chancellor of the Imperial College in 1274, and Wang E who had recommended to Khubilai that he, like Chinese emperors before him, should order the compilation of the records of previous dynasties. After the conquest of the Southern Song, Chinese advisers continued to play a significant role. Ayurbarwada surrounded himself with Chinese scholars and appointed Chinese to senior posts in the secretariat, and his reintroduction of the examinations gave southern Chinese a chance of obtaining office. Tugh Temür also was a patron of Chinese scholarship and he supported a number of Chinese in office, among them the eminent scholar Yu Ji. This is not to suggest that there was no discrimination, but it is possible to argue that Chinese participation in Mongol rule has been underestimated.

With reference to legal treatment the evidence of discrimination is even less convincing. In the past China had permitted ethnic minorities to punish offenders within their own communities according to their own customary law. In the Yuan period Mongols and *semu ren* were tried according to their own Mongolian or Central Asian laws, and Chinese were tried according to Chinese law. This led to some difference in punishment, for example a Chinese offender (but not a Mongol or a Central Asian) in addition to the imposition of the principal punishment was tattooed – a practice which has led writers to assert that legal discrimination was carried out against the Chinese, although such tattooing had in fact been prescribed under Song law. Special courts were established to deal with cases involving two ethnic groups. Mongols did have some legal advantages: in the case of an offence within a mixed marriage the dispute would be adjudicated according to the law of the husband unless the wife happened to be Mongolian, in which case she would have the benefit. In the *Yuan History* it is stated that if a Mongol beat a Chinese, the latter could not fight back, and this has been taken as clear evidence of discrimination. However it has been shown that the Chinese victim was instead provided with a legal remedy for the assault.[14]

On the matter of taxation, the Mongols certainly began with the intention of exploiting the Chinese. Under Ögödei harsh requisitions were replaced with the more orderly form of taxation proposed by Yelüchucai. However his reforms were later abandoned in favour of tax-farming by Muslim entrepreneurs. As north China had already suffered from the disruption of previous conquests and the ravages of natural disasters, the burden of taxation may well have appeared excessive and, under Khubilai and his successors, sporadic attempts were made to moderate it. In the south, although Mongols enjoyed favoured status with regard to taxation, the tax burden on the Chinese population does not appear to have been excessive and the landowners of south China may have benefited considerably from Yuan economic policies.[15] Although excessive taxation was to figure among the reasons given for the fall of the dynasty, the evidence to prove impoverishment of Chinese society and to show that it should be attributed to the exploitation by the Mongols must be regarded as inconclusive.

THE ECONOMY

One view of the consequences of Mongol rule on China is that it inhibited economic growth and even caused regression. This view emphasises that after the Mongol invasion of north China great quantities of arable land were confiscated from Chinese owners and turned into pasture. Much state and private land was given to the Mongol aristocracy and to Buddhist establishments. These actions and heavy taxation ruined many peasants and there was a second wave of migration to the south. The Mongols were ignorant of the need to maintain river defences and as a consequence dikes broke and the Yellow river shifted its course, causing great loss of life. Artisans lost their freedom and became dependents of the Mongols. Even the incorporation of China into the Mongol empire brought no marked benefit as almost all the trade was in the hands of foreigners. The profits of trade were taken out of China and there was a drain on metallic currency, which led to the use of paper money and subsequently to inflation. The Mongol government permitted corruption on a vast scale and the impoverishment that this caused was exacerbated by the Mongol love of splendour epitomised by the building of Dadu and the demands made for its supply.[16]

The evidence that the Mongol invasion had a catastrophic effect on north China appears to be strong, and the calculation that in the Yuan period there was a sharp population decline seems well founded. However, to conclude that the economic impact was purely negative would appear to be too sweeping. Under Khubilai steps were taken to promote economic recovery. In the north he sought to foster agriculture, encouraging the formation of groups of fifty households to open up barren land, improve flood control and irrigation, and to increase silk production. He promoted the interests of both merchants and artisans, who under previous dynasties had held low status and suffered numerous restrictions. He supported the *ortogh*, the associations of merchants, mainly Muslims, who handled the trade along the Silk Road. He made wider use of paper currency than ever before and, as this was adequately backed by a silver reserve, it acted as an encouragement to commerce. He also constructed roads, improved canals and developed the postal system. The division of China had been an impediment to trade and its reunification served to encourage economic activity.

However, towards the end of Khubilai's reign economic problems began to multiply. His foreign expeditions and his massive public works programmes, including the extension of the Grand Canal, imposed a heavy burden on state finances which Khubilai dealt with by employing a series of *semu* ministers whose methods of raising revenue earned them a hateful reputation. Khubilai's successors continued to face fiscal problems which were dealt with by raising revenue from monopolies, by currency manipulation and by profiting from the growth of maritime trade. Under Ayurbarwada an attempt was made to carry out a land survey preparatory to revising the land registers to include landholdings that had been omitted fraudulently from the tax schedules. The opposition provoked by this move led to the survey being stopped and thereafter south China's landlords were left to prosper.[17]

These contradictory indicators make it impossible to deliver a confident assessment of the economic effects of Mongol occupation. The economic decline of the north continued, but the prosperity of cities such as Hangzhou indicates that commerce was thriving. The role of the *ortogh* in terms of benefiting or harming the Chinese economy is likewise unclear, although a recent study has suggested that the Mongols' dealings with the *ortogh* did stimulate foreign trade and enrich the treasury.[18] Even less is known for certain about the situation of the rural population. In the north, and to a lesser extent in the south, the Mongols rulers rewarded their followers with appanages, grants of territory which gave them rights over the resident population which became households in bondage. After the conquest the government sought to prevent the excessive exploitation of these households, but the scale of internal migration suggests that they were not very successful. As noted above, the Mongols did encourage agricultural improvement, but the proliferation of peasant uprisings at the end of the Yuan period is an indicator the harshness of rural life. This may have been exacerbated by poor climatic conditions. In the fourteenth century China experienced thirty-five severe winters and in 1332 extraordinarily great rains and river floods are alleged to have brought about the loss of seven million lives and possibly to have a connection with the origin of the Black Death.[19]

RELIGION AND CULTURE

The Mongols practised a form of shamanism, but they made no attempt to impose this on their subjects. Instead the Yuan period was notable for religious freedom, although the Mongols did favour some religions at the expense of others. Their reliance on divination before settling on a course of action led them to make use of Daoist adepts, for example the Daoist patriarch known as Changchun, who had a famous interview with Genghis khan in 1219 and gained a privileged position for Daoists over Buddhists under Mongol rule.[20] The growth in the numbers of clergy led Ögödei in 1229 to issue an edict that all Daoist and Buddhist clergy below the age of fifty should pass an examination on the scriptures of their religion, or lose their tax exemption. Rivalry between Daoists and Buddhists continued under Möngke and between 1255 and 1258 a series of public debates took place between the two sides. The Buddhists claimed that their religion had been slandered by the Daoists' 'conversion of the barbarians' theory, which alleged that Laozi had travelled to India, there transforming himself into the Buddha and adapting his teachings to suit his audience. A more substantive issue was the Buddhist claim for restitution of monastic properties occupied by the Daoists. Khubilai, who presided at the last of these debates, decided in the Buddhists' favour.[21]

At that debate a key role was played by a Tibetan lama named 'Phags-pa. The Tibetan form of Buddhism had a strong appeal for the Mongols, who preferred its colourful ceremonial and emphasis on magic to the more subtle philosophy of Chan Buddhism. In 1260 'Phags-pa was appointed State Preceptor and it was through his actions that Tibetan Buddhism established a firm hold in China and the Mongol emperors received Buddhist legitimation. 'Phags-pa had another claim to fame, for he had invented the most effective alphabet for writing pre-classical Mongolian.[22]

The Mongol attitude towards Confucianism was originally one of contempt, but as the Mongol conquest of China proceeded first Khubilai, and then to a greater extent Ayurbarwada, recognised the value of Confucian officials in government. After the reunification of China Neo-Confucianism, which up to this point had been restricted to the south, made rapid progress in the north and confirmed its claim to be the new orthodoxy.

For Confucian scholars the Mongol conquest presented a dilemma which could never be resolved. Should they accept foreign conquest and utilise their skills to moderate the effect of Mongol rule? Or should they withdraw from government and retreat into the world of scholarly activity? Two famous examples illustrate these opposing responses. On the one hand Xu Heng (1209–81), Khubilai's chancellor at the Imperial College, and a leading intellectual figure in his day, chose to play an active role. His main intellectual contribution was to promote the Neo-Confucian text known as the *Xiaoxue*, the *Elementary Learning*, which was concerned with the moral education of the young, which he said should start with the performance of simple tasks like cleaning the floor. He served the Mongols because this accorded with his sense of Confucian duty which overrode any loyalist claim that the Mongols did not have the mandate of heaven.[23] The figure cited to represent the opposite reaction was Liu Yin (1249–83), who refused to take office under Mongol rule. Liu Yin was also a distinguished scholar who, in 1291, had been invited to become an academician of the Imperial College. He refused, alleging ill-health, and as he died only two years later this may have been the true reason. However the motive for his refusal has become a matter of dispute. An apocryphal story relates how in 1260 Xu Heng visited the 11-year old Liu Yin and was criticised by him for his decision to serve the Mongols. Defending himself, Xu Heng said that if Confucian scholars were not prepared to serve the invaders, the Confucian way 'could not prevail'. When, twenty years later, Liu Yin refused office, he supposedly said that if Confucian scholars did not decline to serve the way 'would not be respected'. Liu Yin's response has been seen as a veiled protest against Mongol rule and has been described as an outstanding example of 'Confucian eremitism', a withdrawal of the scholar from the world of affairs to that of self-realisation.[24]

Another matter of dispute relating to the attitude towards Mongol rule has arisen in the field of drama. In this period the play became firmly established as a literary form. At least 700 plays – or 'mixed entertainment', because they included singing, music and dancing – were written under the Yuan, and of these at least 150 have survived. They are known collectively as the 'Yuan northern drama' as many were written for performance in Beijing, although drama also flourished in Hangzhou and in other cities. Dramatic performances were very popular and a number of cities had theatrical districts which might contain a score of theatres. The plays have remained in performance in China, and Beijing opera is descended from them. Many of the plays have been translated into western languages, and one of them, translated under the title 'The Orphan of Chao' was adapted by Voltaire and performed at his theatre at Ferney.

The dispute concerns the significance of this development. In the past the argument has been put forward that the plays were the product of the frustrated energies of Chinese scholars. Being deprived under the Mongols of access to their natural environment, that of government service, some abandoned the world, turned to scholarly pursuits and became recluses. Others abandoned the world in a different sense, plunging into an unfamiliar environment, that of city life, where they exercised their talents to raise a limited folk art to the status of literature. However, their motives were not entirely escapist, for the argument continues by identifying in the new drama expressions of resentment of Mongol rule. If such political criticism was being expressed, this was ironic, for it was Mongol patronage which sustained the new theatre and it was allegedly for the Mongols' benefit that the new drama was written in the vernacular, they being unable to understand classical Chinese.

This interpretation has not stood up well to recent investigation. It is now clear that Yuan drama did not emerge as a response to the effects of the Mongol invasion, but was the outcome of a long theatrical development. There is some evidence to show that literati interest in writing for the theatre increased under the Yuan and that there was a degree of collaboration between actors and playwrights in the production of new plays. This development, however, was related to the changing role of the writer. The Yuan period saw not only an efflorescence of dramatic literature, but also a notable advance in fiction, the common element being that both forms of literature were written in the vernacular. The suggestion that Yuan drama 'was to be the weapon of the conquered'[25] is even harder to sustain. The texts themselves rarely contain any direct political allusions and these may have been added in later editions. Moreover, in the past the literati had found in the standard poetic forms ample opportunity to express their feelings.[26]

CHINA'S CONTACT WITH THE OUTSIDE WORLD IN THE YUAN PERIOD

During the thirteenth century the *pax mongolica* permitted travellers for the first time to move safely between China, western Asia and Europe. At the same time the Mongol rulers encouraged the settlement in China of foreigners, in particular western Asians. Their heavy reliance on foreign advisers diverted some of the Chinese animosity away from the Mongols and towards the incomers.

All Muslims in China were grouped as *semu*, and treated as a separate class with special privileges. Many were merchants and those who assisted the government did so mainly because of their financial abilities. Others were experts in fields as diverse as astronomy, medicine, armaments and architecture. The financial experts in particular incurred the odium of the Chinese. Khubilai employed as his finance minister Ahmad, later denounced as the first of three villainous ministers of the dynasty for his oppressive taxation and nepotism. Under Khubilai the merchant associations known as *ortogh* were established in China. They financed the caravans which crossed the deserts to the West carrying Chinese silks and ceramics. In return they were given tax-farming privileges, which again excited Chinese hostility. Until the end of the Yuan dynasty Muslims continued to hold positions of importance at the Mongol court, though as the court became more sinicised greater trust was placed in Chinese advisers.[27]

Another dramatic consequence of the freedom of travel was the arrival of the first Europeans in China and the journeying of Chinese and others to the West. Three motives for these travels may be distinguished. Probably the most common, though the least recorded, was the desire for trade. A political motive can be discerned in the response to the rise of Islam and to the crusades, with both East and West looking for allies. Associated with this hope there was a third motive, that of proselytism. The first of these dramatic journeys was made by the famous Daoist priest Changchun who had an audience with Genghis khan at Kabul in 1222 and gained a privileged position for Daoism under Mongolian rule. The first European to reach the Mongol court at Karakorum was a Franciscan monk, John of Plano Carpini. He had been sent by Pope Innocent IV on a diplomatic mission to the Mongols and was present at the enthronement of Güyüg khan in 1246. He was followed by William of Rubruck, who reached Karakorum in 1253 and made an important record of the Mongol way of life.

It was at this point that the Polo family made its enterprising journeys. The brothers Maffeo and Niccolo, both Venetian merchants, reached Khanbalik in 1262 and were received by Khubilai khan. When they went back to Europe four years later it was with a request from Khubilai that they returned with 'up to a hundred men learned in the Christian religion, well versed in the seven arts, and skilled to argue and demonstrate plainly to idolaters . . . that their religion is utterly mistaken'.[28] They returned to China in 1271, without the scholars, but with Niccolo's son Marco, and remained for the next twenty years in the East. Marco Polo's *Travels* gave a lively impression of Cathay, as north China was known to Europeans at the time, and of Khubilai's court. He described Hangzhou, or as he termed it 'the splendid city of Kinsai' in words which indicated that it far surpassed his native Venice. His accounts are full of superlatives and doubts have been raised about their reliability, there even being speculation whether he actually reached China. It is certainly surprising that he did not remark upon Chinese writing, nor upon the habit of drinking tea. Nevertheless there is sufficient independent evidence to show that he was in China during the reign of Khubilai, although he may not have visited all the places he described.[29] In the meantime the first recorded journey to Europe of a person born in China took place. In 1287 Rabban Sauma, a Turk born in China, reached Naples and then travelled to Paris where he was greeted by the French king Philip IV and went on to Bordeaux where he met Edward I, King of England.[30]

The Franciscan mission to China was continued by Friar John of Montecorvino, who reached China by sea and arrived at Khanbalik in 1295. There he established a mission and made some converts, although he found himself competing with the Nestorians for the court's favour. After twelve years he was made archbishop of Khanbalik and his mission survived into the second half of the fourteenth century. Another Franciscan, Friar Odoric of Pordenone, spent time in Guangzhou and in Khanbalik and left a travel narrative which described those features of Chinese life which later became the stereotype of western concepts of China. Another interesting record was left by Ibn Batuta, who had been born in Tangier and travelled widely, reaching China near the end of the Yuan period.

THE DECLINE AND EXPULSION OF THE YUAN DYNASTY

Explanations of why the Yuan dynasty came to an end have most commonly been expressed from the perspective of China and have tended to emphasise the dynastic decline of the Yuan and the strength of Chinese resentment of the Mongol presence, culminating in the expulsion of the invaders. From what has already been said it will be clear that the degree of sinicisation of the Mongols and the strength of Chinese resentment of their presence are matters difficult to quantify. Nevertheless, despite the efforts of Khubilai and Ayurbarwada to claim legitimacy as Chinese emperors, despite the substantial adoption of Chinese bureaucratic traditions, despite the co-operation, at least to a degree, of Chinese in government, the Mongol court and the Mongol nobility remained alien to the Chinese and were bound to fail as rulers. Behind that failure other changes were taking place, of which three in particular will be discussed.

The first is the undeniable evidence of the declining ability of the Mongol rulers. The murderous intrigues which beset the court were matched by a fragmented and increasingly ineffective administration. Toghon Temür, the last Yuan emperor, showed little aptitude for rule. He relied heavily on chief councillors and the last effective Mongol administrator, Toghto, was dismissed in 1354, an action which precipitated the disintegration of the government.

A second important reason for the Mongol withdrawal was their loss of military advantage. The Mongol position had been achieved by military conquest and, notwithstanding the efforts made to present themselves as legitimate Chinese rulers, had been maintained by military power. After the conquest a complex process took place involving the reorganisation of the Mongol forces and the absorption of the Chinese armies. Out of this emerged four main military formations: the Mongol army; the Mongol forces of the five clans used to garrison conquered areas; the Han army composed of Chinese and non-Chinese, including Qidan, from north China; and the Newly-adhered armies composed of Chinese from the south. Although the Mongols did make use of conscription, for the most part the rank and file of these units were drawn from hereditary military households. These households (apart from the Newly-adhered forces) were given grants of land and were supposedly self-sustaining. Many military households had the services of slaves, sometimes former war captives, and received tax exemptions. In return Chinese military households were expected to provide one soldier for service, whereas in Mongol households there was nearly universal conscription of males. The officer class was treated separately and has been described as a 'self-perpetuating salaried aristocracy'. Officers were members of the Chinese imperial bureaucracy and were paid a salary according to their rank. This position they could pass on to their sons.[31]

It is clear that the Mongol military system deteriorated fairly quickly. A fundamental weakness lay in the inadequate funding of the military households. The Mongol military households, which should have been the core of the Mongol system, were ill-equipped to sustain themselves by farming. The sons of the households were conscripted and their labour force, that is to say their slaves, frequently fled. By the 1290s there were many records of impoverishment, including an extraordinary decree of 1291 which forbade the exportation of Mongolian men and women as slaves to India and Islamic countries. Military standards fell and evidence suggests that intermarriage with Chinese was common. By the end of the dynasty Mongol military families were probably 'not much different from poor Chinese peasants'. Moreover, the garrison system, which had been created to repress internal disturbances had been allowed to decay. In Kublai's reign it had been effective in quelling frequent disturbances, but by the 1340s this capacity had completely disappeared.[32]

A third significant issue concerns the character of the rebellions which became increasingly frequent from the 1330s and which were eventually to overwhelm the dynasty. The most important of these are known as the Red Turban rebellions, after the characteristic headdress of the adherents. These rebellions had a common origin in religious sectarianism and the Red Turban movement was supposedly founded by Peng Yingyu who had transformed the Maitreya cult of the White Lotus sect into an ideology of rebellion.

In the 1340s manifestations of the Red Turban movement sprang up in several places in the Huai region and subsequently elsewhere. By the 1350s two main wings of the movement had appeared, one on the middle Yangzi and the other in the Huai valley. In 1351 the latter wing profited from the unrest caused by the massive conscription of labour to re-route the Yellow river. Some of these uprisings were clearly messianic, following the White Lotus tradition and announcing the imminent coming of the Maitreya Buddha. Others were more obviously class-based and were directed against landlords and officials. The rebels themselves were referred to as 'shiftless elements', and included bandits, idlers, salt smugglers and of course peasants, who were described as deluded. Although this was a great popular rebellion it lacked effective leadership and clear political objectives. These weaknesses enabled the Yuan government to follow the traditional pattern and to allow the gentry to raise peasant militia forces, a stratagem which by 1354 had largely pacified the region.[33] But then a second round of disturbances began, in which various surviving rebel leaders contended for power, and sought allies among local gentry militia leaders. The most successful exponent of this stratagem was Zhu Yuanzhang, who in 1368 was to ascend the throne as first emperor of the Ming dynasty.

This complex sequence of events has been subject to Marxist interpretations and rebuttals. The earlier rebellions have been described as class wars directed against the landlord class, but the later rebellions have been identified as a national struggle against the Mongols with the rebels, in particular Zhu Yuanzhang, deserting their class and siding with the landlords to expel the foreigners. The claim that the rebellions were motivated by ethnic or nationalist feeling is difficult to sustain. Rebel ideology made little if any reference to it, and it has been pointed out that Zhu Yuanzhang made use of defecting Mongols and even ennobled Mongols who gave him meritorious service.[34]

THE IMPACT OF THE MONGOL OCCUPATION OF CHINA

Before concluding this discussion of the Mongol dynasty a further word should be said on the impact that this event had on the development of China. As indicated earlier, the traditional emphasis has been to speak dismissively of the whole episode and to define its impact in entirely negative terms. It is clear however that this was a period in which important developments took place, among them being the rise of literature and drama using the colloquial language.

This point may be supported by citing two other changes which were of importance for China's future development. The first of these concerns the military establishment.

Up to the Yuan period, for much of the previous one thousand years, the military system considered as the norm was the conscript army, this conforming to the classical ideal expressed in the phrase 'the union of the soldiery and the peasantry'. This system, which could only work effectively under a strong and efficient government, had been abandoned by the Tang, and the late Tang and Song governments had relied instead on mercenaries. This had imposed an immense financial burden on the state. The arrival of the dynasties of conquest introduced a new principle of military organisation, that of hereditary military families. This principle was to be adopted by both the Ming and the Qing and played a part in ensuring dynastic strength and encouraging despotic tendencies.[35]

Another example of a long-standing influence can be found in the development of the Chinese legal tradition under the Mongols. Later Chinese scholars were inclined to speak contemptuously of the legal codes drawn up under the Yuan. A Qing scholar wrote of the *Institutions of the Yuan Dynasty* that it was 'minute, rustic and confusing'. Nevertheless it can be shown that under the influence of Mongol customary law, important legal innovations occurred which were retained by later dynasties. One example of this is the use of supplemental penalties, that is to say penalties additional to, or alternative to, the substantive punishment prescribed for the offence. These penalties might be financial, for example the requirement to pay 'nourishment expenses' while the injured person was being treated, or they might be physical, the imposition of retaliatory punishment on certain classes of wrongdoers.[36]

CHAPTER ELEVEN

THE MING DYNASTY

The Ming dynasty extended from 1368 to 1644. Its founder, Zhu Yuanzhang, reigned as the Hongwu emperor until 1398. He was succeeded by his grandson, but in 1403 the throne was usurped by his fourth son, who ruled as the Yongle emperor from 1403 to 1424. These two reigns are seen as the period of the dynasty's greatest vigour, for this was the age of the oceanic voyages and of achievement in various fields. There followed a long period of slow decline in terms of effective government. In the latter half of the sixteenth century there was a period of reform, but under the Wanli emperor and subsequent rulers the pace of decline quickened. The dynasty proved incapable of meeting challenges from within and without and in 1644 was overthrown by peasant rebellion and replaced by the Manchu Qing dynasty. In the south the Southern Ming survived until 1662, when the last emperor of the dynasty, who had fled to Burma, was captured and put to death.

THE FOUNDING OF THE DYNASTY

Edward Dreyer traced the origins of the Ming dynasty back to the 1350s and to 'an obscure band of dislocated soldiers'.[1] The founder of the dynasty, Zhu Yuanzhang, had been born of a very poor family near Fengyang in modern Anhui. Both his parents died in a famine and Zhu entered a Buddhist monastery as a novice. Later he resorted to begging. In 1352, when he was twenty-five, he joined the Red Turban rebels led by Guo Zixing. Zhu showed military ability and also became connected to Guo by marriage. Zhu began to gather his own circle of advisers and administrators and this support, in addition to his military following, enabled him to achieve a degree of independence. From 1355 he offered allegiance to the rebellion headed by Han Liner, the leader of a rebel group, who had declared himself emperor of a restored Song dynasty. In the meantime Zhu developed his own base at Nanjing which he had captured in 1356. A key feature of his strategy was to fuse together his military machine and the support of local gentry.[2] He also fostered a reputation for having a concern for the condition of the people and went out of his way to establish good relations with eminent scholars.[3]

By 1360 the key struggle for power was centred on the Yangzi valley, which was divided between three regimes, the Ming,[4] the Han and the Wu. Zhu Yuanzhang's main rival Chen Youliang, another former Red Turban rebel, had proclaimed himself emperor of the Han dynasty. The principal battles of what has become known as the

180

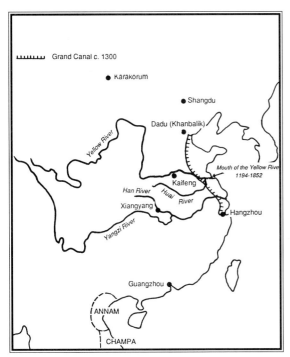

22 China under the Yuan (Mongol) dynasty, 1279–1368

23 Ivory figure of a seated official from the Ming dynasty

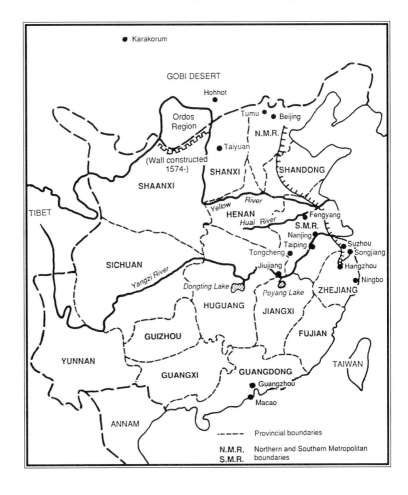

24 China in the early Ming
period

25 The Humble Administrator's Garden, Suzhou; early sixteenth century

他也忙然
閃我又顚蹎不跌倒
步虎直攔兩拳他退
當頭砲勢衝人怕進
須相應
捉兔硬開弓手脚必
下掌摘打其心拿鷹
拘彎肘出步顚剁搬

26 Soldiers drilling in the martial arts; Qi Jiguang's New Treatise on Tactics *(O/C 15291.a.18)*

27 Restored section of the Great Wall near Badaling, north-west of Beijing

Ming-Han war took place between 1360 and 1363. The sequence began with the Han, who had a strong naval force, sailing down the Yangzi and seizing the important city of Taiping. They then moved on to attack Nanjing, the Ming capital, but suffered a serious defeat, with the loss of a considerable number of ships. It was now the Ming leaders' turn to go on the offensive and in September 1361 the Ming fleet sailed upriver, achieved a naval victory and obtained the surrender of Jiujiang. Chen Youliang retreated upriver, and Zhu Yuanzhang, aware of the danger of being absent from Nanjing for a long time, was forced to return to his base. In 1363 the final, famous battle took place on Lake Poyang. By this time the Han had built a new fleet, their ships were large three-decked galleasses with iron-sheathed turrets for archers and sterns high enough to overtower city walls. The Ming fleet was composed of smaller, but more numerous ships. A four-day battle on the lake, in which the Ming used fireships effectively, weakened but did not destroy the Han fleet. However, it was now trapped in the lake and when it tried to break out it was annihilated and in that same action Chen Youliang was killed.[5]

The way was now open for Zhu Yuanzhang to exploit the situation he had created. Between 1365 and 1367 he defeated the Wu regime, the key campaign being the siege and capture of Suzhou. There now remained the final settlement with the Yuan government, which by this time had influence only in the area around Beijing. Late in 1367 Zhu Yuanzhang dispatched expeditions to the north and to the south. So confident was he of their success that in January 1368 he formally ascended to the imperial throne. Such confidence was not misplaced, for the southern expedition quickly brought the south under Ming rule and the northern expedition captured Beijing, the Yuan court fleeing to Inner Mongolia.

THE ESTABLISHMENT OF THE DYNASTY: THE REIGN OF HONGWU, 1368–98

The new emperor, who took the reign name of Hongwu, had a choice of three traditions on which to model his empire. The first was implicit in the name chosen for the dynasty, *ming*, signifying 'bright' or 'brightening', which might be taken as a reference to Manichaeism, or to Maitreyan Buddhism, with which the successful rebellion had previously been associated. However it was soon clear that the emperor no longer had any sympathy for sectarian religion. The second choice was to aspire to recreate the Confucian empire of previous Chinese dynasties. Although Hongwu was prepared to play that role, he was always to treat Confucian officials with deep suspicion. The third choice was the obvious one, but it was also the one which traditional historiography has denied to be the one Hongwu pursued. It was to rule according to the precedent set by the Yuan dynasty. It has been argued that in virtually every essential field, in government institutions and in social and military organisation, the first emperor of the Ming followed practices employed by and often initiated by the Mongols.[6]

His first task was to obtain the military security of the empire and this meant striking at the Mongol court which he did successfully in 1370. The next target was the Yuan loyalist Kökö Temür, who, in the final years of the Yuan dynasty, had been a regional powerholder in the area around Taiyuan, but with Hongwu's victory had been forced to move north. In 1372 a large expeditionary force was sent across the Gobi desert to Karakorum to deal with him. After an initial victory it suffered a disastrous reverse. Kökö Temür died in 1375, but the threat from the Mongols continued until 1388, when Lan Yu crossed the Gobi and achieved a major victory which fragmented the Mongol leadership and ended the Mongol threat for a generation. Meanwhile campaigns were conducted against independent regimes in the south–west and by 1390 the modern provinces of Sichuan and Yunnan had been brought firmly under Ming control.

Such extensive military operations demanded an effective military establishment. Hongwu recognised the need to develop a system which did not ruin the economy, which provided for the demobilisation of troops and which offered adequate rewards to his generals. The solution he arrived at was clearly derived from the precedent set by the Yuan. Known as the *weiso* system, literally 'guards' and 'battalions', it evolved from the military units which had surrendered to the Ming on the establishment of the dynasty. Their leaders had been assured that their commands would be made permanent and that their units would be kept intact. The consequence was the hereditary succession of military commanders. As their soldiers could not be disbanded, it was necessary to provide for their upkeep, and this was achieved by making the armies self-sufficient through the military colony system. The first generals included the 'dislocated soldiers' who had joined Zhu Yuanzhang before 1355. Later generals were awarded noble titles and stipends. Important though this military establishment was, it was clearly subject to imperial control, and from about 1372 its influence was overtaken by that of the civil government.[7]

In its early stages the Ming system of government also owed much to the Yuan precedent. At central government level the emperor retained the secretariat, with its two chief councillors or prime ministers, and the subordinate six ministries which carried out routine administration. At what was to become the provincial level he retained the branch secretariats, although in 1376 he added military and surveillance agencies alongside them to ensure control. A civil service was created to staff these positions, although initially only in 1373 was the examination system used to select candidates.

The period of consolidation came to an abrupt end in 1380 when Hu Weiyong, the senior chief councillor, was put on trial for plotting to assassinate the emperor and to overthrow the dynasty. The charges were almost certainly fabricated, but they illustrate Hongwu's fear of any challenge to his authority. For his supposed crimes Hu Weiyong was executed and perhaps 15,000 others put to death. The secretariat and the office of chief councillor were abolished and henceforth Hongwu resorted to direct rule. In his attempt to keep all affairs of state under his personal supervision, he undertook an immense administrative burden. It was recorded that in one ten-day period towards the end of his reign he received 1,660 documents relating to 3,391 matters which required an imperial decision.[8] At the same time he maintained a punishing schedule of audiences, which kept him in touch with his officials although he did not leave the capital Nanjing.

In the latter part of his reign Hongwu introduced measures which were to have a marked influence on the developing character of the imperial system of government. On his orders a comprehensive overhaul of the land and tax system was inaugurated. Population statistics were entered in the Yellow Registers and the ownership of land was recorded on the Fish-scale Charts and Registers (so called because the topographical charts resembled fish skin in appearance).[9] Alongside these registers, two other systems were introduced to allocate responsibility for tax payment: under the 'tax-captain system' wealthy families were made responsible for the collection of taxes in their area, and under the *lijia* system, peasant households were organised into groups of ten families which were mutually responsible for the payment of taxes and the performance of labour services. The compilation of these registers required an immense effort and provided an unprecedentedly detailed set of statistics, but the records were not updated accurately after Hongwu's death. It may be that the effort was misplaced for another reason. The level of land tax was relatively low, which limited the government's potential revenue and its ability to promote economic improvement.[10]

The second example of Hongwu's intervention concerned the examination system. In 1384 the examinations were revived and thereafter were held at regular intervals. At the same time, throughout the empire, there was an expansion of the government schools which enabled talented young men to compete for office. The curriculum they studied was based on the Confucian classics. In this way a Confucian civil bureaucracy, which was to remain a feature of the empire for the next six hundred years, was created. It must not be supposed, however, that Hongwu intended that these measures should encourage any challenge to his autocracy. This bureaucracy was created to carry out his instructions, not to initiate policy.

Hongwu died in 1398 after a short illness. His personality and the achievements of his reign have long been the subject of debate. There can be few comparable cases of a person of so humble a background and so lacking in prepossessiveness – he had a high forehead, thick nose and protruding jaw – achieving so exalted a position and leaving so distinctive a legacy. On the negative side he has been denounced for having betrayed his social class by relying on the support of the landlords and gentry. He has been accused of paranoia for his distrust of any person he thought opposed to him. On occasions he sank to depths of vindictiveness and cruelty, none worse than the purge he ordered in 1393 after he had executed Lan Yu, one of his foremost generals. On the positive side, he established the most durable dynasty in Chinese history and laid the foundations for what was later to be defined as the requirements of good government.

THE REIGN OF YONGLE, 1402–24

Hongwu was succeeded by his grandson, who in a short reign as the Jianwen emperor tried to rule with the support of Confucian officials and attempted to break the power of the princes who had been granted fiefs by his grandfather. In this he achieved some degree of success, but he was finally defeated by one of those princes, his uncle the Prince of Yen, and reportedly died in a fire at the imperial palace. His uncle thereupon took the throne and was subsequently given the reign name of Yongle.

Yongle proved to be the epitome of the strong second emperor of a dynasty. He began his reign by reducing the bodyguards of the surviving princes and transferring the princes themselves to strategically less important regions. This averted the danger of a challenge to the throne from a member of the imperial clan. He reorganised the machinery of central government, ostensibly to restore the practices of his father which he declared had been disregarded by his predecessor. In fact he introduced a grand secretariat, a revised version of the body which his father had angrily dismissed in 1380. To this secretariat were appointed seven grand secretaries, all with impeccable Confucian backgrounds. A feature of his reign was the long tenure of office enjoyed by his senior officials and this ensured a degree of political stability. A more sinister method of protecting his position was achieved through using the the imperial bodyguard to investigate suspected cases of opposition, a role which was also performed by the palace eunuchs.

Through these reforms he ensured the safety of the throne, and this permitted him to concentrate on military security and expansion, with particular reference to the northern frontier, his own main power base. It was this concern which lay behind the decision to transfer the capital from Nanjing to Beijing, a process commenced in 1402 but only completed in 1421. It involved a massive movement of workmen to the site of the new capital and a major task of constructing new buildings. The Forbidden City of today retains the layout as determined by Yongle, and the Hall of Supreme Harmony stands where the emperor sat enthroned on important state occasions, at the symbolic centre of the capital and of the empire. To supply Beijing it was necessary to accomplish another major task, the restoration of the Grand Canal, which was completed by 1415.[11]

In the meantime Yongle had turned his attention to frontier affairs. At the beginning of his reign the imminent threat came from the Mongol ruler known in the West as Tamerlane, who in the late fourteenth century had established a mighty empire in central Asia and who, in 1404, advanced on China only to die before he had effected an invasion. To the north-east, in what is now Jilin and Inner Mongolia, the Jurchen and Urianghad were persuaded to accept Chinese overlordship by the award of titles and the presentation of gifts. Further west along the frontier were the Mongol tribes now known as the Oirat and the Tatar, the latter including the remnants of the Yuan forces. It was against these that Yongle decided to make a demonstration of China's military power. Five times, between 1410 and 1424, he personally led expeditions across the desert to chastise them. Each expedition required an extraordinary commitment of men and material and involved considerable hardship: the emperor himself died when he returned from the fifth expedition. No major victory was achieved despite this massive expenditure of effort, but the campaigns did ensure that the Mongols would remain divided and unable to threaten China for a generation.[12] Such an outcome was more beneficial than the result of the intervention in Annam in 1407. A Chinese force, sent to there to restore the person believed to be the true claimant to the Annamese throne, was ambushed and the pretender killed. In retaliation Yongle sent two large armies which overran Annam, but he then rashly decided to make the country a province of China. Rebellion against the Chinese presence broke out in 1418 and China was forced to withdraw in 1427–8.

The most spectacular of Yongle's foreign initiatives was the dispatch of the famous oceanic expeditions. The motives behind these have never been entirely clear. A legend ascribes them to a search for his predecessor the Jianwen emperor, who, it was said, had not died in Nanjing but, disguised as a monk, had fled overseas. A more plausible reason was Yongle's desire to enhance his reputation and his claim to legitimacy – for it could not be forgotten that he was an usurper – by securing tributary relations with a large number of states. Another possible motive was that of commercial advantage, prompted in particular by the conquests of Tamerlane which had cut the continental silk route. From 1405 onwards seven maritime expeditions were sent out, six of them in the Yongle period. Most of these were headed by the grand eunuch Zheng He and they were very substantial affairs, the first expedition, according to the record, comprising 317 ships and 27,870 men.[13] In the course of these voyages Zheng He himself reached Hormuz and detachments from the fleets followed the African coast as far south as Malindi and also reached Jidda. The account of the voyages was written by Ma Huan, his interpreter, who was a Muslim and was probably among the group which visited Mecca. Ma Huan made a careful record of the products of the countries visited and the customs of the peoples who lived in them, noting for example the practice of *suttee* on Java and the skill of the jewellers of Aden.

As there is some doubt about why the expeditions were sent, so too is there debate about why they were suspended. One probable reason is that the voyages were closely connected with Yongle's political agenda, and after his death the motivation of seeking recognition no longer applied. The issue of cost and economic benefit is difficult to determine, for the expeditions were financed by eunuch agencies and no record was made of profit and loss. However, Yongle's construction of a new capital, his campaigns in Mongolia, and other costly projects did draw criticism from officials and did lead to retrenchment immediately after his death.[14] The discontinuation of these voyages was to have a significant long-term effect. In the Yongle reign China held an unrivalled position as the leading commercial power throughout Asia and as the leading naval power in the Indian Ocean as far as the African coast. This advantage was to be surrendered on the eve of the western penetration of the Indian Ocean and China was to retire into semi-isolation.

THE MIDDLE YEARS OF THE MING DYNASTY: FOREIGN RELATIONS

A striking feature of the Ming period is the contrast between the aggressive, expansionist policies pursued by the early emperors and the passive, defensive policies followed by their successors. An indication, and perhaps an explanation, of this change can be found in the events of the reign of Zhengtong emperor, who came to the throne as a minor in 1436. At that time the dominant group among the Mongols were the Oirat, who had developed an important trade with China by providing horses in exchange for tea. In the 1440s a new Oirat leader, Esen, had unified the Mongol tribes and had begun to encroach on Chinese territory. Early in Zhengtong's reign the most powerful influence at the Ming court was the chief eunuch Wang Zhen and his self-seeking influence is suspected in what was to follow. In 1448 an Oirat tribute mission to the Ming court was treated discourteously. Esen's response was to launch a major attack on the important market town of Datong to the north-east of Beijing. This prompted Zhengtong, perhaps on the advice of Wang Zhen, to take the extraordinarily risky step of placing himself at the head of the army which was to advance against Esen. Commanding a force of perhaps half a million men, he set out on what was intended to be a short and glorious campaign. Instead his forces were first ambushed and then surrounded by the Mongols at Tumu, some seventy miles north-west of Beijing. The army was destroyed, the senior officers and officials were killed, vast quantities of booty were seized, and the emperor was led off into captivity. In Beijing opposing views were put forward on what to do, with one suggestion being that the capital should be abandoned. To this Yu Qian, the vice-minister of war, reportedly replied:

Those talking about moving south should be beheaded. The capital is the foundation of the empire. Once you move it the empire is lost.
Don't you know what happened to the Song after it moved south?[15]

For his determined response, which ensured that Beijing did not fall, Yu Qian was to become a symbol of national resistance and popular hero of opera. His stand has been seen as marking the end of a characteristic feature of the early Ming period, the dominance of an élite of hereditary military officers. This dominance had already been eroded, but the disgrace of the fiasco at Tumu allowed Yu Qian to assume leadership. Through the rest of the imperial period the civil bureaucracy was to retain this superiority over the military command.[16]

The Tumu incident had other important consequences. In Beijing the decision was taken not to await the outcome of the attempt to ransom the emperor, but instead, in defiance of tradition, to place the emperor's half-brother on the throne. The new emperor, who assumed the reign name of Jingtai, took vigorous steps to stabilise the government and to deal with the Mongol threat. The deposed emperor was released, but kept away from all political power. For a time, the recent disaster united the court and encouraged a mood of reform. But then factional struggles resumed, often connected with the former emperor. In 1457, at a time when Jingtai was ill, a swift coup d'état placed the former emperor back on the throne. There followed a period of violent settlement of scores. Yu Qian, held largely responsible for the deposition, was condemned to death for treason. The purge weakened the government and left the restored emperor and later Ming emperors very much in the hands of factions of eunuchs and officials.

Another consequence of the Tumu disaster related to frontier defence. Although the fiasco had occurred because of one foolish decision, the danger from the Oirat derived from a deeper cause. A crucial element in the balance of power between the settled territory of China and the society of the steppe was the control of the steppe transition zone. Hongwu, recognising this, had not only campaigned against the Mongols, but had also established a defence line comprising eight outer garrisons to maintain control of the Ordos region. For reasons which are not clear, Yongle abandoned these garrisons and thus relinquished Chinese control of the steppe transition zone. At about the same time the shortcomings of the *weiso* system, which could not produce enough trained and mounted soldiers for defence, had started to emerge. The Tumu disaster, which destroyed the dynasty's military prestige, also forced the adoption of a defensive strategy.[17] In the next twenty years many suggestions were put forward on how the Ordos region, now increasingly occupied by Mongols, might be recovered. It was conceded that to mount a major campaign against them would be enormously expensive and would impose an unacceptable burden on the local population. In 1472 Wang Yue, one of the ablest generals of the day, gained an important victory over the Mongols near Red Salt Lake. Two years later, using the respite so gained, Yu Zijun, an official with long experience of working in the area, commenced the project he had long recommended, the construction of a wall which ran for 566 miles from north-eastern Shaanxi to north-western Ningxia. Together with a shorter wall constructed by Wang Yue these fortifications created a barrier which cut the Ordos off from the south. This was the beginning of the Great Wall as it is known today. Although not recognised at the time, its construction marked a decisive shift in strategy towards the nomadic societies of the steppe. The wall was a defensive construction. Its building implied a policy of exclusion, which repudiated previous attempts to establish working relations with the nomads through the promotion of trade and diplomacy.[18]

MING ABSOLUTISM

The phrases 'Ming absolutism' and 'Ming despotism' are used to refer to the unchecked growth of imperial power from the late fourteenth century. Absolutism refers to the development of institutions which enhanced imperial power, whereas despotism may also imply the abuse of power by an individual ruler. Monarchical absolutism was implicit in the doctrine of the mandate of heaven, but early emperors had had any absolutist tendencies limited by the presence of an aristocracy. With the decline of the aristocracy and the increased reliance on a civil bureaucracy, the potential for absolutism increased, but it was moderated by the Confucian concept of an ideal ruler who emphasised benevolence and righteousness. Under the Song, absolutist tendencies had been encouraged by two developments: on the one hand reformers like Wang Anshi promoted the idea that, to meet the crisis which they believed threatened the state, the legal and fiscal powers of central government should be increased; on the other hand the opponents of the reformers, like Sima Guang, rejected practical reform but promoted the exaltation of the ruler.[19]

Dynasties of conquest, which derived from the tribal society of the steppe, continued to rely on tribal chieftains for their support, and as a consequence were not in themselves absolute. However, it is commonly alleged that the Yuan dynasty, because of its indifference to Chinese values and to Chinese standards of government, and because of its neglect of the civil bureaucracy, encouraged the tendency towards absolutism. Hongwu's decision in 1380 to abolish the secretariat and the office of chief councillor has been regarded as an important step along that same road. The emperor was also a despot, carrying out pogroms, operating a secret police organisation, known as the Brocade Uniform Guard, and instituting a literary inquisition to search out any written slights cast on the ruler.

A discussion of Ming absolutism is not complete without reference to the role of the eunuchs, often seen as the sinister agents of imperial despotism. Eunuchs had been employed at court from as early as the eighth century BC. As no uncastrated male was permitted to enter the imperial palace, eunuchs had exceptional opportunities to ingratiate themselves with emperors, or even more commonly to ally themselves with empresses and consorts, in a common front against the bureaucrats, who despised the eunuchs for lack of breeding and education. Eunuchs had played an important role in court politics in the late Tang period, but their influence had declined under the Song. Although many eunuchs served at the Yuan court they exerted little influence on the emperor. When Hongwu came to the throne, being aware that eunuchs in the past had meddled in politics, he issued an edict restricting them to household tasks. In 1384 he had an iron tablet engraved with the inscription 'Eunuchs are forbidden to interfere with government affairs. Those who attempt to do so will be subjected to capital punishment.'[20] However Yongle, who had gained the throne with the assistance of the eunuchs, used them in important and confidential posts. Mention has already been made of the eunuch Zheng He's leadership of the maritime expeditions. A more sinister role was played by the Eastern Depot, the headquarters of the secret police in Beijing, which was controlled by the eunuchs and which reported solely to the emperor. Under Xuande (reigned 1426–35) another means of keeping the eunuchs under control was removed, in that the prohibition on eunuchs receiving a literary education was relaxed.[21]

The consequences of these changes was felt later in the dynasty, with the emergence of eunuch dictators. The first of these was Wang Zhen, whose disastrous encouragement of Zhengtong to attack the Oirat has already been noted. He had been one of the first eunuchs to attend the palace school for eunuchs and had been the emperor's first tutor. This enabled him to establish an ascendancy over the emperor. His appointment as head of the palace eunuch establishment, and hence of the Eastern Depot, gave him control of the Brocade Uniform Guard. Against such a system of influence senior bureaucrats could do little. This concentration of power recurred in later reigns when the emperor, either through incompetence, or through indifference to the duties of his office, allowed a eunuch dictator to emerge. In the middle years of the dynasty the most notorious instance of this occurred in the reign of Zhengde (r. 1506–21). The eunuch Liu Jin dominated the court and used the emperor's authority to extort money to cover the emperor's extravagances. He instituted a reign of terror against any officials who dared to oppose him and eventually incited a revolt. In 1510 he was charged with plotting to kill the emperor and to seize the throne, and for this he was put to death. An even more notorious case, indeed the most notorious case of eunuch dominance in Chinese history, occurred in the Tianqi reign (1621–7). The eunuch dictator Wei Zhongxian gained total control of the emperor and the government: the abuses which he encouraged and the brutal suppression of opposition which he practised were subsequently regarded as having played an important part in the decline and fall of the dynasty.

Absolutism implies the failure of the checks on the arbitrary use of power. In imperial China the formal agency for maintaining such checks was the censorial system, the functions of which were to maintain surveillance of government activities, to impeach or censure officials whose conduct had been exposed as unsatisfactory, and to make recommendations for change, which could include remonstrances directed against the conduct of emperor. This system was of great antiquity for it can be traced back to the Qin. It was strengthened during the Yuan period, although the duty of remonstrance was neglected, and it continued to be a standard and important branch of early Ming government. The censorate might be expected to challenge absolutism, if absolutism implied a departure from the principles of Confucian government. It has been shown that in the period 1424–34 the censorate was reformed, and that in routine matters it appeared to operate efficiently, although it failed to remonstrate with the emperor on matters of personal conduct and neglected to challenge the increase in eunuch power. However a century later, in the time of Wei Zhongxian, although the censorate was ostensibly still active, it appeared incapable of making an effective protest against the excesses of the eunuch dictator.[22]

A discussion of Ming absolutism, with its reference to abuses of power, emphasises negative aspects of Ming government. This is not a balanced judgment to make on the dynasty before its final decline. Despite occasional aberrations, imperial absolutism provided great stability and a quality of administration which was probably not matched by any other state in the world at that time. Moreover absolutism did not imply that there was no consultation in the decision-making process. One study of how Ming foreign policy decisions relating to war and peace were made concluded that, far from being taken in an arbitrary fashion by the emperor or by his favourite, decisions were only arrived at after many people had been consulted, and after long deliberations and careful calculations of the chances of success had taken place.[23]

DEMOGRAPHIC, ECONOMIC AND FISCAL DEVELOPMENTS UNDER THE MING

As a result of Hongwu's policy of requiring the compilation of the Yellow Registers, the population statistics of the early Ming period are very full and probably fairly accurate. Allowing for under-registration, the population of China towards the end of the fourteenth century was probably somewhat over 65,000,000. Subsequently, because of various practices, including deliberate under-reporting and avoidance of registration, the system of population registration became obsolete. The official record showed the population in the late Ming as amounting to only 60,000,000 people. In fact by about 1600, after two centuries of comparative peace, the population had reached approximately 150,000,000. Although the data does not allow any close analysis of population distribution, it seems likely that in that period growth rates were higher in the south than in the north, although the population of the north, which had been decimated at the time of the Mongol invasions, had made a recovery.[24]

The main reasons why this linear growth of population had been possible were prolonged peace and an increase in the food supply. In the eleventh century early-ripening rice, which permitted double-cropping, was introduced from Champa and subsequently underwent further improvement. Under the Ming the sixty-day variety was gradually disseminated to Guangdong and Guangxi and then to other provinces. New crops, for example sorghum, known as the millet of the Sichuan basin, which had been introduced in or before the Yuan period, was now grown more extensively. In the sixteenth century sweet potato, maize and peanuts, all of which came from America, crops which could be grown in dry conditions, were brought to China. Accompanying these improvements in planting materials there were significant advances in farming methods including the extension of irrigation and the increased use of fertiliser.[25]

This reference to the dynamic changes in cropping patterns occurring over the centuries of Ming rule hints at the problem of making generalisations about economic change over so large an area and over so long a period. A recent study of Hunan has shown that at the beginning of the Ming period that province, which was to become a major rice-producing area, was only populated with any degree of density in the counties around the Dongting Lake. By 1582 the proportion of cultivated land had increased considerably and land clearance had spread along the tributaries which fed into the lake. Hunan was now known as a grain-exporting province, but it was still referred to as a place where 'grain is cheap, land is abundant, there are no people to cultivate it, and people do not set a high value on land.'[26] The experience of Hunan was repeated in other parts of the country. In the Ming period migration on a large scale took place to frontier regions, particularly to the west and south-west, to the north-west, and overseas to Taiwan. Much of this migration was the voluntary movement of families in search of better land, and is therefore unrecorded and difficult to estimate. However some migration was state sponsored. Hongwu, for example, had 150,000 families moved to the Huai region, his own birthplace. Yongle moved large numbers of artisans to Beijing to work on his new imperial capital.

The great majority of the population depended on agriculture and lived in the countryside. Nevertheless in the Ming period important industrial and commercial changes took place. One of these was the development of the cotton textile industry. Cotton had been introduced into China during the Tang dynasty and by the Ming period cotton production had spread over a very wide area. However it was only in Songjiang prefecture in the Yangzi delta that a cotton industry developed. This area was economically advanced and some technological transfer may have taken place from the silk industry of Suzhou. It has been suggested that the high level of land tax imposed on the region may have played a part in encouraging the switch away from agriculture to industrial production, although this is disputed. Cotton textile production had first developed as a means of supplementing household income and the whole process of production had been carried out in the household. By the fifteenth century a division of labour was being practised and a wide variety of cotton cloth was being produced. Spinning remained largely a rural activity, but weaving became a professionalised urban industry. Alvaro Semedo, a Portuguese Jesuit missionary living in Shanghai, estimated that in 1621 there were 200,000 looms operating in Shanghai and its administrative area. Gradual advances in the technology in use, increases in the supply of raw cotton and improvements in distribution enabled the increase in demand to be met and the price of cotton cloth to remain relatively stable. These factors, together with the continued availability of cheap labour, may explain why this important industry continued to grow in size but did not pass beyond the stage of handicraft-style production.[27]

In the Ming period the trend towards large-scale urbanisation, which had been noticeable in the Song and Yuan periods, may have slowed or even stopped. Instead, from the sixteenth century, the trend was the proliferation of smaller market towns. This type of development was very noticeable in the more advanced regions, for example around Shanghai. An important function of these towns was to provide a market close enough for spinners and weavers to make daily trips to obtain their raw materials and to trade their finished products. More generally the increase in market towns was a symptom of increasing trade, and the growth in the numbers and wealth of merchants.[28]

It is against this background that one should consider Ming policies relating to currency and taxation. Despite the overall growth of the economy, in many respects these policies were a continuation of the past. The Ming administration has been described as committed to preserving a 'village commodity economy', an outlook which made it reluctant to promote the advanced sectors of the economy, that is to say industrial development and foreign trade, and thus widen the economic gap between different parts of the empire. An example of this outlook can be found in the dynasty's failure to work out an effective monetary policy. The paper currency, which had been introduced under the Yuan with some degree of success, was under the Ming to cause long-term damage to government finances. Hongwu circulated paper currency in large quantities which provoked a serious monetary inflation and eventually the currency lost all commercial value. Copper cash, which for a time had been proscribed, returned to use, but the quantity minted was quite inadequate. Gradually bulk silver came to be used as a form of currency, the unit being the tael or ounce of silver, but this never became a proper coinage.

The main source of government revenue under the Ming, as under previous dynasties, was the land tax. The system under which it was levied was modified by Hongwu, who established tax quotas for each province and prefecture and who, in 1393, declared that the total quotas, amounting to 32,789,000 piculs of grain (a picul equalled 107.4 litres), should be regarded as fixed permanently. In addition the dynasty levied various requisitions on labour and basic commodities, most importantly on salt. It has long been supposed that these levies, even at the beginning of the dynasty, amounted to a heavy burden of taxation, and that by the end of the period they had become so oppressive that they played an important part in the Ming collapse.

More recently it has been argued that the value of the taxes which actually reached the government, amounting to perhaps ten per cent of agrarian output, was in fact rather low. It was sufficient to pay the costs of a government which ran a self-sufficient army and which maintained only a thin veneer of administration, but it was quite inadequate to allow the government to play an active role in developing the economy, although no such policy would have been given serious consideration. However, although the official levels of taxation were relatively light, a whole array of additional impositions and forms of unauthorised taxation were added to the total tax bill and this burden fell disproportionately on those least able to pay. As a consequence tax evasion and tax arrears were serious problems.[29]

In the sixteenth century, beginning from 1531, a protracted attempt was made to revise the system of taxation. The measures taken became known as the Single-Whip reform, the term implying the combination of various levies into a single payment. In fact the reform covered four separate measures: the elimination of the service levy, that is to say the labour service imposed on adult males between the ages of sixteen and sixty, including services relating to the *lijia* system, which in effect became defunct; the simplification and amalgamation of land tax rates; the payment of the taxes in silver; and changes in the arrangements for the collection of taxes. The implications of these reforms are not easy to assess. They have been regarded as an extremely important turning point and as the beginning of the modern land tax system.[30] The requirement that taxes be paid in silver has been seen as accelerating the process of the monetisation of the economy and as sounding the death knell of whatever remained of the natural economy.[31] At one time Marxist historians maintained that the reforms had been beneficial to the poor, because they had relieved them of labour services. More recently the stress has been on the limitations of the reforms. These were never consolidated or applied consistently. Taxation was non-progressive and made no provision for destitution. It failed to take advantage of the growth of the economy and did not provide the government with a surplus which might have allowed it to invest. In fact, Ming financial administration was more concerned with maintaining political stability than with allowing the state to act as an agent of change and improvement. Its legacy was an attitude of complacency which prevented government in China from taking an active role in the economy until modern times.[32]

SOCIAL AND LITERARY CHANGES IN THE MING PERIOD

The founder of the Ming dynasty set out to restore social stability and to that end he introduced a form of village government which was intended to promote harmony and to suppress disorder. Under the *lijia* system the entire population was divided into groups of one hundred and ten families. The ten most wealthy families represented the community to the local magistrate and carried out duties on his behalf. Community chiefs settled disputes and also relayed the moral exhortations of the emperor to the population. The remaining one hundred families were divided into ten groups of ten, and each group supplied a headman who organised the group in carrying out a variety of labour duties.[33]

In the Ming period there emerged fully the status group most commonly known in the west as the gentry. The term is used to translate the Chinese term *shenshi*, literally 'officials and scholars' and in its narrow definition it refers to those individuals who had obtained the formal educational qualifications to make them eligible for office. A broader definition of the gentry presents them as a class which owed its position to the possession of large landed estates, their wealth giving them access to education and thence to influence. The gentry was not a large group. One estimate put their numbers at the end of the Ming period at perhaps 2 per cent of population and at rather less than a quarter of a million families.[34]

A detailed survey of Tongcheng county in Anhui has provided an insight into the character of this élite. Tongcheng was a county of academic distinction, but the total number of persons with degrees of any kind amounted to only 1,800 out of a population of over 200,000. However these degree-holders belonged to the important families and lineage organisations of the county. Their families saw the obtaining of degrees not as an end in itself, but as a means of achieving office and exercising influence. In fact obtaining degrees and holding office were not the only means whereby lineages could exert influence. Some notable lineages owed their social position to organisation and corporate wealth and to systematic intermarriage with other powerful lineages. In these operations the ownership of land was a factor of considerable importance. It has been shown that the fortunes of the great families of Tongcheng county were originally based on land and that subsequently they went to great pains to protect and increase their estates. It has been suggested that the insecurity of basing a lineage's fortunes on examinations and office was an important factor in promoting lineage organisation and in particular the administration of a charitable estate for the support of the lineage. Tongcheng's important lineages were established by the middle or late Ming period and there was little evidence of subsequent upward, or indeed of subsequent downward movement.[35]

The evidence of Tongcheng county leads to a reappraisal of two views on gentry status and social mobility. The first is the argument put forward by Chang Chung-li that gentry income came largely from gentry status rather than from the ownership of land. He suggested that, in the nineteenth century, 'The gentry's control of Chinese society, including its economic aspects, was not dependent on landowning. . . . A gentry member was not necessarily a landlord, nor was a landlord necessarily a member of the gentry.'[36]

The second view concerns social mobility into the élite. Ho Ping-ti, who wrote the best-known study on this topic, noted how Confucian ideology asserted that there should be equal educational opportunity for all. China's competitive civil service examination system seemed to be the perfect embodiment of that principle. He analysed the social composition of the 14,562 men who obtained the *jinshi* 'advanced scholar' degree between 1371 and 1904, placing them into three categories: candidates whose families during the three preceding generations had failed to produce a single holder of the *shengyuan*, the elementary degree; those who in the same period had produced a holder of the elementary degree, but no holder of a higher degree or of office; and those whose families had produced one or more holders of a higher degree or office. He found that in the Ming period 49.5 per cent of *jinshi* fell into the first two categories and 50.5 per cent into the third, whereas the figures for the same categories under the Qing were 37.6 per cent and 62.4 per cent. The most marked evidence of upward mobility came in the early Ming period, that is between 1371 and 1496, when 57.6 per cent of *jinshi* came from the first category. This he took as evidence of an unparalleled instance of upward social mobility in a major society prior to the industrial revolution.[37] However the case of Tongcheng suggests that in the early Ming, and indeed throughout the Ming-Qing period, class structure in the county was much more stable and less mobile than has been argued, and that the stability of the élite was based on the ownership of land.

A statistical analysis can give one a view of Ming society. A more vivid, if more subjective, impression may be obtained from contemporary literature. The Ming period was the time when colloquial fiction, in the form of short stories and novels, came into its own. These had their origin in the plot books used by storytellers and they give a vivid picture of life, particularly as it was lived by the inhabitants of the cities of the lower Yangzi. In the late Ming period collected editions of these stories were made, for example by Feng Menglong (1574–1646), a scholar and failed examination candidate who lived in Suzhou. One such story, entitled 'The Pearl-sewn Shirt', was typical of the genre in that it told of an illicit passion which nevertheless served as a moral tale. It concerned a woman named Fortune, whose husband was a travelling vendor. While he was absent on a journey she was seduced by a merchant who used the services of an old dame as a go-between. The affair was revealed when the pearl-sewn shirt of the title, which Fortune had given to her lover, was recognised by her husband. The story concluded rather improbably with a reconciliation between husband and wife. A notable feature of the story is its lively depiction of the female characters, above all that of the go-between, who like the Wife of Bath in Chaucer's *Canterbury Tales*, used confessions of her own youthful indiscretions to prompt a response from her audience.[38] Such tales may be contrasted with many other Ming stories and accounts which deal with female virtue, but which place the emphasis on a heroine dedicated to the Confucian virtues, who is prepared to undergo horrific ordeals in their defence. Ming local histories all contain biographies of virtuous women, and of the thirty-six thousand women so described, a third of them are recorded as having committed suicide, or being murdered, while resisting rape.[39]

Alongside the development of the short story came the emergence of the full-length novel. Of the four famous novels of the Ming period three evolved from earlier oral versions. The earliest extant printed version of *The Romance of the Three Kingdoms* was published in 1522, but handwritten copies of the novel, set in the turbulent last years of the Later Han dynasty, had been circulating long before this. The same was true of *Water Margin*, the tale of 108 outlaws in the days of the Northern Song, which had been in circulation for almost a century and a half before it was published in 1540 and then went through ten editions in the next century. The *Journey to the West*, known also as *Monkey*, was written down by Wu Cheng'en and published in 1592, but was based on earlier versions. It gave a highly fictionalised version of the travels to India of the Buddhist monk Xuan Zang. The fourth novel, an original work, the notorious *Jin Ping Mei*, was both pornographic and also the world's first realistic social novel.[40] Taken together these works have been described as the only great heritage of novels found in a premodern civilisation outside Europe.[41]

FOREIGN CONTACTS IN THE LATER MING PERIOD

After the discontinuation of the oceanic voyages in 1436, the Ming dynasty had presented a defensive attitude towards the outside world. One aspect of this had been the restriction of foreign commerce to trade carried out by tribute missions; another had been the adoption of conciliatory policies in relations with the steppe nomads. However, these policies were to be subverted by developments in the middle of the sixteenth century.

To the north, the key development came in the early 1540s with the unification of the Mongols under Altan khan. He established his capital at Hohhot in what is now Inner Mongolia and began to employ Chinese in his administration. When his requests for the resumption of trade, which had been cut off in about 1500, were refused, he made a series of raids into China. This provoked an important clash at the Jiajing (r. 1522–66) emperor's court between the grand secretary Xia Yan, a reputedly upright official and Yan Song, his main rival, later to be castigated as a villain. In 1547 Xia Yan obtained the emperor's support for an ambitious plan to recover the Ordos area. However the following year the plan was suddenly abandoned and Xia Yan executed. The dispute left the court paralysed, which allowed Altan to make further successful raids, culminating in 1550 with a sortie to the walls of Beijing. Raiding continued for the next twenty years, and the Chinese response was a second major programme of wall construction. Finally, in 1571, an agreement was made with Altan which for the time being quietened the situation.[42]

A second border threat was eventually dealt with more effectively, although this was not to the credit of the court. From early in the sixteenth century raiders, often described as pirates although their objective was as much smuggling as piracy, had been making raids on the south-eastern coast of China. The official reaction to this was to prohibit overseas trade. From the 1540s Japanese smugglers began to trade with China, exchanging silver for Chinese silk. As the trade grew in importance, so did the disorder associated with it

唐三藏不動色空心

28 The Journey to the West, *showing Pigsy being trapped into accepting food, while Monkey and Tripitaka (Xuan Zang) look on; eighteenth century (O/C 15271.c.13)*

29 *The Hall of the Supreme Harmony, Forbidden City, Beijing*

30 The Temple of Heaven, Beijing

31 Porcelain production at Jingdezhen, Jiangxi province, late Ming dynasty; woodblock prints (O/C 15226.b.19)

and in 1548 a piratical attack on Ningbo caused extensive damage. This was the first of a series of major raids in which cities were captured and looted and officials put to death. The marauders were commonly described as *wokou* or Japanese pirates. The situation only improved when a number of able commanders, the best-remembered being Qi Jiguang, developed new methods of combating the raiders. Rather than use soldiers from hereditary military families Qi Jiguang raised a volunteer force from Zhejiang, trained them in the proper use of weapons, instilled a harsh discipline and above all encouraged teamwork. He made a limited use of firearms, observing that as muskets had a tendency to explode, soldiers did not dare hold them in both hands and that consequently their aim was poor. More through persistence than any other factor, Qi Jiguang demonstrated to the raiders that their activities were no longer profitable. But the real reason why piracy stopped was that in 1567 the ban on foreign trade was rescinded.[43]

One other foreign contact initially went almost unnoticed. The first Portuguese reached China in 1514, and three years later Tomé Pires, who bore a letter from the king of Portugal, landed at Guangzhou and was allowed to proceed to Beijing although he was later expelled. Thereafter Portuguese traders arrived with increasing frequency and having failed to settle at Ningbo began to congregate at Macao. In the 1550s they were given permission to reside there and in 1574 a wall was erected to seal off the settlement and the Portuguese were permitted to administer it as a self-governing enclave. In the meantime the Jesuit mission to Japan had been established and in 1577 Alessandro Valignano, the Jesuit Visitor to the Indies, arrived at Macao. He was followed in 1582 by Matteo Ricci, who eventually obtained permission to reside permanently in Beijing and from there to extend the Jesuit mission to the court. Ricci's strategy for obtaining conversions was to make a cultural accommodation with the Chinese. He studied the Chinese classics and offered to the Chinese his knowledge of western mathematics and science. He described his approach in his journal:

> In order that the appearance of a new religion might not arouse suspicion among the Chinese people, the Fathers did not speak openly about religious matters when they began to appear in public. What time was left to them, after paying their respects and civil compliments and courteously receiving their visitors, was spent in studying the language of the country, the methods of writing and the customs of the people. They did, however, endeavor to teach this pagan people in a more direct way, namely, by virtue of their example and by the sanctity of their lives.[44]

DECLINE AND FALL OF THE MING DYNASTY

The events which culminated in the fall of the Ming dynasty may be summarised briefly. Two long-reigning emperors, Jiajing (r. 1522–66) and Wanli (r. 1573–1620) both withdrew for long periods of time from active participation in government.

During the reign of Jiajing there had been the Mongol raids headed by Altan and the attacks of the Japanese pirates. The emperor did not concern himself with these matters, but instead became increasingly concerned with Daoist practices for achieving immortality and this led to his consumption of elixirs which made him ill. For many years he left Yan Song in charge of affairs, a man who enjoyed a reputation for corruption and treachery and for avoiding the real problems of government. Jiajing's grandson Wanli started his reign more promisingly. Between 1573 and 1582 he had the benefit of the services of Zhang Juzheng, whose administration has been described as 'a last radiant glow in the twilight of the Ming dynasty.'[45] It was notable principally for an austerity programme which restored government finances, but it did not introduce any new measures to deal with the deep-seated problems which beset the dynasty. But after Zhang Juzheng's death the emperor increasingly handed over administrative tasks to eunuchs. The Wanli emperor was credited with having conducted three successful campaigns in the latter part of his reign. The most significant of these was the response to the Japanese invasion of Korea in 1592, which involved the dispatch of major and costly expeditions and was only concluded in 1598 by a Japanese withdrawal after the death of Hideyoshi. In the last years of the reign a political crisis associated with the Donglin academy divided the court into factions and paralysed government.

The Tianqi emperor who came to the throne in 1620 has been described as 'a dim-wit interested mainly in carpentry'[46] His reign was marked by the ascendancy of Wei Zhongxian, the most notorious of the eunuch dictators. His successor Chongzhen was more capable, but was unable to combat the succession of crises which now hit the dynasty. The growing threat from the Manchus was made explicit in 1629 by a raid south of the Great Wall which undermined confidence in the armed forces. In the years that followed a series of droughts and famines led to the rise of rebellion, initially in Shaanxi but later spreading across the North China Plain. By the early 1640s two rebel leaders were prominent. Li Zicheng, whose father had been a rich peasant and who had served in the government postal service, emerged as a contender for the throne. He represented himself as a friend of the poor and ordered that in places which he had captured the people should be exempt from taxes for three years. The other rebel leader, Zhang Xianzhong, known as the 'Yellow Tiger' was notorious for his cruelty. By 1643 Li had occupied Henan and the dynasty's control was crumbling. In the following year he declared the establishment of a new dynasty and entered Beijing. The emperor, deserted by his supporters, hanged himself. Meanwhile Zhang Xianzhong had established his own regime in the south-west with its capital at Chengdu.

The most frequently cited explanation for this dramatic sequence of events has been to invoke the process of the dynastic cycle. In its traditional form this emphasised personal factors, the weakness of the later emperors and the machinations of their ministers and the eunuchs, most notably Yan Song and Wei Zhongxian. To this may be added the record of court extravagance and the consequent oppressive taxation, giving rise to the great peasant rebellions which toppled the dynasty. A more impersonal version of this cycle would note how the first rulers of a dynasty were able to command and to innovate, whereas later rulers became captives of their advisers and of the policies which could only be reformed by attacking vested interests.

A more complex political explanation of the fall of the dynasty has derived from a discussion of the Donglin movement. This movement took its name from the Donglin academy, near Wuxi in the Yangzi delta. The academy provided a focus for scholars and officials who were alarmed by what they saw as a deterioration in standards in public life and who argued for a moral revival and a return to Confucian education and values. Sympathisers with these ideas were dominant in government in the early part of Tianqi's reign, but the tide turned when Wei Zhongxian gained power and carried out a purge of Donglin supporters. The significance the movement had for the decline of the dynasty has been defined variously. Donglin leaders have been described as representing a landowning class reacting against Ming absolutism. Their protest against what they saw as arbitrary and unacceptable actions on the part of the monarch – in particular his attempt to change the order of succession – was part of a move aimed at transforming government from an autocracy to a form which reflected their interests. Other suggestions are that the confrontation arose over political issues or because the factions had a regional alignment. In fact, there was only one issue which united the Donglin supporters and that was opposition to Wei Zhongxian. Analyses of Donglin supporters and their opponents has not revealed any clear regional attachment. Charles Hucker argued that the differences between the factions were essentially moral and that the Donglin supporters represented traditional Confucian morality, which demanded resoluteness and integrity, pitted against the Ming power structure, which at that stage in the dynasty did not permit success to any but the unprincipled. Whatever its origins, the Donglin movement divided the court and encouraged factionalism. Even after the death of Wei Zhongxian, during the reign of Tianqi, 'partisan bickering had become a habit', detaching scholars and officials from the dynasty and paving the way for the switch of allegiance which occurred in 1644.[47]

A different type of explanation for the fall of the dynasty begins with reference to the population rise and then draws attention to the evidence of deteriorating climate and catastrophic epidemics which swept the country in the late Ming period. It includes reference to the effects of China's early involvement in world trade, which brought an influx of silver and which stimulated commercial regions along the south-east coast. At first this had a beneficial effect on government which enjoyed increased revenues. However, economic growth slowed in the early seventeenth century and government expenditure rose with the costs of the Korean campaigns and the gross extravagance of the Wanli emperor. These factors may have amounted to a form of seventeenth-century crisis, comparable in some ways with developments in Europe at the same time.[48]

Why did popular rebellions arise and topple the dynasty? Economic hardship certainly played a part in this process. The rebellions had their origin in northern Shaanxi, an impoverished area which had experienced none of the economic growth which had benefited some other regions, notably the lower Yangzi valley. Another underlying cause was the decline of standards of local administration, with many official posts left unfilled. In 1628 a drought in the area was followed by a famine which might have been averted if local officials had done their duty. Disorder broke out involving peasants, bandits, and soldiers who had deserted their units. The senior official sent to deal with the rebellion initially extended an offer of peaceful surrender towards the rebels, with some degree of success. But in 1629 the first Manchu raid into north China wrecked the pacification programme. The government now switched its policy to that of total suppression but this resulted in the rebel bands moving out of their base area and becoming mobile raiders, often mounted on horseback. Government forces had no answer to this situation and a combination of bad planning, institutional weakness and personal failures allowed the rebellions to survive. At first there was no immediate risk of the rebellions overthrowing the dynasty. However in 1641 Li Zicheng, by now the most prominent rebel leader, captured Luoyang and began to attract gentry members to his cause, who suggested that to gain popular support he should improve his image. Li then set himself the task of capturing Kaifeng, which he did after a protracted siege and at the cost of a major disaster, for during the campaign the Yellow river defences were breached and many thousands of lives were lost. Later the same year he also captured Xi'an. By now the Ming government was incapable a putting an effective force into the field and the fall of Beijing in the following year was a foregone conclusion.[49]

A final reason for the fall of the dynasty, albeit an indirect one, was the rise of Manchu power. In 1619 the Wanli emperor had been persuaded to launch an attack against the Manchu leader Nurhaci. At the time China's state finances were in crisis and the emperor was unwilling to contribute from his own substantial reserves to the cost of the campaign. As a consequence a silver surcharge was added to the land tax, which was unpopular if not exhorbitant. The campaign itself was a disaster and it encouraged the Manchus to attack Chinese territory. In 1629, as mentioned above, they made the deep raid which interrupted the attempt to suppress rebellion in Shaanxi. The continued threat from the Manchus necessitated maintaining a large part of the dynasty's military strength along the northern frontier, rather than deploying it against the rebels. This was of crucial importance in the final days of the dynasty. One of the last effective forces on the imperial side was that commanded by Wu Sangui and stationed near Shanhaiguan. In April 1644, Wu was reportedly about to submit to Li Zicheng, who was holding his father hostage. Instead, in a famous act of treachery, he cast his lot in with the Manchu leader Dorgon. In the following month Manchu troops, with the assistance of Wu Sangui's soldiers, inflicted a crushing defeat on the rebels. The way was now open for the Manchu invasion of China.

CHAPTER TWELVE

THE QING DYNASTY

The events which culminated in the Manchu conquest of China occupied only twelve years, from 1640 to 1652. However, the establishment and consolidation of the Qing dynasty, the 'great enterprise' as Frederic Wakeman described it,[1] occupied a much longer time, from the Manchu capture of Fushun in 1618 to the defeat of the Three Feudatories and of Zheng Chenggong on Taiwan in the 1680s.

By then the Kangxi emperor was on the throne. His reign, from 1662 to 1722, established the character of Manchu rule in China. He was succeeded by his fourth son, who reigned as the Yongzheng emperor between 1723 and 1735. After him came the Qianlong emperor who, after ruling for sixty years, abdicated in 1795 rather than exceed the record of his grandfather, although he, or rather his favourite Heshen, retained power until the emperor's death in 1799. In these three reigns the Chinese empire reached its greatest extent, its population attained its massive quality, and its culture acquired those characteristics which were to determine its modern transformation.

Some writers regarded the Manchu conquest as a victory of barbarism over culture, as an opportunistic victory achieved with great cruelty which established a foreign despotism over a subjugated people. This view became popular at the end of the nineteenth century, when anti-Manchuism became an important component of nationalism. In the manifesto of the Revolutionary Alliance promulgated in 1905 Sun Zhongshan (Sun Yat-sen) declared:

The Manchus of today were originally the eastern barbarians beyond the Great Wall. They frequently caused border troubles during the Ming dynasty; then when China was in a disturbed state they came inside [the Great Wall], conquered China, and enslaved our Chinese people. Those who opposed them were killed by the hundreds of thousands, and our Chinese have been a people without a nation for two hundred and sixty years.[2]

Modern western interpretations have tended to play down the subjugation, if not the cruelty, of the conquest. Emphasis has been placed on the continuities between Ming and Qing and on the collaboration between the Chinese élite and the conquerors. Certainly there were acts of heroic resistance and examples of irreconcilable hostility, but there were also many examples of Chinese submitting to the Manchus and serving them faithfully.

THE RISE OF THE MANCHUS

The Manchus were originally a Jurchen people, that is to say near relatives of the peoples that had founded the Jin dynasty in 1122. Although skilled in mounted archery, the Jurchen were not steppe nomads. They practised agriculture, traded extensively with China and sent tributary missions to Beijing. The Jianzhou Jurchen, the group directly ancestral to the Manchus, emerged in the late sixteenth century in Jilin, in the region known as the Changbaishan, the Long White Mountains. Its people formed an administrative unit, a commandery, within the Ming framework for the control of this region, which was based essentially on the principle of divide and rule.

The fortunes of this group were to be determined largely by the efforts of one man, Nurhaci (1559–1626), the creator of the Manchu state and founder of the Qing dynasty. In his early life he struggled to avenge the murder of his father and grandfather by a neighbouring tribal leader and through his efforts became recognised as the leader of the Jianzhou Jurchen. His success in defeating a bandit group and releasing some Chinese captives led in 1590 to his heading a tribute mission to Beijing. In the following years he grew rich from the trade in ginseng and his ambition led him to attack the tribes to the north. His rapid rise to power, his establishment of a capital, the development of his military capacity, all alarmed the Chinese and ensured that a confrontation would take place. In 1618 Nurhaci listed 'Seven Great Vexations' against the Ming, a list of supposed insults and grievances. He called upon the commander of Fushun, the key garrison town and horse-trading centre of Liaodong, to surrender, which he did. Nurhaci treated him with respect and offered him one of his granddaughters in marriage. Within two years Nurhaci had defeated the Chinese force sent to chastise him and had brought most of Liaodong under his control.[3]

In his later years Nurhaci transformed his confederation of Jianzhou Jurchen tribes and their supporters into a Manchu state (although the name Manchu was only adopted in 1635). In 1601 Nurhaci ordered a registration of the people and then divided the population into *niru*, meaning 'arrows', each composed of 300 households of warriors, this being the first step towards the creation of a new military organisation. Five *niru* formed a battalion and ten battalions formed a banner. At first the Manchu people as a whole were divided into four banners, with four more created in 1615. It has been suggested that the banner organisation was an adaptation of the Chinese *weisuo* system. Both systems were civil as well as military organisations, both embodied a military bureaucracy, both were intended to be self-regulating and self-supporting. However the systems had an important difference: unlike the Chinese *weisuo* the Manchu banners did not have a fixed regional base. The introduction of the banners was part of a more general policy of adopting bureaucratic and imperial features derived from the Chinese state. In 1616 offices of government were created and Nurhaci assumed the title of emperor and founder of a dynasty. Increasingly Chinese were brought into the Manchu administration, a tendency which accelerated after the

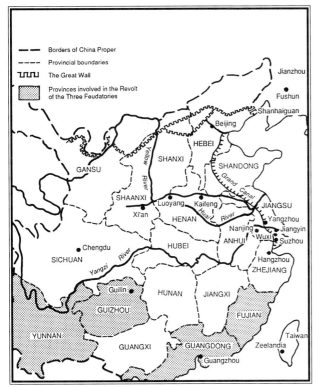

32 *China in the seventeenth century: the Manchu invasion and the revolt of the three feudatories*

33 *Statue of Li Zicheng, in the outskirts of Beijing*

34 *Mu Lan, who disguised herself as a soldier to relieve her father from doing military service; woodblock print from* Biographies of Exemplary Women, *1779 (O/C 15291.a.18)*

35 Chinese export watercolours, c. 1795. Clockwise from top left: Watering tea-plants; Official of the Top Rank; Merchant; Lady of the first Rank.

capture of Fushun. With Liaodong under his control, Nurhaci began to organise the Chinese population as well into banners and the same process was applied to the Mongol tribes that had joined him. At first Nurhaci offered a policy of equality towards the Chinese, but frequent cases of poisoning and a Chinese revolt in 1625 caused him to revert to a policy of racial discrimination. Nurhaci died in 1626, but the process of adopting Chinese methods of government continued under his son Abahai. In 1631 he introduced the six ministries modelled on the Ming administration and in 1636 he formally announced the establishment of the Qing or 'pure' dynasty. In short, before the conquest of China Proper began, the Manchu rulers had already moved away from their traditional clan system of government towards the adoption of Chinese administrative methods. They had also gained valuable experience of ruling a sedentary Chinese population with the help of Chinese collaborators. This debt to Chinese practice led Franz Michael to declare, 'It was the Chinese system, Chinese officials and Chinese ideas that enabled the Manchus to conquer China.'[4] However this view has been challenged as overemphasising the sinicisation of the Manchus both before and after the conquest.[5]

THE MANCHU CONQUEST OF CHINA

Although a Manchu conquest of China had long been anticipated, and major raids into northern China had taken place from early in Abahai's reign, the opportunity for conquest derived from the situation which presented itself in the last years of the Ming dynasty. In 1643 Abahai died. Because his heir was a child, Dorgon, another son of Nurhaci, became regent. The capture of Beijing by Li Zicheng and the death of the Ming emperor forced Dorgon to decide whether the time was ripe for the abandonment of the traditional policy of profitable raiding and instead to risk an invasion. His decision to do the latter was perhaps based on Wu Sangui's offer of an alliance against Li Zicheng, for it has been argued that the Manchu forces were not strong enough to defeat both Wu Sangui and Li Zicheng.[6]

The combined armies inflicted a crushing defeat on Li Zicheng's troops and Dorgon immediately pressed on to Beijing. The rapid sequence of events had left officials quite uncertain how to respond to the Manchu advance. Dorgon seized this opportunity to bring the Chinese élite over to his side. His first proclamation in part read:

The empire is not an individual's private empire. Whosoever possesses virtue holds it. The army and people are not an individual's private army and people. Whosoever possesses virtue commands them. We now hold it. We took revenge upon the enemy of your ruler-father in place of your dynasty. We burned our bridges behind us, and we have pledged not to return until every bandit is destroyed. In the counties, districts, and locales we pass through, all those who are able to shave their heads and surrender, opening their gates to welcome us, will be given rank and reward, retaining their wealth and nobility for generations. But if there are those who resist us disobediently, then when our Grand Army arrives, the stones themselves will be set ablaze and everyone will be massacred.[7]

The response of the rest of the country to the Qing conquest was a complex mixture of resistance and of compliance. Once the Manchu forces had routed Li Zicheng's troops, their next objective was the occupation of the Yangzi valley, the Ming court having fled, in the first instance, to Nanjing. In May 1645 Manchu forces commanded by Dodo besieged Yangzhou, the defence of which was led by the famous Ming loyalist general Shi Kefa. Although the defenders had a new Portuguese type of cannon, such was the ferocity of the Manchu assault that the siege only lasted a week. Shi Kefa was captured but, unlike many other generals, he refused to change sides. He was thereupon executed and Yangzhou delivered over to an infamous ten-day massacre, intended to deter further resistance.[8] This certainly worked in the case of many cities, where the inhabitants were quick to post notices signifying 'surrendering people' on the city gates. Nevertheless instances of resistance occurred, notably at Jiangyin and Jiading.

The famous outburst of resistance at Jiangyin, which is a hundred miles upriver from Shanghai, was apparently sparked off by the Manchu hair-cutting order. After Nanjing had fallen, the Qing authorities had ordered other administrative centres in the region to hand over their tax and population registers, this being the first step towards obtaining the co-operation of the local élite in the orderly transfer of power. The Jiangnan authorities appeared to have no problem with complying with this instruction. But shortly afterwards, in July 1645, the news arrived that the Qing government had also issued a proclamation stating that the regulation requiring men to wear their hair in the Manchu style – that is to say to shave their head at the front and grow a pig-tailed queue at the back – was to be enforced immediately. Anyone found not to have complied with the regulation was to be treated as a bandit. Opposition to this order led to the formation of a resistance movement in Jiangyin. Qing troops were dispatched to subdue the city and this was done ruthlessly with the alleged loss of up to 100,000 lives. Much has been written about the tragedy of Jiangyin, but it has been shown that the resistance was not a clear example of collective loyalism against a foreign invader. Divisions existed among the local élite of Jiangnan and the slaughter was actually perpetrated by Chinese troops.[9]

After the capture of Nanjing, Ming successor regimes fled south. In 1650 Qing forces commanded by Shang Kexi, a Chinese military commander who had switched to the Manchu side in 1634, captured Guangzhou after a prolonged siege and massacred the inhabitants. Ming resistance continued but was now confined to the fringes of the empire. The last Ming emperor was pursued to Burma and captured and executed there in 1662. In the meantime another form of resistance to the Qing had appeared in the person of Zheng Chenggong, known in the West as Koxinga. From about 1646 he led a resistance movement along the coast of Fujian, his long survival depending considerably on his use of sea-power, a form of warfare with which the Manchus were not familiar. In 1659 a large naval force under his command sailed up the Yangzi and besieged Nanjing, but he received little encouragement from the local gentry and had to abandon the attack. Before his death in 1662 he captured the Dutch fort of Zeelandia on Taiwan. His son continued the resistance and in retaliation the Qing resorted to the draconian policy of forcing the coastal population of the area to abandon their settlements and to remove ten miles inland. Koxinga is remembered to this day as the hero of a puppet play by the Japanese dramatist Chikamatsu (Koxinga's mother was Japanese). He has also been celebrated in modern times by both Nationalists and Communists. The former have identified him as an early anti-Manchu nationalist, while the latter have claimed him as an early anti-imperialist. One might suggest that his real intentions were not to expel the Manchus but to carve out an independent kingdom for himself.[10]

THE CONSOLIDATION OF MANCHU RULE: 1644–89

From the moment that the Manchus entered Beijing, and Abahai's son was proclaimed emperor, using the reign title of Shunzhi, the Manchu leaders had to decide how they would rule China. The responsibility for making this decision fell on the regent Dorgon. It was under his direction that the conquest of China and the destruction of Ming resistance was pursued. At the same time he established the general line that was to be taken towards the conquered. The central feature of this was that the Manchus would retain all essential elements of Ming rule, and it was this which has led to the conquest being described as 'the least disruptive transition from one major dynasty to another in the whole of Chinese history.'[11] Dorgon immediately made it clear that he would welcome the services of former Ming officials and a very substantial number of officials, particularly from the north and especially from Shandong, became 'twice-serving ministers'. The examination system was continued and in the palace examinations of 1646 the dominance of the north was apparent, although this was later to shift to the south.[12] From the beginning of the Manchu period the principle of a Manchu-Chinese diarchy, that is to say the duplication of senior appointments by the appointment of a Manchu and a Chinese, was adopted. The main administrative arrangements and the system of checks and balances were retained. An extensive programme of reform derived from suggestions made by former Ming officials was initiated.[13] Finally the Shunzhi emperor was carefully instructed in the performance of his role as a Confucian emperor, a part which he played willingly.

Nevertheless Dorgon was a Manchu and he was determined to maintain the ethnic distinction and dominance of the Manchus. In the early years of his regency, the requirement that Chinese wear the queue was extended and enforced throughout the country, the popular saying being 'off with your hair, or off with your head'. Extensive tracts of land in north China were confiscated from Chinese owners and distributed among Manchu princes and generals. Although the diarchic system appeared to offer the Chinese a substantial role in government, the top metropolitan positions, the positions of power, were kept in Manchu hands.[14] Moreover, the impression that the Manchus accepted the return of a large number of Chinese into positions of responsibility is misleading. Most of the Chinese who supported the new dynasty were Chinese bannermen, that is to say members of the eight Chinese banners formed in 1642, which had fought alongside the Manchus in the conquest and which had then supplied military and civil personnel to the conquerors. Chinese bannermen, because of their reliance on the Manchus, were more trustworthy than Chinese officials who had changed sides.

Dorgon died on the last day of 1650, while on a hunting expedition. His ambitious manoeuvring, followed by his sudden death, precipitated a sharp factional struggle among the Manchu élite, which was temporarily resolved by the success of the faction which had coalesced around Shunzhi. In 1651 the young emperor – he was then thirteen years old – gave his support to a public denunciation of Dorgon, who allegedly had tried to make himself emperor. Shunzhi began to take an active part in government and between 1652 and 1655 a series of important institutional reforms were introduced, many of which, as previously under Dorgon, were suggested by 'twice-serving ministers'.[15] These reforms concerned such practical matters as water conservancy and grain tribute transportation, as well as the improvement of the tax registers and tax collection and the suppression of corruption. Of these the land tax reforms were the most significant, for they increased the number of *ding*, that is adult males liable to labour service, by 60 per cent and nearly doubled the registered acreage of land liable to tax. At the same time Shunzhi initiated measures to curb the activities of the Manchu aristocracy and took the controversial step of re-introducing the eunuch directorates in the Forbidden City.[16]

Shunzhi is also remembered on a more personal note for his love for his consort, the Empress Xiaoxian. This romance has been supposed, probably incorrectly, to have been the subject of the famous Qing novel *The Dream of the Red Chamber*. Xiaoxian died in 1660 and the extravagance of her funeral aroused the resentment of Shunzhi's mother.

Shunzhi died, probably of smallpox, in February 1661. His will named as his heir his seven-year-old son, who was to reign as the celebrated Kangxi emperor. This was one of the few true statements in the document, which was based on the emperor's testament, but which had been mendaciously embroidered by the four regents and his mother, the Grand Empress Dowager. In the will the Shunzhi emperor reproached himself for having rejected his Manchu heritage, for unfilial conduct towards his mother and for excessive interest in Chinese matters. This abject self-criticism may be contrasted with the flattering portrait of the emperor presented by the Jesuit missionary Adam Schall, who held a privileged position at court because of his knowledge of astronomy. At one time an intimacy had sprung up between the emperor and the elderly missionary. The emperor had called Schall 'grandfather' and Schall had entertained hopes that the emperor, of whom he approved strongly, might convert to

Christianity. This was not to be and later the emperor became more interested in Chan Buddhism.[17]

Between 1661 and 1669, while the new emperor was a minor, power was held by the four regents known collectively as the Oboi regency after one of their number. This period was marked by a sharp policy shift, away from accommodation with the Chinese system and towards a greater emphasis on Manchu dominance. The first step was to abolish the eunuch directorates, which allegedly threatened to restore one of the worst features of the Ming dynasty, although Shunzhi's true purpose in establishing them may have been to create an organisation that was independent of the Manchu élite. Steps were also taken to reduce the influence of the Jesuits, and Buddhist advisers were also dismissed. This was only the beginning of the promotion of a Manchu 'reign of virtue'. At the metropolitan level of government a determined effort was made to increase the importance of Manchu representation at the expense of Chinese institutions. The most notable example of this was the reform of the Council of Deliberative Officials to make it a forum where senior Manchu military and civil leaders could discuss issues and formulate policy. At the same time steps were taken to reverse changes made by Shunzhi and to reduce the power of key elements retained from Ming metropolitan government. In particular the Grand Secretariat and the Hanlin Academy were abolished, and the Censorate was greatly reduced in influence. Two other reforms carried the Manchu emphasis even further. In Ming China a system of evaluation of officials had operated, which covered a wide variety of criteria and which permitted self-assessment. After 1662 the criteria for performance were restricted to the fulfilment of tax quotas and the completion of criminal cases, and evaluation was placed solely in the hands of senior officials. Another reform concerned the examination system, where the syllabus was amended by the abolition of the formal 'eight-legged essay', and a sharp reduction was made in the quotas for the *jinshi* degree.[18]

Alongside these metropolitan policies the Oboi regents sought to affirm Manchu superiority in the provinces. As few Manchus had the administrative experience and linguistic skills to enable them to occupy senior provincial posts, there was no alternative to relying on Chinese bannermen as governors-general and governors. Under Dorgon there had been an assumption that their loyalty was beyond question, but by the time of the Oboi regency, their intermediate position led to their being treated with a degree of mistrust. At the start of the regency almost all senior provincial officials were replaced, and their successors were kept under close supervision and expected to enforce policies strictly. The demand for the prompt payment of taxes had alienated the Chinese élite in several places and provoked a particularly sharp reaction in Zhejiang and Jiangnan, leading to many individuals being punished with the loss of their degrees.[19] Another example of the severity of Manchu rule was the previously-mentioned adoption in 1661–2 of the policy of removing the coastal population some ten miles inland to prevent Ming loyalists, and in particular Zheng Chenggong, from obtaining supplies.[20]

By the late 1660s the Oboi regency had been replaced by a faction grouped around Oboi, whose pursuit of his private ambitions had alienated both Chinese and Manchus. In 1667 the Grand Empress Dowager secured an agreement that the emperor should assume personal command while continuing to be advised by the regents. Two years later the emperor ordered the arrest of Oboi and a purge of his supporters. It was at this point that the Kangxi emperor began to rule in his own right.

The final stage in the consolidation of Manchu rule was accomplished in the first fifteen years of Kangxi's reign and it involved military, political and cultural initiatives. The military action derived from a situation which dated back to the pacification of the south. At that time the Manchus had relied on Chinese collaborators to gain control. Of these Shang Kexi, Kong Youde and Geng Zhongming had all come from Shandong and had joined forces with the Manchus in the 1630s. To their number should be added Wu Sangui who had changed sides in 1644. All four men had played a key role in the conquest of north China and all had been rewarded with the title of prince. In 1649 they were sent to the south with broad discretionary powers to eliminate Ming resistance and to establish Manchu control. Kong Youde was surrounded by Ming forces at Guilin and committed suicide, but the other three not only subdued resistance but also carved themselves out semi-independent fiefdoms: Wu Sangui in Yunnan and Guizhou, Shang Kexi in Guangdong, and Geng Jingzhong, the grandson of Geng Zhongming, in Fujian. Each commanded his own forces and was allowed to raise taxes through monopolies and to administer his territory very much as he saw fit.

Concern over the independence of the three feudatories was expressed from the early 1660s, one cause of complaint being the very high cost of their military expenditure. However it was only in 1673 that an opportunity to take action arose. Shang Kexi requested permission to retire because of old age, his intention being to hand his position over to his son. His example prompted an offer of retirement from the other feudatories. Wu Sangui assumed that he would be reinstated, but Kangxi, largely on his own initiative, refused to comply, thus forcing the issue and precipitating a rebellion.[21]

The rebellion of the Three Feudatories lasted eight years and was the most serious threat to the survival of the dynasty. Wu Sangui commanded a large army and he could hope to capitalise on anti-Manchu feeling. He declared the establishment of a new dynasty, the Zhou, gained widespread support in Yunnan and Guizhou, and his armies marched unopposed into Hunan. Before the end of 1674 much of south and west China was in rebellion. The initial threat was met with indecision at court and rumours circulated that the Manchus were about to abandon Beijing. However Kangxi responded by taking personal control of military strategy, and the crisis was relieved when Shang Kexi declared his continued loyalty to the Manchus, so denying the rebels control of Guangdong. Moreover Wu Sangui failed signally to win over anti-Manchu Ming loyalist scholars.[22] In the prolonged struggle which followed a key factor in favour of the Qing dynasty was that Jiangnan, the economic heartland of the empire, remained loyal. This gave the government the resources to pay more troops and to equip them with artillery, designed by Father Verbiest, the Jesuit missionary who was also President of the Tribunal of Mathematics.[23] Military campaigns were supplemented by propaganda which offered an amnesty to the population of the provinces that had been drawn into the rebellion. By the time of Wu Sangui's death in 1678 the rebellion was in effect defeated.

The consolidation of the Qing empire required success in two further campaigns. The first was the subjugation of Taiwan, now held by Zheng Jing, son of the famous Zheng Chenggong, who had allied himself with Geng Jingzhong, one of the three feudatories. This was achieved in 1683, by negotiation rather than by conquest. As the island no longer represented a threat the intention at first was to abandon it. However it was claimed that if it was abandoned it might be re-occupied by the Dutch, who for some years after 1624 had maintained a trading colony on its south-western coast. So in 1684 Taiwan was incorporated into the empire as a prefecture of Fujian province and the policy of removing the coastal population was rescinded.

The second campaign was directed against a relatively new threat. In 1643 Cossacks engaged in the fur trade had reached the Amur river. Taking advantage of Manchu preoccupation elsewhere they established a trading post at Nerchinsk and then a fortress at Albazin. The Kangxi emperor took a personal interest in the situation and resolved to halt Russian encroachment either by diplomatic means or by force. The indigenous population was enrolled in new Manchu banners and the Russian settlers were warned that they must either accept Chinese suzerainty of the area or withdraw. Having concluded that negotiation had failed, the emperor ordered the capture of Albazin. Aware of a growing threat from the Dzungar in the west, Kangxi quickly authorised the negotiation of the Treaty of Nerchinsk. This agreement, which was negotiated in 1689, was China's first treaty with a western state and her first treaty concluded on terms of diplomatic equality with another power. Under it Russia recognised the Amur basin as Qing territory and the two countries made arrangements for trade.[24]

THE LATER YEARS OF KANGXI'S REIGN, 1689–1722

The Kangxi emperor has been described as 'probably the most admirable ruler of the entire later imperial age.'[25] His commitment to his responsibilities was prodigious. The early Qing emperors dealt personally with many aspects of government business. The Kangxi emperor claimed that on some days during the rebellion of the Three Feudatories he had handled five hundred items of business. Even in normal times he read and corrected some fifty memorials a day.[26] At the same time he carried out numerous regular duties, including receiving officials and envoys from foreign states, performing religious ceremonies, reviewing judicial decisions and supervising the highest stages of the examination system. In addition he travelled widely, claiming to have travelled two thousand *li* in each of the four cardinal directions. His tours involved hunting expeditions and military exercises, and he made a point of meeting the people and expressing an interest in their welfare, farming methods, tax burden and similar matters.

Being a Manchu ruler, it was inevitable that Kangxi would be concerned about military affairs and at the time of the rebellion of the Three Feudatories he had taken his role as commander-in-chief very seriously. As a consequence of those campaigns important changes occurred in the size and relative importance of the two main military organisations. At first Kangxi relied heavily on the banner formations and by 1684 the number of banner troops had risen to about 315,000. But as the campaign continued greater use was made of Chinese forces, known as the army of the Green Standard, which at one point reached a total of 900,000 men, though this was later reduced by a third. After the suppression of the rebellion the roles of the two formations stabilised. Banner forces for the most part were stationed in the north, around Beijing and in Manchuria, but seven cities in central and southern China were also garrisoned by banner troops. The army of the Green Standard was more widely scattered and its units placed under the command of both civil and military officials. Apart from garrison duties, its men took on a variety of responsibilities including postal functions and guarding buildings. These changes demonstrate that in the latter part of his reign Kangxi was sufficiently confident of the loyalty of his Chinese subjects to entrust the security of the south largely to their keeping.[27]

The reason why Kangxi's envoys had been quick to negotiate the Treaty of Nerchinsk with the Tsar was the fear of Russian support for the Dzungar, the western Mongols who, under the leadership of Galdan, threatened to unite the other Mongol tribes under their control. However the Dzungar failed in their efforts to win over the Khalkha or eastern Mongols, and moreover they were divided among themselves and this gave Kangxi an opportunity to settle the issue. In 1696, and again in the following year, he personally led campaigns against Galdan which resulted in the latter's defeat and later suicide. Afterwards he wrote:

> Now Galdan is dead, and his followers have come back to their allegiance. My great task is done. In two years I made three journeys, across deserts combed by wind and bathed with rain, eating every other day, in the barren and uninhabitable deserts – one could have called it a hardship but I never called it that; people all shun such things but I didn't shun them. The constant journeying and hardship has led to this great achievement. I would never have said such a thing had it not been for Galdan.[28]

The Dzungar were the last major threat to Qing China out of Inner Asia.[29] Because they had made an alliance with Tibet the Qing court then found it necessary to send expeditions against the Tibetans and eventually, in 1728, to establish a permanent garrison in Lhasa and to appoint an imperial resident there. These were the first expansionist moves which, during the eighteenth century, were to double the area of the Chinese empire.

In many respects the practice of government under Kangxi continued on the lines established under the Ming. However some features were novel and have been the subject of scholarly interest. One such feature, which sheds light on the relationship between Manchus and Chinese, was the role of the *baoyi* or bondservant.

Bondservants were originally household slaves of diverse ethnic origin. However after the Manchu expansion in the 1620s their numbers came to include many Chinese and they were incorporated into the banner system. After the Manchu conquest, and particularly after the death of the Shunzhi emperor, there was a reaction against a revival of eunuch influence at court. Bondservants now took over the main tasks which had been carried out by eunuchs under the Ming, although eunuchs remained an essential part of court personnel.[30] Because of the past danger from eunuch power, this change may have improved the dynasty's chances of survival, but it also strengthened the trend towards autocracy.

Bondservants came to play a key role in the Imperial Household Department, the department which handled the emperor's personal affairs. Most of those who served in the department were bondservants from the upper three, or imperial banners. This was a large and complex department which by the end of Kangxi's reign employed nearly one thousand officials. It was an informal and private institution and members of its staff owed everything to their master who was also the emperor. It might be described as a microcosm of the Manchu–Chinese state, for in organisation it reflected the Chinese bureaucratic administrative apparatus, whereas in personnel it derived from the banner system. In the eighteenth century the department assumed a wider role, and bondservants were appointed to important financial positions often in the provinces. There they acted as the emperor's trusted agents and remitted funds back to his personal treasury. A famous example of this type of appointment was the Cao family, who were bondservants of the Plain White Banner. For much of the time between 1663 and 1728 members of the family held the post of textile commissioner in Nanjing, in charge of the management of government silk factories, until the family then fell into disgrace. Its days of prosperity and decline were to be the background for Cao Xueqin's famous novel, *The Dream of the Red Chamber*, known also as *The Story of the Stone*.[31]

The use of bondservants was connected with a significant development in government practice concerning communications. The official system used by the Ming and continued under the Qing was one of open communication through regular bureaucratic channels. This system was inevitably cumbersome and confined by precedent; it belonged to what has been denominated as the 'outer-court', and was centred on the operations of the bureaucracy. As under previous dynasties, there was also an 'inner court' centred on the emperor and including the Imperial Household Department. To circumvent the procedures of the outer court, Kangxi began to use what became known as the 'palace memorial', the emperor's private mode of communication with correspondents. The first of these correspondents were bondservants serving the emperor in provincial appointments in the south, among them Cao Yin, the textile commissioner at Suzhou. Initially the correspondents reported on the weather, and in particular sent information on droughts and floods – which may seem surprising until it is recalled that Kangxi, like previous emperors, believed in the significance of omens and was fond of repeating that 'if our administration is at fault on earth, Heaven will respond with calamities above'. Later some correspondents were provincial officials and their reports contained a wider range of information, including informal comments on fellow officials. Such a system was a valuable aid to the development of autocratic government which was to progress further in the following reign.[32]

The Manchu willingness to make use of the services of foreigners was illustrated by their response to the Jesuit mission to China. Mention has already been made of Adam Schall, tutor to the Shunzhi emperor and director of the Bureau of Astronomy. After Shunzhi's death Schall was attacked by Chinese astronomers and accused of high treason. He was found guilty, although the punishment was stayed. His successor, Ferdinand Verbiest, challenged Chinese astronomers to a demonstration of skills and having defeated them, was himself appointed director of the astronomical bureau, a post he held until 1687. Kangxi employed other Jesuits who had skills in mathematics, architecture and painting. In return for their assistance, the emperor allowed Christianity to be promoted and in 1692 promulgated an 'edict of tolerance'. On the vexed question of whether Christian converts should continue to perform Confucian rites and practise ancestor worship, a formulation drawn up by the Jesuits in Beijing and agreed by the emperor read:

that Confucius was honored by the Chinese as a master, but his name was not invoked in prayer for the purpose of gaining happiness, rank, or wealth; that worship of ancestors was an expression of love and filial remembrance, not intended to bring protection to the worshiper; and that there was no idea, when an ancestral tablet was erected, that the soul of the ancestor dwelt in that tablet. And when sacrifices were offered to Heaven it was not the blue existent sky that was addressed, but the lord and creator of all things. If the ruler Shangdi was sometimes called Heaven, *Tian*, that had no more significance than giving honorific names to the emperor.[33]

Although the transmission of ideas between East and West was not as smooth as depicted by either side, for each had its own agenda, these years marked the closest point yet achieved to a mutual understanding.

This understanding was not to last. Dominican and Franciscan missionaries criticised the Jesuit strategy of accommodation to the Chinese way of life and commitment to the service of the Manchu emperor. By the beginning of the eighteenth century the Jesuits had lost influence in Rome and their willingness to compromise with the Chinese practice of ancestor worship was condemned by the Inquisition. In an attempt to settle the controversy the Pope sent a special legate, Charles Maillard de Tournon, to the Qing court. He was received in audience by Kangxi but it soon became clear that no agreement was possible. The legate rejected the formulation which had been agreed regarding rites. The emperor would not countenance any claim of equality between the Pope and himself, nor that the Pope should assert any authority over Christian missionaries in China. In 1706 Kangxi ordered that all missionaries must accept the agreed formulation and undertake to remain in China for life. If they did not agree they should leave. Maillard de Tournon countered by forbidding missionaries to accept. This disagreement precipitated what became known as the Rites Controversy, which culminated in 1742 with the Pope issuing the bull *Ex Quo Singulari*, which condemned all forms of accommodation with Chinese rites.

An important underlying issue during the reign concerned government revenue and in particular the level of the land and labour-service taxes. One of Kangxi's best-known measures was the decision taken in 1712 to use the previous year's *ding* figures, that is the number of adult males paying tax, as the permanent basis for computing the labour-service tax. As increases in land and labour taxes were regarded as a major cause of dynastic instability, such a measure would appear to be enlightened and a gesture of confidence in the willingness of the state to curb its fiscal demands. However, the truth of the matter was somewhat different, for Kangxi had inherited, and then left to his successors, a legacy of chronic fiscal shortage. The fundamental reason for this was the difficulty of wresting an adequate revenue from an impoverished peasant economy. Chinese governments lacked an income sufficient to administer the country effectively, let alone enough to provide a surplus to invest in economic improvement. At the beginning of the Ming period Hongwu had recognised this in part, when he overhauled the tax system and fixed the land tax at a relatively low level. In the late sixteenth century the fiscal measures known as the Single-Whip reforms improved things a little, by consolidating some taxes and requiring their payment in silver. But this still left many anomalies and had one unexpected result: because revenues were now collected in silver rather than in kind, it became much easier for central government to appropriate resources which had in the past been used to maintain the local administration. Local officials were forced to find new sources of revenue to run their offices and this they did through the collection of a variety of surcharges. When the Manchus came to power they had continued Ming fiscal practices, but the costs of pacification, the maintenance of the Three Feudatories and then the suppression of their rebellion, all had imposed heavy burdens on the treasury. Kangxi had commanded frugality in government expenditure and efforts had been made to encourage land reclamation and settlement. These measures had enabled the government to remain solvent, but the dramatic declaration of 1712 flew in the face of the reality of the tax situation and exacerbated the constraints on the fiscal system at a time when the population was climbing steadily.[34]

Another recurrent problem, one which clouded Kangxi's final years, was the settlement of the succession. Emperors tended to have a large progeny: Kangxi had thirty-five sons, of whom twenty lived beyond the age of eleven, and twenty daughters, of whom only eight reached maturity.[35] According to Manchu custom a successor was elected by the elders of a tribe from all the sons of the previous ruler, but by Chinese tradition only sons born of the empress, the sole legitimate wife of the emperor, were eligible to succeed, with the firstborn enjoying priority.[36] Following the latter principle the emperor's heir apparent was his second son Yinreng, born in 1674, whose mother was the empress Xiaocheng, who had died at his birth. Yinreng was given an indulgent upbringing but after he had reached adulthood tensions arose between him and his father. Nevertheless Kangxi appointed Yinreng regent when he was away campaigning against Galdan. However the incessant factional struggles at court ensured that no opportunity would be lost in informing the emperor of any shortcoming in the heir apparent. In 1697 Yinreng was accused of some serious but unspecified misconduct and later he came under suspicion of involvement in a plot on his father's life. More damaging complaints were made after the emperor's southern tour of 1707, alleging that Yinreng was engaged in a frenzied search for 'pretty girls' and 'fair-looking boys'.[37] In the following year Kangxi publicly denounced Yinreng for his immorality, extravagance and usurpation of imperial privileges, and ordered him to be put in chains and imprisoned. He was later reinstated, on the grounds that he must have been possessed by evil spirits, but he was finally deposed in 1712. For a quarter of a century the issue of the succession fuelled factional struggles at Kangxi's court, and for the last ten years of his reign the emperor had no acknowledged heir apparent, which created an atmosphere of uncertainty about the future.

In 1717 Kangxi issued a valedictory edict in which he wrote:

I am already old, and have reigned long, and I cannot foretell what posterity will think of me. Besides which, because of what is going on now, I cannot hold back my tears of bitterness; and so I have prepared these notes to make my own record, for I still fear that the country may not know the depth of my sorrow.[38]

He died a disillusioned old man, yet his official reputation maintained that he was an outstanding emperor. Undoubtedly his conscientiousness, his attempt to be impartial between Manchus and Chinese, his efforts to fulfil the obligations of a Confucian emperor, all justify this high reputation. But if a broader view is taken of the achievements of his reign it must be said that the glory of it concealed serious and unresolved problems.

THE REIGN OF THE YONGZHENG EMPEROR, 1722–35

Kangxi's successor was his fourth son, Yinzhen, who reigned as the Yongzheng emperor. His reign was much shorter than that of his father, and was also more controversial. He was alleged to have usurped the throne and then to have disposed of his brothers and rivals ruthlessly. Thereafter he pursued his objectives single-mindedly, strengthening the autocratic character of the imperial institution. This negative verdict may be contrasted with the claim that he was 'the greatest centralizer and stabilizer' of the Qing dynasty, and that he 'revitalized the state administration, and fostered a time of economic prosperity'.[39]

The question of his succession and treatment of his brothers may be dealt with first. The argument that Yongzheng usurped the throne is based on suggestions that the intended successor was Yinti, Kangxi's fourteenth son, who was unable to enforce his claim because he was absent from Beijing at the crucial moment of his father's final illness. According to some accounts Kangxi's death was sudden and even accelerated by Yinzhen, who then seized the throne and fabricated evidence to prove that the late emperor had named him as his successor in the presence of several of his sons. The usurpation thesis has been challenged, one view being that Yinzhen succeeded because his actions were more astute than those of his rivals, another that there is evidence to show that he was indeed Kangxi's chosen successor. The allegations of usurpation are discredited as the work of southern intellectuals who had found favour under Kangxi but who were to be set aside by Yongzheng.[40] As for the accusation of ruthlessness, there was certainly some truth in that. Eight of his brothers died during his reign and Yinti was kept in confinement for most of that time. The most notorious incident was Yongzheng's imprisonment of Kangxi's eighth and ninth sons who both died in captivity under suspicious circumstances. However, an autocratic emperor could not tolerate any challenge to his position and his ruthless actions can be matched by the trust and affection he bestowed on Yinxiang, Kangxi's thirteenth son, until he died in 1730.

The more important estimate of Yongzheng concerns his achievements as a ruler. Undoubtedly in his reign a number of valuable reforms were introduced. In 1723 he started a new system for nominating the heir apparent. Under this the ruler selected his heir from among his eligible sons and then, without revealing his choice, placed the name in a sealed box which was only to be opened upon the emperor's death. Such a method might prevent the growth of factions centred on those Manchu princes who had a claim to the throne. A similar objective lay behind a reform of the banner system under which command of the five inferior banners, the banners loyal to the imperial princes, was taken out of their hands and put under bureaucratic control.

Two other areas of reform were more complex and more difficult to assess. One of these concerned the effective operation of the offices of central government. It has been noted earlier how in the later years of Kangxi's reign the system of palace memorials was introduced, and how this enabled the emperor to receive confidential information. Under Yongzheng, in response to the increasing volume of work and the need to deal rapidly with military emergencies, a form of response to such memorials was introduced. Known as a 'court letter' this was an informal and secret communication. In an early surviving example Yongzheng wrote to Yue Zhongqi, the governor-general of Sichuan:

Because I have so many edicts, there is no time personally to write on the memorials. [I just] orally tell the grand secretaries [that is, those on duty in the inner court] what to send in a court letter.[41]

The next development was the creation of a consolidated agency to handle the business of the inner court, the institution to be known as the Grand Council. It has often been claimed that the Grand Council was the creation of Yongzheng and that it came into being in 1729, with the establishment of the Military Finance Section set up in the inner court to deal with matters relating to the campaign against the Dzungar. Recent research suggests a more complex and evolutionary origin. Under Yongzheng several informal, and in the first instance temporary, bodies were created to handle the Dzungar campaign, the reason being that this was an ambitious and costly venture, liable to be undermined by embezzlement. However it was only in the early years of Qianlong's reign that these separate groups were consolidated into what is recognisably the Grand Council.

Another fundamental reform initiated in Yongzheng's reign concerned taxation. He had inherited a fiscal system which impoverished peasants, enriched wealthy landowners and left both central and local government inadequately supplied with funds to carry out their responsibilities. Two particular problems may be identified: the imposition on peasants of substantial surcharges on top of the regular taxes, and the apportionment of tax revenue between central and local government, with perhaps only 21 per cent of the land and head taxes being retained to support local administration, and much of this being used for purposes properly described as the responsibilities of central government.[42]

The key measure promoted by Yongzheng concerned what was known as the meltage fee. In theory this was the surcharge levied to cover the losses caused by melting down the broken silver used for the payment of tax and casting it into ingots to be remitted to central government. This surcharge, which in some provinces was a heavy burden on those least able to pay, was a tolerated abuse and much of it went on customary gifts to officials to supplement their entirely inadequate salaries. The reforms sponsored by Yongzheng legalised the meltage fee at a lower rate and prohibited or reduced the customary gifts. The legalised meltage fee was to be retained locally and used for public welfare projects and to supplement officials' salary, the additional payment being described as *yanglian*, that is to 'nourish incorruptibility'.

How effective were these reforms? It has been claimed that they consolidated Yongzheng's power, improved state finances and enhanced the common people's well-being.[43] They have been described as marking an important step in the development of the modern state in which the concept of government responsibility went beyond the collection of taxes and the maintenance of public order, to include an element of social responsibility. Certainly until the last decades of the eighteenth century public finances were much improved, the treasury was in surplus and it was possible to grant tax remission to areas hit by famine. But it has also been admitted that the effect of the reforms did not last and that the problems which had prompted them returned before the end of the century. Moreover it has been suggested that these problems were in fact insoluble: China was an agrarian society, with only a limited overseas trade. Almost to the end of the dynasty the yield of its agrarian taxes exceeded that of commercial taxes.[44] This tax base was too narrow and incapable of bearing a high level of taxation. It yielded less than 5 per cent of the gross national product – insufficient to finance a modern government or to promote industrialisation.[45]

It would be unfair to judge Yongzheng's reign solely on these grounds, for his achievement in several other spheres should also be taken into account. The common theme in these activities, as in the case of his administrative and fiscal reforms, was the extension of imperial power. He pursued a vigorous policy towards the ethnic minorities in the south. The traditional means of controlling these minorities, for example the Miao, Yao and Lolo peoples, whose main centres of population were in Guangxi, Guizhou, Yunnan and Sichuan, was the *tusi* or tribal headman system, under which a senior member of the community was given an official rank and title, which was usually hereditary.[46] The headman was expected to maintain peace, but otherwise the community was allowed to remain undisturbed. Such a policy might allow sufficient control in the early stages of Chinese expansion, but by the Qing period this was no longer the case. The loyalty of some tribes had come under suspicion at the time of the rebellion of the Three Feudatories. In addition economic motives, for example the demand for copper from Yunnan, may in part explain the forward move. But the underlying reason was the undesirability of allowing tribal chiefs to exercise feudal power within the confines of a centralised empire. Under Yongzheng, Oertai, a Manchu who had unusually passed the *juren* examination, was promoted to acting governor-general of Yunnan and Guizhou with the specific task of 'pacifying' the Miao, abolishing the hereditary headmen and bringing the ethnic minorities into the provincial administrative system. His responsibilites were later extended to Guangxi and over a period of six years he forcibly expanded the power of central government in the region.

Yongzheng was very aware of the importance of asserting ideological conformity. In 1670 Kangxi had circulated the famous Sacred Edict which contained sixteen maxims defining appropriate behaviour. Early in his reign Yongzheng went further, issuing the *Amplified Instructions on the Sacred Edict*, which included his own commentaries on his father's work, with an additional emphasis on the importance of loyalty to the sovereign. These precepts were to be recited aloud publicly and memorised by scholars. Yongzheng was sensitive to any sign of residual anti-Manchu sentiment as well as any accusation that he had usurped the throne, and certain vindictive acts may be attributed to this. One such occurred in the case of the seventeenth-century scholar Lu Liuliang, who had included some anti-Manchu comments in his essays and who had famously stipulated in his will that he should not be buried in any clothes of Manchu design. His writings inspired a Hunanese scholar named Zeng Jing to plot a rebellion against Yongzheng. In 1729 he tried to involve Yue Zhongqi, governor-general of Sichuan and Shaanxi, in his plans. Yue betrayed the plot and Yongzheng wreaked a dreadful revenge not on Zeng Jing but on Lu Liuliang, ordering the destruction of his writings, the dismemberment of his corpse and the punishment of his descendants. But he dealt leniently with Zeng Jing, using him as an example in an ideological campaign intended to forestall any further criticism of Yongzheng himself or of the Manchus. After the Lu Liuliang affair Yongzheng produced a book justifying Manchu rule of China on orthodox Confucian grounds, claiming that it was the virtue of their rulers which had led to the mandate of heaven being transferred to them.

QING CHINA AT ITS HEIGHT: THE REIGN OF QIANLONG, 1736–95

If Yongzheng may be said to have consolidated the Manchu position on the Chinese throne, it was his fourth son, who ruled as the Qianlong emperor, who profited from his endeavours. Qianlong's reign was the longest, and in some ways the most glorious, in Chinese history. During those years China's boundaries reached their widest extent, her population attained a new high point, a prolonged period of internal peace occurred, and feats of scholarly and artistic achievement were recorded. On the other hand, and with hindsight, it has been argued that it was under Qianlong that the evidence of dynastic decline can first be detected, and even more serious threats to the imperial system and China's traditional society began to emerge.

What sort of person was this occupant of the Chinese throne? Because the identity of the heir to the throne was a secret, the future Qianlong emperor had been given the same education as his half-brother. This was an education designed to produce a monarch who had learnt the Chinese classics and who had studied the orthodox Zhu Xi commentaries, who was familiar with history and the arts as well as adept in the military skills expected of a Manchu ruler. It was an education which stressed historical precedents and the ethical basis of imperial role. From it Qianlong learned of the importance of the emperor's personal example and the necessity of his using ministers of high talent. In the first decade of his reign these lessons appeared to have been well learned, for he relied on experienced statesmen, such as Oertai, and he pursued modest objectives. But in the middle years his principal minister, Yu Minzhong, never dared to disagree with him, and Qianlong assumed a large personal role in making policy decisions. His energy was extraordinary, for apart from dealing with the massive quantities of paperwork which reached him, he emulated his grandfather in making six major tours and in directing military campaigns. These were expensive operations and were accompanied by increasing extravagance at court. In his final years Qianlong fell under the influence of his favourite, Heshen, and all semblance of practising what he had been taught seemed to be lost.[47] However his abdication in 1796, a gesture of piety towards his grandfather, the length of whose reign he did not wish to outstrip, was a remarkable assertion of the continued strength of the concept of a Confucian monarch.

In terms of the practice of government Qianlong's reign saw a consolidation of the centralising tendencies which had been a marked feature of his father's rule. The most obvious example of this was the development of the Grand Council from the inner-court groups developed under Yongzheng. The council, which acted in secret and was frequently presided over by the emperor himself, handled all the most important business of the day, from the conduct of military campaigns to the promotion of literary enterprises. It was a relatively small body, usually having five or six members, which made it practicable for it to accompany the emperor on tour. Although Manchus remained the dominant ethnic group on the council, through it Chinese officials gained new influence on policy-making. Ironically, as the council increased its effectiveness during the course of the reign, it reduced the need for the emperor's personal intervention, a factor which was to become significant under the less capable successors of Qianlong.[48]

Under Qianlong the operation of the bureaucracy remained largely unchanged. At the centre routine business was handled by the six boards or ministries, which had limited authority because senior provincial officials were answerable directly to the emperor. Qianlong continued the established policy of making these appointments without distinction between Chinese and Manchus. Nevertheless, an important change in the ethnic composition of this essential group was taking place. Chinese bannermen, who at the beginning of the dynasty had occupied the majority of the appointments as governors-general and governors now lost their dominance. New appointees were for the most part Manchu or Han Chinese. This alteration epitomised the changing relationship between the Manchu ruling class and its Chinese subjects: Manchus were now sufficiently sinicised and sufficiently administratively skilled to take on these posts and at the same time the dynasty no longer feared sharing key provincial appointments with Han Chinese.[49]

During Qianlong's reign, and under his patronage, the arts and literature flourished. The emperor himself practised painting and calligraphy. He claimed to be an arbiter of taste, calling for paintings in the imperial collection to be displayed before him so that he could endorse them with his own inscriptions and seals. Among the artists he approved was the Italian Jesuit Giuseppe Castiglione, who became a court painter.[50] For the same reason he wrote prose and verse, leaving some 42,000 verses attributed to him. He commissioned major scholarly enterprises, the largest being the *Siku quanshu*, the *Complete Library of the Four Branches of Literature*, compiled between 1773 and 1782. This was a collection of 3,500 literary works representing the best in the Chinese literary tradition. Collecting and editing these works and transcribing them to make seven copies provided work, often of a routine kind, for an army of scholars.

The making of this collection preserved many rare works, but it also had a more sinister purpose, for its compilation was used to carry out a literary inquisition. Books were searched for any hint of disrespectful comments about the Manchus. These were either expunged or the destruction of the book itself was ordered: in this way over two thousand works of literature were suppressed. In addition punishment was meted out to all held responsible for the offensive publication.

This aspect of the enterprise has led to a conflict of views. Writing in the 1930s, L. Carrington Goodrich saw the literary inquisition as the major reason for the compilation of the *Complete Library*, and identified Qianlong as the instigator of this censorship, his purpose being to establish greater control over the lives and thoughts of his subjects. Goodrich concluded that its effects were to further estrange the Manchus and the Chinese, to cause a great gap in Chinese literature and to intimidate a generation of Chinese writers. He suggested that it played a part in bringing about a spirit of revolt which became manifest in the nineteenth century.[51] More recently, R. Kent Guy has pointed out that the scholars who undertook the compilation were not doing so for self-seeking or craven motives, and that the suppression of material offensive to the Manchus was only a small part of the project. They co-operated with enthusiasm because the work gave them an opportunity to review texts on a larger scale than it would be possible for them to do as individuals, and in the course of their review they could select among the ancient texts those which most closely supported their opinions.[52]

How powerful were the intellectual currents during these years? In the early Qing period much scholarly activity had been expended on what were known as *kaozheng*, literally 'search for evidence', studies – careful textual studies of the Confucian classics. It has been argued that this type of work, exemplified by the compilation of the *Complete Library*, coupled with the effects of the examination system and the rising competition for scholarly employment, had by the eighteenth century led to the dominance of an inward-looking conservatism and a sterile quest for minute and often trivial knowledge. On the other hand a more positive view has been taken of *kaozheng* studies. It has been suggested that textual studies required empirical methods and exact scholarship, qualities quite foreign to the tradition of Confucian scholarly enquiry. Although only a minority of students became involved in these studies, in Jiangnan an academic community developed and scholarly research and teaching were promoted. Among the subjects studied were mathematics and astronomy; information from Jesuit sources was incorporated and a sense of progress was asserted.[53]

Under Qianlong the Qing empire in Inner Asia achieved its greatest extent. By 1800 Chinese Inner Asia comprised four main areas: Manchuria, Mongolia, Xinjiang and Tibet. Manchuria was treated as a Manchu homeland and restraints were imposed on Han Chinese immigration, although settlers had already arrived in Fengtian in considerable numbers. Mongolia was garrisoned by Qing forces, but there was no longer any danger from Mongol warriors. Mongol society was now divided into banners and Mongol nobles held ranks in the Qing aristocracy. Another means of control lay through Qing patronage of Lamaism or Tibetan Buddhism. The opulent Lama Temple in

Beijing, which has recently been restored, provides a vivid glimpse of how effectively this was done. Further to the west Qianlong consolidated his father's success, waging further campaigns which established China as the dominant power in Central Asia. Between 1755 and 1757 the Dzungar were finally subdued and subsequently an administrative centre was established at Ili and military units stationed in that region. Further campaigns confirmed Chinese dominance in Eastern Turkestan. This newly acquired territory, which amounted to approximately six million square miles, was named Xinjiang, the 'new frontier'. Finally there was the question of Tibet. In 1750 the Chinese position of influence achieved under Kangxi was threatened by a civil war. Qianlong's response was to have the Dalai Lama installed as both civil and spiritual leader of his country while at the same time keeping him firmly under Chinese control.[54]

The Qing continued the Ming procedures for the conduct of relations with foreigners and under Qianlong these reached a new level of formality. Foreign relations were conducted through the tributary system, an expression of Chinese cultural superiority over barbarians, which was modified to suit the needs of the Manchus. Under this system, states in a tributary relationship with China sent embassies to the Qing court at fixed intervals, the most frequent embassies being those of Korea which sent an annual tribute mission. The ceremony for the presentation of tribute was prescribed in minute detail, indicative of the moral value of the transaction for the rulers of China. Nevertheless it was also true that the granting of permission to trade was an important economic benefit to tributary states and of course to China as well.[55]

In the eighteenth century western commercial contacts with China increased, particularly because of the rising demand for tea. On the British side the monopoly of the trade was held by the British East India Company, which was also the effective government of large parts of India. The Chinese government confined the trade to southern ports and required foreign merchants to observe protocol when dealing with officials. The latter requirement infuriated Admiral George Anson, commanding a British squadron preying on Spanish shipping, who was kept waiting at Macao in 1743 after he had requested permission to refit his ship. The account of his voyage, which became a best-seller, included a hostile view of the Chinese which marks the beginning of a significant deterioration in western attitudes towards China. In 1759 a British trader named James Flint, sent to China by the East India Company to request an expansion of trade, reached Tianjin, only to be imprisoned and expelled. From 1760 foreign maritime trade was restricted to Guangzhou and had to be conducted with the Chinese merchant monopoly, known as the Cohong or Hong merchants, who operated under official supervision.

These measures indicated that the Qing government was determined to preserve the tributary system as the method of dealing with the barbarians from the Western Ocean, even though it had previous treated Russian envoys on a basis of equality. It was this which guaranteed the failure of the Macartney mission which reached Qianlong's court at Rehe in 1793. The mission had been sent by the British government to request better trading facilities. The barge which carried the mission sailed up the Bei river displaying flags bearing the inscription 'The English Ambassador bringing Tribute to the Emperor of China'. Considerable pressure was brought to bear on Macartney to observe the ceremonial required of a tributary mission and that in particular he should perform the *koutou*, the ritual three prostrations and nine head knockings. Macartney refused to do this and was only willing to treat the Qianlong emperor as he would his own sovereign, which was by going down before him on one knee. In the end the emperor agreed to this modification and Macartney was received at an audience. But in all other respects the visit was treated as a tribute mission, and all Macartney's requests were rejected.[56]

The key economic development of the eighteenth century was the massive increase in population. Between the end of the seventeenth century and the end of the eighteenth, the population of China approximately doubled from about 150 million to over 300 million. It continued to grow at a somewhat slower rate until the middle of the nineteenth century. This growth derived mainly from a decline in the mortality rate, although the reason for this is not entirely clear. It may be connected with the diffusion of new crops from America and with the prolonged peace of the eighteenth century. Such growth imposed an increasing strain on resources which was partly relieved by internal migration, the most important movements in the Qianlong period being to less developed parts of China, particularly to the upper Yangzi region, Taiwan and southern Manchuria. The clearing of new land in these areas provided good opportunities for pioneering farming families, though in time their activities were to cause disastrous erosion and flooding.[57] The increase in the area of land under cultivation and increases in output per acre produced a growth in food supply which, well into the eighteenth century, outstripped population growth. The evidence from various parts of the country suggests a rising standard of living and a general increase of wealth. But it has been calculated that at some point between 1750 and 1775, the optimum point was passed and the law of diminishing returns ensured that a slow decline in the amount of food available per head of population began to occur.[58]

Nevertheless an observer might be forgiven for regarding the economy of China under Qianlong as thriving. Commerce flourished, and a banking system had appeared which advanced loans and remitted funds, so encouraging long-distance trade. It was true that the monetary system in other respects remained poorly developed and that transportation depended heavily on the river and canal system. At the same time several important industries were flourishing, notably porcelain and iron and most importantly textiles. This evidence has encouraged a further debate on why China did not experience an industrial revolution, this time referring to the eighteenth century. The Marxist interpretation, as represented in China, has been to assert that the 'sprouts of capitalism' were emerging in China at this time, but they failed to develop because of the combined repressive effects of Qing feudalism and foreign capitalism. Western economic historians have been less willing to identify such 'sprouts of capitalism' and have tended to point out that it is more surprising that Europe did experience an industrial revolution than that China did not. Nevertheless they have identified a number of obstacles to industrialisation. One of these allegedly was the Chinese character: that although the Chinese had the capacity to invent new machinery, they lacked the entrepreneurial instinct to capitalise on their inventions. Another was the social system and the cultural values which it endorsed, in other words blame was laid on Confucianism and on the attitudes of officials. The third obstacle was government, the accusation being that the government failed to create the infrastructure necessary to foster industrialisation. Perhaps the most convincing argument is that put forward by Mark Elvin referring to the 'high-level equilibrium trap.' He suggested that the fundamental obstacle to China's industrialisation at this time was a positive, not a negative feature. It was the ability of the Chinese economy to respond effectively to any bottlenecks in production. For example, food output was increased by a constant series of small improvements which utilised the potential of traditional technology without resorting to the possibilities of modern science. In a similar manner, textile production was expanded not by importing cotton or by introducing machinery, but by using beancake fertiliser to increase the cotton crop, and by using moist underground cellars to enable cotton spinning to be carried out in the dry north. By these means the economy could continue to expand without going through a fundamental change. Such a process could continue, albeit with declining living standards, until either a Malthusian check reduced the population, or an exogenous shock forced the introduction of new technology.[59]

So far the description of Qianlong's reign has emphasised the successful extension of the imperial power and the prevalence of the dominant culture, an emphasis which reflects the assertions of official history. Over recent years a number of studies have appeared which explore the extent and character of dissent and of opposition during this period. One such study considered social criticism, taking as its starting point the famous novel *Rulin waishi, The Scholars*, written by Wu Jingzi in the 1740s. The book's main target was the civil service examination system and the appointment to office of those who had succeeded in it. Wu Jingzi himself was a failed examination candidate and his father, who had passed, made no progress in his career. The ironic description of a character in *The Scholars* may be based on Wu Jingzi's perception of his father:

> When he was an official he showed no respect at all for his superiors, but instead just schemed to please the common people. And every day he spouted that nonsense about "fostering filiality and brotherhood" and "encouraging agriculture." These phrases are merely educational topics and flowery terms for use in essays, but he took them seriously. Since his superiors didn't approve, they dismissed him from office.[60]

Wu Jingzi satirised the operation of the examination system and in particular how it rewarded incompetence, but his criticism went deeper than merely protesting against the faults of a system of selection. The novel has been interpreted as a covert attack on Manchu rule, or on feudal exploitation, but perhaps it is better described as an expression of social criticism and as evidence of an intellectual unease which contrasted sharply with the complacent and conservative attitudes of the dominant culture.

Two other themes are prominent in the novel and may be related to tensions in Chinese society in the eighteenth century. The first was that of the position of women. It has been argued that while the subordination of women can be traced far back in Chinese history, that subordination was never stronger than under the Qing. Under the Manchus foot-binding became more popular, increased restrictions were placed on women mixing with men in public, and the pressure on widows to remain faithful to their husband's memory, even if this meant preferring suicide to dishonour, became increasingly strong.[61] In *The Scholars* Wu Jingzi attacked widow suicide and portrayed women as capable of intelligence and cultural refinement, often at the expense of boorish men. His contemporary, the poet and essayist Yuan Mei, wrote in the same vein, attacking the traditional view that 'absence of talent in women is synonymous with virtue'.[62] In the eighteenth century an increasing number of women received some education, although it was assumed that this would confirm their subordinate position in the society. However, before the end of the century, a debate had arisen over the content of women's learning which has been seen as marking a significant stage in the development of a female consciousness in China.[63]

The second issue related to popular religion. In *The Scholars*, Wu Jingzi had made satirical comments about supernatural religious beliefs, for example fortune-telling and geomancy. In so doing he echoed the scepticism publicly expressed by Confucian intellectuals, although in private they often followed the same practices. His scepticism was based on evidence of the inefficacy of such procedures rather than on any increase in scientific knowledge or rationalism. Popular religion continued to be strongly supported and incipient social strains – what has been called a 'premonitory shiver' on the eve of China's tragic modern age[64] – were revealed not by a rejection of popular religion, but by a manifestation of the strength of its hold on the population. The reference is to the sorcery scare of 1768, when a rumour began to circulate in the lower Yangzi region alleging that sorcerers were roaming the land and stealing men's souls by clipping off the ends of their queues. As the rumour spread, and as supposed instances of soul-stealing multiplied, the emperor himself, believing that soul-stealing masked sedition, urged provincial officials to apprehend suspected sorcerers. They complied in a routine fashion and by the autumn the scare had died down. Nevertheless the scare may be interpreted as having a wider significance, a response to 'danger from persons unknown and forces unseen'. It might be seen as a reflection of a changing economy, population pressure, increased migration and the growth of an underclass of displaced persons.[65]

The same factors may have been relevant to the rebellion, known as the Wang Lun uprising, which broke out in Shandong in 1774. This was the precursor of the much larger White Lotus Rebellion of 1796–1804, with which it shared a common ideology. The White Lotus religion had first appeared in the sixteenth century, mainly in the north of China. In normal times members of White Lotus sects practised various life-prolonging and salvation-inducing arts. At other times sects became the nuclei of millenarian movements which might also become anti-dynastic rebellions. Because of this danger the state suppressed such cults when discovered, and the action taken in the years preceding the Wang Lun uprising against two other White Lotus groups may have alarmed the sectarians. However, the reason for their actions given by those involved in the uprising was their belief in the imminence of the millennium. With this inspiration, in the summer of 1774 Wang Lun's followers seized three local towns, killing officials, releasing prisoners and appropriating grain and silver reserves. Their apparent goal was to seize Beijing, but they failed to achieve their first major target, the capture of the important city of Linqing. The account of the attack on Linqing reveals what importance both sides placed on ritual and magic in these affairs. Wang Lun had recruited women to his sect and the attackers made conspicuous use of magical arts. To negate their use of magical power the defenders likewise used women and Wang Lun himself noted that 'on the city wall there were women wearing red clothing but naked from the waist down, bleeding and urinating in order to destroy our power.'[66] Eventually the Qing government managed to concentrate sufficient well-armed forces against the rebels to defeat them. Wang Lun and many of his followers died in the fighting, but other rebels were captured and punished with methodical severity.

This uprising has been described as the 'first crack in the smooth facade' of the high Qing. Perhaps that is to put it too dramatically: the military ineffectiveness displayed by banner and army of the Green Standard troops was nothing new; the uprising was eventually quelled and it was not followed by a wave of popular movements.[67]

However the facade was damaged by a different type of threat, that occasioned by the rise to power of Heshen, the emperor's favourite. Heshen, who had been born in 1750, was a Manchu bannerman. He attracted Qianlong's attention in 1772 and was quickly promoted to be a member of the Grand Council. It has often been claimed that his relationship with the emperor was a homosexual one, although this has never been proved. Once he had established himself as the emperor's favourite, he wielded a tremendous amount of influence, being able to secure the appointment of his nominees to key positions and being able to demand lavish bribes from all who needed his support in matters requiring Qianlong's attention. He has been accused of having brought about a disastrous fall in the standards of government by his demands on officials for bribes. As these demands were passed on to the people, this was said to have aroused discontent leading to rebellion, the reference being to the outbreak of the White Lotus rebellion. It was further alleged that the reason why it took so long to suppress that rebellion was because Heshen and his friends were embezzling vast sums from the military appropriations. The situation became even worse after Qianlong's abdication, when Heshen was effectively regent, profiting from the retired emperor's increased senility. Immediately after Qianlong's death in 1799 Heshen was forced to commit suicide, leaving a fortune estimated at 80,000,000 taels.

Heshen's career poses a conundrum: was he the cause or a symptom of the dynastic decline that began to manifest itself in the last year's of Qianlong's reign? It has been argued that there are too many other explanations for the beginning of dynastic decline to justify heaping much of the blame onto one man – that being the verdict of traditional Chinese historiography which has tended to lay blame on the moral shortcomings of the individual. Certainly the emperor himself should share the responsibility because he failed to respect the principle of taking advice from loyal ministers. But that was a principle to which the Manchu emperors only paid lip service. If they chose to ignore it and exercise their autocratic powers there was little that could be done by officials to stop them.[68] To blame Heshen for a disastrous increase in official corruption is to ignore evidence of earlier evidence of embezzlement of funds intended for military purposes, for example for the suppression of uprisings of aboriginal tribes in western Sichuan in 1747–9 and 1771–6. It is also to misunderstand the reason why corruption existed, which was not necessarily because officials and their assistants were venal, or because the standards of government had declined. It arose from the system itself, which did not recognise the tension between a bureaucratic imperial state which operated on detailed and impersonal regulations, and the individual interests of those affected by its operation. What was condemned as corruption might be described as the use of inducements to make this system work, and for this reason the suggestion that the Qing government collapsed because it became increasingly corrupt has been rejected.[69]

But even blaming the autocracy and citing corruption as evidence of the beginnings of dynastic decline would not be enough to explain the deep crisis which was now beginning to emerge, albeit largely unnoticed. In the eighteenth century the Qing empire had been in its glory. In the nineteenth century the same empire was to experience internal humiliation and external defeat. The point of change between those two conditions had now been reached.

NOTES

INTRODUCTION

1. Quoted in John Meskill, *The Pattern of Chinese History: Cycles, Development, Stagnation?* (Lexington, D.C. Heath, 1968), pp. 2–3.
2. Edwin O. Reischauer and John K. Fairbank, *East Asia: The Great Tradition* (Boston, Houghton Mifflin, 1960), pp. 115–18.
3. Gungwu Wang, *The Structure of Power in North China during the Five Dynasties* (Kuala Lumpur, University of Malaya Press, 1963), pp. 1–6.
4. Wolfram Eberhard, *A History of China*, fourth edition (London, Routledge and Kegan Paul, 1977).
5. Hisayuki Miyakawa, 'An outline of the Naito hypothesis and its effects on Japanese studies of China', *Far Eastern Quarterly*, 14.4, 1955, pp. 533–52.
6. Basil Guy, *The French Image of China Before and After Voltaire* (Geneva, 1963).
7. Hélène Carrère d'Encausse and Stuart R. Schram, *Marxism and Asia: An Introduction with Readings* (London, Allen Lane, 1969), pp. 7–8.
8. Karl A. Wittfogel, *Oriental Despotism: A Comparative Study of Total Power* (New Haven, Yale University Press, 1957, 1970). See also Wittfogel, 'Chinese society: An historical survey', *Journal of Asian Studies*, 16.3, May 1957, pp. 343–64.
9. Etienne Balazs, 'China as a permanently bureaucratic society', in Etienne Balazs, *Chinese Civilization and Bureaucracy* (New Haven, Yale University Press, 1964, 1967), p. 21.
10. Peter C. Perdue, *Exhausting the Earth: State and Peasant in Hunan 1500–1850* (Cambridge, Massachusetts, Harvard University Press, 1987).
11. Richard von Glahn, *The Country of Streams and Grottoes: Expansion, Settlement, and the Civilizing of the Sichuan Frontier in Song Times* (Cambridge, Massachusetts, Harvard University Press, 1987); Hugh R. Clark, *Community, Trade, and Networks: Southern Fujian Province from the Third to the Thirteenth Century* (Cambridge, Cambridge University Press, 1991).
12. G. William Skinner, *The City in Late Imperial China* (Stanford, Stanford University Press, 1977).
13. Susan Naquin and Evelyn S. Rawski, *Chinese Society in the Eighteenth Century* (New Haven, Yale University Press, 1987), pp. 138–216.

CHAPTER ONE

1. Louisa G. Fitzgerald Huber, 'The relationship of the Painted Pottery and the Lung-shan cultures', in David N. Keightley ed., *The Origins of Chinese Civilization* (Berkeley, University of California Press, 1983), pp. 177–216.
2. K.C. Chang, 'Sandai archaeology and the formation of states in ancient China: processual aspects of the origin of Chinese civilization', in Keightley ed., *The Origins of Chinese Civilization*, pp. 495–521.
3. Paul Wheatley, *The Pivot of the Four Quarters: A Preliminary Enquiry into the Origins and Character of the Ancient Chinese City* (Edinburgh, Edinburgh University Press, 1971) p. 58.
4. Noel Barnard, 'Further evidence to support the hypothesis of indigenous origins of metallurgy in ancient China' and Ursula Martius Franklin, 'On bronzes and other metals in early China', both in Keightley ed., *The Origins of Chinese Civilization*, pp. 237–77.
5. Kwong-yue Cheung, 'Recent archaeological evidence relating to the origin of Chinese characters', in Keightley ed., *The Origins of Chinese Civilization*, pp. 323–91.
6. David N. Keightley, *Sources of Shang History: The Oracle-Bone Inscriptions of Shang China* (Berkeley, University of California Press, 1978), pp. 57, 59.
7. Wheatley, pp. 52–63.
8. David N. Keightley, 'The Late Shang state: when, where, and what?' in Keightley ed., *The Origins of Chinese Civilization*, pp. 523–64.
9. Ping-ti Ho, *The Cradle of the East* (Hong Kong, The Chinese University of Hong Kong, 1975), pp. 354–7.

CHAPTER TWO

1. At least twenty different dates have been proposed for the conquest of the Shang by the Zhou, ranging from 1122–1018 BC.
2. Herrlee G. Creel, *The Origins of Statecraft in China, Vol. I, The Western Chou Empire* (Chicago, University of Chicago Press, 1970), pp. 42–3.
3. D.C. Lau trans. and ed., *Mencius* (Harmondsworth, Penguin, 1970), p. 128.
4. Wolfram Eberhard, *A History of China*, fourth edition (London, Routledge & Kegan Paul, 1977), p. 23.
5. Edward L. Shaughnessy, 'Historical perspectives on the introduction of the chariot into China', *Harvard Journal of Asiatic Studies*, 48.1, June 1988, pp. 189–237.
6. Franz Michael, *China Through the Ages* (Boulder, Westview Press, 1986), p. 27.
7. Jacques Gernet, *A History of Chinese Civilization* (Cambridge, Cambridge University Press, 1985), p. 53.
8. Kwang-chih Chang, *The Archaeology of Ancient China*, third edition (New Haven, Yale University Press, 1977), pp. 346–76.
9. Henri Maspero, *La Chine antique* (Paris, Boccard, 1927), p. 66.
10. Derk Bodde, 'Feudalism in China', in Rushton Coulborn ed., *Feudalism in History* (Hamden, Connecticut, Archon Books, 1965), pp. 49–92.
11. Quoted in Bodde, p. 58.
12. Charles O. Hucker, *China's Imperial Past* (London, Duckworth, 1975), p. 33.
13. Cho-yun Hsu and Katheryn M. Linduff, *Western Chou Civilization* (New Haven, Yale University Press, 1988), p. 147.
14. Lau, *Mencius*, p. 177.
15. Cho-yun Hsu, *Ancient China in Transition* (Stanford, Stanford University Press, 1965), p. 118.
16. Gernet, p. 62.
17. Hsu, *Ancient China*, p. 35.
18. Xueqin Li, *Eastern Zhou and Qin Civilizations* (New Haven, Yale University Press, 1985), pp. 315–29.
19. Li, pp. 371–98.
20. Hsu, *Ancient China*, p. 56.
21. Derk Bodde, 'The state and empire of Ch'in', in *CHC*, 1, p. 24.
22. Hsu, *Ancient China*, p. 13.
23. Bodde, 'The state and empire of Ch'in', pp. 99–100.
24. Hsu, *Ancient China*, p. 71.
25. Hsu, *Ancient China*, p. 1.
26. Lau, *Mencius*, p. 101.
27. Hsu, *Ancient China*, p. 121.
28. D.C. Lau trans. and ed., *Confucius: The Analects* (Harmondsworth, Penguin, 1979), p. 10.
29. R. Dawson, *Confucius* (Oxford, Oxford University Press, 1981), p. 11.
30. Lau, *Confucius: The Analects*, p. 114.
31. Lau, *Confucius: The Analects*, p. 121.
32. W.T. de Bary et al. eds., *Sources of Chinese Tradition*, I (New York, Columbia University Press, 1960), p. 40.
33. D.C. Lau trans. and ed., *Lao Tzu: Tao Te Ching* (Harmondsworth, Penguin, 1975), p. 11.
34. Lau, *Lao Tzu*, p. 57.
35. Lau, *Lao Tzu*, p. 121.
36. From the *Chuang Tzu* trans. by Arthur Waley, in Cyril Birch ed., *Anthology of Chinese Literature* (New York, Grove Press, 1965), p. 82.
37. Lau, *Confucius: The Analects*, p. 143.
38. Lau, *Mencius,* p. 82.
39. Lau, *Mencius*, p. 49.
40. Quoted in de Bary, *Sources of Chinese Tradition*, I, p. 127.
41. De Bary, *Sources of Chinese Tradition*, I, p. 133.

CHAPTER THREE

1. Derk Bodde, 'The state and empire of Ch'in', in *CHC*, 1, p. 20.
2. Charles O. Hucker, *China's Imperial Past* (London, Duckworth, 1975), p 43.

3. Bodde, 'The state and empire of Ch'in', p. 20.

4. *Shiji*, quoted in Bodde, 'The state and empire of Ch'in', pp. 31–2.

5. J.J.L. Duyvendak, *The Book of Lord Shang* (London, Arthur Probsthain, 1928), p. 2.

6. Duyvendak, p. 159.

7. Yu-ning Li ed., *Shang Yang's Reforms and State Control in China* (White Plains, New York, M.E. Sharpe, 1977), pp. lxxvii–lxxx.

8. Xueqin Li, *Eastern Zhou and Qin Civilizations* (New Haven, Yale University Press, 1985), p. 429.

9. Li ed., *Shang Yang's Reforms*, p. 78.

10. Derk Bodde, *China's First Unifier: A Study of the Ch'in Dynasty as Seen in the Life of Li Ssu 280?–208 BC* (Leiden, 1938, reprinted Hong Kong, Hong Kong University Press, 1967), p. 129.

11. Bodde, 'State and empire of Ch'in', p. 47.

12. Li Ssu, 'Memorial on annexation of feudal states', in T. de Bary et al eds., *Sources of Chinese Tradition*, I (New York, Columbia University Press, 1960), pp. 139–40.

13. Bodde, *China's First Unifier*, pp. 178–9.

14. Bodde, *China's First Unifier*, pp. 168–9.

15. Li, *Eastern Zhou and Qin Civilizations*, pp. 240–6.

16. Arthur Waldron, *The Great Wall of China* (Cambridge, Cambridge University Press, 1992).

17. Herold J. Wiens, *Han Chinese Expansion in South China* (Shoe String Press, n.p., 1967), pp. 130–3.

18. De Bary, *Sources of Chinese Tradition*, I, p. 141.

19. Ulrich Neininger, 'Burying the scholars alive: On the origins of a Confucian martyr's legend', in Wolfram Eberhard, Krzysztof Gawlikowski and Carl-Albrecht Seyschab eds., *East Asian Civilizations: New Attempts at Understanding Traditions, 2: Nation and Mythology* (Munich, Simon and Magiera, 1983).

20. Bodde, *China's First Unifier*, p. 121.

21. Quoted in Wen Fong ed., *The Great Bronze Age of China: An Exhibition from the People's Republic of China* (London, Thames and Hudson, 1980), pp. 356–7.

22. J.P. Harrison, *The Communists and Chinese Peasant Rebellions* (London, Gollancz, 1970), p. 279.

23. De Bary, *Sources of Chinese Tradition*, I, pp. 150–6.

24. Harrison, p. 220.

25. Xueqin Li ed., *The First Emperor of China* (White Plains, New York, International Arts and Sciences Press, 1975), p. lxiv.

26. Bodde, 'The state and empire of Ch'in', pp. 89–90.

CHAPTER FOUR

1. Cho-yun Hsü, *Han Agriculture: The Formation of Early Chinese Agrarian Economy (206 BC–AD 220)* (Seattle, University of Washington Press, 1980), p. 3.

2. Michael Loewe, *Chinese Ideas of Life and Death: Faith, Myth and Reason in the Han Period (202 BC–AD 220)* (London, George Allen & Unwin, 1982), p. 3.

3. Loewe, *Chinese Ideas of Life and Death*, p. 116. See also Michael Loewe, *Ways to Paradise: The Chinese Quest for Immortality* (London, George Allen & Unwin, 1979), pp. 17–59.

4. Loewe, *Ways to Paradise*, pp. 60–85.

5. De Bary, *Sources of Chinese Tradition*, I, pp. 154–5.

6. The Empress Lü was said to have been bitterly jealous of a concubine of Liu Bang, the Lady Qi. After Liu Bang's death, she poisoned the concubine's son and caused the lady herself to be seized, and had her hands and feet cut off and her organs of speech and hearing destroyed. She was then thrown on a dunghill. The empress invited her own son, the emperor, to go and see the 'human sow'. The sight drove the emperor mad. See W.F. Mayers, *The Chinese Reader's Manual* (Shanghai, American Presbyterian Press, 1874; Taipei, Literature House Ltd, 1964), p. 144.

7. Hans Bielenstein, *The Bureaucracy of Han Times* (Cambridge, Cambridge University Press, 1980), pp. 125–31.

8. Michael Loewe, 'The concept of sovereignty', in *CHC*, 1, p. 732.

9. A.F.P. Hulsewé, 'Ch'in and Han law', *CHC*, 1, pp. 520–44.

10. Nancy Lee Swann, *Food and Money in Ancient China: The Earliest Economic History of China to AD 25* (Princeton, Princeton University Press, 1950), pp. 174–5.

11. Michael Loewe, *Everyday Life in Early Imperial China During the Han Period 202 BC–AD 220* (London, Carousel, 1973), pp. 128–36.

12. Ying-shih Yü, 'Han foreign relations', *CHC*, 1, pp. 377–462.

13. Michael Loewe, *Crisis and Conflict in Han China 104 BC–AD 9* (London, George Allen & Unwin, 1974), pp. 11–13.
14. Burton Watson trans., *Courtier and Commoner in Ancient China: Selections from the* History of the Former Han *by Pan Ku* (New York, Columbia University Press, 1974), p. 56.
15. De Bary, *Sources of Chinese Tradition*, I, pp. 162–3.
16. Ch'i-yün Ch'en, 'Confucian, Legalist, and Taoist thought in Later Han', *CHC*, 1, p. 769.
17. De Bary, *Sources of Chinese Tradition*, I, p. 189.
18. Hulsewé, 'Ch'in and Han law', *CHC*, 1, p. 534.
19. Loewe, *Crisis and Conflict in Han China*, pp. 37–90.
20. Loewe, *Crisis and Conflict in Han China*, p. 114.
21. Loewe, *Crisis and Conflict in Han China*, pp. 139–40.
22. Hu Shih, 'Wang Mang, the socialist emperor of nineteen centuries ago', *Journal of the North China Branch of the Royal Asiatic Society*, 59, 1928, pp. 218–30.
23. Charles O. Hucker, *China's Imperial Past* (London, Duckworth, 1975), p. 129.
24. Hans Bielenstein, 'Wang Mang, the restoration of the Han dynasty and Later Han' *CHC*, 1, p. 239.
25. De Bary, *Sources of Chinese Tradition*, I, pp. 180–2.
26. Ban Gu, *Hanshu*, de Bary, *Sources of Chinese Tradition*, I, p. 226.
27. Sadao Nishijima, 'The economic and social history of Former Han', *CHC*, 1, p. 589.
28. Hucker, *China's Imperial Past*, p. 130.
29. Franz Michael, *China Through the Ages* (Boulder, Westview Press, 1986), pp. 80–1.
30. Bielenstein, 'Wang Mang', p. 239.
31. James P. Harrison, *The Communists and Chinese Peasant Rebellions* (London, Gollancz, 1970), p. 281.
32. Bielenstein, 'Wang Mang', p. 275.
33. Patricia Ebrey, 'The economic and social history of Later Han', *CHC*, 1, p. 614.
34. Etienne Balazs, 'Political philosophy and social crisis at the end of the Han dynasty', in Etienne Balazs, *Chinese Civilization and Bureaucracy* (New Haven, Yale University Press, 1967), pp. 198–205.
35. Zhongshu Wang, *Han Civilization* (New Haven, Yale University Press, 1982), p. 207.
36. Balazs, 'Political philosophy', p. 192.
37. Rafe de Crespigny, *Northern Frontier: The Policies and Strategy of the Later Han Empire* (Canberra, Australian National University, 1984), pp. xiii, 417–25.
38. Balazs, 'Political philosophy', pp. 192–3.
39. Bielenstein, 'Wang Mang', pp. 289–90.

CHAPTER FIVE

1. For example, L. Carrington Goodrich, *A Short History of the Chinese People*, third edition (London, Harper Torchbooks, 1959), p. 84.
2. Mark Elvin, *The Pattern of the Chinese Past* (London, Eyre, Methuen, 1973), p. 20.
3. E.O. Reischauer and John K. Fairbank, *East Asia: The Great Tradition* (Boston, Houghton Mifflin Company, 1960), pp. 128–9.
4. Wolfram Eberhard, *A History of China*, fourth edition (London, Routledge and Kegan Paul, 1977), p. 114.
5. Patricia Buckley Ebrey, *The Aristocratic Families of Early Imperial China: A Case Study of the Po-ling Ts'ui Family* (Cambridge, Cambridge University Press, 1978), pp. 16–19.
6. Eberhard, p. 119.
7. Eberhard, p. 143.
8. W.J.F. Jenner, *Memories of Loyang: Yang Hsüan-chih and the Lost Capital (493–534)*, (Oxford, Clarendon Press, 1981), p. 28.
9. Eberhard, p. 144.
10. Charles O. Hucker, *China's Imperial Past* (London, Duckworth, 1975), p. 183.
11. Reischauer and Fairbank, p. 158.
12. Jenner, p. 38.
13. Jenner, Appendix III.
14. Guo Xiang, *Commentary on the Zhuangzi*, quoted in de Bary, *Sources of Chinese Tradition*, I, p. 243.
15. Zong Bing, *Introduction to Landscape Painting*, quoted in de Bary, *Sources of Chinese Tradition*, I, p. 254.

16. Kenneth K.S. Chen, *Buddhism in China: A Historical Survey* (Princeton, Princeton University Press, 1964), pp. 124–8.
17. Jenner, p. 148.

CHAPTER SIX

1. Arthur F. Wright, 'The Sui dynasty (581–617)', in *CHC*, 3 pp. 57–61.
2. Arthur F. Wright, *The Sui Dynasty* (New York, Knopf, 1978), p. 84.
3. Wright, 'The Sui dynasty', p. 106.
4. Wright, quoting Xiao Yu's reply to the Tang Emperor Taizong in 621, *The Sui Dynasty*, p. 71.
5. Wright, *The Sui Dynasty*, p. 173.
6. Howard J. Wechsler, *Mirror to the Son of Heaven: Wei Cheng at the Court of T'ang T'ai-tsung* (New Haven, Yale University Press, 1974), p. 16.
7. Howard J. Wechsler, 'The founding of the T'ang dynasty: Kao-tsu (reign 618–26),' *CHC*, 3, p. 161.
8. William Frederick Mayers, *The Chinese Reader's Manual* (Shanghai, American Presbyterian Mission Press, 1874; Taipei, Literature House, 1964), p. 122.
9. Arthur F. Wright, 'T'ang T'ai-tsung: The man and the persona', in John C. Perry and Bardwell L. Smith eds., *Essays on T'ang Society: The Interplay of Social, Political and Economic Forces* (Leiden, E.J. Brill, 1976), pp. 17–32.
10. Wright, 'T'ang T'ai-tsung', p. 26.
11. Wright, 'T'ang T'ai-tsung', p. 29.
12. Quoted in Wechsler, *Mirror to the Son of Heaven*, p. 84.
13. Wei Zheng's posthumous reputation led to him being transformed into a Daoist adept and a door god. In the Cultural Revolution he was praised by Mao Zedong's opponents as an example of someone who dared to criticise the emperor, by implication someone who would have dared to criticise Mao. See Wechsler, *Mirror to the Son of Heaven*.
14. D.C. Twitchett, *Financial Administration under the T'ang Dynasty*, second edition (Cambridge, Cambridge University Press, 1970), pp. 1–16.
15. David G. Johnson, *The Medieval Chinese Oligarchy* (Boulder, Westview Press, 1977), pp. 28–30, 48–50.
16. Ichisada Miyazaki, *China's Examination Hell: The Civil Service Examinations in China* (New Haven, Yale University Press, 1981), p. 113.
17. Stanley Weinstein, *Buddhism under the T'ang* (Cambridge, Cambridge University Press, 1987), p. 12.
18. D.C. Twitchett and Howard J. Wechsler, 'Kao-tsung (reign 649–83) and the empress Wu: the inheritor and the usurper' in *CHC* 3, p. 244.
19. Twitchett and Wechsler, p. 258.
20. Twitchett and Wechsler, p. 251.
21. C.P. FitzGerald, *The Empress Wu* (London, Cresset Press, 1956), p. 31.
22. Twitchett and Wechsler, p. 273.
23. Johnson, pp. 128–9.
24. Twitchett, *Financial Administration*, p. 75.
25. FitzGerald, p. 116.
26. FitzGerald, p. 163.
27. FitzGerald, pp. vii, 197–8.
28. Richard W.L. Guisso, 'The reigns of the empress Wu, Chung-tsung and Jui-tsung (684–712)' in *CHC*, 3, and R.W.L. Guisso, *Wu Tse-t'ien and the Politics of Legitimation in T'ang China* (Washington, Western Washington, 1978).
29. D.C. Twitchett, 'Hsüan-tsung (reign 712–56),' *CHC*, 3, pp. 462–3.
30. Edwin G. Pulleyblank, *The Background of the Rebellion of An Lu-shan* (Oxford, Oxford University Press, 1955), pp. 47–8, 192–5.
31. Pulleyblank, *Background to the Rebellion*, pp. 30–2.
32. Twitchett, *Financial Administration*, pp. 87–9.
33. Pulleyblank, *Background of the Rebellion*, p. 59.
34. Mayers, p. 6.
35. Pulleyblank, *Background of the Rebellion*, p. 59.
36. Twitchett, 'Hsüan-tsung', p. 402.
37. Edwin G. Pulleyblank, 'The An Lu-shan Rebellion and the origins of chronic militarism in Late T'ang China', in Perry and Smith, pp. 39–40.

38. Translated by Witter Bynner in Cyril Birch, compiler and editor, *Anthology of Chinese Literature: From Early Times to the Fourteenth Century* (Harmondsworth, Penguin Books, 1967), p. 282.
39. Pulleyblank, *Background of the Rebellion*, p. 1.
40. Pulleyblank, *Background of the Rebellion*, p. 27.
41. C.A. Peterson, 'Court and province in mid- and late T'ang', in *CHC*, 3, pp. 471–2.
42. Peterson, pp. 485–6.
43. Twitchett, *Financial Administration*, pp. 39–40.
44. C. A. Peterson, 'The Restoration completed: Emperor Hsien-tsung and the provinces', in Wright and Twitchett, *Perspectives on the T'ang* (New Haven, Yale University Press, 1973), pp. 151–91.
45. Edwin O. Reischauer, *Ennin's Travels in T'ang China* (New York, Ronald Press, 1955), p. 7.
46. Reigned 846–59, to be distinguished from his famous predecessor who reigned 712–56.
47. Robert M. Somers, 'The end of the T'ang', *CHC*, 3, 682–789.

CHAPTER SEVEN

1. Denis Twitchett, 'Introduction', *CHC*, 3, p. 33.
2. Arthur F. Wright, 'Changan', in Arnold Toynbee ed., *Cities of Destiny* (London, Thames and Hudson, 1967), p. 143.
3. Edward H. Schafer, *The Golden Peaches of Samarkand: A Study of T'ang Exotics* (Berkeley, University of California Press, 1963), p. 142.
4. Edward H. Schafer, *The Vermilion Bird: T'ang Images of the South* (Berkeley, University of California Press, 1967), p. 230.
5. For an account of his journey see Arthur Waley, *The Real Tripitaka and Other Pieces* (London, George Allen and Unwin, 1952). Waley called Xuan Zang 'Tripitaka', a Sanskrit word meaning 'three baskets', referring to the triple canon of Buddhist scriptures.
6. Waley, p. 39.
7. René Grousset, *In the Footsteps of the Buddha* (London, George Routledge and Sons, 1932), pp. 270–84.
8. C.P. FitzGerald, *The Southern Expansion of the Chinese People* (London, Barrie and Jenkins, 1972), p. 2.
9. Schafer, *The Vermilion Bird*, pp. 45–7.
10. Mark Elvin, *The Pattern of the Chinese Past* (London, Eyre Methuen, 1973), pp. 204–9.
11. Herold J. Wiens, *Han Chinese Expansion in South China*, (Hamden, Connecticut, Shoe String Press, 1967), pp. 272–4.
12. Hugh R. Clark, *Community, Trade, and Networks: Southern Fujian Province from the Third to the Thirteenth Century* (Cambridge, Cambridge University Press, 1991), pp. 19–37.
13. FitzGerald, p. 77.
14. FitzGerald, pp. 60–6.
15. Thomas J. Barfield, *The Perilous Frontier: Nomadic Empires and China* (Oxford, Basil Blackwell, 1989), pp. 9, 131.
16. Barfield, p. 49.
17. Barfield, p. 145.
18. Quoted in René Grousset, *The Empire of the Steppes: A History of Central Asia* (New Brunswick, Rutgers University Press, 1970), p. 102.
19. Quoted in Barfield, pp. 146-7.
20. Howard J. Wechsler, 'T'ai-tsung (reign 626–49) the consolidator', in *CHC*, 3, p. 230 and n.
21. Richard W.L. Guisso, 'The reigns of the empress Wu, Chung-tsung and Jui-tsung 684–712', in *CHC* 3, p. 285.
22. Michael T. Dalby, 'Court politics in late T'ang times', in *CHC*, 3, p. 677.
23. Barfield, p. 155.
24. Quoted in Grousset, *The Empire of the Steppes*, p. 122.
25. Barfield, p. 12.
26. From the *Liao Shih*, quoted in Barfield, p. 172.
27. John Whitney Hall, *Japan from Prehistory to Modern Times* (Tokyo, Charles E. Tuttle, 1971), p. 40.
28. Ryusaku Tsunoda, W.T. de Bary and Donald Keene compilers, *Sources of Japanese Tradition* (New York, Columbia University Press, 1964), I, p. 47.
29. Mikiso Hane, *Premodern Japan: A Historical Survey* (Boulder, Westview Press, 1991), p. 34.
30. Edwin O. Reischauer, *Ennin's Travels in T'ang China* (New York, The Ronald Press, 1955), pp. 272–94.
31. Gungwu Wang, 'Ming relations with Southeast Asia: A background essay' in J.K. Fairbank ed., *The Chinese World*

Order: Traditional China's Foreign Relations (Cambridge, Massachusetts, Harvard University Press, 1968), pp. 34–62.

32. Sechin Jagchid and Van Jay Symons, *Peace, War, and Trade along the Great Wall: Nomadic-Chinese Interaction through Two Millennia* (Bloomington, Indiana University Press, 1989), pp. 1–23.

CHAPTER EIGHT

1. From Jacques Gernet, *Les aspects économiques du Bouddhisme dans la société chinoise du Ve au Xe siècle*, Saigon, 1956 as summarised in Arthur F. Wright, 'T'ang T'ai-tsung and Buddhism', in Arthur F. Wright and Denis Twitchett eds., *Perspectives on the T'ang* (New Haven, 1973), p. 241.
2. Kenneth K.S. Chen, *Buddhism in China: A Historical Survey* (Princeton, Princeton University Press, 1964), p. 204.
3. Chen, p. 204.
4. De Bary, *Sources of Chinese Tradition*, I, p. 292.
5. Stanley Weinstein, *Buddhism under the T'ang* (Cambridge University Press, Cambridge, 1987), p. 4.
6. Weinstein, p. 26.
7. Weinstein, pp. 60–1.
8. Weinstein, p. 84.
9. Weinstein, p. 91.
10. De Bary, *Sources of Chinese Tradition*, I, p. 373.
11. Edwin O. Reischauer trans., *Ennin's Diary: The Record of a Pilgrimage to China in Search of the Law* New York, The Ronald Press, 1955, p. 361.
12. De Bary, *Sources of Chinese Tradition*, I, pp. 380–2.
13. John T. Meskill ed., *An Introduction to Chinese Civilization* (Lexington, Columbia University Press, 1973), pp. 110–11.
14. Charles O. Hucker, *China's Imperial Past* (London, Duckworth, 1975), p. 219.
15. A.C. Moule, *Christians in China Before the Year 1550* (London, Society for Promoting Christian Knowledge, 1930), pp. 38–9.
16. F.S. Drake, 'Mohammedanism in the T'ang dynasty', *Monumenta Serica*, VIII, 1943, pp. 1–40.
17. De Bary, *Sources of Chinese Tradition*, I, p. 370.
18. David McMullen, *State and Scholars in T'ang China* (Cambridge, Cambridge University Press, 1988).
19. Charles Hartman, *Han Yü and the T'ang Search for Unity* (Princeton, Princeton University Press, 1986), pp. 1–3.
20. De Bary, *Sources of Chinese Tradition*, I, p. 375.
21. David McMullen, 'Han Yü: An alternative picture', *Harvard Journal of Asiatic Studies,* 49.2, Dec. 1989, pp. 603–57.
22. Wu-chi Liu, *An Introduction to Chinese Literature* (Bloomington, Indiana University Press, 1966), p. 69.
23. Tao Qian, 'Two poems on returning to dwell in the country', translated by William Acker, in Cyril Birch, compiler and editor, *Anthology of Chinese Literature: From the Earliest Times to the Fourteenth Century* (New York, Grove Press 1965), p. 183.
24. Stephen Owen, *The Great Age of Chinese Poetry: The High T'ang* (New Haven, Yale University Press, 1981), pp. 3–6.
25. Owen, p. 39.
26. Owen, p. 109.
27. Translated by William Acker, Birch, p. 232.
28. Arthur Cooper, *Li Po and Tu Fu* (Harmondsworth, Penguin Books, 1973), p. 109.
29. Cooper, pp. 18–19.
30. Owen, pp. 197–8.
31. Arthur Waley, *The Life and Times of Po Chü-i, 772–846 AD* (London, George Allen and Unwin, 1949), p. 163.
32. Liu, p. 92.
33. Trans. by Waley, Birch, p. 277.
34. A.C. Graham, *Poems of the Late T'ang* (Harmondsworth, Penguin Books, 1981), p. 117.
35. Birch, pp. 258–9.
36. Edward H. Schafer, *The Vermilion Bird: T'ang Images of the South* (Berkeley, University of California Press, 1967), p. 143.
37. For a translation by Waley of 'The Story of Miss Li', see Birch, pp. 300–13.
38. William Dolby, *A History of Chinese Drama* (London, Paul Elek, 1976), pp. 5–8.
39. Arthur F. Wright, 'Changan', in Arnold Toynbee, *Cities of Destiny* (London, Thames and Hudson, 1967), p. 146.

40. Michael Sullivan, *The Arts of China* (London, Sphere Books, 1973), p. 127.

41. Sullivan, p. 134.

42. Michael Sullivan, 'The heritage of Chinese art', in Raymond Dawson ed., *The Legacy of China* (Oxford, Oxford University Press, 1964), p. 226.

43. Dong You (active 1119–26), quoted in Arthur Waley, *An Introduction to the Study of Chinese Painting* (London, 1923), p. 117.

44. Max Loehr, *The Great Paintings of China* (Oxford, Phaidon, 1980), pp. 41–6.

45. William Watson, *Style in the Art of China* (Harmondsworth, Penguin Books, 1974), Plates 101 a, b.

46. Jessica Rawson ed., *The British Museum Book of Chinese Art* (London, British Museum Press, 1992), pp. 232–4.

47. Rawson, p. 145.

CHAPTER NINE

1. E.O. Reischauer and J.K. Fairbank, *East Asia: The Great Tradition* (Boston, Houghton Mifflin Company, 1960), p. 194.

2. Winston W. Lo, *An Introduction to the Civil Service of Sung China* (Honolulu, University of Hawaii Press, 1987), p. 56.

3. Gungwu Wang, *The Structure of Power in North China during the Five Dynasties* (Kuala Lumpur, University of Malaya Press, 1963).

4. E.A. Kracke, Jr., *Civil Service in Early Sung China, 960–1067* (Massachusetts, Harvard University Press, Cambridge, 1953, 1968), p. 1.

5. John W. Chaffee, *The Thorny Gates of Learning in Sung China: A Social History of Examinations* (Cambridge, Cambridge University Press, 1985), pp. 47–65.

6. Thomas H.C. Lee, *Government Education and Examinations in Sung China* (Hong Kong, The Chinese University Press,1985), pp. 22–3, 62–3.

7. Kracke, pp. 194–5.

8. Chaffee, p. 182.

9. Figures from a study by Sun Kuo-tung, quoted in Lee, pp. 211–15.

10. Etienne Balazs, 'A forerunner of Wang An-shih', in Etienne Balazs, *Chinese Civilization and Bureaucracy: Variations on a Theme* (New Haven, Yale University Press, 1967).

11. James T.C. Liu, *Ou-yang Hsiu: An Eleventh-Century Neo-Confucianist* (Stanford, Stanford University Press, 1967), pp. 52–64.

12. De Bary, *Sources of Chinese Tradition*, I, p. 414.

13. Quoted in James T.C. Liu, *Reform in Sung China: Wang An-shih (1021–1086) and his New Policies* (Massachusetts, Harvard University Press, Cambridge, 1959), p. 49.

14. Quoted in John Meskill ed., *Wang An-shih: Practical Reformer?* (Boston, D.C. Heath and Company, 1963), p. 21.

15. Quoted in Meskill, p. 25.

16. Meskill, p. 39.

17. Liu, *Reform in Sung China*, p. 13.

18. Meskill, pp. 77-81.

19. Meskill, pp. 82–90.

20. Liu, *Reform in Sung China*, pp. 114–16.

21. Ray Huang, *China: A Macro History* (New York, M.E. Sharpe Inc., 1989), pp. 118–21.

22. Kao Yu-kung, 'A study of the Fang La rebellion', *Harvard Journal of Asiatic Studies*, 24, 1962–3, pp. 17–63.

23. See chapter 7.

24. Otherwise 'Jürched'.

25. Jing-shen Tao, *The Jurchen in Twelfth-Century China: A Study of Sinicization* (Seattle, University of Washington Press, 1976), pp. 3–13.

26. Tao, p. 34.

27. Herbert Franke, 'The Jin dynasty', in *CHC*, 6, pp. 215–320.

28. Tao, pp. 92–4.

29. Hellmut Wilhelm, 'From myth to myth: The case of Yüeh Fei's biography', in Arthur F. Wright and Denis Twitchett eds., *Confucian Personalities* (Stanford, Stanford University Press, 1962), pp. 146–61, and James T.C. Liu, 'Yüeh Fei (1103–1141) and China's heritage of loyalty', *Journal of Asian Studies*, 31.2, Feb. 1972, pp. 291–7.

30. James T.C. Liu, *China Turning Inward: Intellectual-Political Changes in the Early Twelfth Century* (Cambridge, Massachusetts, Harvard University Press, 1988), p. 83.

31. Richard L. Davis, *Court and Family in Sung China, 960–1279: Bureaucratic Success and Kinship Fortunes for the Shih of Ming-chou* (Durham, Duke University Press, 1986), p. 85.
32. Davis, p. 86.
33. Herbert Franke, 'Chia Ssu-tao (1213–1275): A "bad last minister"?', Wright and Twitchett, *Confucian Personalities*, pp. 217–34.
34. Franke, 'Chia Ssu-tao', pp. 226–9.
35. Mark Elvin, *The Pattern of the Chinese Past* Eyre (London, Methuen, 1973), pp. 111–99.
36. Elvin, p. 179.
37. Etienne Balazs, 'The birth of capitalism in China', in Balazs, *Chinese Civilization and Bureaucracy*, pp. 34–54.
38. Peter J. Golas, 'Rural China in the Song', *Journal of Asian Studies*, 39.2, 1980, pp. 291–325.
39. Robert Hartwell, 'A revolution in the Chinese iron and coal industries during the northern Sung, 960–1126 AD', *Journal of Asian Studies*, 21, 1961–2, pp. 153–162.
40. Robert P. Hymes, *Statesmen and Gentlemen: The Elite of Fu-chou, Chiang-hsi, in Northern and Southern Sung* (Cambridge, Cambridge University Press, 1986).
41. Davis, p. xv.
42. Golas, p. 302.
43. Etienne Balazs, 'Chinese towns' in Etienne Balazs, *Chinese Civilization and Bureaucracy*, pp. 66–78. See also Jacques Gernet, *Daily Life in China on the Eve of the Mongol Invasion 1250–1276* (London, George Allen & Unwin, 1962).
44. Patricia Buckley Ebrey, *The Inner Quarters: Marriage and the Lives of Chinese Women in the Sung period* (Berkeley, University of California Press, 1993), pp. 4–6.
45. Ebrey, pp. 261–71.
46. Liu, *China Turning Inward*, pp. 55–80.
47. De Bary, *Sources of Chinese Tradition*, I, pp. 457–60, 465–70.
48. Wei-ming,Tu 'The Confucian tradition in Chinese history', in Paul S. Ropp ed., *Heritage of China: Contemporary Perspectives on Chinese Civilization* (Berkeley, University of California Press, 1990), pp. 112–37.
49. Michael Sullivan, *The Arts of China* (London, Sphere Books, 1973), p. 159.
50. Quoted in Joseph Levenson, *Modern China and its Confucian Past* (New York, Anchor Books, 1964), p. 29.
51. Peter C. Swann, *Art of China Korea and Japan* (London, Thames and Hudson, 1963), p. 137.

CHAPTER TEN

1. Jacques Gernet, *A History of Chinese Civilization* (Cambridge, Cambridge University Press, 1985), pp. 360–84.
2. Ray Huang, *China: A Macro History* (New York, M.E. Sharpe Inc., 1989), p. 147.
3. F.W. Mote, 'The growth of Chinese despotism: A critique of Wittfogel's theory of oriental despotism as applied to China', *Oriens Extremus*, 8.1 (August 1961), pp. 1–41.
4. John D. Langlois Jr ed., *China under Mongol Rule* (Princeton, Princeton University Press, 1981), pp. 3–21.
5. F.W. Mote, 'Chinese society under Mongol rule, 1215–1368', in *CHC*, 6, pp. 618–22.
6. Thomas Allsen, 'The rise of the Mongolian empire and Mongolian rule in north China', in *CHC*, 6, pp. 321–413.
7. Igor de Rachewiltz, 'Yeh-lü Ch'u-ts'ai (1189–1243): Buddhist idealist and Confucian statesman', in Arthur F. Wright and Denis Twitchett eds., *Confucian Personalities* (Stanford, Stanford University Press, 1962), pp. 189–216.
8. Herbert Franke, *From Tribal Chieftain to Universal Emperor and God: The Legitimation of the Yüan dynasty* (Verlag der Bayerischen Akademie der Wissenschaften, Munich, 1978), p. 38.
9. De Rachelwiltz, p. 214.
10. Hok-lam Chan, 'Chinese official historiography at the Yüan court: The composition of the Liao, Chin, and Sung histories', in Langlois, *China Under Mongol Rule*, pp. 56–106.
11. Mote, 'Chinese society under Mongol rule', pp. 651–3.
12. Paul Heng-chao Ch'en, *Chinese Legal Tradition under the Mongols: The Code of 1291 as Reconstructed* (Princeton, Princeton University Press, 1979), p. xvi.
13. Ch'i-ing Hsiao, 'Mid-Yüan politics', in *CHC*, 6, pp. 490–560.
14. Ch'en, pp. 80–8.
15. Elizabeth Endicott-West, 'The Yüan government and society', in *CHC*, 6, p. 613.
16. Witold Rodzinski, *A History of China* Volume I, (Oxford, Pergamon Press, 1979), pp. 184–5.
17. Endicott-West, 'The Yüan government and society', p. 613.
18. Elizabeth Endicott-West, 'Merchant associations in Yüan China: The *Ortoy*', *Acta Asiatica*, 2.2, 1989, pp. 127–54.

19. H.H. Lamb, *Climate: Past and Future* (London, Methuen, 1977), II, pp. 447, 456.
20. de Rachewiltz, pp. 195–8.
21. Yün-hua Jan, 'Chinese Buddhism in Ta-tu: The new situation and new problems', in Hok-lam Chan and Wm. Theodore de Bary eds., *Yüan Thought: Chinese Thought and Religion Under the Mongols* (New York, Columbia University Press, 1982), pp. 390–3.
22. Herbert Franke, 'Tibetans in Yüan China', in Langlois ed., p. 306.
23. Wing-tsit Chan, 'Chu Hsi and Yüan Neo-Confucianism', in Chan and de Bary, pp. 197–231.
24. Wei-ming Tu, 'Towards an understanding of Liu Yin's Confucian eremitism', in Chan and de Bary, pp. 233–77.
25. *Six Yüan Plays* translated with an introduction by Liu Jung-en, (Harmonsdworth, Penguin books, 1972), p. 10.
26. Stephen H. West, 'Mongol influence on the development of Northern Drama', in Langlois ed., pp. 434–65.
27. Morris Rossabi, 'The Muslims in the early Yüan dynasty', in Langlois ed., pp. 257–95.
28. *The Travels of Marco Polo*, translated and with an introduction by Ronald Latham (Harmondsworth, Penguin Books, 1958), p. 36.
29. John W. Haeger, 'Marco Polo in China? Problems with internal evidence', *Bulletin of Sung and Yuan Studies*, 14, 1978, pp. 22–30.
30. Morris Rossabi, *Voyager from Xanadu: Rabban Sauma and the First Journey from China to the West* (New York, Kodansha International, 1992).
31. Ch'i-ch'ing Hsiao, *The Military Establishment of the Yüan Dynasty* (Cambridge, Massachusetts, Harvard University Press, 1978), pp. 3–32.
32. Hsiao, pp. 32, 62–3.
33. John W. Dardess, 'The transformations of messianic revolt and the founding of the Ming dynasty', *Journal of Asian Studies*, 29.3, 1970, pp. 539–58.
34. Charles O. Hucker, *The Ming Dynasty: Its Origins and Evolving Institutions* (Ann Arbor, The University of Michigan Center for Chinese Studies, 1978), p. 24.
35. Hsiao, pp. 3–8.
36. Ch'en, pp. 41–67.

CHAPTER ELEVEN

1. Edward L. Dreyer, *Early Ming China: A Political History 1355–1435* (Stanford, Stanford University Press, 1982), p. 237.
2. John W. Dardess, 'The transformations of Messianic revolt and the founding of the Ming dynasty', *Journal of Asian Studies*, 29.3, 1970, pp. 539–58.
3. Frederick W. Mote, 'The rise of the Ming dynasty' in *CHC*, 7, pp. 11–57.
4. The term is used anachronistically to denote Zhu Yuanzhang's regime.
5. Edward L. Dreyer, 'Military origins of Ming China', *CHC*, 7, pp. 58–106.
6. Dreyer, *Early Ming China*, pp. 69–70, 155–6.
7. Dreyer, *Early Ming China*, pp. 76–87; Romeyn Taylor, 'Yüan origins of the *wei-so* system', in Charles O. Hucker ed., *Chinese Government in Ming Times: Seven Studies* (New York, Columbia University Press, 1969), pp. 23–40.
8. Charles O. Hucker, *The Ming Dynasty: Its Origins and Evolving Institutions* (Ann Arbor, Center for Chinese Studies, University of Michigan, 1978), p. 43.
9. Ray Huang, *Taxation and Governmental Finance in Sixteenth-Century Ming China* (Cambridge, Cambridge University Press, 1974), p. 42.
10. Ray Huang, 'Fiscal administration during the Ming dynasty', in Hucker ed., *Chinese Government in Ming Times*, pp. 73–128.
11. Edward L. Farmer, *Early Ming Government: The Evolution of Dual Capitals* (Cambridge, Massachusetts, Harvard University Press, 1976), pp. 114–28.
12. Hok-lam Chan, 'The Chien-wen, Yung-lo, Hung-hsi, and Hsüan-te reigns, 1399–1435', in *CHC*, 7, pp. 182–304.
13. J.V.G. Mills trans. and ed., *Ma Huan, Ying-yai sheng-lan: The Overall Survey of the Ocean's Shores [1433]* (Cambridge, Cambridge University Press, 1970), p. 10.
14. Hok-lam Chan, p. 278.
15. Farmer, p. 133.
16. Dreyer, *Early Ming China*, p. 252.
17. Frederick W. Mote, 'The T'u-mu incident of 1449' in Frank A. Kierman and John K. Fairbank eds., *Chinese Ways in Warfare* (Cambridge, Massachusetts, Harvard University Press, 1974), pp. 243–72.

18. Arthur Waldron, *The Great Wall of China: From History to Myth* (Cambridge, Cambridge University Press, 1992), pp. 91–107.

19. Frederick W. Mote., 'The growth of Chinese despotism: A critique of Wittfogel's theory of Oriental Despotism as applied to China, *Oriens Extremus*, 8.1, 1961, pp. 1–41.

20. Albert Chan, *The Glory and Fall of the Ming Dynasty* (Norman, University of Oklahoma Press, 1982), pp. 18, 32.

21. Hok-lam Chan, p. 287.

22. Charles O. Hucker, *The Censorial System of Ming China* (Stanford, Stanford University Press, 1966), pp. 147–51; 232–4.

23. Jung-pang Lo, 'Policy formulation and decision-making on issues respecting peace and war', in Hucker ed., *Chinese Government in Ming Times*, pp. 41–72.

24. Ping-ti Ho, *Studies on the Population of China, 1368–1953* (Cambridge, Massachusetts, Harvard University Press, 1974), pp. 258–65.

25. Dwight H. Perkins, *Agricultural Development in China, 1368–1968* (Edinburgh, Edinburgh University Press, 1969), pp. 5–78.

26. Peter C. Perdue, *Exhausting the Earth: State and Peasant in Hunan, 1500–1850* (Cambridge, Massachusetts, Harvard University Press, 1987), p. 49.

27. Sadao Nishijima, 'The formation of the early Chinese cotton industry', in Linda Grove and Christian Daniels eds., *State and Society in China: Japanese Perspectives on Ming-Qing Social and Economic History* (Tokyo, University of Tokyo Press, 1984), pp. 17–77. See also Ramon H. Myers, *The Chinese Economy: Past and Present* (Belmont, Wadsworth Inc., 1980), pp. 96–8.

28. Mark Elvin, *The Pattern of the Chinese Past* Eyre (London, Methuen, 1973), pp. 268–76.

29. Huang, *Taxation and Governmental Finance*, pp. 182–9.

30. Fang-chung Liang, *The Single-Whip Method of Taxation in China* (Cambridge, Massachusetts, Harvard University Press, 1970), p. 1.

31. Lloyd E. Eastman, *Family, Fields, and Ancestors: Constancy and Change in China's Social and Economic History, 1550–1949* (Oxford, Oxford University Press, 1988), p. 139.

32. Huang, *Taxation and Governmental Finance*, pp. 130, 313–23.

33. Hucker, *The Ming Dynasty*, pp. 55–6.

34. Huang, *China: A Macro History*, p. 161.

35. Hilary J. Beattie, *Land and Lineage in China: A Study of T'ung-ch'eng County, Anhwei, in the Ming and Ch'ing Dynasties* (Cambridge, Cambridge University Press, 1979).

36. Chung-li Chang, *The Chinese Gentry: Studies on Their Role in Nineteenth-Century Chinese Society* (Seattle, University of Washington Press, 1967), p. xvii.

37. Ping-ti Ho, *The Ladder of Success in Imperial China: Aspects of Social Mobility, 1368–1911* (New York, Columbia University Press, 1967), pp. 92–105, 256.

38. Cyril Birch, *Stories from a Ming Collection: Translations of Chinese Short Stories Published in the Seventeenth Century* (New York, Grove Press, Inc., 1958), pp. 37–96.

39. Katherine Carlitz, 'Desire, danger, and the body: stories of women's virtue in late Ming China', in Christina K. Gilmartin et al eds. *Engendering China: Women, Culture, and the State* (Cambridge, Massachusetts, Harvard University Press, 1994), pp. 101–24.

40. Wu-chi Liu, *An Introduction to Chinese Literature* (Bloomington, Indiana University Press, 1966), pp. 195–237.

41. Charles O. Hucker, *China's Imperial Past: An Introduction to Chinese History and Culture* (London, Duckworth, 1975), p. 406.

42. Waldron, *The Great Wall*, pp. 122–39.

43. Ray Huang, *1587, A Year of No Significance: The Ming Dynasty in Decline* (New Haven, Yale University Press, 1981), pp. 156–74.

44. Quoted in Jonathan Spence, *The China Helpers: Western Advisers in China 1620–1960* (London, The Bodley Head, 1969), pp. 6–7.

45. Ray Huang, 'The Lung-ch'ing and Wan-li reigns, 1567-1620', in *CHC*, 7, p. 522.

46. Edwin O. Reischauer and John K. Fairbank, *East Asia: The Great Tradition* (Boston, Houghton Mifflin, 1960), p. 341.

47. Charles O. Hucker, 'The Tung-lin movement of the late Ming period' in Fairbank ed., *Chinese Thought and Institutions* (Chicago, University of Chicago Press, 1957), pp. 132–62.

48. Frederic E. Wakeman, 'China and the seventeenth-century crisis', *Late Imperial China*, 7.1, June 1986, pp. 1–26.

49. James Bunyan Parsons, *The Peasant Rebellions of the Late Ming Dynasty* (Tucson, University of Arizona Press), 1970.

CHAPTER TWELVE

1. Frederic Wakeman, *The Great Enterprise: The Manchu Reconstruction of Imperial Order in Seventeenth-Century China*, two volumes (Berkeley, University of California Press, 1985).
2. Quoted in J. Mason Gentzler ed., *Changing China: Readings in the History of China from the Opium War to the Present* (New York, Praeger Publishers, 1977), p. 135.
3. Franz Michael, *The Origin of Manchu Rule in China* (John Hopkins Press, 1942, reprinted New York, Octagon Press, 1972), pp. 39–47; Wakeman, *The Great Enterprise*, I, pp. 23–66.
4. Michael, p. 79.
5. Robert B. Oxnam, *Ruling from Horseback: Manchu Politics in the Oboi Regency 1661–1669* (Chicago, University of Chicago Press, 1975), pp. 5–6.
6. Angela Hsi, 'Wu San-kuei in 1644: A reappraisal', *Journal of Asian Studies* 34.2, Feb. 1975, pp. 443–53.
7. Quoted in Wakeman, *The Great Enterprise*, I, pp. 316–17.
8. Wakeman, *The Great Enterprise*, I, pp. 556–69.
9. Frederic Wakeman, 'Localism and loyalism during the Ch'ing conquest of Kiangnan: The tragedy of Chiang-yin', in Frederic Wakeman and Carolyn Grant eds., *Conflict and Control in Late Imperial China* (Berkeley, University of California Press, 1975), pp. 43–85.
10. Ralph C. Croizier, *Koxinga and Chinese Nationalism: History, Myth and the Hero* (Cambridge, Massachusetts, Harvard University Press, 1977). See also John E. Wills, 'Maritime China from Wang Chih to Shih Lang: themes in peripheral history', in Jonathan D. Spence and John E. Wills eds., *From Ming to Ch'ing: Conquest, Region, and Continuity in Seventeenth-Century China* (New Haven, Yale University Press, 1979), pp. 201–38.
11. Charles O. Hucker, *China's Imperial Past: An Introduction to Chinese History and Culture* (London, Duckworth, 1975), p. 295.
12. Wakeman, *The Great Enterprise*, II, pp. 886–9.
13. Wakeman, *The Great Enterprise*, I, pp. 458–61.
14. Oxnam, pp. 41–3.
15. Wakeman, *The Great Enterprise*, II, pp. 909–11.
16. Wakeman, *The Great Enterprise*, II, pp. 1013–5; 1058–9.
17. Oxnam, pp. 50–63.
18. Oxnam, pp. 64–89.
19. Oxnam, pp. 90–117; Lawrence D. Kessler, *K'ang-hsi and the Consolidation of Ch'ing Rule 1661–1684* (Chicago, University of Chicago Press, 1976), pp. 30–9.
20. Kessler, pp. 39–46.
21. Wakeman, *The Great Enterprise*, II, pp. 1099–102.
22. Kessler, pp. 85–6.
23. Wakeman, *The Great Enterprise*, II, pp. 1110–12.
24. Kessler, pp. 97–103.
25. Hucker, p. 297.
26. Jonathan D. Spence, *Emperor of China: Self-Portrait of K'ang-hsi* (London, Jonathan Cape, 1974), p. 46.
27. Kessler, pp. 105–11.
28. Spence, *Emperor of China*, p. 22.
29. Morris Rossabi, *China and Inner Asia: From 1368 to the Present Day* (London, Thames and Hudson, 1975), p. 141.
30. Preston M. Torbert, *The Ch'ing Imperial Household Department: A Study of Its Organization and Principal Functions, 1662–1796* (Cambridge, Massachusetts, Harvard University Press, 1977), pp. 14–39.
31. Jonathan D. Spence, *Ts'ao Yin and the K'ang-hsi Emperor: Bondservant and Master* (New Haven, Yale University Press, 1966, 1988).
32. Silas H.L. Wu, *Communication and Imperial Control in China: Evolution of the Palace Memorial System 1693–1735* (Cambridge, Massachusetts, Harvard University Press, 1970).
33. Spence, *Emperor of China*, p. 79.
34. Madeleine Zelin, *The Magistrate's Tael: Rationalizing Fiscal Reform in Eighteenth-Century Ch'ing China* (Berkeley, University of California Press, 1984), pp. 1–24.
35. Pei Huang, *Autocracy at Work: A Study of the Yung-cheng Period, 1723–1735* (Bloomington, Indiana University Press, 1974), p. 27 and n. 2.
36. Silas H.L. Wu, *Passage to Power: K'ang-hsi and His Heir Apparent, 1661–1722* (Cambridge, Massachusetts, Harvard University Press, 1979), p. 23.
37. Wu, *Passage to Power*, p. 95.
38. Spence, *Emperor of China*, p. 145.

39. Huang, p. 21.
40. Huang, pp. 78–80; Wu, *Passage to Power*, pp. 179–83.
41. Quoted in Beatrice S. Bartlett, *Monarchs and Ministers: The Grand Council in Mid-Ch'ing China, 1723–1820* (Berkeley, University of California Press, 1991), p. 104.
42. Zelin, pp. 29–32.
43. Huang, p. 272.
44. Zelin, pp. 303–8.
45. Susan Naquin and Evelyn S. Rawski, *Chinese Society in the Eighteenth Century* (New Haven, Yale University Press, 1987), p. 219.
46. See chapter 7.
47. Harold L. Kahn, *Monarchy in the Emperor's Eyes: Image and Reality in the Ch'ien-lung Reign* (Cambridge, Massachusetts, Harvard University Press, 1971), p. 181.
48. Bartlett, pp. 180, 266–7, 278.
49. Lawrence D. Kessler, 'Ethnic composition of provincial leadership during the Ch'ing dynasty', *Journal of Asian Studies*, 28.3, May, 1969, pp. 489–511.
50. Kahn, p. 136.
51. L. Carrington Goodrich, *The Literary Inquisition of Ch'ien-lung* (1935, New York, Paragon Book Reprint, 1966).
52. R. Kent Guy, *The Emperor's Four Treasuries: Scholars and the State in the Late Ch'ien-lung Era* (Cambridge, Massachusetts, Harvard University Press, 1987).
53. Benjamin A. Elman, *From Philosophy to Philology: Intellectual and Social Aspects of Change in Late Imperial China* (Cambridge, Massachusetts, Harvard University Press, 1984).
54. Joseph Fletcher, 'Ch'ing Inner Asia *c.* 1800' in *CHC*, 10, pp. 35–106.
55. John K. Fairbank and Ssü-yu Teng, 'On the Ch'ing tributary system,' in John K. Fairbank and Ssü-yu Teng, *Ch'ing Administration: Three Studies* (Cambridge, Massachusetts, Harvard University Press, 1968), p. 112–13.
56. Wang Tseng-tsai, 'The Macartney Mission: a bicentennial review', in Robert A. Bickers ed., *Ritual and Diplomacy: The Macartney Mission to China 1792–1794* (London, The British Association for Chinese Studies and Wellsweep, 1993), pp. 43–56.
57. Lloyd E. Eastman, *Family, Fields, and Ancestors: Constancy and Change in China's Social and Economic History, 1550–1949* (Oxford, Oxford University Press, 1988), pp. 3–14.
58. Ping-ti Ho, *Studies on the Population of China, 1368–1953* (Cambridge, Massachusetts, Harvard University Press, 1967), p. 270.
59. Mark Elvin, *The Pattern of the Chinese Past* (London, Eyre Methuen, 1973), pp. 298–315.
60. Paul S. Ropp, *Dissent in Early Modern China: Ju-lin wai-shih and Ch'ing Social Criticism* (Ann Arbor, University of Michigan Press, 1981), p. 60.
61. Paul S. Ropp, 'The seeds of change: reflections on the condition of women in the early and mid-Ch'ing', *Signs: Journal of Women in Culture and Society*, 2.1, Autumn 1976, pp. 5–23.
62. Arthur W. Hummel ed., *Eminent Chinese of the Ch'ing Period (1644–1912)* (Washington, United States Government Printing Office, 1943–4; Taipei, Literature House, 1964), p. 956.
63. Susan Mann, 'Learned women in the eighteenth century,' in Christina K. Gilmartin, Gail Hershatter, Lisa Rofel and Tyrene White eds., *Engendering China: Women, Culture and the State* (Cambridge, Massachusetts, Harvard University Press, 1994), pp. 27–46.
64. Philip Kuhn, *Soulstealers: The Chinese Sorcery Scare of 1768* (Cambridge, Massachusetts, Harvard University Press, 1990), p. 1.
65. Kuhn, pp. 30–48, 223.
66. Susan Naquin, *Shantung Rebellion: The Wang Lun Uprising of 1774* (New Haven, Yale University Press, 1981), p. 101.
67. Naquin, pp. 148–64.
68. David S. Nivison, 'Ho-shen and his accusers: ideology and political behavior in the eighteenth century,' in David S. Nivison and Arthur F. Wright eds, *Confucianism in Action* (Stanford, Stanford University Press, 1959), pp. 209–43.
69. Albert Feuerwerker, *State and Society in Eighteenth-Century China: The Ch'ing Empire in Its Glory* (Ann Arbor, Center for Chinese Studies, University of Michigan, 1976), pp. 73–5.

SELECT BIBLIOGRAPHY

GENERAL WORKS

S.A.M. Adshead, *China in World History* (London, Macmillan, 1988).

Thomas J. Barfield, *The Perilous Frontier: Nomadic Empires and China* (Oxford, Basil Blackwell, 1979).

Kenneth K.S. Ch'en, *Buddhism in China: A Historical Survey* (Princeton, Princeton University Press, 1964).

H.G. Creel, *Chinese Thought: From Confucius to Mao Tse-tung* (London, Methuen, 1962).

W.T. de Bary, Wing-tsit Chan and Burton Watson, *Sources of Chinese Tradition,* two volumes (New York, Columbia University Press, 1960).

Lloyd E. Eastman, *Family, Fields and Ancestors* (Oxford, Oxford University Press, 1988).

Wolfram Eberhard, *A History of China*, fourth edition (London, Routledge & Kegan Paul, 1977).

Mark Elvin, *The Pattern of the Chinese Past* (London, Eyre, Methuen, 1973).

J.K. Fairbank ed., *The Chinese World Order* (Cambridge, Massachusetts, Harvard University Press, 1968).

John King Fairbank, *China: A New History* (Cambridge, Massachusetts, Harvard University Press, 1992).

Jacques Gernet, trans. J.R. Foster, *A History of Chinese Civilization* (Cambridge, Cambridge University Press, 1985).

James P. Harrison, *The Communists and Chinese Peasant Rebellions: A Study in the Rewriting of Chinese History* (London, Gollancz, 1970).

Ping-ti Ho, *Studies on the Population of China, 1368-1953* (Cambridge, Massachusetts, Harvard University Press, 1959, 1967).

Charles O. Hucker, *China's Imperial Past: An Introduction to Chinese History and Culture* (London, Duckworth, 1975).

Sechin Jagchid and Van Jay Symons, *Peace, War and Trade along the Great Wall: Nomadic Chinese Interactions through Two Millennia* (Bloomington, Indiana University Press, 1989).

Wu-chi Liu, *An Introduction to Chinese Literature* (Bloomington, Indiana University Press, 1966).

Michael Loewe, *Imperial China: The Historical Background to the Modern Age* (London, George Allen and Unwin, 1966).

John T. Meskill, *An Introduction to Chinese Civilization* (Lexington, D.C. Heath, 1973).

Franz Michael, *China Through the Ages: History of a Civilization* (Boulder, Westview Press, 1986).

Ichisada Miyazaki, trans. Conrad Schirokauer, *China's Examination Hell: The Civil Service Examinations of Imperial China* (New Haven, Yale University Press, 1981).

Ramon H. Myers, *The Chinese Economy: Past and Present* (Belmont, Wadsworth, 1980).

Dwight H. Perkins, *Agricultural Development in China, 1368–1968* (Chicago, Aldine, 1969).

E.O. Reischauer and John K. Fairbank, *East Asia: The Great Tradition* (Boston, Houghton Mifflin, 1960).

Paul S. Ropp ed., *Heritage of China: Contemporary Perspectives on Chinese Civilization* (Berkeley, University of California Press, 1990).

Morris Rossabi, *China and Inner Asia from 1368 to the Present Day* (New York, Pica, 1975).

Jonathan D. Spence, *The Search for Modern China* (London, Hutchinson, 1990).

Arthur Waldron, *The Great Wall of China: From History to Myth* (Cambridge, Cambridge University Press, 1990).

Arthur F. Wright, *Buddhism in Chinese History* (Stanford, Stanford University Press, 1959, 1970).

The Cambridge History of China

Abbreviated as *CHC*, 1, etc. General editors Denis Twitchett and John K. Fairbank (Cambridge, Cambridge University Press, 1978–).

Volume 1: *The Ch'in and Han Empires, 221* BC–AD *220* edited by Denis Twitchett and Michael Loewe, 1987 [*CHC*, 1].

Volume 3: *Sui and T'ang China, 589–906, Part I,* edited by Denis Twitchett, 1979 [*CHC*, 3].

Volume 6: *Alien Regimes and Border States, 710–1368,* edited by Denis Twitchett, 1994 [*CHC*, 6].

Volume 7: *The Ming Dynasty 1368–1644, Part 1,* edited by Frederick W. Mote and Denis Twitchett, 1988 [*CHC*, 7].

WORKS BY CHAPTER

Introduction
John Meskill, *The Pattern of Chinese History: Cycles, Development, or Stagnation?* (Lexington, D.C. Heath, 1968).

Chapter One
Kwang-chih Chang, *The Archaeology of Ancient China*, third edition (New Haven, Yale University Press, 1977).

Ping-ti Ho, *The Cradle of the East: An Inquiry into the Indigenous Origins of Techniques and Ideas of Neolithic and Early Historic China, 5000–1000 BC* (Hong Kong, The Chinese University of Hong Kong, 1975).

David N. Keightley ed., *The Origins of Chinese Civilization* (Berkeley, University of California Press, 1983).

William Watson, *Early Civilization in China* (London, Thames and Hudson, 1966).

Paul Wheatley, *The Pivot of the Four Corners: A Preliminary Enquiry into the Origins and Character of the Ancient Chinese City* (Edinburgh, Edinburgh University Press, 1971).

Chapter Two
Rushton Coulborn ed., *Feudalism in History* (Hamden, Connecticut, Archon, 1965).

Herrlee G. Creel, *The Origins of Statecraft in China: Vol 1, The Western Chou Empire* (Chicago, University of Chicago Press, 1970).

Raymond Dawson, *Confucius* (Oxford, Oxford University Press, 1981).

Cho-yun Hsu, *Ancient China in Transition: An Analysis of Social Mobility, 722–222 BC* (Stanford, Stanford University Press, 1965).

Cho-yun Hsu and Katheryn M. Linduff, *Western Chou Civilization* (New Haven, Yale University Press, 1988).

D.C. Lau trans. and ed., *Mencius* (Harmondsworth, Penguin, 1970).

D.C. Lau trans. and ed., *Lao Tzu: Tao Tě Ching* (Harmondsworth, Penguin, 1975).

D.C. Lau trans. and ed., *Confucius: The Analects* Harmondsworth, Penguin, 1979).

Xueqin Li, trans. K.C. Chang, *Eastern Zhou and Qin Civilizations* (New Haven, Yale University Press, 1985).

Chapter Three
Derk Bodde, *China's First Unifier: A Study of the Ch'in Dynasty as Seen in the Life of Li Ssu 280?–208 BC* (Leiden, 1938; Hong Kong, Hong Kong University Press, 1967).

J.J.L. Duyvendak, *The Book of Lord Shang: A Classic of the Chinese School of Law* (London, Probsthain, 1928).

Wen Fong, *The Great Bronze Age of China: An Exhibition from The People's Republic of China* (London, Thames and Hudson, 1980).

Yu-ning Li, *The First Emperor of China* (White Plains, New York, International Arts and Sciences Press, 1975).

Yu-ning Li ed., *Shang Yang's Reforms and State Control in China* (White Plains, New York, M.E. Sharpe, 1977).

Chapter Four
Hans Bielenstein, *The Bureaucracy of Han Times*, (Cambridge Cambridge University Press, 1980).

T'ung-tsu Ch'ü, ed. Jack L. Dull, *Han Social Structure* (Seattle, University of Washington Press, 1972).

Rafe de Crespigny, *Northern Frontier: The Policies and Strategy of the Later Han Empire* (Canberra, Australian National University, 1984).

Cho-yun Hsü, ed. Jack L. Dull, *Han Agriculture: The Formation of Early Chinese Agrarian Economy (206 BC–AD 220)* (Seattle, University of Washington Press, 1980).

Michael Loewe, *Everyday Life in Early Imperial China During the Han Period 202 BC–AD 220* (London, Carousel, 1973).

Michael Loewe, *Crisis and Conflict in Han China 104 BC–AD 9* (London, George Allen and Unwin, 1974).

Michael Loewe, *Ways to Paradise: The Chinese Quest for Immortality* (London, George Allen and Unwin, 1979).

Michael Loewe, *Chinese Ideas of Life and Death: Faith, Myth and Reason in the Han Period (202 BC–AD 220)* (London, George Allen and Unwin, 1982).

Zhongshu Wang, trans. K.C. Chang et al, *Han Civilization* (New Haven, Yale University Press, 1982).

Chapter Five
Patricia Buckley Ebrey, *The Aristocratic Families of Early Imperial China: A Case Study of the Po-ling Ts'ui Family* (Cambridge, Cambridge University Press, 1978).

W.J.F. Jenner, *Memories of Loyang: Yang Hsüan-chih and the Lost Capital (493–534)* (Oxford, Clarendon Press, 1981).

Chapters Six to Eight

Arthur Cooper, *Li Po and Tu Fu* (Harmondsworth, Penguin, 1973).

F.S. Drake, 'Mohammedanism in the T'ang Dynasty', *Monumenta Serica*, 8, 1943, 1–40.

Hilda Ecsedy, 'Cultivators and barbarians in ancient China', *Acta Orientalia Hungaricae* (Budapest), 27, 1974, 327–49.

C.P. FitzGerald, *The Empress Wu* (London, The Cresset Press, 1956).

C.P. FitzGerald, *The Southern Expansion of the Chinese People* (London, Barrie and Jenkins, 1972).

A.C. Graham, *Poems of the Late T'ang* (Harmondsworth, Penguin, 1981).

R.W.L. Guisso, *Wu Tse-t'ien and the Politics of Legitimation in T'ang China* (Washington, Western Washington Press, 1978).

Charles Hartman, *Han Yü and the T'ang Search for Unity* (Princeton, Princeton University Press, 1986).

Robert M. Hartwell, 'Demographic, political and social transformations of China, 750–1550', *Harvard Journal of Asiatic Studies*, 42.2, December 1982, 365–442.

David Hawkes, *A Little Primer of Tu Fu* (Oxford, Clarendon Press, 1969).

David G. Johnson, *The Medieval Chinese Oligarchy* (Boulder, Westview, 1977).

Colin Mackerras, *The Uighur Empire (744–840): According to the T'ang Dynastic Histories* (Canberra, Australian National University, 1968).

David McMullen, *State and Scholars in T'ang China* (Cambridge, Cambridge University Press, 1988).

Stephen Owen, *The Great Age of Chinese Poetry: The High T'ang* (New Haven, Yale University Press, 1981).

John C. Perry and Bardwell L. Smith eds., *Essays on T'ang Society: The Interplay of Social, Political and Economic Forces* (Leiden, E.J. Brill, 1976).

Edwin G. Pulleyblank, *The Background of the Rebellion of An Lu-shan* (London, Oxford University Press, 1955).

Edwin G. Pulleyblank, 'The An Lu-shan Rebellion and the origins of chronic militarism in late Tang China', in John Curtis Perry and Bardwell L. Smith eds, *Essays on T'ang Society* (Leiden, E.J. Brill, 1976).

Edwin O. Reischauer, *Ennin's Travels in T'ang China* (New York, Ronald Press, 1955).

Edwin O. Reischauer, *Ennin's Diary: The Record of a Pilgrimage to China in Search of the Law* (New York, Ronald Press, 1955).

G.W. Robinson, *The Poems of Wang Wei* (Harmondsworth, Penguin, 1973).

Edward H. Schafer, *The Golden Peaches of Samarkand: A Study of T'ang Exotics* (Berkeley, University of California, 1963).

Edward H. Schafer, *The Vermilion Bird: T'ang Images of the South* (Berkeley, University of California, 1967).

Denis C. Twitchett, *Financial Administration under the T'ang Dynasty*, second edition (Cambridge, Cambridge University Press, 1970).

Arthur Waley, *The Life and Times of Po Chü-i 772–846 AD* (London, George Allen and Unwin, 1949).

Arthur Waley, *The Poetry and Career of Li Po, 701–762 AD* (London, George Allen and Unwin, 1950).

Arthur Waley, *The Real Tripitaka and Other Pieces* (London, George Allen and Unwin, 1952).

Arthur Waley, *Ballads and Stories from Tun-huang: An Anthology* (New York, Macmillan, 1960).

Howard J. Wechsler, *Mirror to the Son of Heaven: Wei Cheng at the Court of T'ang T'ai-tsung* (New Haven, Yale University Press, 1974).

Stanley Weinstein, *Buddhism under the T'ang* (Cambridge, Cambridge University Press, 1987).

Herold J. Wiens, *Han Chinese Expansion in South China* (Hamden, Connecticut, Shoestring, 1967).

Arthur F. Wright, 'Symbolism and function: Reflections on Ch'ang-an and other great cities', *Journal of Asian Studies* 14.4, 1965, 667–79.

Arthur F. Wright, *The Sui Dynasty* (New York, Knopf, 1978).

Arthur F. Wright and Denis Twitchett eds, *Perspectives on the T'ang* (New Haven, Yale University Press, 1973).

Chapter Nine

Peter K. Bol, *"This Culture of Ours": Intellectual Transitions in T'ang and Sung China* (Stanford, Stanford University Press, 1992).

John C. Chaffee, *The Thorny Gates of Learning in Sung China* (Cambridge, Cambridge University Press, 1985).

Richard L. Davis, *Court and Family in Sung China, 960–1279: Bureaucratic Success and Kinship Fortunes for the Shih of Ming-chou* (Durham, Duke University Press, 1986).

Patricia P. Ebrey, *Family and Property in Sung China: Yüan Tsai's Precepts for Social Life* (Princeton, Princeton University Press, 1984).

Jacques Gernet, trans. H.M. Wright, *Daily Life in China on the Eve of the Mongol Invasion, 1250–1276* (London, George Allen and Unwin, 1962).

Richard von Glahn, *The Country of Streams and Grottoes: Expansion and Settlement, and the Civilizing of the Sichuan Frontier in Song Times* (Cambridge, Massachusetts, Harvard University Press, 1987).

Robert P. Hymes, *Statesmen and Gentlemen: The Elite of Fu-chou, Chiang-si, in Northern and Southern Sung* (Cambridge, Cambridge University Press, 1986).

E.A. Kracke, *Civil Service in Early Sung China, 960–1067* (Cambridge, Massachusetts, Harvard University Press, 1953).

Thomas H.C. Lee, *Government, Education and Examinations in Sung China* (Hong Kong, The Chinese University Press, 1985).

James T.C. Liu, *Reform in Sung China, Wang An-shih, 1021–1086 and His New Policies* (Cambridge, Massachusetts, Harvard University Press, 1959).

James T.C. Liu, *Ou-yang Hsiu, An Eleventh Century Neo-Confucianist* (Stanford, Stanford University Press, 1967).

James T.C. Liu, *China Turning Inward: Intellectual-Political Changes in the Early Twelfth Century* (Cambridge, Massachusetts, Harvard University Press, 1988).

James T.C. Liu and Peter J. Golas eds., *Change in Sung China: Innovation or Renovation?* (Lexington, Massachusetts, 1969).

Winston W. Lo, *An Introduction to the Civil Service of Sung China, with Emphasis on Its Personnel Administration* (Honolulu, University of Hawaii Press, 1987).

Brian E. McKnight, *Village and Bureaucracy in Southern Sung China* (Chicago, University of Chicago Press, 1971).

John Meskill, *Wang An-shih: Practical Reformer?* (Boston, D.C. Heath, 1963).

Thomas A. Metzger, *Escape from Predicament: Neo-Confucianism and China's Evolving Political Culture* (New York, Columbia University Press, 1977).

Morris Rossabi, *China among Equals: The Middle Kingdom and Its Neighbors* (Berkeley, University of California Press, 1983).

Yoshinobu Shiba, trans. Mark Elvin, *Commerce and Society in Sung China* (Ann Arbor, University of Michigan, 1970).

Jing-shen Tao, *The Jurchen in Twelfth-Century China: A Study of Sinicization* (Seattle, University of Washington Press, 1976).

Gungwu Wang, *The Structure of Power in North China during the Five Dynasties* (Stanford, Stanford University Press, 1967).

Chapter Ten

Paul Heng-chao Ch'en, *Chinese Legal Tradition under the Mongols* (Princeton, Princeton University Press, 1975).

John W. Dardess, *Conquerors and Confucians: Aspects of Political Change in Late Yüan China* (New York, Columbia University Press, 1973).

Ch'i-ch'ing Hsiao, *The Military Establishment of the Yüan Dynasty* (Cambridge, Massachusetts, Harvard University Press, 1978).

John D. Langlois ed., *China under Mongol Rule* (Princeton, Princeton University Press, 1981).

Chapter Eleven

William Atwell, 'International bullion flows and the Chinese economy circa 1530–1650', *Past and Present*, 95, May 1982, 68–90.

William Atwell, 'Some observations on the "Seventeenth-Century Crisis" in China and Japan', *Journal of Asian Studies*, 45.2, February 1986, 223–44.

Ralph C. Croizier, *Koxinga and Chinese Nationalism: History, Myth and the Hero* (Cambridge, Massachusetts, Harvard University Press, 1977).

John Dardess, *Confucianism and Autocracy: Professional Elites and the Founding of the Ming Dynasty* (Berkeley, University of California Press, 1983).

Edward Dreyer, *Early Ming China: A Political History, 1355–1435* (Stanford, Stanford University Press, 1982).

Helen Dunstan, 'The late Ming epidemics: A preliminary survey', *Ch'ing-shih wen-t'i*, 3, 1975, 1–59.

Joseph Esherick and Mary Rankin eds., *Chinese Local Elites and Patterns of Dominance* (Berkeley, University of California Press, 1990).

Edward L. Farmer, *Early Ming Government: The Evolution of Dual Capitals* (Cambridge, Massachusetts, Harvard University Press, 1976).

Linda Grove and Christian Daniels eds, *State and Society in China: Japanese Perspectives on Ming-Qing Social and Economic History* (Tokyo, University of Tokyo Press, 1984).

Philip C.C. Huang, *The Peasant Family and Rural Development in the Yangzi Delta, 1350–1988* (Stanford, Stanford University Press, 1990).

Ray Huang, *Taxation and Governmental Finance in Sixteenth-Century Ming China* (Cambridge, Cambridge University Press, 1974).

Ray Huang, *1587, A Year of No Significance: The Ming Dynasty in Decline* (New Haven, Yale University Press, 1981).

Charles O. Hucker, *The Censorial System of Ming China* (Stanford, Stanford University Press, 1966).

C.O. Hucker ed., *Chinese Government in Ming Times: Seven Studies* (New York, Columbia University Press, 1969).

Charles O. Hucker, *The Ming Dynasty: Its Origins and Evolving Institutions* (Ann Arbor, University of Michigan Press, 1978).

J.V.G. Mills, *Ma Huan: Ying-yai sheng-lan, "The Overall Survey of the Ocean's Shores" [1433]* (Cambridge, Cambridge University Press, 1970).

Masao Mori, 'The gentry in the Ming', *Acta Asiatica*, 38, 1980, 31–53.

James B. Parsons, *The Peasant Rebellions of the Late Ming Dynasty* (Tucson, University of Arizona Press, 1970).

Lynn A. Struve, *The Southern Ming, 1644–1662* (New Haven, Yale University Press, 1984).

Frederic Wakeman, 'China and the seventeenth-century crisis', *Late Imperial China*, 7.1, June, 1986, 1–26.

Chapter Twelve

Beatrice S. Bartlett, *Monarchs and Ministers: The Grand Council in Mid-Ch'ing China (1723–1820)* (Berkeley, University of California Press, 1991).

Jerry Dennerline, *The Chia-ting Loyalists: Confucian Leadership and Social Change in Seventeenth-Century China* (New Haven, Yale University Press, 1981).

J.K. Fairbank and S.Y. Teng, *Ch'ing Administration: Three Studies* (Cambridge, Massachusetts, Harvard University Press, 1960).

Albert Feuerwerker, *State and Society in Eighteenth-Century China: The Ch'ing Empire in its Glory* (Ann Arbor, University of Michigan Press, 1976).

L. Carrington Goodrich, *The Literary Inquisition of Ch'ien-lung* (1935, New York, Paragon Book Reprint, 1966).

R. Kent Guy, *The Emperor's Four Treasuries: Scholars and the State in the Late Ch'ien-lung Era* (Cambridge, Massachusetts, Harvard University Press, 1987).

Ping-ti Ho, 'The significance of the Ch'ing period in Chinese history', *Journal of Asian Studies*, 26.2, February 1967, 189–95.

Pei Huang, *Autocracy at Work: A Study of the Yung-cheng Period, 1723–35* (Bloomington, Indiana University Press, 1974).

Harold L. Kahn, *Monarchy in the Emperor's Eyes: Image and Reality in the Ch'ien-lung Reign* (Cambridge, Massachusetts, Harvard University Press, 1971).

Lawrence D. Kessler, 'Ethnic composition of provincial leadership during the Ch'ing dynasty, *Journal of Asian Studies*, 28.3, May 1969, 489–511.

Lawrence D. Kessler, *K'ang-hsi and the Consolidation of Ch'ing Rule, 1661–1684* (Chicago, University of Chicago Press, 1978).

P.A. Kuhn, *Soulstealers: The Chinese Sorcery Scare of 1768* (Cambridge, Cambridge University Press, 1990).

Susan Naquin, *Shantung Rebellion: The Wang Lun Uprising of 1774* (New Haven, Yale University Press, 1981).

Susan Naquin and E.S. Rawski, *Chinese Society in the Eighteenth Century* (New Haven, Yale University Press, 1987).

D.S. Nivison, 'Ho-shen and his accusers: ideology and political behavior in the eighteenth century', in David S. Nivison and A.F. Wright eds., *Confucianism in Action* (Stanford, Stanford University Press, 1959).

Paul S. Ropp, *Dissent in Early Modern China: Ju-lin wai-shih and Ch'ing Social Criticism* (Ann Arbor, University of Michigan Press, 1981).

J.D. Spence, *Ts'ao Yin and the K'ang-hsi Emperor: Bondservant and Master* (New Haven, Yale University Press, 1966).

J.D. Spence, *Emperor of China: Self-Portrait of K'ang-hsi* (London, Jonathan Cape, 1974).

Jonathan Spence and John Wills eds., *From Ming to Ch'ing: Conquest, Region, and Continuity in Seventeenth-Century China* (New Haven, Yale University Press, 1979).

Preston M. Torbert, *The Ch'ing Imperial Household Department* (Cambridge, Massachusetts, Harvard University Press, 1978).

Frederic Wakeman, *The Great Enterprise: The Manchu Reconstruction of the Imperial Order in Seventeenth-Century China*, two volumes (Berkeley, University of California, 1985).

Silas H.L. Wu, *Communication and Imperial Control in China: Evolution of the Palace Memorial System 1693–1735* (Cambridge, Massachusetts, Harvard University Press, 1970).

Madeleine Zelin, *The Magistrate's Tael: Rationalizing Fiscal Reform in Eighteenth-Century Ch'ing China* (Berkeley, University of California, 1984).

INDEX